Internet of Things

This book is a compendium of various applications and current progress in a powerful technology known as the Internet of Things (IoT). IoT provides a system of interconnecting things such as vehicles, electrical equipment, agriculture devices, etc. Such items are allocated with the computing device so that they can use a network to transfer data to one another and automate their actions on certain events.

Internet of Things: Applications for Sustainable Development will throw light on recent developments in the latest field and will be of great interest to know various application areas for sustainable development. This book mainly focuses on the current state of the art, including protocol design and low-cost sensor design, for the sustainable development of society using IoT.

The sustainable development areas include climate, healthcare systems, electrical systems, and energy that can meet present and next-generation advancement using IoT. Sustainable development faces various issues, challenges, opportunities, and future enhancements with the latest technologies, hardware, and software.

Features:

- A real-world problem-solving approach for diversified problems
- Potential contributors from industries/academia have been given the opportunity to publish their work
- Identification of various challenges in IoT for future contributions
- Diversified coverage of the book, including applications, securities, industrialization, automation, etc
- IoT for the sustainable development areas

This book will offer strong support as a reference book for students, practitioners, researchers, and scientific investigators worldwide, as well as anyone who wants to set up IoT-enabled industries. It provides pertinent industries with new ideas and innovations to visionaries.

Chapman & Hall/CRC Internet of Things: Data-Centric Intelligent Computing, Informatics, and Communication

The role of adaptation, machine learning, computational Intelligence, and data analytics in IoT Systems is becoming increasingly essential and intertwined. The capability of an intelligent system is growing depending upon various self-decision-making algorithms in IoT Devices. IoT-based smart systems generate a large amount of data that traditional data processing algorithms and applications cannot process. Hence, this book series involves different computational methods incorporated within the system with the help of Analytics Reasoning, learning methods, Artificial intelligence, and Sense-making in Big Data, which is most concerned in IoT-enabled environments.

This series focuses on attracting researchers and practitioners in Information Technology and Computer Science in the intelligent computing paradigm, Big Data, machine learning, Sensor data, the Internet of Things, and data sciences. The main aim of the series is to make available a range of books on all aspects of learning, analytics, advanced intelligent systems, and related technologies. This series will cover the theory, research, development, and applications of knowledge, computational analytics, data processing, and machine learning algorithms as embedded in engineering, computer science, and Information Technology.

Series Editors:

Souvik Pal
Sister Nivedita University, (Techno India Group), Kolkata, India

Dac-Nhuong Le
Haiphong University, Vietnam

Internet of Things and Data Mining for Modern Engineering and Healthcare Applications
Ankan Bhattacharya, Bappadittya Roy, Samarendra Nath Sur, Saurav Mallik and Subhasis Dasgupta

Energy Harvesting: Enabling IoT Transformations
Deepti Agarwal, Kimmi Verma and Shabana Urooj

SDN-Supported Edge-Cloud Interplay for Next Generation Internet of Things
Kshira Sagar Sahoo, Arun Solanki, Sambit Kumar Mishra, Bibhudatta Sahoo and Anand Nayyar

Internet of Things: Applications for Sustainable Development
Niranjan Lal, Shamimul Qamar, Sanyam Agarwal, Ambuj Kumar Agarwal and Sourabh Singh Verma

Artificial Intelligence for Cognitive Modeling: Theory and Practice
Pijush Dutta, Souvik Pal, Asok Kumar and Korhan Cengiz

Internet of Things
Applications for Sustainable Development

Edited by
Niranjan Lal
Shamimul Qamar
Sanyam Agarwal
Ambuj Kumar Agarwal
Sourabh Singh Verma

CRC Press
Taylor & Francis Group
Boca Raton London New York

CRC Press is an imprint of the
Taylor & Francis Group, an **informa** business

A CHAPMAN & HALL BOOK

Cover Image Credit: Shutterstock.com

First edition published 2023
by CRC Press
6000 Broken Sound Parkway NW, Suite 300, Boca Raton, FL 33487-2742
and by CRC Press

4 Park Square, Milton Park, Abingdon, Oxon, OX14 4RN

CRC Press is an imprint of Taylor & Francis Group, LLC

© 2023 selection and editorial matter, Niranjan Lal, Shamimul Qamar, Sanyam Agarwal, Ambuj Kumar Agarwal and Sourabh Singh Verma; individual chapters, the contributors

---

Library of Congress Cataloging-in-Publication Data

Names: Lal, Niranjan, editor.
Title: Internet of things : applications for sustainable development /
edited by Niranjan Lal, Shamimul Qamar, Sanyam Agarwal, Ambuj Kumar
Agarwal, Sourabh Singh Verma.
Other titles: Internet of things (CRC Press)
Description: First edition. | Boca Raton : Chapman & Hall/CRC Press, 2023. |
Series: Internet of things: data-centric intelligent computing, informatics, and communication |
Includes bibliographical references and index. | Identifiers: LCCN 2022044739 (print) |
LCCN 2022044740 (ebook) | ISBN 9781032128986 (hbk) | ISBN 9781032129228 (pbk) |
ISBN 9781003226888 (ebk)
Subjects: LCSH: Internet of things.
Classification: LCC TK5105.8857 I56455 2023 (print) | LCC TK5105.8857 (ebook) |
DDC 004.67/8--dc23/eng/20221128
LC record available at https://lccn.loc.gov/2022044739
LC ebook record available at https://lccn.loc.gov/2022044740

ISBN: 978-1-032-12898-6 (hbk)
ISBN: 978-1-032-12922-8 (pbk)
ISBN: 978-1-003-22688-8 (ebk)

DOI: 10.1201/9781003226888

Typeset in Palatino
by KnowledgeWorks Global Ltd.

Contents

Preface

The proposed book is intended to cover the vast and fast-growing fields of the Internet of Things (IoT) with the latest advancements for sustainable development in many areas. This book is meant to serve its readers as a textbook and reference book. It will also prove to be a boon for research scholars and will open new avenues in next-generation technologies. To realize the full potential of the IoT paradigm, it is necessary to address several challenges and develop suitable conceptual and technological solutions for tackling them. This book also focuses on various issues, challenges, and difficulties in implementing IoT in areas for organizations.

The book on the above theme aims to enable researchers to build connections and share their knowledge for the betterment of society for sustainable development. This book features innovative research on product design and lifecycle, smart cities, agriculture, environment automation, healthcare, farming wearables, climate, healthcare system, transportation, city, electrical, e-governance renewable energy, and eco-system for sustainable growth. This book is a critical reference source for academicians, professionals, engineers, technology designers, analysts, and students. It includes high-quality application chapters, survey and tutorial papers, case studies, and short research notes reflecting IoT for sustainable development.

The primary goal of this book is to highlight the literature reviews on the IoT, its various application architectures, and the latest technologies that address challenges. We expect the book to serve as a reference for bachelor's students, master's students, Ph.D. students, researchers, academicians, and industry persons involved in IoT and sustainable development with the integration of the latest technologies.

Organization of the Book

This book contains 20 chapters written by experts in the IoT field. The book topic started with an essential application for sustainable development with advanced implementations. Chapter 1 presents the various important applications of Internet of Things. Chapters 2 and 3 cover IoT applications in smart homes and smart grids. Chapter 4 provides insights about IoT and machine learning; Chapter 5 discusses the AIC algorithm for online cashback; Chapters 6–20 cover the various application for the sustainable development in smart monitoring and controlling systems, water management, agriculture, smart farming, designing of single-bit six transitory using IoT and smart irrigation system and also cover the role of IoT and human for the development of the sustainable community, and further covers industrial IoT and also includes IoT for health monitoring, various challenges, solution, and opportunities for global sustainable development.

Editor Biographies

Dr. Niranjan Lal did his Ph.D. in Computer Science and Engineering. He has completed M. Tech from Guru Gobind Singh Indraprastha University (GGSIPU), Delhi, and did B.E. from Rajasthan University. Presently he is working as an Associate Professor in Computer Science and Engineering at SRMIST, Delhi NCR Campus, Ghaziabad, Uttar Pradesh, India. He has more than 14 years of experience in IT and academics. His research areas are network security, wireless sensor networks, cloud computing, dataspaces, android application development, information retrieval, machine learning, IoT, and blockchain. He presently guides four Ph.D. students at Mody University of Science and Technology. He is a highly disciplined and organized person. He has organized more than 15 conferences/seminars and workshops. He has chaired more than eight conferences as special sessions and delivered six keynote addresses. He serves in an advisory capacity in several international journals as an editorial member and at international conferences as a general chair and technical program committee/organizing committee. He has published more the 30 papers in national and international conferences and journals.

Dr. Shamimul Qamar has been recognized as an eminent scholar in the field of Electronics & Computer Engineering; he did his B. Tech from MMMEC Gorakhpur, M. Tech from AMU, Aligarh, and earned his Ph.D. degree from IIT Roorkee with a highly honorable grade. He is currently working as a Computer Science and Engineering Professor at Faculty of Sciences & Managements, Dhahran Al Janub, King Khalid University, Abha, Saudi Arabia. Prof. Qamar has a wide teaching experience in various engineering colleges. He has research interests in communication and computer networks, multimedia applications, Internet applications, satellite networks, DSP, and image processing. He has published several research papers in reputed national/international journals and conferences. He served as a consultant at Jackson State University, USA. He is a reviewer of IJCSIS, USA. He has written some textbooks and chapters in Electronics and Computer Engineering. He is also a technical program committee member at the international mobility conference in Singapore. He is a lifetime member of international association of engineers and a life member of Indian Society for Technical Education. His technical depth and interest resulted in setting up a research lab according to the latest technical innovations. Along with this, he has actively participated in various technical courses workshops, seminars, etc., at the IITs.

Dr. Sanyam Agarwal is working as Professor and Director at ACE College of ENGG. & MGMT., Agra, UP, India. He has more than 24 years of experience and expertise in his area. He has published many papers in national and international journals and conferences. It has been a tremendous experience. After his graduation, he joined the IT industry and worked there for seven years in the field of marketing from marketing executive to country head. There he got a chance to communicate with a variety of people on different aspects of products, services, and a lot more. His start in the education industry was in a really very different environment where he got a chance to enhance his teaching skills, learning skills, and technical skills. Updating the knowledge base has been a very wonderful experience, just to cater for the project-based learning because the scenario is changing from day-to-day basis. So yes, one has to keep pace with the ongoing system and a change of policies in the education system is highly required.

Dr. Ambuj Kumar Agarwal secured his Ph.D. degree in the field of Computer Science and Engineering. He has 17 years of experience in academics, research, administration, and industries. He is currently working in the Department of Computer Science and Engineering, School of Engineering and Technology, Sharda University, Greater Noida, India. His research area includes software engineering, cloud computing, software testing, and information hiding. He has served as a chairperson and technical committee member for various international conferences. He has authored more than 40 papers in the journals, conferences, and book chapters related to his research. He has served as a chairperson and technical committee member for various international conferences. He has published more than ten Australian and Indian patents.

Dr. Sourabh Singh Verma is currently working as Assistant Professor at the School of Computing & IT, Manipal University, Jaipur (an A+ NAAC accredited university). He has more than 17 years of experience in academics. Before joining Manipal University, Jaipur, he served at the prestigious Mody University, Sikar, for 15 plus years in the Computer Science Department as an Assistant Professor. He has guided more than ten M. Tech. dissertation theses. His areas of interest include machine learning, ad hoc networks, and security. He has published research articles in various international journals and conferences. Dr. Verma has two software copyrights under his name. He has served as a reviewer for various international journals and conferences. Dr. Verma was also honored as the Best Young Researcher (Male) by Global Education and Corporate Leadership Awards (GECL) 2018.

Contributors

Sanju Joseph Abraham
Saintgits College of Engineering
Kottayam, Kerala, India

Alaknanda J Adur
Surana College
Peenya, Bengaluru, India

Reeya Agrawal
GLA University
Mathura, Uttar Pradesh, India
and
National Institute of Technology
Patna, Bihar, India

Khushi Akhoury
Vellore Institute of Technology
Chennai, Tamil Nadu, India

Aswin Anand
SRM Institute of Science and Technology
Kattankulathur, Tamil Nadu, India

Kiruba B
Sri Krishna College of Engineering and
    Technology
Coimbatore, Tamil Nadu, India

Nishant Bhardwaj
Raj Kumar Goel Institute of Technology
Ghaziabad, Uttar Pradesh, India

Amitabh Bhargava
Graphic Era (deemed to be University)
Dehradun, Uttarakhand, India

Deepshikha Bhargava
DIT University
Dehradun, Uttarakhand, India

Dhananjay Bhatkhande
Vishwakarma University
Pune, Maharashtra, India

Bhupal Bhattacharya
Raiganj University
Raiganj, West Bengal, India

Haleshi Chalwadi
Davangere University
Davanagere, Karnataka, India

Pinkie Cherian
St Joseph's College for Women
Alappuzha, Kerela, India

Pooja Chitravelan
Vellore Institute of Technology
Chennai, Tamil Nadu, India

Raajasubramanian D
Annamalai University
Chidambram, Tamil Nadu, India

Sivakumar D
Annamalai University
Chidambaram, Tamil Nadu, India

Rahul Dandautiya
Chandigarh University
Mohali, Punjab, India

Juliya V Devasia
St Teresa's College
Ernakulam, Kerela, India

Ritismita Devi
Assam Down Town University
Guwahati, Assam, India

Fantin Irudaya Raj E
Dr. Sivanthi Aditanar College of Engineering
Thoothukudi, Tamil Nadu, India

Viswanathan Ganesh
Chalmers University of Technology
Gothenburg, Sweden

A. Govindasamy
Government Arts College
Tindivanam, Tamil Nadu, India

Ankit Gupta
Raj Kumar Goel Institute of
    Technology
Ghaziabad, Uttar Pradesh, India

Dhawal Gupta
Scientist – E Cyber Law
MEITY (GoI)
New Delhi, India

Priya Gupta
UCL, IRIS
University College London
London, United Kingdom

Sunil Gupta
UPES
Dehradun, Uttarakhand, India

Jasmine Selvakumari Jeya I
Hindusthan College of Engineering and
    Technology
Coimbatore, Tamil Nadu, India

Siddharth Jabade
Vishwakarma University
Pune, Maharashtra, India

Varsha Jayaprakash
Vellore Institute of Technology
Chennai, Tamil Nadu, India

Smita Joshi
G.H. Patel College of Engineering and
    Technology
Anand, Gujarat, India

Narendra K
Annamalai University
Chidambaram, Tamil Nadu, India

Pratibha Kantanavar
R. V. College of Engineering
Bangalore, Karnataka, India

Monit Kapoor
Chitkara University
Rajpura, Punjab, India

Shraddha Khamparia
Vishwakarma University
Pune, Maharashtra, India

Bui Huy Khoi
Industrial University of HCM City
Ho Chi Minh City, Vietnam

M S Kirtan
Raj Kumar Goel Institute of Technology
Ghaziabad, Uttar Pradesh, India

Shrikaant Kulkarni
Vishwakarma University
Pune, Maharashtra, India

Manicka Raja M
Sri Krishna College of Engineering and
    Technology
Coimbatore, Tamil Nadu, India

Manjushree M
Rotary Educational Society
Mandya, Karnataka, India

Appadurai Mangalraj
Dr. Sivanthi Aditanar College of Engineering
Thoothukudi, Tamil Nadu, India

Sujatha Manohar
Vellore Institute of Technology
Chennai, Tamil Nadu, India

Shabana Mehfuz
Jamia Millia Islamia
New Delhi, India

Ansu Anna Moncy
Vellore Institute of Technology
Chennai, Tamil Nadu, India

Akkalakshmi Muddana
Gitam Deemed University
Hyderabad, Telangana, India

Priya Nakade
Vishwakarma University
Pune, Maharashtra, India

Nguyen Ngan
Industrial University of HCM City
Ho Chi Minh City, Vietnam

Midhila P
Sahrdaya College of Engineering and
Technology
Thrissur, Kerala, India

Aarthi R
Annamalai University
Chidambaram, Tamil Nadu, India

Farah Fathima Raheem
Saintgits College of Engineering
Kottayam, Kerala, India

Sindhu Rajendran
R. V. College of Engineering
Bangalore, Karnataka, India

Manoj Kumar S
KPR Institute of Engineering and
Technology
Coimbatore, Tamil Nadu, India

Srinivasan S
Annamalai University
Chidambaram, Tamil Nadu, India

Vaishnav Nair S
Saintgits College of Engineering
Kottayam, Kerala, India
and
Government Arts College for Women
Krishnagiri, Tamil Nadu, India

Harshil Sathwara
G.H. Patel College of Engineering and
Technology
Anand, Gujarat, India

Hitesh Kumar Sharma
UPES
Dehradun, Uttarakhand, India

Manmohan Sharma
Manipal University Jaipur
Jaipur, Rajasthan, India

Senthilmurugan Solamalai
SRM Institute of Science and
Technology
Kattankulathur, Tamil Nadu, India

Reet Singh
Vellore Institute of Technology
Chennai, Tamil Nadu, India

Sangeeta Singh
National Institute of Technology
Patna, Bihar, India

Sidharth Sivanraj
Saintgits College of Engineering
Kottayam, Kerala, India

Annapoorani Subramanian
Vellore Institute of Technology
Chennai, Tamil Nadu, India

CVSR Syavasya
Gitam Deemed University
Hyderabad, India

Polly Thomas
Saintgits College of Engineering
Kottayam, Kerala, India

Sonali Vyas
UPES
Dehradun, Uttarakhand, India

Mehwash Weqar
Jamia Millia Islamia
New Delhi, India

Anshul Yadav
Raj Kumar Goel Institute of Technology
Ghaziabad, Uttar Pradesh, India

R K Yadav
Raj Kumar Goel Institute of Technology
Ghaziabad, Uttar Pradesh, India

1

Importance and Applications of Internet of Things (IoT)

Midhila P, Manjushree M, Raajasubramanian D, Srinivasan S, Haleshi Chalwadi, Ritismita Devi, Alaknanda J Adur, and Narendra K

CONTENTS

1.1 Introduction

Internet of Things (IoT) delineates the integration of computing devices, embedded computing systems, and data conveyance technologies that collect and exchange data, promoting dramatic changes in people's lifestyles by enabling sophisticated technologies based on sustainability. IoT-based multiple devices communicate effectively with objects, processes or people, helping the global networking infrastructure to bring about substantial changes in cognitive and lifestyle factors based on sustainability across the globe. IoT is an ideal technology platform that provides multiple benefits by updating IoT devices according to changes in the environment providing advanced and structured optimization, supporting human well-being through automated technologies and facilitating effective monitoring and management of innovative real-world applications such as water and wastewater management systems, agricultural practices, wildlife, marine life, waste management system, air quality management, home automation, irrigation, solar energy utilization and

DOI: 10.1201/9781003226888-1

automation of building to communicate effectively with networks independent of human activities and transmit indispensable data in support of taking decisions.

The IoT architecture has three layers:

1. The perception layer: The perception layer is the lowest layer, which has sensors, actuators or other IoT devices. These devices collect data from different environments and communicate the information to the subsequent layer (the network layer).
2. The network layer: The network layer is involved in processing a massive amount of data and transmitting the data obtained from the perception layer to the application layer.
3. The application layer: The application layer manages all intelligent applications such as smart home, smart building, smart city, smart agriculture, intelligent transportations, smart wearables, smart hospitals and other cognitive applications.

IoT devices have a remarkable impact on human life (Khalil et al., 2021) as it senses and dispatches data to a server as pertinent real-time information. IoT data collection process ensures proper management and data transmission using sensors that detect changes in environments. Sensors can be broadly divided into analogue sensors and digital sensors. Temperature sensors, ultrasonic, pressure, infrared, proximity and humidity sensors are a few of the innovative IoT-based sensors available in the market. Consumer IoT platforms allow multiple device interconnectivity with greater intelligence, facilitating consumer interaction with device manufacturers through third-party developers and service providers. IoT brings decentralized heterogeneous clever networking tactics, bringing intelligence and visibility converging internet technologies and Information and Communication Technology (ICT), which enhances the contentment of society, industries, academicians and researchers. IoT technologies are also deployed to ameliorate the living standards, enhancing environmental sustainability (Table 1.1).

TABLE 1.1

Examples of Sensors Used in IoT, Their Functions and Applications

S. No	Types of Sensor	Sensor Functions	Applications
1.	Temperature sensor	Measure the amount of heat	Environmental, health and agricultural sectors
2.	Humidity sensor	Detect the amount of water vapour in atmosphere	Heating, vents, smart buildings, smart houses, smart hospitals, agricultural sector
3.	Pressure sensor	Detects pressure fluctuations in gases	Industries
4.	Proximity sensors	Detects nearby objects	Safety and security systems
5.	Location sensor	Detects position of objects	Network/Wi-fi services
6.	Image sensors	Images to electrical signals	Digital cameras
7.	Infrared sensors		Healthcare sector (monitor blood pressure)
8.	Optical sensors	Record the quantity of light	Smart vehicles, Smart cities, health sector etc.
9.	Chemical sensors	Detects chemical levels in liquid/gas	Industries, smart home, healthcare sectors etc.
10.	Gyroscope sensors	Capture data on the angular velocity	Robotics, automated vehicles etc.

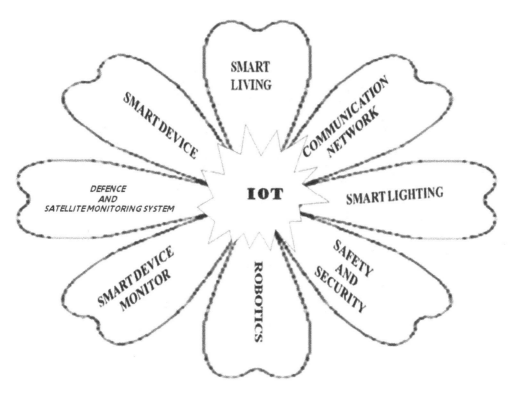

FIGURE 1.1
IoT opportunities and impacts.

This chapter presents the importance and applications of IoT technology (Figure 1.1), emphasizing the further scope of IoT to develop end-to-end energy-efficient techniques, interoperability and cost-effective solutions considering sustainability with improved privacy and security with a contemporary network architectural status. This chapter also reviews the current situation and advanced real-time communication technologies implemented across the globe. Finally, the chapter features the real-time execution of IoT technologies in high-level intelligence platforms such as cognitive IoT (CIoT) and artificial intelligence (AI).

1.2　IoT and Its Significance

IoT is a nascent technology with an ecosystem of IoT-based devices that have transformed traditional living concepts into an advanced lifestyle to provide sustainability-based social, economic and environmental benefits. Smart cities, smart homes, smart buildings, smart agricultural systems, smart healthcare systems, smart wearables, smart irrigation and smart transportation, enabling internet-based technologies, are some of the IoT-based transformations to provide technological and social perspectives to change the traditional way of living into an advanced digital lifestyle (Figure 1.2). IoT technologies optimize productivity, escalate product quality, minimize environmental hazards and take the edge off resources to make life more innovative, accessible and dynamic.

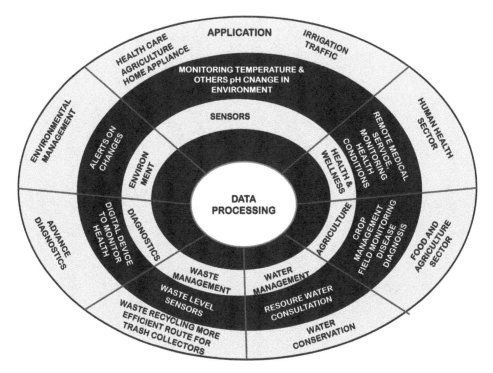

FIGURE 1.2
IoT platform importance and applications.

1.3 Role of the IoT in Sustainable Development

Over the last centuries, the long-term nature of climate changes has led to an increased concentration of greenhouse gases (GHGs) affecting global temperatures (Agrimonti et al., 2020). Due to the strong dependence of humans on climate, it is imperative to provide foundations for practical approaches to enable sustainable development integrating renewable energy systems reducing GHG emissions. IoT-based approaches offer opportunities for integrating technologies necessary to solve significant problems of population growth with an ecosystem of internet-enabled devices and ensure balanced economic development reducing the effects of global warming (Nizetic et al., 2019). Over the past decade, researchers and engineers have been trying to bridge challenging tasks such as climate change effects and sustainable practices. Many IoT-based technological advancements have addressed humanity's most significant challenges ranging from climate changes to contemporary living based on sustainable architecture. Improving sustainability through sustainable energy and electric systems amends the implementation of energy-efficient systems using IoT technologies, cognitive automation, AI and real-time monitoring (Andronie et al., 2021). Advancing IoT technologies in smart farming satisfies extensive demand for nutrients with expanding population and interminable urbanization concepts (Inderwildi et al., 2020; Li et al., 2020; Lyons and Lăzăroiu, 2020). Advancing towards sustainable development focusing on meeting the urban needs reinforces reduced emissions, industrial decarbonization and climate change mitigation, incorporating sustainable strategies based on renewable energy systems (Grondys et al., 2020; Nelson, 2020; Nik et al., 2020).

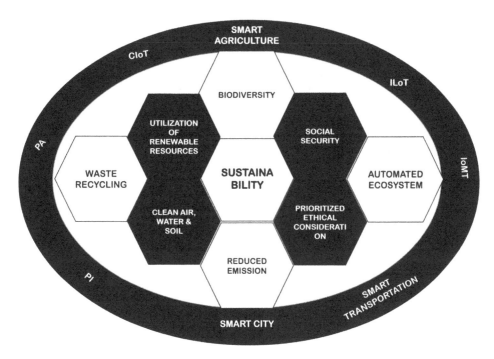

FIGURE 1.3
Next-generation IoT and sustainable urbanization.

Sustainable energy solutions mitigating climate changes remodel energy-efficient transitions featuring IoT technologies such as photovoltaics (PV) and wind generators (Figure 1.3). PV and wind generators can ensure energy efficiency from 35% to 45%, with an average wind competence feature of 20% to 40% extracting deep insights into the need for the proliferation of IoT infrastructure. Excepting the concerns of greenhouse emissions, there is also a persistent ascent of hazardous pollutants such as N_2O, CH_4, fertilizers, pesticides, natural gas and oil.

1.4 Role of IoT in Environment Management

Recent advancement in technologies and urbanization has brought many environmental concerns such as air pollution, aquatic and marine pollution and energy wastage (Lagerspetz et al., 2019). IoT-based technologies provide environmental cleanliness, reliable and cost-effective energy solutions, automation and digitization of human and industrial activities in a smart city context to take constructive ecological measures to protect nature (Ejaz et al., 2017). IoT technologies are also considered promising for harsh environments such as nuclear storage and high gamma radiation operations.

An extensive, multi-level, secure monitoring network in an IoT-based environmental management system can be accomplished using sensors, constructing an IoT platform with customer support strategies and big data analytics (Gomez et al., 2019). IoT-based environmental technologies have been enforced across variegated smart environments such as smart cities, intelligent healthcare systems and smart wearable technologies, weather monitoring systems, precision agriculture, disaster management and smart warning systems (Bibri, 2018). The application of IoT-based technologies has become decisive in environmental management systems to evolve and stimulate innovative principles and processes in sustainable development. The recent trends in human population growth and consequent demand for food and energy-efficient engineering technologies have become crucial determinants of a strategic new environment.

1.5 Role of IoT in Energy Management

Platitudinous use of vehicles is the primary reason for the energy crisis, and IoT technologies represent a feasible way to promote energy conservation through smart transportation and traffic management. IoT-based transportation systems play a crucial role in traffic management through real-time monitoring of transportation systems. Real-time data processing offers smart parking and intelligent transportation applications to take decisions such as cost-saving options, faster routes or a shorter distance (Mohanty, 2016).

Smart city is enabled with IoT system to track down pollution, energy usage, demand of individual buildings, vehicles through sensors connected to each buildings, logistics and energy network systems. These connections ensure many energy supplies and distribution systems applications to create an energy-efficient smart city ecosystem (Motlagh et al., 2020). A smart grid is an electrical grid used in IoT-based electricity delivery systems that use remote control and automation to monitor and manage electricity. Innovative grid-based digital technologies have an advantage over the conventional approaches in creating

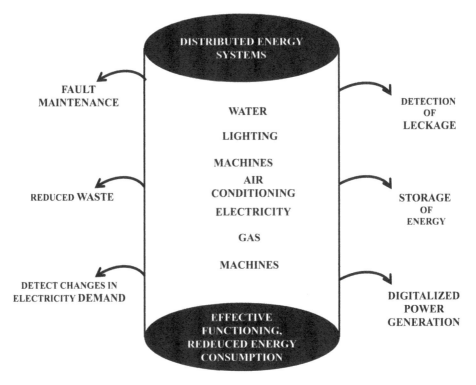

FIGURE 1.4
Importance of IoT in the energy sector.

a widely distributed automated energy delivery network that intelligently responds to changes adapting to energy-efficient conservation strategies such as energy efficiency, energy utilization, cost-effectiveness and reduced emissions (Figure 1.4).

1.6 Importance of IoT in Industries

IoT-based computer paradigms having the potential to accelerate intelligent industrial processing technologies through advanced analytics platforms have fuelled the creation of an IoT subcategory known as the industrial IoT (IIoT). IIoT is a coalescence of automated machinery, control systems and IoT devices. IIoT would be a significant constituent in the forthcoming industrial revolution offering high industrial productivity, superior asset management, sensor-based preventive and predictive sustentation delivering insights into industrial automation, reduced labour cost and customer transactions.

IIoT is a high-level IoT architecture consisting of internet-connected automated machinery that aims to bring IoT-based industrial applications to increase production yield, improve product quality and reduce errors (Chalapathi et al., 2021). IIoT system-elevated progress in industries has a plethora of advantages in logistics, performance of the industrial machinery and real-time innovative industrial processing. IIoT-based industrial processing at the entire life cycle, creating remarkable market segmentation and sustainable industrial value creation, has transformed industries, enabling competitive manufacturing processes. IIoT underpins contemporary architectural techniques and data management developments that ensure significant future results and assistance for industries and small factories. A decade of technological advancements in IIoT through data management and information services has brought several established IIoT cloud platforms to provide services for smart factories (Yu et al., 2021).

1.7 IoT-Based Smart Agriculture and Water Management Systems

Present-day agricultural practices such as excessive fertilizers, irrigation systems and use of non-renewable energy sources such as fossil fuels for agricultural machines make agriculture a consequential patron of GHG emissions (Heidecke et al., 2018). Also, the enormous use of fertilizers and pesticides in agricultural lands has adjudged a peril to soil health, aquatic systems and ecosystem biodiversity (Agrimonti et al., 2020). Plant factories are an IoT-based imaginative approach to agriculture that enables a closed growing system. A plant factory utilizes an integrated farming system that creates a more consistent atmosphere with artificial light, temperature, relative humidity and CO_2.

Water is vital to support ecosystem functioning and represents all necessities for all living beings (Singh and Ahmed, 2020). There is a mounting demand for water due to an explosion in the human population, and concerns of water quality can be blown up to cause perturbations in water demand management. Aside from water demand management, water resources and water pollution are strongly influenced by human population growth. With the emergence of IoT, tracking water management systems using various sensors is achieving significant milestones for measuring parameters like temperature, relative humidity and pH. Consistently used sensors for the management of water include ultrasonic sensors (to evaluate the water level in a water reservoir), temperature sensors (to measure the temperature of water reservoirs) and pH sensors (to measure the pH of water).

The IoT-based water management systems can be grouped into two categories: water level monitoring systems and water quality monitoring systems (Singh and Ahmed, 2020). Water level monitoring systems perform sensor-based real-time monitoring of water level, while the water quality monitoring systems aim to measure diverse water quality parameters such as pH, total dissolved solids (TDS) and temperature of the water. In addition to offering water level and quality management systems, some other possible applications of IoT in water management include the management of irrigation systems through soil and weather monitoring, water saving etc. Crop monitoring and automation in the agricultural sector play a significant role in various farming activities to increase productivity and accomplish customization without human intervention.

1.7.1 Precision Agriculture (PA) and Precision Irrigation (PI)

Global climate change is having severe impacts on crop quality and agricultural practices. The reduced nitrogen and minerals are overwhelmingly harmful, significantly impacting human health and nutrition. The integration of ICT technologies such as the internet, television, computers, mobile phones, wireless networking system, software and hardware systems, virtual media applications, social networking, satellite systems or other communication technologies in the agriculture sector is known as precision agriculture (PA). Precision agriculture may contribute to food safety (Gebbers and Adamchuk, 2010) and makes farming further convenient and transparent by improved tracking, delineating, documenting the agricultural practices and predictions with the possibility to enhance the quality of farm products (Agrimonti et al., 2020). Automated greenhouses used in PA allow farmers to procure real-time information with the help of low-cost hardware systems (sensors, actuators and communication technologies). The automatic optical sensors and intelligent agricultural systems, intelligent planning, agronomic practices and controlled fertilization will inevitably shape the future of agriculture. Real-time crop monitoring, weather forecasting, intelligent field monitoring, skill-based farm management systems, automated watering and fertilization systems, geolocation of the livestock farming, prediction analytics for crop yield and plant diseases, whole-farm management approach to obtain data on soil temperature, soil conductivity, soil pH, soil nutrients and amount of water in soil are some of the management approaches which rely on PV technology (Ferrández-Pastor et al., 2018).

IoT-based water management enables precision irrigation (PI) as advanced technology to reassure solutions for global demand for water and effective utilization of water resources. PI promises to improve the water use efficiency, crop improvement and automation in agricultural and irrigational sectors. Cutting-edge technologies such as WSN are deputed to monitor irrigation activities, soil moisture and soil temperature, and the data from the sensors are transmitted to the IoT gateway devices through Message Queuing Telemetry Transport (MQTT) standard messaging protocol to take immediate decisions about agricultural activities. Wireless sensor network (WSN) permits smart irrigation management by directly interacting with the environment for real-time monitoring of irrigational activities, water savings and optimization of water usage (Khriji et al., 2020). Smart irrigation and agriculture has been the subject of intensive research and works related to smart farming practices. The efficient utilization of renewable resources has gained momentum globally in recent years. This has led to innovative IoT-based approaches to utilize resources based on sustainable development efficiently. Interaction of farmers with IoT devices enables accurate tracking of endless information about crop details, soil statistics, irrigation decisions, zone-wise watering, remote data monitoring etc. Integration of IoT into machines, sensors and other networking systems leads to the development of smart farming technologies (Pivoto et al., 2018) such as agricultural automation, agribots (robots designed for farming activities to detect weeds or spray pesticides etc.), drones (for visualization, mapping and observing of the farms), sensor-based remote sensing of environmental changes (such as soil pH, temperature, relative humidity, crop growth), weather forecasting (based on which cultivation is done for suitable crops) and computer imaging using cameras (to produce images that are used for predicting the crop growth, detecting plant diseases and improving water-efficient irrigation) (Figure 1.5).

1.8 Importance of IoT in Waste Management

Waste management consists of prevention, recycling, biological treatments and disposal to manage the waste generated from its inception to decomposition, cure or final disposal. Rapid population growth, urbanization, improper collection and discarding of waste, lack of advanced technologies for waste management and uncoordinated proposition to waste collection and disposal threaten the existing waste management systems (Ali et al., 2020). Significant alterations in waste management systems and remodelling approaches are extracting deep insights into IoT-based waste management systems, integrating physical systems, engineering skills and wireless access networks, capitalizing on the potential to transform waste management systems.

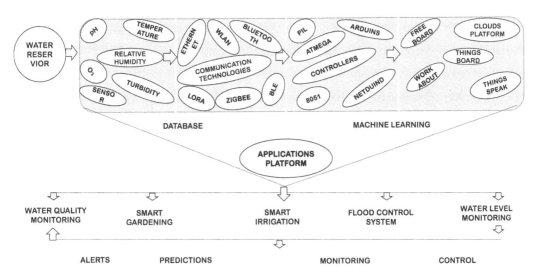

FIGURE 1.5
IoT-based water management system.

1.9 Importance of Intelligent Cities and Smart Homes

A smart city is an infrastructure framework designed by IoT systems, sensor networks, digital cameras and different types of electronic methods to make better and faster decisions based on real-time information to improve the quality of urban life. The smart city concept efficiently employs physical and digital elements to provide necessary interoperable services to customers, which are safe, disciplined, energy-efficient, unified and competent for a sustainable future. The Institute of Electrical and Electronics Engineers (IEEE) envisages a smart city as an urban digital ecosystem that unites technology, government and society to empower citizens, economy, environment and governance. The smart city offers digital solutions for advanced healthcare, smart transportation, intelligent waste management systems and improved lifestyles through practical frameworks that embrace processes and planning mechanisms.

A smart home provides a centralized network of devices and systems to control the operative functions of electronic home appliances such as refrigerators, personal computers, lights, dishwashers and television (Figure 1.6). Smart homes dispense innovative communication and service utilization for security control, automatic control of lighting, gas, home appliances, cameras, doors and windows by both companies and individuals through integrated network environments (Rego et al., 2021). The automatic control of home appliances and electronic devices regularly in an IoT smart home system (IoTSHS) promotes an energy-efficient environment and conservation of natural resources. IoT-based streamlining of the Quality of Services (QoS) through digital imaging, carried on with the aid of wireless micro medical devices (WMMD) in the smart home, ensures swift and safe healthcare practices for patients and healthcare providers (Guo et al., 2019).

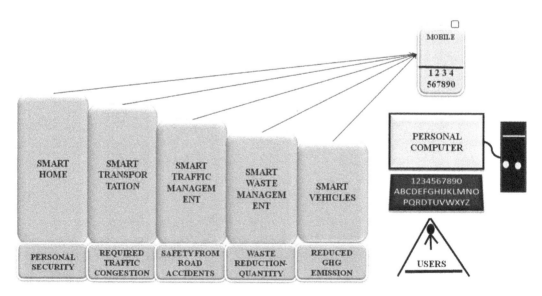

FIGURE 1.6
Smart city ecosystem.

1.10 Importance of Wildlife and Tourism IoT

Wildlife is becoming the global focal point as it helps maintain the ecological balance of nature. Wildlife monitoring and conservation is the most significant concern of offering more incredible sustainable solutions as it provides stability to different functional processes of interrelated renewable resources. IoT-based low-power wide area networks (LPWAN) is an open specification hardware program that monitors wildlife and forest environment (Ojo et al., 2021). Also, the tourism enterprises create an interactive environment with innovation in robust digital learning artistry and IoT-based devices to provide more valuable and reliable information on tourist attractions. Intelligent tourism information provides appealing scientific data to provide travel scams and understand popular tourist attractions (Gao, 2020). Smart devices that can discern animal habits and the environment through automated wireless radio telemetry systems can bridge formidable engineering tasks for the well-being of humans and wildlife.

1.11 IoT in Marine Ecosystem Monitoring

Marine ecosystem monitoring has captivated more attention in recent decades due to growing concern about the changes in the climate and global warming, marine pollution and natural disasters. IoT has become a growing trend in materializing marine environment monitoring systems (Xu et al., 2020). The traditional approaches such as oceanographic and hydrographic equipment used in monitoring the marine environment are expensive, time-consuming and complicated. Compared with these conventional monitoring systems, the new generation IoT devices have much stronger proficiency, enabling smart and precise sensor-based control of objects. Sensors are used to monitor temperature, pressure, salinity, turbidity, dissolved oxygen concentration and pH. IoT technology makes ships intelligent by integrating technologies based on sensor processing, processing functions, RFID and LAN communication network technology, providing data exchange from the IoT platform to the concerned person or device centred on ship area network architecture information (Al-Absi et al., 2020). IoT-based digitalization of the marine ecosystem has laid a strong foundation for improving the data processing management of aquatic environments and technical standards of marine environment monitoring systems, notwithstanding the far-reaching construction of digital ocean (Zixuan et al., 2016).

1.12 Importance of IoT in Air Quality Management

Air pollution refers to the deliverance of finely dispersed substances into the air that can harm the health of humans, animals and other living beings. The all-embracing air pollution problem is also fundamentally altering the environment and public health, creating widespread concerns about social-scientific interventions. This emphasizes the prominence of having sustainable approaches to air quality management (Mahajan et al., 2021).

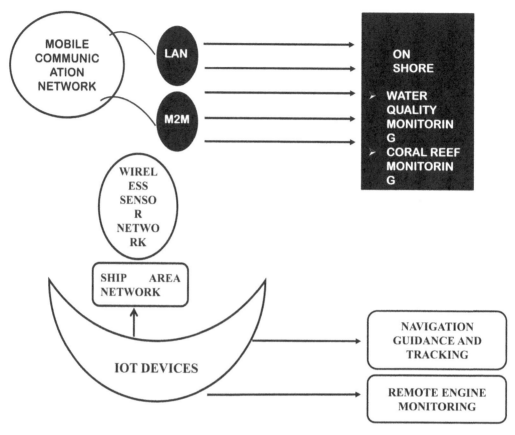

FIGURE 1.7
IoT-based marine environment monitoring systems.

The fundamental strategies to consider in monitoring air pollution management include sustainable energy-efficient environment and transportation, sustainable, cost-effective and energy-efficient buildings and sustainable approaches to reducing air pollution. Low-cost IoT-based air pollution sensors have been deployed in air quality management systems that can sense and interact with their object, environment and users enabling real-time information on air quality of a prescribed regional ecosystem or travel destination and pollution level of a particular region (Figure 1.7). Smart sensors can thus provide extensive monitoring advantages over the available monitoring systems with mediocre precision and low sensitivity (Dhingra et al., 2019).

1.13 Importance of Blockchain Technologies in IoT

The blockchain bridges a string of blocks, where each block is pointed to the preceding block with hash codes or cryptography. Each blockchain block comprises data transactions across several participants and transaction history. The blockchain accomplishes unified identity authentication, stockpile public keys, user-defined data sets and revocation data groups to make a machine-to-machine (M2M) chronicle possible. The system administrators create program-dependent system parameters to deliver private keys to individual users. Malevolent users can be captured and revoked to ensure security and privacy (Yu et al., 2021).

The blockchain will boost power generation and storage through decentralized IoT devices and exchange big data without human intervention in the energy sector. The decentralized devices provide energy utilization, energy distribution and energy flow information. Furthermore, blockchain helps in smart grid-based diagnosis or alimentation of equipment and exchange of software updates maintaining customer satisfaction and trust. Blockchain technology enables stakeholders and enterprises to provide trust protocol and reduce face value in a low-cost IT solution.

1.14 Future Perspectives of IoT

The IoT gives the impression of being poised to traverse into new impetus, proliferating numerous real-world applications ranging from smart home to managing Covid-19 (Ferrag et al., 2021). The impact of IoT on humans will address the burning issues such as sustainability and utilization of renewable resources, bridging the gap between objects and the digital world to ameliorate the standard and productivity of society and industries. However, IoT systems manifest threats due to the integration of numerous devices and advanced networking, including cloud and fog computing and other composite cyber-physical systems. Hence, further research is needed to manipulate the hardware and software systems capitalizing on the possibilities of the IoT system to future-proof sustainable development and urbanization (Figure 1.8).

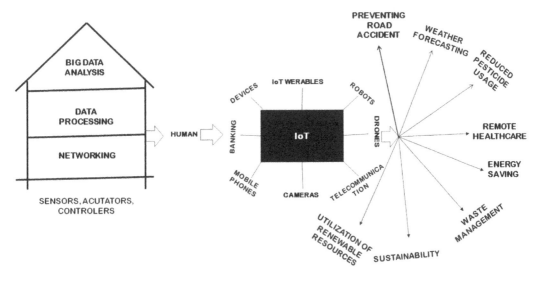

FIGURE 1.8
Future perspectives of IoT.

References

Agrimonti, C., Lauro, M., Visioli, G., **2020**. Smart Agriculture for Food Quality: Facing Climate Change in the 21st Century. Critical Reviews in Food Science and Nutrition. 61(6), 1–11.

Al-Absi, M.A., Kamolov, A., Al-Absi, A.A., Sain, M., Lee, H.J., **2020**. IoT Technology with Marine Environment Protection and Monitoring. International Conference on Smart Computing and Cyber Security: Strategic Foresight, Security Challenges and Innovation. Smartcyber 2020: Proceedings of the International Conference on Smart Computing and Cyber Security. pp. 81–89.

Ali, T., Irfan, M., Alwadie, A. S., Glowacz, A., **2020**. IoT-Based Smart Waste Bin Monitoring and Municipal Solid Waste Management System for Smart Cities. Arabian Journal for Science and Engineering. 45, 10185–10198.

Andronie, M., Lăzăroiu, G., Iatagan, M., Hurloiu, L., Dijmărescu, I., **2021**. Sustainable Cyber-Physical Production Systems in Big Data-Driven Smart Urban Economy: A Systematic Literature Review. Sustainability. 13, 751.

Bibri, S.E., **2018**. The IoT for Smart Sustainable Cities of the Future: An Analytical Framework for Sensor-Based Big Data Applications for Environmental Sustainability. Sustainable Cities and Society. 38, 230–253.

Chalapathi, G.S.S., Chamola, V., Vaish, A., Buyya, R., **2021**. Industrial Internet of Things (IIoT) Applications of Edge and Fog Computing: A Review and Future Directions. Edge and Fog Computing For Security, Privacy and Applications. 83, 293–325.

Dhingra, S., Madda, R.B., Gandomi, A.H., Patan, R., Daneshm, M., **2019**. Internet of Things Mobile–Air Pollution Monitoring System (IoT-Mobair). IEEE Internet of Things Journal. 6(3), 5577–5584.

Ejaz, W., Naeem, M., Shahid, A., Anpalagan, A., Jo, M., **2017**. Efficient Energy Management for the Internet of Things in Smart Cities. IEEE Communications Magazine 55, 84–91.

Ferrag, M.A., Shu, L., Raymond Choo, K.K., **2021**. Fighting COVID-19 and Future Pandemics with the Internet of Things: Security and Privacy Perspectives. IEEE/CAA Journal of Automatica Sinica. 8(9), 1477–1499.

Ferrández-Pastor, F.J., García-Chamizo, J.M., Hidalgo, M.N., Mora-Martínez, J., **2018**. Precision Agriculture Design Method Using a Distributed Computing Architecture on Internet of Things Context. Sensors. 18, 173.

Gao, H., **2020**. Big Data Development of Tourism Resources Based on 5G Network and Internet of Things System. Microprocessors and Microsystems, 80, 103567. ISSN 0141-9331, https://doi.org/10.1016/j.micpro.2020.103567.

Gebbers, R., Adamchuk, V.I., **2010**. Precision Agriculture and Food Security. Science. 327(5967):828–831.

Gomez, C., Chessa, S., Fleury, A., Roussos, G., Preuveneers, D., **2019**. Internet of Things for Enabling Smart Environments: A Technology-centric Perspective. JAISE. 11, 23–43.

Grondys, K., Androniceanu, A., Dacko-Pikiewicz, Z., **2020**. Energy Management in the Operation of Enterprises in the Light of the Applicable Provisions of the Energy Efficiency Directive (2012/27/EU). Energies. 13, 4338.

Guo, X., Shen, Z., Zhang, Y., Wu., T., **2019**. Review on the Application of Artificial Intelligence in Smart Homes. Smart Cities. 2(3), 402–420.

Heidecke, C., Montgomery, H., Stalb, H.,Wollenberg, L. (Eds.), **2018**. International Conference on Agricultural GHG Emissions and Food Security – Connecting Research to Policy and Practice – Volume of Abstracts, Braunschweig: Johann Heinrich von Thunen- €Institut Berlin, Germany.

Inderwildi, O., Zhang, C., Wang, X., Kraft, M., **2020**. The Impact of Intelligent Cyber-Physical Systems on the Decarbonization of Energy. Energy & Environmental Science. 13, 744–771.

Khalil, U., Ahmad, A., Abdel-Aty, A.H., Abo El-Soud, M.W., Zeshan, F., **2021**. Identification of Trusted IoT Devices for Secure Delegation. Computers and Electrical Engineering. 90, 106988.

Khriji, S., El Houssaini, D., Kammoun, I., Kanoun, O., **2020**. Precision irrigation: An IoT-Enabled Wireless Sensor Network for smart Irrigation Systems. Women in precision Agriculture. pp. 107–129.

Lagerspetz, E., Motlagh, N.H., Zaidan, M.A., Fung, P.L., Mineraud, J., Varjonen, S., Siekkinen, M., Nurmi, P., Matsumi, Y., Tarkoma, S., et al., **2019**. MegaSense: Feasibility of Low-Cost Sensors for Pollution Hot-spot Detection. Proceedings of the 2019 IEEE 17th International Conference on Industrial Informatics (INDIN), Helsinki-Espoo, Finland, 23–25 July 2019.

Li, L., Li, X., Chong, C., Wang, C.H., Wang, X., **2020**. A Decision Support Framework for the Design and Operation of Sustainable Urban Farming Systems. Journal of Cleaner Production 268, 121928.

Lyons, N., Lăzăroiu, G., **2020**. Addressing the COVID-19 Crisis by Harnessing Internet of Things Sensors and Machine Learning Algorithms in Data-driven Smart Sustainable Cities. Geopolitics, History, and International Relations. 12, 65–71.

Mahajan, S., Luo, C.H., Wu, D.Y., Chen, L.J., **2021**. From Do-It-Yourself (DIY) to Do-IT-Together (DIT): Reflections on Designing a Citizen Driven Air Quality Monitoring Framework in Taiwan. Sustainable Cities and Society. 66, 102628.

Mohanty, S.P., **2016**. Everything You Wanted to Know about Smart Cities: The Internet of Things Is the Backbone. IEEE Consumer Electronics Magazine. 5, 60–70.

Motlagh, N.H., Mohammadrezaei, M., Hunt, J., Zakeri, B., **2020**. Internet of Things (IoT) and the Energy Sector. Energies. 13, 494.

Nelson, A., **2020**. Smart Transportation Systems: Sustainable Mobilities, Autonomous Vehicle Decision-Making Algorithms, and Networked Driverless Technologies. Contemporary Readings in Law and Social Justice. 12, 25–33.

Nik, V.M., Perera, A., Chen, D., **2020**. Towards Climate Resilient Urban Energy Systems: A Review. National Science Review. 8(3), nwaa134.

Nizetic, S., Djilali, N., Papadopoulos, A.,, Rodrigues, Joel J.P.C., **2019**. Smart Technologies for Promotion of Energy Efficiency, Utilization of Sustainable Resources and Waste Management. Journal of Cleaner Production. 231, 561–595. https://doi.org/10.1016/j.jclepro.2019.04.397.

Ojo, M.O., Adami, D., Giordano, S., **2021**. Experimental Evaluation of a LoRa Wildlife Monitoring Network in a Forest Vegetation Area. Future Internet. 13(5), 115.

Pivoto, D., Waquil, P.D., Talamini, E., Spanhol, C., Corte, V.F.D., Mores, G.D.V., **2018**. Scientific Development of Smart Farming Technologies and Their Application in Brazil. Information Processing in Agriculture. 5, 21–32.

Rego, A., Gonzalez Ramirez, P.L., Jimemez, J.M., Lloret, J., **2021**. Artificial Intelligent System for Multimedia Services in Smart Home Environments. Cluster Computing. 25, 2085–2105.

Singh, M., Ahmed, S., **2020**. IoT Based Smart Water Management Systems: A Systematic Review. Materials Today: Proceedings. https://doi.org/10.1016/j.matpr.2020.08.588.

Xu, G., Shi, Y., Sun, X., Shen, W., **2020**. Internet of Things in Marine Environment Monitoring: A Review. Sensors. 19, 1711.

Yu, K., Tan, L., Aloqaily, M., Yang, H., Jararweh, Y., **2021**. Blockchain-Enhanced Data Sharing With Traceable and Direct Revocation in IIoT. IEEE Transactions on Industrial Informatics. 17, 11.

Zixuan, Y., Zhifang, W., Chang, L., **2016**. Research on Marine Environmental Monitoring System based on the Internet of Things Technology. 2016 IEEE International Conference on Electronic Information and Communication Technology (ICEICT).

2

Smart Homes: Is It a Luxury Anymore?

Annapoorani Subramanian, Khushi Akhoury, Pooja Chitravelan,
Ansu Anna Moncy, Varsha Jayaprakash, Reet Singh, and Sujatha Manohar

CONTENTS

2.1 Introduction

The term 'smart' is widely accepted as a synonym for intelligence. In today's era of continuous technological advancements, smart devices are majorly developed using a representative emerging technology called the Internet of Things (IoT). The IoT is a mesh network of real-world physical objects, vehicles, buildings that are embedded with electronic devices, which enable them to store, share, exchange data and automate any appliance over wireless connection. IoT enlarges the perception of the Internet and, due to this very reason, is very beneficial in smart home automation (Pirbhulal, S., Zhang, H., E Alahi, M. E., Ghayvat, H., Mukhopadhyay, S. C., Zhang, Y. T., & Wu, W., 2016). Smart home automation enables the user to use all the appliances efficiently, conveniently and remotely, while giving a sense of greater comfort as well as security (Edge, M., Taylor, B., Dewsbury, G., & Groves, M., 2000).

DOI: 10.1201/9781003226888-2

People of this generation are in awe of digitalization and look forward to reaping more of its benefits (Hoffman, D. L., & Novak, T., 2016). Many elderly people suffer from a cognitive disability, dementia, loss of clear vision or lack of strength, which makes it difficult for them to perform household chores (Jiang, L., Liu, D. Y., & Yang, B., 2004).

IoT essentially provides a connection between a hub or a network and electrical and electronic devices. This helps in controlling, tracking and locating those devices virtually by the user. IoT is based on the concept of device-to-device connectivity and the development of smart sensors along with various communication techniques, such as Bluetooth, Wi-Fi, supported by cloud computing technologies. These IoT-connected devices collect data, send data and act upon the data they collected. The field of IoT has evolved, but most of the works done so far are based on adopting the IoT technologies for extremely resource-constrained nodes like sensor network node that simply sends the collected data to the base station. There is dearth of work done on applying IoT technologies into embedded devices used by humans including customer appliances. Combining classic smart home techniques, cloud computing, IoT, rule-based event processing and considering the market to smart homes in India, the authors are proposing an advanced smart home technology with the basic components at an affordable rate for customers.

Remote control of the connected appliances with an android device is the main feature. Devices, such as light, fan, air conditioner, will be incorporated with various varieties of sensors and can be controlled and monitored with the help of android devices. Analysing the data collected by these devices will be helpful in monitoring the health of the customers, overall energy consumption of a household etc. This smart home technique is beneficial in many other aspects, such as energy management, utilization of minimal resources, better security. The intention is to provide a solution that is ecologically and economically efficient, which is the need for a country like India. This chapter not only highlights the advancement of technology but also discusses the business model for affordable smart home solutions and various marketing strategies.

2.2 Literature Review

A smart home is an advanced system that involves complete control and automation of various actuators using embedded technologies. Such homes have various smart devices incorporated to control lighting, air conditioning, heating, television, entertainment gadgets, home appliances, such as refrigerators, washing machines and security systems capable of interacting among themselves as well as with the user. The devices can be controlled remotely by mobile or other internet-enabled devices. Such systems include switches and sensors connected to a central unit controlled by the users using a terminal or by a mobile connected to cloud services.

In this section, we first look at the global and Indian scenario of the market for smart homes and then discuss the technology used for the smart home services. The authors acknowledge the existence of smart home solutions in India but highlight the need for an affordable solution and propose a business model for the same.

2.2.1 Global Scenario

With the expanding population of the world, the demand for power is also increasing. The global market size for the smart home market in 2018 was estimated to be between

TABLE 2.1

Top Competitors in the International Market

S. No	Company	Country
1	Johnson Controls International	Ireland
2	Schneider Electric	France
3	Honeywell International Inc.	USA
4	ABB Ltd	Switzerland
5	Crestron Electronics, Inc.	Canada
6	Siemens AG	Germany
7	ADT Corporation	USA
8	Control4 Corporation	USA
9	Samsung Electronics Co., Ltd.	South Korea

$70 billion and $75 billion and is expected to grow at a rate of 13% (Meng, Y., Zhang, W., Zhu, H., & Shen, X. S., 2018). According to CAGR's (Compound annual growth rate) statistical report, the global market is projected to reach USD 119.26 billion by 2022 (Yang, H., Lee, W., & Lee, H., 2018). The smart home market can be geographically distributed into four major categories (North America, Europe, APAC [Asia Pacific Accreditation Cooperation] and ROW [rest of the world]). North America is expected to contribute roughly 40% of the total expenditure followed by APAC 34% and Europe 22%. Major factors contributing to the rise of the smart home market are the growing adoption of smart devices and the rising demand for smart security systems and electronic devices among consumers.

Quoting the estimation provided by NASSCOM (The National Association of Software and Service Companies): 'The IoT market in India is poised to reach USD 15 billion by 2020, accounting for nearly 5 percent of the total global market. With nearly 120 firms offering solutions in the IoT segment, there are tremendous opportunities for further growth' (Chinchane, A., Bani, V. & Sumant, O., 2019).

Table 2.1 lists the companies offering smart home solutions in the international market (Meticulous Blog, 2021; Markets and Markets, 2021; Business Wire, 2019).

2.2.2 Indian Scenario

Although in Indian cities and rural areas, the home automation market is in its developing years, it will expand in the future due to excessive urbanization. Inspired by Government of India programs, such as 'Make in India' and 'Digital India', there have been few smart home start-ups, such as Home Brain, Inoho, Oakter and IFIHomes (Chinchane, A., Bani, V. & Sumant, O., 2019).

- Residential sector: Accounting for almost 60% of the market size, the residential sector in India is the most competitive, having the highest current growth at a CAGR of 35–40%. Out of this, individual homes and villas take up 75–80% and builders for the apartment take around 20% of the market.

- Commercial sector: Accounting for almost 30% of the market size, it is majorly driven by security and access systems. In India, this segment is dominated by companies like Samsung and Bosch.

- Hospitality industry: Accounting for 10% of the market size, the hospitality industry is also anticipated to fuel the demand for home automation systems due to need for differentiation.

TABLE 2.2

Top Indian Home Automation Companies

S. No	Name of Company	Headquarters	Services/Products
1	BuildTrack	Mumbai	Home automation solutions are useful for safety, security, comfort, convenience and power savings for your house
2	Oakter	Noida	Plug and play smart home products. Smart control of up to 40 different varieties of home appliances
3	Smartify	Ahmedabad	A wide range of home automation products and solutions
4	IFI Homes	Bangalore	Switches, solar lights and network security cameras. Focuses on DIY installation and educate users how to install their products
5	SharpNode	Mumbai	Effective solutions for control and security of homes that function on innovative and advanced technologies with the help of IoT
6	Cubical Labs	Delhi	Wireless smart home solutions, curtain closer monitors etc.

The market is currently concentrated in the top ten cities, a few factors being the growth of IT Hubs and HNIs (high net-worth individuals). Low network bandwidth and limited connectivity contribute to the lower level of market penetration of home automation systems in India as compared to other developing nations. Also, usage of non-standard components in smart homes leading to its failure can hamper the growth of the Indian home automation market.

Table 2.2 lists the promising home automation companies in India (Indianweb2, 2016; Things in India, 2020; Startuptalky, 2021).

2.2.3 Technology Used in Smart Home Automation

A home automation system will control lighting, climate, entertainment systems and appliances. It also includes home security, such as access control and alarm systems. The product is operated on the phone in the form of an app. An app associated with the control of appliances is installed by the consumer on their mobiles from which every room in the house can be monitored and controlled. When a customer uses the app, they can remotely operate the fans, light and lock the door just by enabling certain instructions on the app. This app is a combination of AI (artificial intelligence), NLP (natural language processing) and ML (machine learning), together known as chatbot technology. This is enabled with the ability to converse with the users and provide instructions to the IoT-controlled devices, such as sensors, speakers, Bluetooth devices etc. Various technologies and methodologies have been proposed by previous researchers for configuring a smart home. This includes collection of data using various sensors, control of appliances using actuators, voice or multimedia and transfer of data to various platforms using wireless communication technologies. Since IoT devices are comparatively expensive than general home appliances, various approaches are underway to develop standard home appliances as smarter appliances at affordable costs (Lin, Y. W., Lin, Y. B., Hsiao, C. Y., & Wang, Y. Y., 2017; Liu, Q., Yang, X., & Deng, L., 2018). Operational loads of the embedded smart devices are evaluated by obtaining the total and peak power consumption and based on the impact of environmental or atmospheric conditions. This in turn leads to an efficient energy management by utilizing the cutting-edge technologies like IoT and big data analytics across multiple sectors (Pilloni, V., Floris, A., Meloni, A., & Atzori, L., 2016). With the advent of the latest technologies and the concept of smart homes, the exposure of sensitive data and the potential risk for data to be hacked has increased. Thus, security and privacy of users is a key factor to be included in any system as proposed by various researchers. In particular, they have studied various methods to secure the embedded devices, network-level security, secure authentication techniques for IoT devices, secure data uploading methodology and the potential threats caused by malicious hackers to reveal sensitive data (Sivaraman, V., Gharakheili, H. H., Fernandes, C., Clark, N., & Karliychuk, T., 2018).

The increase in crime rates and the feeling of insecurity instilled in the minds of people have eventually led to a surge in economical video surveillance integrated along with real-time data analytics which potentially has the ability to boost the growth of the home automation market in India. Moreover, cost-effectiveness, increase in disposable income and surge in awareness about automated technology are some of the driving factors for the Indian home automation market. In addition to this, improved mobile technology upgrades and availability of improved Wi-Fi access have bolstered the country's smart home automation devices. All of the above factors contribute to the development of India's home automation industry. It is also expected that the current AI-based voice assistants that we use can later act as the brain-voice of the entire home automation system.

2.3 Proposed Smart Home Solution

There is a need for a cost-efficient home automation system that is affordable by the highly populated middle-class segment. This section discusses various aspects of the proposed smart home solution.

2.3.1 Security

- IoT security is an integral part of any IoT-based solution as it prevents leakage of confidential data from reaching the hands of malicious hackers who launch various attacks, like DDoS, Man-in-the-Middle attacks, differential attacks, etc.
- Encryption ensures that the transmitted data can be accessed only by those who have the secret decryption code. The data in transit between a device and its service infrastructure (cloud) is protected.
- Whenever a device is connected to the network, it should be authenticated before the transmission of data. Cryptographic algorithms involving symmetric keys and asymmetric keys such as Triple DES (Data Encryption Standard) are to be utilized for two-way authentication.
- To prevent attacks, secure boot technology would be implemented to prevent hackers from replacing the firmware with malicious versions.
- To mitigate further attacks, we could consider the following legacy cryptographic algorithms (Abu-Tair, M., Djahel, S., Perry, P., Scotney, B., Zia, U., Carracedo, J. M., & Sajjad, 2020):

Block Ciphers:

1.1 Blowfish (Schneier, B., 1933)

1.2 AES128-CBC and AES256-CBC (Daemen, J., Rijmen, V., 2013).

Stream Ciphers:

2.1 Chacha20 (Nir, Y., Langley, A., 2015),

2.2 AES128-CTR, AES256-CTR and DES3 (Smid, M. E., Branstad, D. K., 1988).

2.3.2 Privacy

Most of the consumers are surrendering their privacy to unauthorized softwares and companies even without realizing that their data is being leaked. With the increase in the IoT market, the need for consumer data protection is also highly necessary to ensure that the consumer can handle these devices in a safer manner. Various attacks, such as jamming and spoofing, lead to a decline in the integrity of the users' data (Meng, Y., Zhang, W., Zhu, H., Shen, X. S., 2018). Companies are not very strict about their privacy policies, and even if a detailed explanation is given, they are often unintelligible to a common man. First and foremost, it is very important to analyse the types of possible attacks that can damage any IoT-based solution before implementing protection and privacy schemes. It is more advantageous to perform various activities at the sensor layer as it minimizes privacy breaches rather than a database layer. However, this may reduce the efficiency of the system and result in lower utility. Simple methods, like regular updates of the device, frequent password changes, minimal cloud use, are techniques that can be adopted by consumers to protect their data. Some of the advanced methods adopted for preserving privacy include multiparty and trusted third party computation, homogeneous encryption and anonymization techniques.

2.3.3 Connectivity and Control

The ability to keep all of the technology in your home connected through one interface is a massive stride for technology. The users cannot manage each device individually. It will become a hassle leading to traffic chaos in the smart home network and will end up in energy wastage too. To overcome these problems, it is necessary to build an integrated management system that connects all the IoT devices (Jo, H., Yoon, Y. I., 2018).

2.3.4 Energy Efficiency

If we can have more control over the heating and cooling of homes with a programmable smart thermostat that can study the customer schedules, temperature preferences, record them, then suggest the best energy-efficient settings throughout the day, it will help increase the energy efficiency and help the environment. Lights and motorized shades can be programmed to switch to an evening mode as the sun sets and switch back again to morning mode when the sun rises. Lights can also be turned on and off automatically when the customer enters or leaves the room so that they never have to worry about wasting energy. Figure 2.1 summarizes the suggested solutions to IoT vulnerabilities.

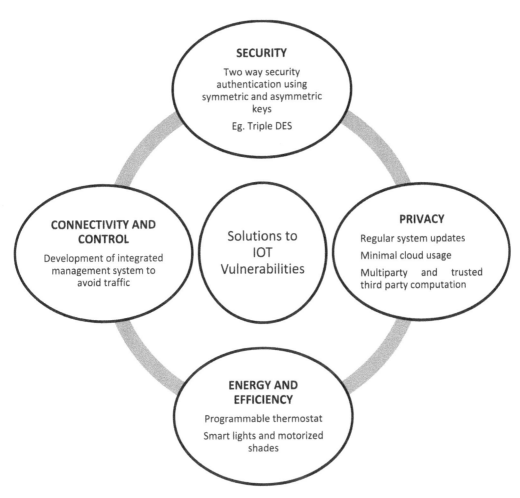

FIGURE 2.1
Solutions to IOT vulnerability.

2.4 Business Model Canvas

The Business Model Canvas (BMC) is a strategic management tool which gives the structure of a business plan. BMC includes some various business aspects which we will discuss in this section. Some of the aspects of the canvas are presented in Figure 2.2.

2.4.1 Envisioning

One of the key motivations for this business is that people are investing more in home automation recently. We are trying to provide affordable smart home services for the Indian community. There are a lot of limitations, such as security concerns, limitations in modifying the existing home appliances to fit into our proposed working methodology. With the help of IoT, the best antivirus software, and advanced sensors, we can overcome most of the limitations.

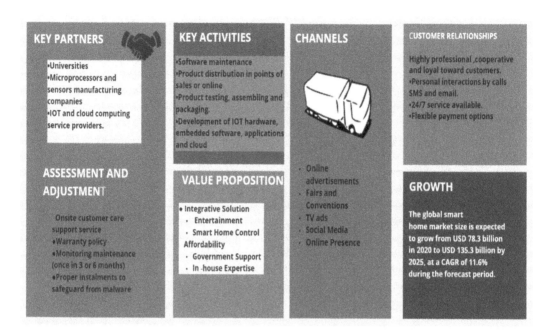

FIGURE 2.2
Business Model Canvas.

2.4.2 Assessing Opportunities

Assessing the marketing opportunities and required resources, among different types of customer segments in the market, the 'strugglers', (poor people struggling for meagre existence) with low incomes are unlikely to adopt smart home technologies. 'Retired renders' (retired people), 'convenience seekers' (People who're not sensitive to prices) and 'greeners' (people who prefer eco-friendly products) are challenging segments. However, 'affluent nesters' (people who have higher income outcomes that invest in improving their homes), 'impressors' (people who have an impressing lifestyle) and 'early adopters' (people who use new products before the majority of other people) are the easiest target market for smart home technologies. A study shows that by 2022, the smart home market in India will reach around $6 Billion. Our competitors will be companies providing smart home technology and products. As the technology underpinning this revolution in how we live continues to get faster and more powerful, we can expect home automation, IoT and AI to offer domestic help in new and innovative ways. Various skills and partners are also required for the complete establishment of this project. Energy efficiency, ease of use for elder people etc. are other areas in which we can attract customers.

2.4.3 Evolving Strategies

2.4.3.1 Value Proposition

Product marketing becomes simple when we emphasise the product's qualities and the fact that it consumes less energy. Other considerations would include its integrative solution, home monitoring, system control and product affordability.

2.4.3.2 Financial

The basic model of complete home automation using the phone will cost roughly Rs. 15,000, with modification depending on the client's budget and needs. The components' total cost would be Rs. 5,500. Additional features will be determined based on the client's budget.

2.4.3.3 Company Goals

One of the important goals is to focus on enhancing residents' safety and security while also improving their quality of life and their convenience at home. Home automation systems can also lead to significant savings on energy.

2.4.4 Operations

The key activities involved in the business are:

1. Software maintenance
2. Product distribution through stores or e-commerce channels
3. Product testing
4. Assembling and packaging
5. Development of IoT hardware
6. Embedded software
7. Web-based applications and cloud platform to manage data
8. Comfort and convenience at affordable costs
9. Energy-efficiency
10. Safety and Security
11. Entertainment

Residential and commercial customers are our two main customer segments. We will rely on online advertisements, fairs and conventions, television commercials, and inbound channels such as SEO and social media for promotion.

The marketing team must focus on retaining existing consumers, establishing long-term relationships with them and ensuring high levels of customer satisfaction. The following are some of the most important customer relationship strategies:

1. Onsite customer care support service
2. Warranty policy
3. Monitoring maintenance (once in three or six months)
4. Proper instalments to safeguard from malware
5. Improvisations and re-vamps based on feedback
6. 24/7 service available
7. Flexible payment options

2.5 Challenges

The issues described below aren't specific to the suggested solution but rather apply to the smart home concept as a whole.

Installation and initial cost: Installing a home automation system can be a significant strain on the property holder, depending on the advancement of the framework. In such a case, you tentatively look for an exterior temporary worker, which will land you up with extensive exploitation of your money, but if you are doing it yourself, it'll take a toll on your time, and it might go wrong due to lack in knowledge and expertise in that region. In spite of the fact that numerous keen home automation gadgets are presently affordable to the people belonging to any strata, totally automating a home is still relatively costly. Most of the computing innovation is effectively progressing and becoming less costly in any automation system due to the advancement in technology and thus will lead to a surge in cheaper and affordable options in the upcoming years.

Complex technology: Where automating everything in life may sound luring, our old school fashioned flip of the switch is distant more helpful than getting your smartphone to turn on and off lights. You should always consider to what extent do you want your home to get automated rather than looking into framework that suites your home (Yang, H., Lee, W., & Lee, H., 2018).

System compatibility: Having control over all the components while automating your home is important, but there are some devices which need different platforms for performing their day-to-day tasks. For instance, the thermostat may require the user to log in to another platform to control the air conditioner, but your security system may need you to access and manage the setting from one location. To fully utilize the comfort of home automation, investing in a centralized platform that controls all systems and gadgets from one location is critical (Ma, L., Li, Z., & Zheng, M., 2019).

Cost: Despite the fact that home automation systems have gotten significantly more affordable in recent years, the cost of purchasing and setting a device can still be expensive. Consumer reports generally have some insights and views about the top home automation systems on the market, including prices.

Security issues: As more people utilize smart home gadgets, security is likely to become a major issue. The huge volume of devices connected and data transmitted across various networks makes the system vulnerable for potential hackers to take control of the system. There will be rise of new security problems, as well as a proliferation of smart home security gadgets and software.

A smart house is made up of several components that may be managed over the internet or Bluetooth, such as cameras, security systems, appliances. Smart home developers and engineers are improving the security algorithms and authentication layers of smart home automation as smart technologies improve. Passwords or biometrics are used to protect most systems nowadays. As a result, smart home hacking is extremely unlikely in the presence of a strong security system. As a result, it's important to understand how to prevent your smart home from being hacked (Ma, L., Li, Z., & Zheng, M., 2019).

App security: The majority of smart home gadgets come with related apps that can be useful to control them. To get this control, apps are given a set of rights that affect the device's operation, for example, the permission to open and close a smart lock that secures the house. If a hacker acquires access to these apps, it can pose a threat to the security, allowing them to obtain access to your house. The easiest approach to avoid this kind of security threats is to keep your apps used for smart home automation as updated as possible and to install some additional software and security applications to protect your device from data theft or illegal access (Ma, L., Li, Z., & Zheng, M., 2019).

Wireless security: Most of the smart devices communicate using wireless technologies like Wi-Fi, ZigBee and Bluetooth. This makes the smart home devices vulnerable to hackers who can intercept and gain access to your devices. Since Wi-Fi is most widely used mode of connection, it is important to secure the Wi-Fi router placed in your home (Ma, L., Li, Z., & Zheng, M., 2019).

Integrated systems: Certain manufacturers provide integrated smart house systems, which allow you to operate all of your smart home devices from a single location. The apparent danger is that if a hacker gains access to your system, they will have total control over your smart house.

Maintenance: Repairing the developed system when it breaks down can be time-consuming and costly. In addition to this, there is a slight possibility for the system to crash which can lead to the failure of the entire system or certain functionalities associated with it. As a result, fixing any form of breakdown can be quite expensive.

Data transmission speed: When transferring a significant amount of data, the network might get congested, slowing down the transmission speed and causing the functions to slow down, depending on the number of systems connected.

Ring connection: When data is connected in the shape of a ring, there may be a delay, which is also dependent on the number of points connected to the network, ultimately resulting in minimal reliability.

Dependency on the Internet: Internet is the backbone for a smart home system. A good reliable and robust internet connection is required to control smart home system. There is no other fall back option to have a smart home system if there is no internet (Ma, L., Li, Z., & Zheng, M., 2019).

Dependency on professionals: It is vital to select a reliable internet service provider to have a continuous and smooth operation of a smart home. Airtel, Jio, ACT, Hathaway and Asianet are some good network providers. An ordinary electrician cannot fix any issue with smart homes. It requires well-trained professionals to resolve any issue with smart homes, and such dependence on them is a drawback that needs to be addressed.

2.6 Conclusion

In this chapter, an affordable, intelligent home framework based on IoT is proposed, as well as a detailed overview of the system's integrated structure is discussed. Since the entire framework is connected to the web, it not only allows for connectivity among different household equipment's, but it also allows for the sharing of all information. The various vulnerabilities in a smart home and solutions to overcome them are discussed. The system proves to be scalable, secure and the availability of a user-friendly interface makes it simple to use without compromising their privacy.

References

Abu-Tair, M., Djahel, S., Perry, P., Scotney, B., Zia, U., Carracedo, J. M., & Sajjad, A. **2020**. "Towards secure and privacy-preserving IoT enabled smart home: Architecture and experimental study". *Sensors*, 20(21), 6131.

BusinessWire(https://www.businesswire.com/news/home/20190418005311/en/European-Smart-Home-Market-Trends-Forecasts-2019-2024-Featuring-Johnson-Controls-Schneider-Honeywell-International-Siemens-and-United-Technologies—ResearchAndMarkets.com). Accessed 7 October 2021.

Chinchane, A., Bani, V., & Sumant, O. **2019**. India Home Automation Market. Allied Market Research, India.

Daemen, J., & Rijmen, V. **2013**. The Design of Rijndael: AES – The Advanced Encryption Standard. Springer Sci. Bus. Media, Germany.

Edge, M., Taylor, B., Dewsbury, G., & Groves, M. **2000**. "The potential for 'smart home's systems in meeting the care needs of older persons and people with disabilities". *Seniors Housing Update, 10*(1), 6–8.

Hoffman, D. L., & Novak, T. **2016**. "How to market the smart home: Focus on emergent experience, not use cases". *Not Use Cases* (January 15, 2016).

Indianweb2 (https://www.indianweb2.com/2016/08/10-promising-home-automation-startups.html). Accessed 7 October 2021.

Jiang, L., Liu, D. Y., & Yang, B. **2004**. "Smart home research". In *Proceedings of 2004 International Conference on Machine Learning and Cybernetics (IEEE Cat. No. 04EX826)* (Vol. 2, 659–663).

Jo, H., & Yoon, Y. I. **2018**. "Intelligent smart home energy efficiency model using artificial TensorFlow engine". *Human-centric Computing and Information Sciences, 8*, 9 (2018), 2–18.

Lin, Y. W., Lin, Y. B., Hsiao, C. Y., & Wang, Y. Y. **2017**. "IoTtalk-RC: Sensors as universal remote control for aftermarket home appliances". *IEEE Internet of Things Journal, 4*(4), 1104–1112.

Liu, Q., Yang, X., & Deng, L. **2018**. "An IBeacon-based location system for smart home control". *Sensors, 18*(6), 1897.

Ma, L., Li, Z., & Zheng, M. **2019**. "A research on IoT based smart home". In *2019 11th International Conference on Measuring Technology and Mechatronics Automation (ICMTMA)* (120–122). doi: 10.1109/ICMTMA.2019.00033.

Markets and Markets (https://www.marketsandmarkets.com/ResearchInsight/building-automation-control-systems-market.asp). Accessed 7 October 2021.

Meng, Y., Zhang, W., Zhu, H., & Shen, X. S. **2018**. "Securing consumer IoT in the smart home: Architecture, challenges, and countermeasures". *IEEE Wireless Communications, 25*, 53–59.

Meticulous Blog (https://meticulousblog.org/top-10-companies-in-smart-home-market/). Accessed 7 October 2021.

Nir, Y., & Langley, A. **2015**. "ChaCha20 and Poly1305 for IETF Protocols". Rfc 7539 (Informational), Internet Eng. Task Force.

Pilloni, V., Floris, A., Meloni, A., & Atzori, L. **2016**. "Smart home energy management including renewable sources: A QoE-driven approach". *IEEE Transactions on Smart Grid, 9*(3), 2006–2018.

Pirbhulal, S., Zhang, H., E Alahi, M. E., Ghayvat, H., Mukhopadhyay, S. C., Zhang, Y. T., & Wu, W. **2016**. "A novel secure IoT-based smart home automation system using a wireless sensor network". *Sensors, 17*(1), 69.

Schneier, B., **1933**. Description of a New Variable-Length Key, 64-Bit Block Cipher (Blowfish). Springer: Berlin/Heidelberg, Germany, pp. 191–204.

Sivaraman, V., Gharakheili, H. H., Fernandes, C., Clark, N., & Karliychuk, T. **2018**. "Smart IoT devices in the home: Security and privacy implications". *IEEE Technology and Society Magazine, 37*(2), 71–79.

Smid, M. E. & Branstad, D. K. **1988**. "Data encryption standard: Past and future. *Proceedings of the IEEE, 76*, 550–559.

Startuptalky (https://startuptalky.com/top-home-automation-companies-india/). Accessed 7 October 2021.

Things in India (https://thingsinindia.in/home-automation-companies-in-india/). Accessed 7 October 2021.

Yang, H., Lee, W., & Lee, H. **2018**. "IoT smart home adoption: The importance of proper level automation". *Journal of Sensors.*, vol. 2018, Article ID 6464036, 11 pages, 2018. https://doi.org/10.1155/2018/6464036

3

Role of IoT in Integration of Smart Home and Smart Grid

Viswanathan Ganesh, Senthilmurugan Solamalai, and Aswin Anand

CONTENTS

3.1 Introduction: Background and Current Research

The evolution of electronic field and computer field have created large opportunities for employment and automation. In the current trend, a number of smart home automation devices have made their strong impact in the style of residences and industries. In industrial terminology, the IoT penetration is considered IoT 4.0, known for its intelligent, interconnected equipment which is capable of autonomously communicating followed by optimization technique for the complete chain. In [1], the application of IoT has been initiated with smart security door lock system, followed by the challenges, issues, and possible solutions for smart home security [2]. In [3], a successful deployment if IoT for a smart home through real-time control mechanism is being considered. The accessibility to automation an IoT is mainly dependent on the cost to be incurred by the customer; therefore, in [4], a low-cost-based IoT applications has been studied. The cost of physical computing platforms can be reduced if the applications are open sourced as stated in [5] providing an opportunity to customize the basic structure for their independent use.

3.2 Need and Role of Sensors

Sensors are defined to be physical devices which can be tuned are integrated to perform various activities depending upon the consumer requirements. Sensors play a key role in all sectors varying from automobile, electrical, mechanical, biomedical, industrial etc.

DOI: 10.1201/9781003226888-3

Modern advancements in field of semiconductors and technology have created a significant impact for the environment and have been a main concern for drastic climatic changes and global warming conditions [6, 7]. As a claim for this, an intergovernmental panel was formed to have a record of recent changes occurred in the climatic conditions due to various factors, such as urbanization, transportation. Various sensors can be utilized for a specific requirement depending upon the cost factor of the consumer. The basic role of sensor is to convert physical signal to electrical or digital signals for successfully transmitting the signals through an Internet of Things (IoT)-supported device. Sensors can be categorized with the requirement of power, contacting type, and physical characteristics measured. As seen in Table 3.1, there are categories of sensors which consume power are known as active sensors, similarly those which do not consume power are known as passive sensors. Sensors which require a physical contact to initiate measurement are known as contact type, on the other hand, sensor which does not require any physical contact to measure the parameter are known as non-contact type. Figure 3.1 depicts that sensor can be categorized on a broad scale with the context of physical parameter, which is to be measured ranging from flow, level, temperature, pressure, displacement, gas, and chemical.

On the other hand, transducers can also be used to convert one form of energy to another, for example: microphone, thermometer, pressure sensor. Similar to sensor, as seen in Table 3.2, transducers can also be categorized into various categories, such as active transducer and passive transducers. Active transducers are those which can work without any external power source, hence also known by the term self-generating type transducer. Concurrently passive transducers need external power source for operation. Similarly based upon the nature of output with respect to time, transducers can further be classified at analogue (continuous) and digital (discrete). Further to the classification of transducers, some of them include a mechanical device acting as a primary transducer which converts physical quantity to mechanical signal, secondary transducer then transforms

TABLE 3.1

Various Categories of Sensors

1. Power requirement	2. Connection type
a. Active sensor	a. Contact type
b. Passive sensor	b. Non-contact type

3. Physical parameter

a. Flow	a. Temperature
i. Differential pressure	i. Thermistor
ii. Position displacement	ii. Thermocouple
iii. Vortex	iii. Infrared radiation
iv. Thermal mass	b. Displacement
v. Electromagnetic	i. Potentiometric
vi. Ultrasonic	ii. Ultrasonic
vii. Anemometer	iii. Photoelectric
b. Level	iv. Capacitive
i. Mechanical	
ii. Magnetic	
iii. Ultrasonic	
iv. Microwave	
v. Radar	

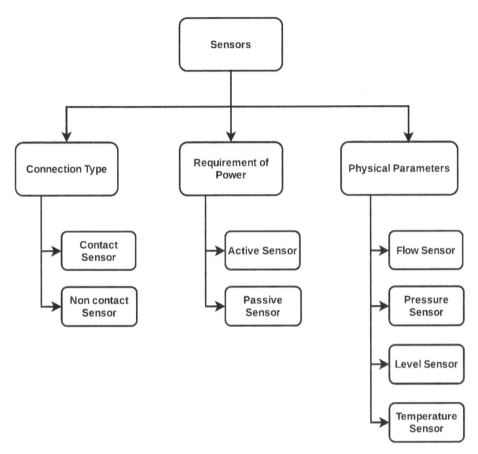

FIGURE 3.1
Classification of sensors.

TABLE 3.2

Various Categories of Transducers

1. Power requirement	**2. Output with respect to time**
a. Active transducer	a. Analogue transducer
i. Piezoelectric	i. Strain gauge
ii. Photovoltaic	ii. LVDT
iii. Electromagnetic	iii. Thermocouple
b. Passive transducer	b. Digital transducer
i. Resistive	i. Shaft encoder
ii. Inductive	ii. Limit switch
iii. Capacitive	iii. Digital tachometer
3. Combinational transducer	**4. Transduction principle**
a. Primary transducer	a. Capacitive transduction
b. Secondary transducer	b. Electromagnetic transduction
	c. Inductive transduction
	d. Piezoelectric transduction
	e. Photovoltaic transduction
	f. Photoconductive transduction

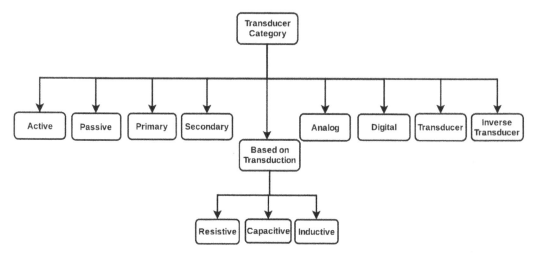

FIGURE 3.2
Classification of transducers.

the mechanical signal to an electrical signal [8, 9]. Transducers can also be classified based on the principle of transduction commonly known as capacitive, electromagnetic, inductive, piezoelectric, photovoltaic, and photoconductive transduction. Figure 3.2 depicts various categories of transducers.

A capacitor essentially consists of a dielectric insulator separated by two conductors (plates). In the process of capacitive transduction, the capacitance changes by either altering the distance between two plates or by providing a dielectric change. Similarly in the process of electromagnetic transduction, the measured quantity is converted into electromagnetic force/voltage by change in the magnetic flux in absence of excitation. In continuation, following section explains the selection and role of sensors in design of an efficient smart home.

3.2.1 Sensors in a Smart Home

Smart home is defined as a combination of efficient and resilient systems. The wise usage of sensors can transform a classic home into a smart home [10]. Various factors must be considered while selection of sensors in the case of domestic purposes, such as cost, multipurpose functionality, durability, and low maintenance. Hence, the main priority of selection of sensors has been considered with common nodes in a house with number of branches extended with various sensors. Figure 3.3 depicts an example of combination of sensors with common nodes.

$$\text{Sensor Importance} = \frac{\text{No of Connected Branches}}{\text{Total No of Branches}} \times 100 \qquad (3.1)$$

As the above equation states, the sensor with the most number of connected branches have the highest importance in the smart home community.

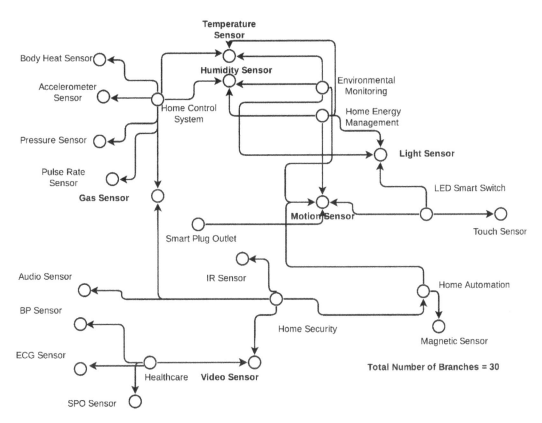

FIGURE 3.3
Sensor connection in smart home.

3.2.2 Sensors in a Smart Grid

On the other hand, certain common sensors are used in the area of smart gird, such as current sensor, over current relay, voltage sensors, phasor measurement units (PMU).

Current sensors are basic devices which can detect electric current flow in a wire and have a capability to generate a signal directly proportional to the current flow. The signal generated can be either analogue or digital.

Over current relay is considered an extended version of current sensor which detects flow of electric current but more frequently considered a protective relay which operates when the current flowing exceeds a preset value. This sensor is mainly used for the successful operation of circuit breaker for cut-off during fault conditions.

Voltage sensors are devices that have the capability to monitor the live voltage level in a circuit. These sensors have capability to monitor and detect AC and DC voltage levels.

Phasor measurement units are devices capable of estimating the magnitude and phasor angle of an electrical phasor quantity by considering a common source of time for proper synchronization. Therefore, these devices are also known as synchrophasor.

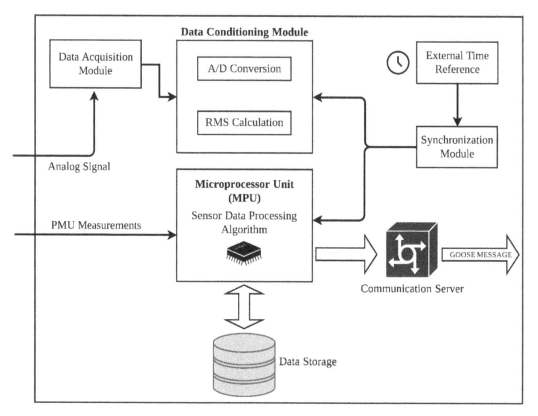

FIGURE 3.4
Working example of a sensor.

3.3 Working of Sensor: Physical Quantity to Data

Figure 3.4 depicts an example of a voltage sensor which begins from measurement of physical quantity to the processing of data and sending of adequate command. Initially, the data from PMU and voltage sensor is received at microprocessor unit (MPU) and data conditioning module, respectively. The role of data conditioning module is to provide A/D conversion and RMS calculation for the analogue signal; on the other hand, the MPU provides the sensor data processing algorithm which is supported by an external time reference and a synchronization module for parallel operation. The data sent out to communication server is stored at the data storage for back up. The communication server is responsible for sending the data to the end user/controls.

3.4 Software Architecture in IoT

There are numerous layers of architecture that facilitate in the connection of various devices at various tiers. It also gives the developer the ability to construct and develop programs at each tier. The user layer is represented by the white block, the runtime layer by the dark blue layer, and the developer layer by the light blue layer. This layer provides architecture for real-time device integration and management in IoT infrastructure, as well as security and safety [11]. The application layer is used by the business layer to get full entry to all other layers. The business layer is concerned with the e-commerce management strategies used by any firm or educational institution to achieve business-related goals. This business layer examines IoT infrastructure and projects future development based on user or device data. The business layer is crucial in managing the whole IoT infrastructure, where real-time data is gathered and processed to give quality services and extend the life of the product or device for stakeholders. This layer will be especially important for the software approach in connecting apps and devices in the IoT infrastructure and offering quality of services (QoS) guarantees [12].

The application layer comprises IoT-specific apps that deliver a variety of services to IoT stakeholders. A wide range of applications are used in a number of disciplines, including

- Smart cities/homes/offices/shops
- Smart agriculture and water management
- Advanced transportation
- Medical and emergency services
- Security systems
- Smart management of energy

Interaction between stakeholders and IoT devices is enabled through the application layer. The apps are built and developed in accordance with the needs of the users. Applications may be built in smaller modules and then distributed to end users for testing and validation. Before the programme is given over to the end user, each unit of the application should be extensively tested. Each sensor in an IoT infrastructure is related with the generation of data and the management of that data by an application. With the proliferation of IoT devices comes an increase in the number of apps that must be managed and monitored in order to prevent overloading the IoT infrastructure. The IoT could also be used to monitor geriatric behaviour for those suffering from a physical or cognitive disease, noting any behavioural changes and analysing the risk associated with them. This assists in the implementation of protections for the elderly and the improvement of decision-making based on their behaviour [13]. The software approach gives a standard set of principles for developers to follow in order to construct standard and reusable applications.

The control layer is in charge of enforcing a set of regulations that govern and manage IoT devices. This layer is concerned with the IoT system's hardware and software components, as well as their associated functions. The control layer is largely responsible for discovering and assessing the interconnections of heterogeneous IoT networks. It also helps with the monitoring and control of a wide range of interoperable devices and applications. This layer supports numerous IoT layers, which is the main challenge with software oriented. This layer is also in charge of numerous network-related functions, such as selecting when and where to receive and send data. The object-oriented approach may be used for software design, classes, and generalization notions that help in the behavioural characterization of the concepts. The software technology adds to a critical way of data retrieval and deployment in IoT architecture [14].

IoT end nodes are managed by the management layer. It is in charge of identifying IoT infrastructure devices and their related functionalities. This layer is focused with device administration and contains a management agent that focuses on communication between various connected devices in IoT architecture. The management layer is responsible for a wide range of management functions in IoT infrastructure, including Mission-Critical IoT, transaction security, and massive data flow [15]. The software solution aids the management layer in detecting the features and functions of IoT devices, allowing devices to be controlled efficiently and identifying uncertainty ranging from unknown device characteristics to emerging IoT data.

In an IoT heterogeneous environment, the data layer is responsible for handling the massive volumes of data created by various devices. The data layer analyses and processes data for the IoT architecture's numerous nodes. The data may be real-time or time-sensitive, and it could be computed locally or centrally on an IoT cloud platform. The data layer is responsible for selecting and delivering data computation via IoT infrastructure. We can now extract metadata, such as MAC address, timestamp, GPS position, and camera settings from IoT data to help in data analysis and organizing [17–21]. This layer is also in charge of classifying data depending on its type, size, efficiency, runtime, and other factors. Based on the objectives of the client, the software approach can provide a choice of patterns and agile-based modelling methodologies for developing, generating, and delivering IoT data. Because data in IoT infrastructure is scalable, scalable application architecture is required to combine multi- and multi-output applications.

The communication and connection layer guarantees that various stakeholders and IoT devices in the IoT infrastructure efficiently communicate. The IoT infrastructure is made up of a number of communication protocol-based heterogeneous networks and the technologies that are used in such networks. Despite the fact that their communication protocols differ, this layer successfully provides a platform for various IoT devices to interact with one another. A modelling tool is included in the software technique for determining the protocol type and incorporating it into IoT infrastructure. It also facilitates in the conveyance of messages and the provision of priority-based services [22, 23].

The security layer is in charge of assuring the security of IoT infrastructure from start to finish. The security layer protects both hardware and software while also allowing them to communicate safely with one another. This layer is responsible for validating various policy certificates, portfolios, and user credentials. This layer contributes to the prevention of malware, e-crime, and the administration of privilege rights. The software technique provides a set of standards that allow security in IoT infrastructure from the demand collection phase through the deployment phase.

The developer enabling layer is in charge of developing apps that are secure, interoperable, and scalable with all IoT layers. This layer works with the other seven layers to ensure that apps and IoT infrastructure stakeholders can communicate reliably. This layer leverages current APIs, SDKs, and DEV tools to build apps that fit the demands of the consumers. The software technique may reduce design and development time by providing reusable items. The software technique enables the developer to construct and implement applications based on design documents and use cases. It also helps with the upkeep of test cases and test scenarios, allowing succeeding developers to follow and update them. Table 3.3 provides the features and benefits of various cloud platforms, such as Google Cloud, Amazon Web Services (AWS), Microsoft Azure IoT Suite, IBM Watson IoT Platform, and Cisco IoT Cloud Connect.

TABLE 3.3

Features and Benefits of Various Cloud Solutions

S. No.	Cloud Solutions for IOT	Features	Benefits
1.	Google Cloud	• Google cloud IOT is most adaptable and industrial ready to deploy and implement IOT solutions without the need of complex infrastructure • The Google cloud platform takes care of the device integration, scalable based on load forecasts, end-to-end security and ensures the communication of the devices • Google IoT Core is a centralized service that establishes bidirectional communication through MQTT and HTTP protocols. This facilitates the customers to integrate the device either to through a gateway or directly to the cloud for real-time data analysis	• Easy access to Google resources • Integration of location intelligence into IoT devices • Accessibility to board range of AI resources • Auto scaling of the infrastructure based on the demand • Data visualization and presentation with no or minimal efforts • End-to End encrypted communication modes • Ease of integration to Android • Cuts cost for server maintenance • Low latency • Performs big data analysis
2.	Amazon Web Services(AWS)	• AWS IOT Core enables the customers to integrate IoT devices without the need dedicated server infrastructure • The message processing power is massive which process trillions message in a secured and reliable fashion when connected to the AWS end points • AWS IoT Core facilitates MQTT (message queuing and telemetry transport), HTTPS (hypertext transfer protocol – secure), MQTT over WSS (WebSockets Secure), and LoRaWAN (low-power long-range wide-area network)	• Open and flexible integration of IOT devices • The complete infrastructure can be accessed at a reduced priced • Availability of the LAAS Architecture for the best logging purposes • Highly secure and data can't be exchanged without a authentication or identity • Easy integration with Alexa • AWS IoT Core simplifies the usage of AWS services, such as AWS Lambda, Amazon Kinesis, Amazon S3, Amazon DynamoDB, Amazon CloudWatch, and Amazon Elasticsearch Service, to create even more powerful IoT applications

(Continued)

TABLE 3.3 (*Continued*)

Features and Benefits of Various Cloud Solutions

S. No.	Cloud Solutions for IOT	Features	Benefits
3.	Microsoft Azure IoT Suite	• Azure IOT suite provides profitable and productive solutions with prebuilt solutions • Establishes a bidirectional communication to identify the state of the device and routes the message to different routes without the need of code • IOT edge module can be integrated to transfer code and REST services • Easily adaptable to new data and new device integration • The Azure Digital Twins service enables you to construct a virtual model of your actual IoT ecosystem and establish dependencies, correlations, and linkages among its components	• Open to third party services • Secured end-to-end data transfers • High availability • Requires minimum coding • Flexible pricing system based on the customer requirements • Prebuild templates such as azure maps can be integrated • Powerful partner network • Ease of building Hybrid IoT modules • Powerful data visualization and analysis
4.	IBM Watson IoT Platform	• IBM Watson enables real-time data streaming by transferring messages MQTT protocol from any sources using platform service • Data analysis can be performed with ease with built-in tools and external technologies • Built-in dashboards for data visualizations • Cognitive systems • The device integration are categorized based customer requirements	• Process untapped data • Highly secure for data transfer • Data analytics can be performed • Improved customer services • Handle huge quantities of data • New features added to analyse weather data
5.	Cisco IoT Cloud Connect	• Cisco IOT enables the acceleration of digital transformation based on the availability of the data • It is integrated with voice assistance • Provides a deep dive report on the devices and IP sessions • Improved customer engagement • Manages the data life cycle • It provides solutions for mobile carriers to create a fantastic IoT experience. It allows you to deploy your devices in a variety of ways	• Scalable to billions of devices and messages • Has rock-solid infrastructure • Low latency in data transfer • Compatible for industrial standards • Help deploying and managing at large scale • Bridges the gap between IT and operations

3.5 Conclusion

The chapter provided an introduction to the role of IoT in various domains of electrical engineering. A detailed focus to smart home and smart grid integration has been explained in various sections for the selection of sensors having the most importance and methods of integration through various available domains of Google Cloud, AWS, Microsoft Azure IoT Suite, IBM Watson IoT Platform, and Cisco IoT Cloud Connect. Various points of comparing and contrasting have been provided as a guide for selection of various cloud solutions. On the other hand, the needs for smart home have been constantly increasing in the coming future for a map to sustainable environment and society.

References

1. Dansana, Debabrata, Brojo Kishore Mishra, K. Sindhuja, and Subhashree Sahoo, 2021. "IoT-Based Smart Security System on a Door Lock Application." In *Next Generation of Internet of Things*, pp. 695–703. Springer, Singapore.
2. Touqeer, Haseeb, Shakir Zaman, Rashid Amin, Mudassar Hussain, Fadi Al-Turjman, and Muhammad Bilal, 2021. "Smart home security: challenges, issues and solutions at different IoT layers." The Journal of Supercomputing 77: 14053–14089. https://doi.org/10.1007/s11227-021-03825-1.
3. Krishnamoorthy, Ramesh, Kalimuthu Krishnan, and C. Bharatiraja, 2021. "Deployment of IoT for smart home application and embedded real-time control system." Materials Today: Proceedings 45: 2777–2783.
4. Mustafa, Bilal, Muhammad Waseem Iqbal, Mohsin Saeed, Abdul Rehman Shafqat, Hasnain Sajjad, and Muhammad Raza Naqvi, 2021. "IOT Based Low-Cost Smart Home Automation System." In *2021 3rd International Congress on Human-Computer Interaction, Optimization and Robotic Applications (HORA)*, pp. 1–6. IEEE.
5. Maceli, Monica G., 2021. "Low-cost physical computing platforms for end-user prototyping of smart home systems." Behaviour & Information Technology 40(10), 997–1007. https://doi.org/10.1080/0144929X.2021.1918248.
6. Laxmi Shawa, Rudra Narayan Sahoo, Hemachandran K and S.K.Nanda, 2021. "Machine Learning Techniques in IoT Applications: A State of The Art." In *IoT Applications, Security Threats, and Countermeasures, (Eds)* Padmalaya Nayak, Niranjan Ray, P. Ravichandran, CRC Press, Boca Raton, Florida, United States.
7. Nguyen, Hoang Phuong, Phan Quang Huy Le, Van Viet Pham, Xuan Phuong Nguyen, Dhinesh Balasubramaniam, and Anh-Tuan Hoang, 2021. "Application of the Internet of Things in 3E (efficiency, economy, and environment) factor-based energy management as smart and sustainable strategy." Energy Sources, Part A: Recovery, Utilization, and Environmental Effects: 1–23. https://doi.org/10.1080/15567036.2021.1954110.
8. Awaar, Vinay Kumar, Praveen Jugge, and Padmalaya Nayak, 2021. "Significance of Smart Sensors in IoT Applications: A State of The Art." In *IoT Applications, Security Threats, and Countermeasures, (Eds)* Padmalaya Nayak, Niranjan Ray, P. Ravichandran, CRC Press, Boca Raton, Florida, United States.
9. Parmar, Monika, and Harsimran Jit Kaur, 2021 "Blockchain-Based Secured Data Transmission of IoT Sensors Using Thingspeak." In *Artificial Intelligence and Speech Technology*, pp. 77–86. CRC Press.
10. Kumari, P., and S. K. Singh, 2021. "Smart Irrigation System Using IoT." In *Smart Computing*, pp. 137–141. CRC Press. https://doi.org/10.1201/9781003167488

11. Chawla, Nidhi, and Surjeet Dalal, 2021. "Edge AI with Wearable IoT: A Review on Leveraging Edge Intelligence in Wearables for Smart Healthcare." In *Green Internet of Things for Smart Cities*, CRC Press, Boca Raton, Florida, United States. pp. 205–231. ISBN: 9781003032397

12. Naudiyal, Reetu, Sandeep Rawat, Safia A. Kazmi, and Rupendra Kumar Pachauri, 2021. "Development of IoT-Based Data Acquisition System for Real-Time Monitoring of Solar PV System." In *Applied Soft Computing and Embedded System Applications in Solar Energy*, pp. 123–137. CRC Press. ISBN: 9781003121237.

13. Kaushik, S., K. Srinivasan, B. Sharmila, D. Devasena, M. Suresh, Hitesh Panchal, R. Ashokkumar, Kishor Kumar Sadasivuni, and Neel Srimali, 2021. "Continuous monitoring of power consumption in urban buildings based on Internet of Things." International Journal of Ambient Energy19(5): 5027–5033.

14. Selvaraj, Yoganand, and Chithra Selvaraj, 2021. "Proactive maintenance of small wind turbines using IoT and machine learning models." International Journal of Green Energy 19(5), 463–475.

15. Garg, Puneet, Shrivastava Pranav, and Agarwal Prerna, 2021. "Green Internet of Things (G-IoT): A Solution for Sustainable Technological Development." In *Green Internet of Things for Smart Cities*, pp. 23–46. CRC Press. ISBN: 9781003032397.

18. Senthilmurugan, Solamalai, Ananthanarayanan Rathinam, Viswanathan Ganesh, and VM Ajay Krishna, 2021. "Simulink Model of Advanced FLISR Intentional Islanding for Smart Distribution Networks." In *2021 7th International Conference on Electrical Energy Systems (ICEES)*, pp. 79–84. IEEE.

17. Ganesh, Viswanathan, S. Senthilmurugan, and Ajit Ram RR, 2021. "Role of green buildings in sustainable living: implementation and impacts." SPAST Abstracts 1, no. 01.

18. Ganesh, Viswanathan, and Ajit Ram RR, 2021. "Role of turbine selection in hydropower and wind power for sustainable living." SPAST Abstracts 1, no. 01.

19. Ganesh, Viswanathan, and S. Senthilmurugan, 2021. "Role and improvements of battery energy storage systems in energy sector." SPAST Abstracts 1, no. 01.

20. Senthilmurugan, S., Viswanathan Ganesh, Shiva Srenivasan Srinivasan, and N. R. S. Lakshanasri, 2021. "A Review on SVC-SVC Interaction." In *The Opportunities of Uncertainties: Flexibility and Adaptation Needed In Current Climate Volume II (ICT and Engineering)*, p. 152. Lulu Publication, North Carolina, United States.

21. Ganesh, Viswanathan, VM Ajay Krishna, and Ajit Ram RR, 2021. "Safety Feature in Electric Vehicle at Public Charging Station." In *2021 7th International Conference on Electrical Energy Systems (ICEES)*, pp. 156–161. IEEE.

22. Ganesh, Viswanathan, and S. Senthil Murugan, 2020, "Growth of Green Building Sector and Sustainable Life." In *IOP Conference Series: Earth and Environmental Science*, vol. 573, no. 1, p. 012033. IOP Publishing.

23. Ganesh, Viswanathan, S. Senthil Murugan, Ajit Ram RR, and Akash Prabhu, 2020. "Smart Grid-Meters and Communications-Design, Challenges, Issues, Opportunities and Applications." In *2020 IEEE International Conference on Advances and Developments in Electrical and Electronics Engineering (ICADEE)*, pp. 1–5. IEEE.

4

IoT and Machine Learning

M S Kirtan, Ankit Gupta, Anshul Yadav, Nishant Bhardwaj, and R K Yadav

CONTENTS

4.1 Introduction

In a digital world, we can make everything talk to each other, like we can make our phones talk to each other, we can make Facebook talk to each other and so on. But when it comes to physical world, we cannot make "things" talk to each other or communicate with each other. By "things" here we are referring to simple objects surrounding us like a light bulb, TV and AC. But now due to our ever-developing technology, we have Internet

DOI: 10.1201/9781003226888-4

of Things (IoT) and machine learning (ML) which allow the "things" for us to be smarter and to connect with each other. Let's discuss more about these technologies in the sections following below.

4.1.1 IoT

Our day-to-day life is more or less dependent on the internet these days. We all know that the internet has mostly been a product for the people. So, all the information, images, videos, games, books, commerce etc. were all created by the people, for the people and about the people. The internet has been one of the most significant and revolutionary technologies ever invented. In fact, nowadays we cannot live without the internet. The internet is like a digital web that has connected our lives to it in one way or another. The computer networking revolution, i.e., the creation of the internet, has changed the world and has opened a new gateway to the development of new technologies. Now just imagine how interesting it would be if we could connect "things" around us like we have connected people using the internet. This new internet will not just connect people but also connect "things" around us; therefore, it is called the IoT. This internet is believed to change the world again. IoT allows "things" to share their data and communicate with other things. Now, one may think about how does that work to make "things" to interact, communicate and collaborate with other "things". Figure 4.1 shows the growth of IoT from year 2010 to 2024.

Well, that's really simple, just like we use our five senses to interact with others, we add the ability to sense, touch, communicate, and control and there we get the opportunity for connecting. Now that we know that any physical device can be a part of IoT just by

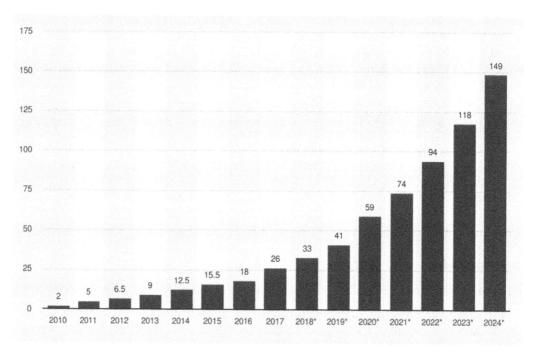

FIGURE 4.1
Growth prediction chart for IoT.

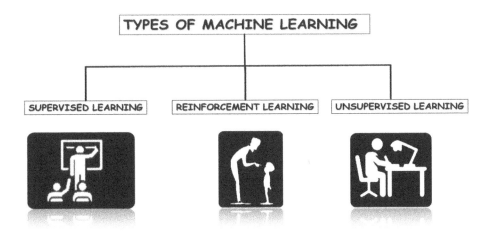

FIGURE 4.2
Types of machine learning.

connecting a sensor to it, by 2021, it was estimated that there will be 59 billion IoT devices worldwide. It has also been forecasted that IoT devices will be generating 180 zettabytes of data by 2025; this was mainly because of an increase in the demand for IoT products due to the COVID-19 pandemic.

4.1.2 Machine Learning

We all know that we as humans learn a lot from our past experiences. Now, just like us what if machines can also learn from the data which is already present? This is what ML is all about. As discussed earlier, it is estimated that there will be 180 zettabytes of data by 2025. That's a lot of data! Now the question is what are we going to do with that data? Obviously, filtering, sorting etc. will be done, but we can also use this data to start training some ML models which will help us to make intelligent decisions that are being generated by our own machines [1]. Figure 4.2 shows the different types of machine learning approaches.

There are three ways in which a machine learns: supervised learning, unsupervised learning and reinforcement learning. Let's understand all of these types briefly one by one [2].

4.1.2.1 Supervised Learning

Supervised learning uses well-labelled data to train the model. Let's take an example to have a much better understanding. For example, the dataset given in the figure below contains different shapes (rectangle, triangle, circle and hexagon). Now, note that the dataset provided here is labelled which is the key point in supervised learning. Now, your ML model will predict the name of the shape which is given as an input. Here, the number of sides of the shape becomes the feature of the shapes and their names as their labels. Figure 4.3 depicted the various supervised learning approaches with labeled data.

When we feed this data to the ML model, it learns which feature is associated with which label, i.e., it learns that the shape with three sides is a triangle and so on. So, here

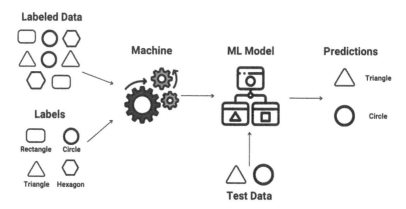

FIGURE 4.3
Simple example for supervised learning.

we conclude on the basis of the number of sides that our model will predict the shape. This was a very simple illustration of how supervised learning is done in real life; much more complex data is used. One of the applications of supervised learning is the Biometric Attendance System.

4.1.2.2 Unsupervised Learning

In unsupervised learning, we provide the data to the machine but we do not specify its features and labels. Instead, the machine decides the features and labels of the data on its own. Market-based analysis is one of the key techniques used by large retailers to uncover an association between items and it all works on unsupervised learning. How does it work? It works by looking for a combination of products that occurs together frequently in the transactions; in simpler words, it helps the retailer to understand the relationship between items that customers buy [3]. Figure 4.4 shows the unsupervised learning with unlabelled data.

4.1.2.3 Reinforcement Learning

Reinforcement learning is feedback-based learning or it works on the principle of feedback. In the illustration below, we can observe how reinforcement learning works. Here, we give water and fire as the input to the machine. Now, the machine will choose either one of the two. If the machine chooses fire, then you give negative feedback, then the machine will

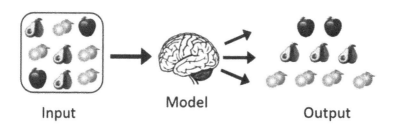

FIGURE 4.4
Simple example for unsupervised learning.

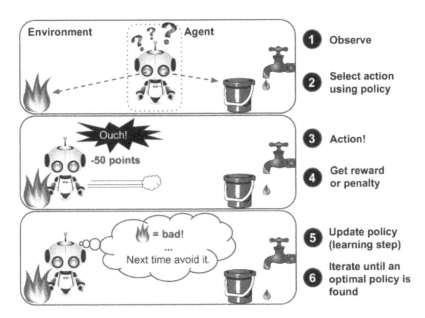

FIGURE 4.5
Simple example for reinforced learning.

learn from it (fire = bad, as illustrated). Next time if the machine comes across a similar situation, then it will choose water instead.

This was a very simple explanation for reinforcement learning, but one of the applications of reinforcement learning is games; the most famous ones are AlphaGo and AlphaGo Zero [4]. Figure 4.5 shows the reinforced learning with learning steps.

4.1.2.3.1 IoT Building Blocks

There is an increase in the use of technology and electronic devices in today's world and one is always witnessed to be surrounded by common electronic devices like smart gadgets, automatic vehicles and smart buildings and others. These devices provide specific services according to the purpose they are designed for, and in order to do so, they are provided or equipped with the software. These physical devices are designed in such a manner that they can overcome almost any geographical boundary and are capable of communicating through strong communication networks, but earlier there were limitations to the connectivity among these physical devices. It was hard for these devices to gain control over devices connected to technologies like Bluetooth, Wi-Fi and other mobile applications. Thus, the concept of IoT is created to overcome these physical geographical boundaries and allow one to connect to anyone on the planet through different physical devices. Different computing technologies like edge computing, fog computing and roof computing are used with the agenda of interconnecting millions of physical devices to an IoT network. The connected physical gadgets in IoT ought to be provided with specific software, sensors and components that are able to support networks. The sensors understand the presence of a physical unit with the help of the software fitted inside it and then utilize this to gain the data needed for the connection. It can be easily seen here that the internet acts as the medium of communication between the various scattered physical devices where every physical unit has a specific identification number. This information gained from the physical devices having a unique identification number is further processed with the help of storage servers on the web and then it is delivered to the correct place at the right time to be used by various applications.

4.1.2.3.2 *IoT Definitions*

The term IoT is hard to define accurately but it portrays a place where any connected device can interact and communicate in a very clever manner. It describes an emerging model which consists of a continuous sequence of distinctive addressable things or physical objects incorporated with sensors, software or other technological devices to connect and exchange information on a worldwide basis over the internet. They form a dynamic network of special devices, connected with each other. These special devices like sensors, objects or even everyday use items with potential computing ability are called IoT. The term IoT is new but the concept of connecting different devices and networks to exchange data or other information has existed for a long time, for example, since the 1970s telephone lines were used to monitor meters on the electric grid. This concept has been further developed into advanced wireless technology and is now used in the industrial sector for monitoring different industrial operations and equipment, and instead of Internet Protocol (IP) and Internet Standards (IS), they use close purpose-built networks. IoT is a popular term nowadays in order to understand circumstances where internet connectivity and computing capability are not limited and extend to various objects [5].

4.1.2.3.3 *IoT Basic Characteristics*

The IoT is a complicated system consisting of various characteristics. These characteristics can be understood with the help of components used in IoT, services provided by the IoT, usability of the IoT and the security provided by the IoT. Since IoT keeps on evolving, it is hard to dictate its features, but there are some common characteristics which are as follows:

- Intelligent data collection and smart handling
- Ability to connect and interconnect
- Availability of things-related services
- Diversity
- Enormous scale

4.2 IoT Technical Landscape

In this part, we cover the evolution of IoT over time, its application structure and driver technologies along with the explanation of the concepts of edge, fog and roof computing in IoT.

4.2.1 Evolution of IoT

The term IoT was firstly introduced by Kevin Ashton who is the co-founder of the Auto-ID centre at MIT. It was referenced with the global standard system for radio frequency identification (RFID) and also several more sensors were invented or created. Then gradually wireless technologies of communication systems like Wi-Fi, Bluetooth, wireless sensor network (WSN) and other cellular technologies contributed to its evolution. The present system of IoT comprises a set of smart devices or things (physical as well as virtual) that are interconnected in a collaborative way working towards one single agenda. The physical devices or things collect data from the surroundings, quantify it and then integrate it smoothly [6]. The data is then easily discoverable, accessible, addressable and managed. There is also a scope of innovation since everything is interconnected. These three technological developments support the evolution of IoT:

- Wi-Fi is a wireless technology mainly used in IoT devices at homes through smartphones, personal computers and other gadgets. The most common Wi-Fi system uses 2.4 GHz frequency band and 5GHz (ISM radio) band for different communication purposes but there is a new and very recent development in Wi-Fi called the Wi-Fi HaLow introduced by Wi-Fi Alliance[7].
- RFID labels are smart standardized tags with the ability to chat with a networked system and are capable of locating the required objects. If seen from a technical perspective, RFID labels are chips with receiving wires that are normally inserted in objects containing electronically stocked data [8].
- NFC (near-field communication) allows different devices to share data when they are in close proximity. It is communication technology. It is mostly used to share personal data, confidential data, financial transactions etc. The RFID system foundation and evolution is discussed in [9].

There are other technological developments as well which support the evolution of IoT such as machine-to-machine (M2M) communication and sensors.

4.2.2 IoT Application Structure and Driver Technologies

The technologies used by an IoT environment are categorized mainly into three groups helping with the data handling process. The three phases of data handling are as follows:

- Data collection phase: The data present in the physical world is being collected in this phase using sensors, RFIDs, actuators, different cameras etc. Short-range or cellular technologies are also used.
- Transmission phase: The collected data is transmitted to the main assistance needed platform across different networks for easy accessibility by the applications.
- Processing, managing and utilization phase: This phase works on the abstract information which is acquired in the transmission phase and it collects all the important information from objects, networks, and services. After this, it offers a loose combination of components like service discovery and service composition.

4.2.3 Concept of Edge, Fog and Roof Computing in IoT

There is an increase in the use of cloud computing in the IT sector but several obstacles like unreliable latency, less mobility support and tracking awareness are still unsolved. Edge, Fog and Roof computing technologies help in addressing these unsolved issues [10]:

- Edge computing is mainly a way to optimize cloud computing. It comprises tags, sensors, tag readers and actuators and other components. It reduces the communication bandwidth of the sensors and the central data as it works near the data source [11].

- Fog computing is described as an extension of the cloud computing pattern. It keeps an eye on cloud computing from the core network to the edge of the network and thus eliminates the repetitive analysis of the information at cloud [12].
- ROOF (Real-time Onsite Operations Facilitation) is a new and very recent federated networking system. It provides precise, alert, decision triggers and very efficient data connectivity to the cloud providers.

4.3 IoT Challenges

IoT proved to be a boon to various domains such as economic, societal, government and research and offers many opportunities to its users but it is also an origin of limitations and challenges.

4.3.1 Technological Challenges

- Interoperability has various meanings in the IoT sector like capability to communicate, exchange data and understand the data. Even though IoT provides data to users very efficiently, there is a problem in understanding that data because there is no universal language present [13].
- Precision is a hard quality to access, especially in areas like health and safety. The data accessed in these areas is time-bound, and as smart as the IoT systems are, they sometimes fail to provide important data timely.
- Data volume and scalability is another challenge faced by IoT. There is an interconnection between all the data, and in the coming years, the data generated due to this interconnectivity will be so high that all the methods of data collection will fail. There is a need for sufficient data collection methods or processes.
- Internet connectivity demanded by IoT needs to be perfect, but in remote areas, there is a lack of internet connectivity.

4.3.2 Security, Privacy and Trust Issues

The data shared in an IoT network is needed to be highly secured. A secure network helps in gaining user's trust and also supports the ethical and privacy aspects. But because IoT systems rely on wireless networks, it is always risked by different types of intrusions like unauthorized access of routers, DOS attacks, traffic injections, brute-force attacks and faulty configurations [14].

4.3.3 Regulatory Challenges

Numerous regulatory challenges are arising due to data ownership and data collection management. There is a debate over what type of data should be collected and how much. This problem is fuelled by the increase in heterogeneous IoT systems. European General Data Protection Regulation (GDPR) was made responsible for the protection of data in May 2018. It is all about privacy and the protection of data. They look over all the auctions where the personal data and activities related to it are involved. They make certain the free flow of personal data between EU member states and give rights to privacy to their citizens, thus affecting the companies who deal with personal data largely.

4.4 IoT Enablers and Solutions

4.4.1 IoT Enablers

A prerequisite that unleashes the potential of the IoT for the masses is the practical viability for IoT system and Application Enabler to enable new things to connect and communicate to the internet. IoT firstly exploits standard protocols and networking technologies. The big enabling technologies and protocols of IoT are NFC, RFID, low-energy Bluetooth, low-energy wireless, low-energy radio protocols and LTE-A [15]. Figure 4.6 depicts various technologies which may be integrated with IoT.

4.4.2 Top Enablers for Internet of Things

- Technology selection and evolution: There are so many options for IoT technologies available in the markets today, but what is important is to go with the mainstream 3GPP technologies for inter-working with advanced technologies like 5G in the future and at the same time providing the highest level of security and protection.
- Industry partnerships: IoT has a large scope and having partnerships to facilitate the development of long-term solutions enablers is necessary. Industry

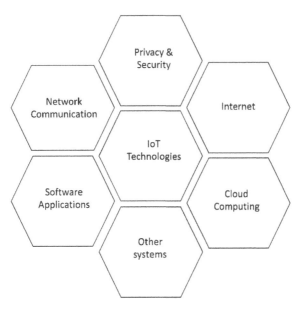

FIGURE 4.6
Enabling technologies in IoT.

partnerships are required for different aspects; an enabler would require them for understanding automobiles and hardware devices to provide an IT system and platform for enabling IoT.

• IT transformation: It is necessary that an IoT enabler has an IT system that can cater to the needs of IoT, mechanisms for flexibility and scalability for admitting billions of devices because if we think about IoT, we are not thinking about humans, so it will not make sense to send a connectivity bill to a sensor. There are certain use cases where a system has to cater to requirements for multi-country solutions like you cannot expect that your connected car stops working when you drive from Malaysia to Singapore [16].

4.5 IoT and Data Protection

The growth of the IoT increases rapidly, which creates substantial opportunities for users to benefit from services that are based on data acquisition and storage, analytics and ML. It is sure that a responsible approach must be taken by service designers to ensure that personal data and privacy are protected for users [17].

4.5.1 GDPR Personal Data

GDPR is GDPR which is a legal framework that sets the guidelines for collection and processing of personal information from individuals. Personal data is the heart of the GDPR. Through GDPR, we get to know what exactly is personal data, that is, information which relates to an identified or identifiable individual [18]. Figure 4.7 depicts the personal data of general data protection regulation.

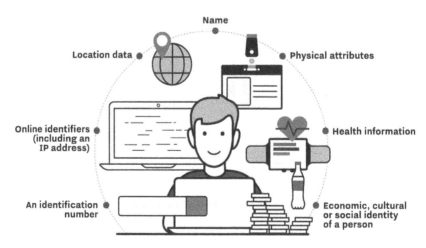

FIGURE 4.7
GDPR personal data.

FIGURE 4.8
Sustainable development with IoT.

4.6 Impact of IoT on Sustainable Development

The industry considers that the IoT is a better opportunity for the present and the future that will digitize so many operations and bring major benefits. But it has also the capability to help combat climate change and protect the environment. In this way, the IoT would impact or affect the sustainability of the planets in different areas, such as water use and energy efficiency [19]. Figure 4.8 shows the sustainable development technologies which may be integrated with IoT.

4.7 IoT Technical Standardization

IoT technology played a vital role in the improvement and growth of the technical standards across the business sector and the rapid spread of internet and the devices connected through it. For the development of IoT and other technologies, initiatives should be taken at the international as well as national levels by elaborating interoperable global standards across the application domain. This will enhance the importance of IoT at the market level.

4.7.1 Technical Standardization Background

The specialized normalization is a benchmark which is created inside the normalization bodies by keeping the interest of partners by giving a specialized or subjective referential norm of items or administrations at various geological levels in their spaces of capability. At worldwide level, the three most perceived Standards Development Organizations (SDOs) are the International Organization for Standardization (ISO), the International Electrotechnical Commission (IEC) and the International Telecommunication Union's Telecommunication Standardization Sector (ITU-T). Additionally, there are some all-around perceived Standardization Organizations at European level as the European

Committee for Standardization (CEN), the European Committee for Electrotechnical Standardization (CENELEC) and the European Telecommunications Standards Institute (ETSI). There is one public guidelines body (NSB) in each country which works at public level while being as a team with European and global normalization associations. For instance, ILNAS is the NSB working at Luxembourg which is likewise an individual from CEN, CENELEC, ETSI, ISO, IEC and ITU-T [20].

4.7.2 Technical Standardization and IoT

Specialized standardization gives a standard level which makes it a successful apparatus against the majority of the difficulties looked by IoT. Electrotechnical Commission has an extremely vital impact in the improvement of IoT innovation at the market level as it helps recognizing specialized principles. These specialized guidelines make a rivalry in the market of IoT by guaranteeing interoperability among IoT arrangements. Normalizations additionally make answer for a sensible expense of IoT framework by giving the data with respect to innovative work cost [21].

4.7.3 National Context of IoT Technical Standardization

The enlisted delegates participate in the specialized normalization under the ILNAS which deals with the National Mirror Committee (NMC) of ISO/IEC JTC 1/SC 41 with the help of ANEC G.I.E. In the normalization work of ISO/IEC JTC 1/SC 41, the agents are permitted to cast a ballot and remark on the recommendations given by the subcommittee and they can likewise engage in the global whole gatherings. With the help of ANEC G.I.E., the normalization exercises of IoT are checked by the ILNAS the monitor refreshes just as giving these updates to the public partners.

4.8 Conclusion

The IoT is a very beneficial tool for our modern world as it helps in the communication between things or devices around us. On the other hand, ML makes it easy for a model to design, test and train the dataset to give desired outcome on the basis of data provided. We basically tried to put some light on the application and implementation of IoT and ML in this chapter. ML Techniques are very helpful in making the IoT devices smart and intelligent. We also discussed about the challenges faced by IoT and its role in the sustainable development of society. Thus, ML techniques are highly preferred for classification and prediction in vast field of applications even if they may not overcome all the challenges faced by IoT.

References

1. Y. Kodratoff, 1993, "Introduction to Machine Learning," Pitman Publishing, London.
2. A. J. Smola and S. Vishwanathan, 2008, "Introduction to Machine Learning," Cambridge University Press, Cambridge University, UK.

3. K. Murphy, 2012, "Machine Learning: A Probabilistic Perspective," MIT Press, Cambridge, MA.
4. R.S. Sutton and A.G. Barto, 1998, "Reinforcement Learning: An Introduction," MIT Press, Cambridge, MA.
5. K. Ashton, 2009, "That "Internet of things" thing: In the Real World Things Matter More than Ideas," RFiD J., vol. 22, no. 7, pp. 97–114.
6. K. Finkenzeller and RFID Handbook, 2010, "Fundamentals and Applications in Contactless Smart Cards, Radio Frequency Identification and Near-Field Communication," Wiley, New York.
7. G. Yovanof and G. Hazapis, 2009, "An architectural framework and enablingwireless technologies for digital cities and intelligent urban environments," Wireless Pers. Commun., vol. 49, no. 3, pp. 445–463.
8. X.L. Jia, Q.Y. Feng and C.Z. Ma, 2010, "An efficient anti-collision protocol for RFID tag identification," IEEE Commun. Lett., vol. 14, no. 11, pp. 1014–1016.
9. J. Buckley (Ed.), 2006, "The Internet of Things: From RFID to the Next-Generation Pervasive Networked Systems," Auerbach Publications, New York.
10. M. Abomhara and G.M. Koien, 2014, "Security and privacy in the Internet of Things: Current status and open issues," in Int'l Conference on Privacy and Security in Mobile Systems PRISMS), 1–8.
11. M. Satyanarayanan, 2017, "The emergence of edge computing computer," Computer, vol. 50, no. 1, pp. 30–39.
12. F. Bonomi, 2011, "Connected vehicles, the internet of things, and fog computing," VANET.
13. R. Roshan, and A. Kr. Ray, 2016, "Challenges and risk to implement IOT in smart homes: An Indian perspective", IJCA (0975–8887), vol. 153, no. 3, p. 16.
14. Y. Lu and L. Da Xu, 2019, "Internet of Things (IoT) cyber security research: A review of current research topics," IEEE Internet Things J., vol. 6, no. 2, pp. 2103–2115.
15. M.G. Seok, and D. Park, 2018, "A novel multi-level evaluation approach for human-coupled IOT applications," J. Ambient Intell. Hum. Comput., pp 1–4.
16. M.-S. Dao, S. Pongpaichet, L. Jalali, K. Kim, R. Jain and K. Zettsu, 2014, "A real-time complex event discovery platform for cyber-physical-socialsystems," in Proceedings of International Conference on Multimedia Retrieval, ACM, 2014, pp. 201.
17. M. Weiser and R. Gold, 1999 "The origins of ubiquitous computing research." at PARC, 1980s, IBM Syst. J., vol. 38, pp. 693–696.
18. A. Gapchup, A. Wani, D. Gapchup and S. Jadhav, 2016, "Health care systems using Internet of things", IJIRCCE, Pune, India, vol. 4, no. 12, 20896–20903.
19. H. Liu, Y. Liu, Q. Wu and S. Ma, 2013, "A heterogeneous data integration model," in Geo-Informatics in Resource Management and Sustainable Ecosystem. Springer, Berlin, Heidelberg, pp. 298–312.
20. J. Belissent, 2010, "Getting Clever about Smart Cities: New Opportunities Require New Business Models," Forrester Research, Inc., Cambridge, MA.
21. 2007, WSN for Smart Cities: Amaretto, San Diego, CA, USA.

5

AIC Algorithm for Online Cashback: Evidence from Vietnam

Nguyen Ngan and Bui Huy Khoi

CONTENTS

5.1 Introduction

In Vietnam, the cashback wave has been introduced since 2016 and putatu.com is the pioneer website in this campaign, helping Vietnamese people catch up with the trend (VTV 2017). Launched in January 2017, after two months of launch, more than 2,000 people have made thousands of transactions with a value of up to 12 billion VND via putatu.com. The amount of user savings has reached 500 million (VTV 2017). Nowadays, cashback is becoming more and more popular, especially when there is the appearance of shopping through e-wallets: MoMo, Moca, ZaloPay, and Shopback. With bill payment via e-wallet or with affiliate applications, customers can get 10%–20% cashback, even when buying data,

DOI: 10.1201/9781003226888-5

phone cards, game cards, restaurant reservations, flight tickets, movie tickets (Thanhnien 2020). PVcomBank is one of the banks that has applied this program to customers and, in the first month of opening, the bank estimated to refund customers VND 100 million (PVcombank 2020). In December 2019, Shopback began its beta program in Vietnam, drawing almost 800,000 users and more than 150 partners. ShopBack Vietnam saw a 1.5-fold increase in monthly sales and orders. To date, more than VND 4 billion has been reimbursed to ShopBack users in Vietnam (BaoCongthuong 2020). Cashback applications appeared in Vietnam as a tool to help business partners save costs in marketing and promoting products and services for the online shopping segment and attracting potential customers, potential, increase revenue and this is a potential form of promotion in the Vietnamese market.

In the e-commerce market, customers benefit from their transactions on linked websites or apps. Combining traditional techniques, such as word of mouth, is critical for the success of this company model because it can increase and strengthen client loyalty (Ballestar et al. 2018). By using this method, both the business and the affiliate gain from the affiliate's e-commerce transactions, resulting in a win-win situation for both the client and the business. Customers' social networks are likewise growing and becoming more active (Ballestar et al. 2016). The study (Ballestar et al. 2018) showed that the important role of customers in using cashback applications determines customer behavior and activities for e-commerce channels. Vana et al. (2018) analyzed cashback incentives that increase a consumer's likelihood of purchasing e-commerce sites and increase the size of that transaction, according to dashboard data from a large refund company. Cashback payments increase a consumer's probability of purchasing e-commerce sites and increase the size of that transaction, regardless of impact. The adoption of cashback apps is similar to other types of online or offline marketing in terms of effectiveness (Christino et al. 2019).

The refund application or website is already present and popular in developed countries such as the US, UK, Singapore. In Vietnam, this type of payment method was introduced in 2016 by putatu.com, but its level of popularity has only exploded in recent years. Specifically, in 2020, when many website applications are launched such as Shopback, Accumulation, Cashback, Clingme (Demaitinh 2020).

The cashback program is a strategy that is not too new to countries around the world and there are many studies on this strategy. However, each study gives different results on factors affecting the intention or behavior of customers. Much of the difference is in the geographic, economic, and customer segmentation that researchers choose. In Vietnam, according to the research, the author found that this is a new market, there are still limited research topics on this issue. So from that, the author formed the idea of researching the topic of the refund program. Therefore, this study focuses on AIC algorithm for online cashback. The following is the order in which this chapter is presented: The first section gives an overview of the study, Section 5.2 presents a review of literature on the variable used in this research, and Section 5.3 presents the methodology. Results and analysis with some discussion and implications are offered in Section 5.4. Lastly, Section 5.5 accomplishes this chapter.

5.2 Literature Review

5.2.1 Using Behavior of Cashback (UBC)

Commerce-related business models that connect companies with customers help them improve their purchasing decisions (Barnes-Vieyra and Claycomb 2001). Vana et al. (2018)

show that cashback payments increase the likelihood of repeat purchases and that customer behavior is significantly different from those without it, as they are not only performing transactions more diversified but also important in the items that need economic investment. Customers benefit from cashback programs because they make the purchasing process easier and provide financial incentives (Ballestar et al. 2016). Consumers are easily seduced by savings, which benefits them because they have the freedom to spend or store the money in any way they see fit (Vana et al. 2018). Consumers often assume they are a customer of that business. Before making a purchase, consumers often search for the products they need to buy on e-commerce channels to see if the product is in stock. Consumers tend to remember cashback programs only when they receive a notification (reminder) from a refund program (Venkatesh et al. 2012, Christino et al. 2019,). Thus, the behavior of using the cashback application is the ability to use the cashback application depending on the benefits that the cashback application brings such as helping customers save, and the convenience of using the product.

5.2.2 Ease of Use (EU)

Potential users are more likely to embrace and use innovative technology solutions that are viewed as easy to use and less difficult (Davis 1989). In the TAM (Technology Acceptance Model), according to Davis (1989), "perceived ease of use is the degree to which a person believes that using a particular system will be effortless". Perceived ease of use (EU) of technology will have an effect or influence on behavior and activities, i.e., the higher the perceived EU of a system, the higher the users' information level (Sayekti and Wijayanti 2018). EU is implicit as the ease with which users perceive a technology to be used, which is the trust that using a specific organization will be easy (Alalwan et al. 2018). Perceived EU helps users have a positive attitude toward the service, thereby enhancing the intention to use (Widyanti and Usman 2019). Consumers often think that mobile apps, such as cashback programs, are easy to use (Arora et al. 2020). According to Bai (2015), websites, applications with a beautiful interface will attract more customers. Davis (1989) mentioned that consumers find it difficult to remember passwords or technology-related security. Kaur and Jain (2016) argue that customers feel that online payment will be useful for online shopping. Thus, it can be seen that "Ease of use" is an intimate factor with the behavior of using the cashback program. Because consumers in today's technology era feel it is easy and necessary to use applications and programs to serve their online shopping needs.

5.2.3 Personal Capacity (PC)

Personal capacity (PC) relates to how confident consumers are that they have the necessary skills or knowledge to effectively participate in and use a particular service area (Walker and Johnson 2006). A personal capability to estimate consumers' competence to accomplish tasks derived from social perception (Alalwan et al. 2016). When it comes to new technology, the easier it is for a person to use a specific program, the better their cognitive-behavioral performance is (Zhang et al. 2017). Capacity is "the ability, subjective or natural condition available to perform a certain activity" such as thinking capacity, financial capacity. Consumer technology skills are now good. And customers easily adapt to newly launched technology applications. They believe that they can always use a new technology application. More than that, they feel comfortable when many services are connected with technology applications (Walker and Johnson 2006, Christino et al. 2019). With the era of technology and modernization, consumers always equip themselves with knowledge and updates on the launch of new technologies to serve themselves, as well as shortening the time to perform a certain job just by manipulating applications and technology on mobile devices. Thus, the "personal capacity" of customers always goes hand in hand with user behavior. They feel that they perform well or can perform a certain technology, the higher the behavior of using that technology.

5.2.4 Perceived Risk (PR)

Compared with product risk, consumers' perception of personal information disclosure risk had a greater impact on Internet shopping decisions (Eggert 2006). Consumers may face risks throughout the purchasing process if they are aware that they have no control over their purchase or that the consequences of making a poor decision could be disastrous (Al Kailani and Kumar 2011). Perceived risk (PR) is another factor affecting personal enjoyment and motivation. The degree to which a consumer perceives the overall negativeness of an action is referred to as PR (e.g., purchasing, using, or disposing of a product/service), based on an assessment of the outcomes, and the probability of these outcomes (Zhang 2010). Types of risks act as barriers to conducting transactions on the Internet, influence online product purchase behavior, and determine consumers' choice of purchasing channels (Tandon et al. 2016). PR is defined as the possibility of a negative outcome as a result of an action (Mohseni et al. 2018). PR has a direct effect on use and intention to use (Aminu et al. 2019). Consumers' PRs will influence consumers' attitudes and interests in online shopping (Ghachem et al. 2019). Customers feel insecure when providing personal information to apply for cashback programs. They worry that when they provide personal information to refund programs, their information will be used for other purposes. Besides, they also feel worried that the refund programs will be faulty (Walker and Johnson 2006, Christino et al. 2019). According to Abrar et al. (2017), consumers feel worried when the product is not correct or unsatisfactory (damaged, wrong size, not like the picture) after completing the transactions and making payment entirely online. It can be noticed from there that when performing the activity of using consumers, they will worry about the risks when connecting to applications and technologies. These are all things that can make them hesitate or decide not to use that application or technology. Technology businesses should pay attention to this issue because it is also a way to build trust with customers

5.2.5 Using Intention of Cashback (UIC)

According to behavioral theory, using intention has a direct influence on the performance of the behavior. When a customer has an intention toward a certain product or service, the ability to buy and use the product or service is very high (Lee 2010). Research on consumer intention to use has broader implications than behavior and will often have a positive impact on individual actions. Intention to use is defined as an active decision that reveals an individual's behavior depending on the product (Ross 2021). According to Ajzen (1991), the intention is energizing and indicates a person's eagerness to engage in a specific behavior. It is understood as a person's determination to act in a certain way (Ramayah et al. 2010). Using intention is the consumer behavior of using the app in the future. They will use technology to make online shopping. And when they make good use of the technology, they will intend to continue using that technology (Venkatesh et al. 2012, Christino et al. 2019). In short, intention to use represents what the individual wants to use in the future (Mouakket 2015).

5.3 Methods

5.3.1 Sample Approach

The data collection method is by questionnaire, a survey designed on Google Drive and sending surveys through social networks Facebook and Zalo. The answers will be updated as soon as the surveyor completes the questionnaire. The statistics of sample characteristics are listed in Table 5.1.

Table 5.1 shows that the results for the sexes of men and women are almost equal. However, there are more men than women, with men accounting for 54.2% of the total and women accounting for 45.8%. The age group of 18–29 years old accounted for 97.2% of the total, while the age group of 30–44 years old accounted for 2.8%. The remaining age groups did not. This result for the age group of 18–29 years old is the most prominent age of exposure and use of online shopping and payment. Research results on the structure of monthly income, we see that out of 107 people surveyed, there are 34 people with income under 3 million, accounting for 31.8%, people with income from 3 million to 6 million have 34 people account for 32.7%, there are 29 people with incomes from 6 to under 12 million, accounting for 27.1%, the rest accounting for 8.4% are people with incomes over 12 million.

To assess the amount of consent for the linked elements, we employ a 5-point Likert scale. As a result, the 5-point Likert scale is used in this paper to assess the level of permission for all observed variables, with 1 denoting disagreement and 5 denoting agreement (see Table 5.2).

5.3.2 Blinding

For the duration of the study, all study staff and participants were blinded. The participants in the study had no contact with anyone from the outside world.

TABLE 5.1

Statistics of Sample

Characteristics		Amount	%
Sex	Male	58	54.2
	Female	49	45.8
Age	18–29	104	97.2
	30–44	3	2.8
Monthly income	Below 3 million VND	34	31.8
	3–6 million VND	35	32.7
	6–12 million VND	29	27.1
	Over 12 million VND	9	8.4

TABLE 5.2

Factor and Item

Factor	Item
Ease of use (EU)	Mobile tech apps, such as cashback programs, are simple to utilize in my opinion.
	I find apps that have a nice, easy-to-use interface are more appealing to me.
	Passwords, technology-related security issues, and applications such as cashback programs are all difficult for me to remember.
	I feel using online payment will be useful for online shopping.
Personal capacity (PC)	My technology skills are good.
	I can quickly learn new technology applications, such as online shopping or online payment, and adapt quickly.
	I believe I will be able to use freshly released technological applications, such as online shopping and payment apps.
	When various services are linked to technology applications, such as online buying or online payment, I feel at ease.
Perceived risk (PR)	When I provide personal information to apply for a cashback program, I feel uneasy (such as bank details, phone number, address).
	I am worried that the cashback application will fail (For example: not receiving the money, much longer time to receive the money than expected).
	I'm concerned that if I participate in the cashback program, my personal information will be utilized for unknown purposes.
	I feel worried when the product is incorrect or unsatisfactory (damaged, wrong size, not like the picture) after completing online transactions and online payments.
	I feel insecure when providing personal information to apply for a cashback program (such as bank details, phone number, address).
Using intention of cashback (UIC)	I will use the cashback program in the future.
	On my purchases, I'll make every effort to use cashback programs.
	I continue to use the regular cashback programs.
Using behavior of cashback (UBC)	I am a cashback program customer.
	Before buying, I often search the e-commerce site to see if the product is still available or out of stock.
	I only remember the cashback program when I receive a notification (reminder) from the application or website of these programs.

5.4 Results

5.4.1 Akaike Information Criterion Selection

The R program used AIC (Akaike Information Criteria) to select the optimal model. The AIC has been utilized for model selection in the theoretical environment (Mai et al. 2021). When multicollinearity occurs, the AIC method can handle several independent variables. AIC can be used to estimate one or more dependent variables from one or more independent variables using a regression model. The AIC is an important and useful metric for finding a complete and simple model. Based on the AIC information standard, a model with a lower AIC is picked. The best model will come to an end when the minimum AIC value is obtained (Burnham and Anderson 2004, Khoi 2021).

TABLE 5.3

Akaike Information Criterion Selection

Model	AIC
UBC = f (EU + PC + PR + UIC)	−140.17
UBC = f (EU + PC + PR)	−141.96
UBC = f (PC + PR)	−142.52

TABLE 5.4

The Coefficients

UBC	Estimate	Std. Error	T	p-Value	Decision
Intercept	1.16025				
PC	0.29019	0.07045	4.119	0.000000	Accepted
PR	−0.42578	0.06250	6.813	0.000000	Accepted

Every step of the search for the best model is documented in R reports. The initial step is to use AIC = −142.52 for UBC = f (PC + PR) to analyze all 06 independent variables in Table 5.3.

The p-value of less than 0.05 exists for two variables (Hill et al. 2018), as a result, they are linked to using behavior of cashback (UBC), which is in Table 5.4. PC and PR impact using behavior of cashback (UBC). EU and using intention of cashback (UIC) do not influence UBC.

5.4.2 Variance Inflation Factor

Multicollinearity occurs when the independent variables in regression models have a high degree of correlation. If the variance inflation factor (VIF) coefficient is greater than ten, Gujarati and Porter (2009) found evidence of multicollinearity in the model. The VIF for the independent variables is less than ten according to Table 5.5 (Miles 2014), indicating that the independent variables are not collinear.

TABLE 5.5

Model Test

VIF	PC		PR	
		1.267508		1.267508
Heteroskesdaticity	Goldfeld-Quandt test		chi2	p-value:
			0.97345	0.5383
Autocorrelation	Durbin-Watson		Test for autocorrelation	
		2.0046		p-value: 0.4953
Model evaluation	Adjusted R-squared		F-statistic	p-value:
		0.5116	56.51	0.0000

5.4.3 Heteroskesdaticity

The random error must be constant, according to one of the key concepts of the traditional linear regression model (Homoskedasticity). In practice, this assumption is unlikely to be correct. When the variance of the random error for each observation is different, heteroscedasticity develops. Because the p-value for the Goldfeld-Quandt test is 0.97345 and greater than 0.05 (Godfrey 1978), in Table 5.5, there is no heteroskedasticity.

5.4.4 Autocorrelation

Durbin-Watson (DW) value is in the range from 0 to 4. If the DW value is in the range of 1.5–2.5, there will be no autocorrelation, if the smaller the value, the closer to zero the parts will be the error is positively correlated, close to 4 means that the error parts are negatively correlated. Because the p-value = 0.4953 is greater than 0.05, the DW test (2.0046) reveals that there is no autocorrelation in the model in Table 5.4 (Durbin and Watson 1971).

5.4.5 Model Evaluation

According to Table 5.5's findings, PC and PR impact UBC is 51.16% in Table 5.5. R^2 (R square) ranges from 0 to 1, the closer to 1, the more significant the model, and vice versa, the closer to 0, the weaker the model significance. p-Value of the F test is used to test the fit of the regression model p-value < 0.05 the multiple linear regression model fits the data set and can be used. The model is statistically significant, according to the aforementioned analysis (Greene 2003).

5.4.6 Discussion

The AIC algorithm for the UBC revealed that there are two independent factors. Because their p-values are less than 0.05, PC has a positive impact on the UBC and PR has a negative impact on the UBC. In descending order, compare the influence degree of these two variables on the UBC: PC (–0.42578), PR (0.29019). Thus, all relationships are accepted at the 95% confidence level.

5.5 Conclusion

The chapter builds on previous studies: Christino et al. (2019) study shows that the factors affecting cashback application such as habit, social influence, and other behavioral aspects, this chapter is based on the UTAUT2 research model, which has successfully demonstrated that customer behavior is closely related to technology. Ballestar et al. (2016) found that customer engagement on cashback programs has a positive impact on customer loyalty and profitability for both customers and businesses. Ballestar et al. (2018) apply the concepts of trustworthiness, social systems, consumer growth, and interaction to see that the role of customers depends on the customer's position in the social network. This chapter also displays that the more consumers trust, the more engaged, more transactional, and the level of engagement with the cashback program is also related to the multi-transaction of the program. Finally, research by Vana et al. (2018) has proven that it is useful for businesses and companies to cooperate with cashback programs. This study found that the success of cashback programs was generally similar to that of previously recognized online and offline promotions. The studies have been successful in developed countries, but for Vietnam, the refund program is still new, with the author's research, the two factors "personal capacity" and "perceived risk" are a strong influence on the "behavior of using" cashback program of customers.

5.5.1 Limitations and Next Research Directions

Firstly, this study was conducted in a relatively short time of only five months, the time limitation has more or less affected the process of selecting the research model and building the most suitable scale, the time of collecting survey collection also affects the results of research on factors. Secondly, in the process of carrying out the research, the author also encountered certain difficulties such as having difficulty accessing leading experts, limited meeting time as well as not being able to fully comprehend all the relevant topics. The process of collecting secondary data also faces many difficulties because some agencies in Vietnam have not disclosed data transparently and clearly. Thirdly, the number of samples of 107 that the author studied is not large enough, this number of samples only represents a small part of the population, not the general population of the entire population of consumers living in Vietnam. And because the epidemic is quite serious, it is also limited in the direct survey process, surveys only used on social networks are also a limitation. Therefore, the number of consumers invited to respond to the survey cannot fully assess the consumer behavior of using the cashback program in Vietnam. To complete the research model and achieve better results, the next research topic on the behavior of using the consumer cashback program: Research studies with a larger number of samples to achieve a higher level of satisfaction better overall representation; research on a larger scale in Vietnam, with many types of consumers to increase the diversity of survey subjects; it is possible to focus on researching each separate consumer object to devise a specific strategy for each different consumer group.

5.6 Authors Contribution

The paper is co-authored by three people. B.H. Khoi assisted in the data analysis and collection of research-related references. N.T. Ngan assisted in the data collection and revision of the text. A data survey was done by B.H. Khoi.

Acknowledgment

Industrial University of Ho Chi Minh City, Vietnam, is funding this study.

References

Abrar, Kashif, Muhammad Naveed, and Ifra Ramay. 2017. "Impact of perceived risk on online impulse buying tendency: An empirical study in the consumer market of Pakistan." *Journal of Accounting & Marketing* no. 6 (3):246.

Ajzen, Icek. 1991. "The theory of planned behavior." *Organizational Behavior and Human Decision Processes* no. 50 (2):179–211.

Al Kailani, Mahmud, and Rachna Kumar. 2011. "Investigating uncertainty avoidance and perceived risk for impacting Internet buying: A study in three national cultures." *International Journal of Business and Management* no. 6 (5):76.

Alalwan, Ali Abdallah, Yogesh K Dwivedi, Nripendra P Rana, and Raed Algharabat. 2018. "Examining factors influencing Jordanian customers' intentions and adoption of internet banking: Extending UTAUT2 with risk." *Journal of Retailing and Consumer Services* no. 40: 125–138.

Alalwan, Ali Abdallah, Yogesh K Dwivedi, Nripendra PP Rana, and Michael D Williams. 2016. "Consumer adoption of mobile banking in Jordan: Examining the role of usefulness, ease of use, perceived risk and self-efficacy." *Journal of Enterprise Information Management* no. 29 (1): 118–139.

Aminu, Suraju Abiodun, Olusegun Paul Olawore, and Adesina Emmanuel Odesanya. 2019. "Perceived risk barriers to Internet shopping." *KIU Journal of Social Sciences* no. 5 (2):69–81.

Arora, Neerja, Garima Malik, and Deepak Chawla. 2020. "Factors affecting consumer adoption of mobile apps in NCR: A qualitative study." *Global Business Review* no. 21 (1):176–196.

Bai, Jianyong. 2015. How the Electronic Commerce Enterprise Attract More Customers. In *Paper Read at 2015 International Conference on Management Science and Innovative Education*.

Ballestar, María Teresa, Pilar Grau-Carles, and Jorge Sainz. 2018. "Customer segmentation in e-commerce: Applications to the cashback business model." *Journal of Business Research* no. 88:407–414.

Ballestar, María Teresa, Jorge Sainz, and Joan Torrent-Sellens. 2016. "Social networks on cashback websites." *Psychology & Marketing* no. 33 (12):1039–1045.

BaoCongthuong. 2020. *Shopback cashback platform officially launched in Vietnam (Vietnamese)*. Available from https://congthuong.vn/nen-tang-hoan-tien-shopback-chinh-thuc-ra-mat-tai-viet-nam-141780.html.

Barnes-Vieyra, Pamela, and Cindy Claycomb. 2001. "Business-to-business e-commerce: Models and managerial decisions." *Business Horizons* no. 44 (3):13–20.

Burnham, Kenneth P, and David R Anderson. 2004. "Multimodel inference: Understanding AIC and BIC in model selection." *Sociological Methods & Research* no. 33 (2):261–304.

Christino, Juliana Maria Magalhães, Thaís Santos Silva, Erico Aurélio Abreu Cardozo, Alexandre de Padua Carrieri, and Patricia de Paiva Nunes. 2019. "Understanding affiliation to cashback programs: An emerging technique in an emerging country." *Journal of Retailing and Consumer Services* no. 47:78–86.

Davis, Fred D. 1989. "Perceived usefulness, perceived ease of use, and user acceptance of information technology." *MIS Quarterly* vol. 13 (3): 319–340.

Demaitinh. 2020. *Six best cashback apps in Vietnam today (Vietnamese)*. Available from https://demaitinh.vn/6-ung-dung-hoan-tien-cashback-tot-nhat-hien-nay-tai-viet-nam.

Durbin, James, and Geoffrey S Watson. 1971. "Testing for serial correlation in least squares regression. III." *Biometrika* no. 58 (1):1–19.

Eggert, Axel. 2006. "Intangibility and perceived risk in online environments." *Journal of Marketing Management* no. 22 (5–6):553–572.

Ghachem, Lassaad, Costinel Dobre, Reza Etemad-Sajadi, and Anca Milovan-Ciuta. 2019. "The impact of cultural dimensions on the perceived risk of online shopping." *Studia Universitatis Babes-Bolyai, Negotia* no. 64 (3): 7–28.

Godfrey, Leslie G. 1978. "Testing for multiplicative heteroskedasticity." *Journal of Econometrics* no. 8 (2):227–236.

Greene, William H. 2003. *Econometric Analysis*: Pearson Education India.

Gujarati, Damodar N, and Dawn C Porter. 2009. *Basic Econometrics*, International Edition: Mc Graw-Hill.

Hill, R Carter, William E Griffiths, and Guay C Lim. 2018. *Principles of Econometrics*: John Wiley & Sons.

Kaur, Baljeet, and Tanya Jain. 2016. "Attracting customers' to online shopping using mobile apps: A case study of Indian market." In *Securing Transactions and Payment Systems for M-commerce*, 117–140. IGI Global.

Khoi, Bui Huy. 2021. "Factors influencing on university reputation: Model selection by AIC." In *Data Science for Financial Econometrics*, 177–188. Springer.

Lee, CS. 2010. "Study on the decision factors for customer satisfaction and repurchase intention in high-speed internet access service: Focus on the company, product and customer service." *The e-Business Studies* no. 11 (4):275–289.

Mai, Dam Sao, Phan Hong Hai, and Bui Huy Khoi. 2021. Optimal Model Choice Using AIC Method and Naive Bayes Classification. In *IOP Conference Series: Materials Science and Engineering*.

Miles, Jeremy. 2014. "Tolerance and variance inflation factor." *Wiley StatsRef: Statistics Reference Online*.

Mohseni, Shahriar, Sreenivasan Jayashree, Sajad Rezaei, Azilah Kasim, and Fevzi Okumus. 2018. "Attracting tourists to travel companies' websites: The structural relationship between website brand, personal value, shopping experience, perceived risk and purchase intention." *Current Issues in Tourism* no. 21 (6):616–645.

Mouakket, Samar. 2015. "Factors influencing continuance intention to use social network sites: The Facebook case." *Computers in Human Behavior* no. 53:102–110.

PVcombank. 2020. *Cashback – Promotion trend with many benefits for consumers*. Available from https://www.pvcombank.com.vn/tin-tuc/tin-pvcombank/hoan-tien-xu-huong-khuyen-mai-nhieu-loi-ich-cho-nguoi-tieu-dung-1577.html.

Ramayah, T, Noor Hazlina Ahmad, and May-Chiun Lo. 2010. "The role of quality factors in intention to continue using an e-learning system in Malaysia." *Procedia-Social and Behavioral Sciences* no. 2 (2):5422–5426.

Ross, Stanley C. 2021. *Organizational Behavior Today*: Routledge.

Sayekti, F, and LE Wijayanti. 2018. The Influence of Perception of Usefulness (PoU) and Perceived Ease of Use (PEU) on the Perception of Information System Performance. In *Paper Read at Increasing Management Relevance and Competitiveness: Proceedings of the 2nd Global Conference on Business, Management and Entrepreneurship (GC-BME 2017)*, August 9, 2017, Universitas Airlangga, Surabaya, Indonesia.

Tandon, Urvashi, Ravi Kiran, and Ash N Sah. 2016. "Understanding online shopping adoption in India: Unified theory of acceptance and use of technology 2 (UTAUT2) with perceived risk application." *Service Science* no. 8 (4):420–437.

Thanhnien. 2020. *Cashback – Promotion trend with many benefits for consumers (Vietnamese)*. Available from https://thanhnien.vn/tai-chinh-kinh-doanh/hoan-tien-xu-huong-khuyen-mai-nhieu-loi-ich-cho-nguoi-tieu-dung-1292140.html.

Vana, Prasad, Anja Lambrecht, and Marco Bertini. 2018. "Cashback is cash forward: Delaying a discount to entice future spending." *Journal of Marketing Research* no. 55 (6):852–868.

Venkatesh, Viswanath, James YL Thong, and Xin Xu. 2012. "Consumer acceptance and use of information technology: Extending the unified theory of acceptance and use of technology." *MIS Quarterly* no. 36 (1):157–178.

VTV. 2017. *Viet Startup brings the world's popular cashback model to Vietnam (Vietnamese)*. Available from https://vtv.vn/kinh-te/startup-viet-mang-mo-hinh-cashback-thinh-hanh-tren-the-gioi-ve-viet-nam-20170420080544875.htm.

Walker, Rhett H, and Lester W Johnson. 2006. "Why consumers use and do not use technology-enabled services." *Journal of Services Marketing* no. 20 (2):125–135.

Widyanti, Jovita, and Osly Usman. 2019. *Leverage of Perceived Usefulness, Perceived Ease of Use, Information Quality, Behavioral Intention towards Intention to Use Mobile Banking*. Perceived Ease of Use, Information Quality, Behavioral Intention towards Intention to Use Mobile Banking (December 27, 2019).

Zhang, Lin-lin. 2010. Measuring Perceived Risk of Securities Investment Based on Disposition Effect. In *Paper Read at 2010 International Conference on E-Product E-Service and E-Entertainment*.

Zhang, Peiyao, Nan Li, Dongping Fang, and Haojie Wu. 2017. "Supervisor-focused behavior-based safety method for the construction industry: Case study in Hong Kong." *Journal of Construction Engineering and Management* no. 143 (7):05017009.

6

IoT-Driven Smart Pisciculture Monitoring and Control System

Polly Thomas, Vaishnav Nair S, Sanju Joseph Abraham, Farah Fathima Raheem, and Sidharth Sivanraj

CONTENTS

DOI: 10.1201/9781003226888-6

6.1 Introduction: Background and Current Developments

Farming our own crops has been one of the most historic steps man has taken in the path to evolution. Agriculture has always been one of the backbone sectors in India and at present contributes about 17% to the country's GDP (Gross Domestic Product) and employment to over 60% of the population. Although farming on land has been around for as long as we can remember farming in water has only been around for a few centuries. It wasn't until the 1800s that commercial fish farming came into the fray. Aquaculture contributes about 1.0% to Indian GDP and is steadily rising at over 10.8% per year. Aquaculture is in high demand throughout the world due to depletion of marine fish by overfishing. Rearing fish for profit has evolved from selling goldfish in a bowl to farming thousands of kilograms of fish in water bodies spanning hundreds of acres. Fish farming done on a large scale, if done right, is highly profitable but it requires the pond or fish tank to be set up correctly. An improperly setup or poorly maintained fish farm can spell disaster for aquatic life. As water volume decreases, key parameters will change quickly. Also farmers are faced with sudden and erratic climate changes. Therefore, it is very important to measure key water quality parameters and carry out corrective actions accordingly. Many studies indicate that larger water volumes are better for fish health as the increased water volume prevents a drastic change in key quality parameters over a short span of time [1, 2]. In addition to a larger water volume, two other key aspects of fish farming are the sensing of a wide range of key water quality parameters and informing the farmers of the same and the corrective actions required in case of a sharp decline in water quality. It is not always possible to be present in person near the farm and so if an undesired scenario arises it could go unnoticed. To avoid this, several solutions based on IoT (Internet of Things) have been proposed [3–5]. However, most systems employ only basic testing [6, 7]. Some systems provide trivial control based on threshold values [8]. Based on IoT, we propose a smart pisciculture monitoring and control system that allows for the pisciculture system to transmit sensor data to the farmers as well as help the farmers actuate the control motors in response to an unwanted change in key water quality parameters in real time. One of the main features of this system is the presence of both an automatic mode and a manual mode. Manual control uses nontrivial intelligence for controlling the motors. The sensors of the system don't simply return raw data but allow for the farmers to understand how their farms are interacting with the environment and how the key quality parameters are changing with time. One of the main issues that fish farm owners face is poor water quality of the farm. Although sensors exist to measure these changes, there is no good way to set up the control system for optimal water quality management.

6.2 Dissolved Gases and Their Effect on Water Quality

Some dissolved gases are essential to aquatic life, whereas some gases if found in higher quantities will be toxic to the fish. Dissolved gases such as oxygen, carbon dioxide and ammonia all constitute towards the stress levels of aquatic life. These gases are described in this section.

6.2.1 Oxygen

Oxygen is the vital driving force of all life on earth. Every living environment requires a steady oxygen supply to maintain life. Decreased oxygen concentrations along with increased carbon dioxide levels can cause suffocation [9]. DO (dissolved oxygen) levels vary according to the fish species and its weight. Some fish have additional systems allowing them to live in mildly hypoxic (oxygen deprived) conditions whereas for some others without such special organs or systems, a hypoxic environment spells imminent danger [7]. However, well-equipped a species may be, negative effects occurring due to hypoxia will start to occur if the oxygen tensions drop below the organism's biological demand. Depending on the species, dissolved oxygen should be higher than certain concentrations (usually 2–5 mg/L) to avoid oxygen starvation.

6.2.2 Carbon Dioxide

Increased carbon dioxide levels can cause suffocation and lower the pH of water which can eventually lead to acidic water, suffocation and eventual death. High carbon dioxide in water may lead to acidosis which happens when the exchange of carbon dioxide between the fish's blood and surroundings is hindered. To avoid this, fish have to regulate their blood bicarbonate levels. If the high carbon dioxide levels are accompanied by other factors such as low dissolved oxygen, it can lead to lower oxygen affinity and oxygen carrying capacity of the blood. Although the toxic carbon dioxide levels permissible vary depending on the fish, an amount of up to 30ppm or 30 mg/L is considered safe for most fish species [3].

6.2.3 Ammonia

Ammonia is mainly found in the water as a by-product of organic decomposition of dead matter and uneaten food. Nitrate compounds exist in water mainly in two forms: free ammonia (NH_3) which is the toxic component and ammonium ($NH4^+$) [1]. TAN (total ammonia nitrogen) levels and the percentage concentrations of toxic free ammonia and ammonium depend on temperature [10] and pH [4]. Free ammonia build-up is one of the main concerns for a closed tank with aquatic life. High ammonia levels cause increase in ATP (Adenosine triphosphate) levels and may even cause tissue necrosis which increase energy requirement further. Constant high levels of ammonia can cause fish to be lethargic, lose appetite, become diseased and eventually die. Decomposition of organic matter (fish excrement, uneaten food caused mainly by overfeeding) as well as usage of chemically treated water can also cause excessive ammonia levels [8]. Ammonia poisoning can also be caused due to some bacterial colonies dying because of using chemicals or as an effect of not changing the water at regular intervals. Prolonged durations of high ammonia concentrations are harmful for the fish and if ammonia levels reach 1 ppm then the water must be changed immediately.

6.3 Effect of Water Quality Parameters on Aquatic Life

To properly understand how to implement a system capable of water quality assessment and control for a wide variety of parameters, it is essential to understand how these parameters affect the aquatic life and also how they interact with each other to facilitate the increase or decrease of other parameters.

6.3.1 Temperature

Extreme changes in temperature or rapid changes are more harmful for fish than constant exposure to high or low temperatures. Studies have shown that aquatic life shows best health when the temperatures are within optimal range of the species. The correct temperature range increases health and immune functions [3, 8, 10]. Optimal temperature ranges from 20 to 32°C for most species. Temperature also interacts with other factors.

6.3.2 pH

Dissolved carbon dioxide causes carbonic acid that acidifies the water, decreasing the overall pH [11]. Low pH can also indicate increased levels of hydrogen sulphide. It also ceases proton movement from the fish body. A higher pH coupled with temperature rise can accelerate formation of toxic free ammonia [5]. Sudden changes of pH can cause changes in blood pH, increased stress and ultimately death. The comfortable pH range is from 6.5 to 8.5.

6.3.3 TDS and EC

Electrical conductivity (EC) is related to total dissolved solids (TDS) and general water hardness [12]. An increased conductivity generally means that there is a higher level of dissolved particles in the water. This is a very important parameter to monitor. Comfortable values of EC range from 100 to 350 µS/cm for freshwater species (Labeo catla, tilapia) and go up to 800 µS/cm for marine species (chromide). TDS is affected by pollutants and microparticles. If the TDS is high, water needs to be replaced to reduce TDS and keep the fish healthy. If the TDS drops below the required levels, suitable chemicals or bicarbonates have to be added to increase the general hardness of the water.

6.3.4 Salinity

Salinity is an important aspect of fish farming, especially if the farm is situated near a coastal area. Fish have to balance out the osmotic potential between their blood and the water in order to regulate the ion exchange through their bodies. If the salinity goes above or below the required levels then this can conflict with their ion pathways and can cause stress and unwanted health hazards for the fish. Increased salinity levels along with higher temperature levels can reduce dissolved oxygen levels in the water [13]. Salinity concentration is generally measured in practical salinity units (PSU). Measuring salinity holds value especially in situations where fresh water fish are farmed near coastal areas.

6.4 System Control and Actuators

The proposed system measures the pond water parameters and alerts the farmer when a parameter exceeds a predefined threshold. This is also accompanied by suggested corrective action if needed. The system allows for manual control of the pond should the farmer wish to intervene in any situation. The current version of the system can control aeration, circulation and evaporation and water level. Out of these, water level is controlled automatically and the water lost by evaporation is replenished periodically according to pre-set conditions. Water should be changed periodically according to the species and stocking density of the pond.

6.4.1 Circulation and Evaporation

Increased water movement has many positive benefits on the fish. Although the swimming area remains the same, increased water movement brings the fish one step closer to the behaviour of its natural habitat. By swimming against or through moving water, fish get the required physical engagement that is essential for good growth and health. A stagnant water body will have areas of increased ammonia concentration. Water movement also helps remove stratification which is the separation of water into two immiscible layers in a standing water body based on temperature. Agitating the water is sufficient to release a considerable amount of the dissolved ammonia present in water as long as the pH is below 9. Carbon dioxide can also be released by agitating the surface of water. Installing motorized paddle sets to induce a rolling motion of water is also very useful in producing basic circulation as well as agitating the water, breaking the surface and promoting gas exchange between the water and the atmosphere.

6.4.2 Water Level

Water level helps reveal signs of excessive water loss through evaporation. The water level, though not as important as other parameters, helps us to assess the conditions of the pond based on the other parameters as concentrations of other parameters usually increases slightly as the water level decreases [1]. In the proposed system, the water level is controlled automatically and water is replaced manually. The system alerts the farmer if there is a sudden drop of water level but is automated and doesn't require intervention. This is especially useful in situations where fish are farmed in makeshift tanks made of less durable materials.

6.4.3 Aeration

Aeration is an important factor in fish farming. Natural water bodies have many different ways to replenish the dissolved oxygen levels in them. Artificial ponds however require periodic oxygenation as there is no method to replenish the dissolved oxygen. During daytime, phytoplankton and plants carry out photosynthesis and replenish the oxygen but at night the oxygen levels don't get replenished. Moreover, respiration and other biochemical activities can cause oxygen to drop [13]. Although some fish species can survive in hypoxic conditions, there are some species such as shrimp mostly farmed near coastal areas that require near perfect oxygen control to sustain life [14].

6.5 Creating the System

The proposed system is a microcontroller and IoT-based smart pisciculture monitoring and control system designed for reducing the workload on farmers by employing sensors, motors and an IoT framework to periodically measure water quality parameters and make available the data to the farmer in real time. The advantage of this system is that it allows the farmer to make informed decisions to control the water quality based on these values and control up to three motors, namely for aeration, circulation and water level control. A detailed description of the system design is discussed in the following sections.

6.5.1 Microcontroller Unit

The Arduino and ESP (esp8266) modules are connected via serial communication to control the whole process. This is established via the SoftwareSerial library. The Arduino consists of multiple digital and analogue pins operating at 5V. The ESP has a single analogue pin and multiple digital pins that work in the 3.3V range. The Arduino handles all the outputs of the sensors for the system and computes the values and sends them to the ESP. The ESP relays this information to the ThingSpeak server where these values are stored using the ThingSpeak API (application programming interface) and channel write keys.

6.5.2 IoT System

The Wi-Fi-based ESP acts as the controlling unit for IoT operations for the system [11]. It acts as the bridge between the relay module controlling the motors and the android application used to control the motors in real time. The system transmits data to the ThingSpeak server channel dedicated to receiving the data sent by the ESP and relays that data to the app. This is done with the help of API keys. The app is updated with data periodically while the controlling feature is always in operational mode.

6.5.3 Sensors and Value Computation

There are four sensors to provide values of temperature, TDS, EC, salinity and pH and carefully devised mathematical equations to provide an approximate and fairly accurate readings for DO and ammonia.

6.5.3.1 Temperature

The temperature sensor used is the DS18B20 waterproof sensor shown in Figure 6.1. It is the modified version of the DS18B20 ambient temperature sensor. It is a digital sensor with an operating range of 3.3–5V and runs in parasitic mode due to an open drain port or open collector configuration. Hence to obtain the value for the inbuilt register, we need to give an active high signal to the output pin of the sensor. The sensor consists of a low temperature coefficient oscillator and a high temperature coefficient oscillator both connect to separate counters. These oscillators produce pulses according to their coefficient systems and the difference is used to compute the timing sequence and step count used to compute the temperature value. The main advantage of the sensor is that it can carry out temperature readings in fewer than 750ms.

FIGURE 6.1
DS18B20 waterproof temperature sensor.

6.5.3.2 pH

pH sensing is done via a pH sensor which is an analogue sensor with 3.3–5V operating range. It has its own signal smoothing circuit and uses a Bayonet Neill–Concelman (BNC) connector to connect to a glass type electrode. The general working principle depends upon exchange of ions from sample solution to buffer solution inside the glass electrode through the glass membrane. An increase in acidity of the sample increases the voltage while a basic solution decreases the voltage. The pH sensor type referred in this work is shown in Figure 6.2.

6.5.3.3 TDS, EC and Salinity

The TDS sensor module is employed to carry out the duty of measuring the TDS, EC and salinity values of the water. Figure 6.3 shows the TDS sensor used in this work. It is an

FIGURE 6.2
pH sensor.

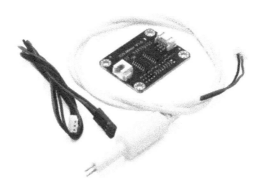

FIGURE 6.3
TDS sensor.

analogue sensor with an operating range of 3.3–5V and gives an output of around 0–2.3V. The sensor senses electrical conductivity of the water using the two electrodes and outputs that value with a standard temperature compensation which is unique to the sensor. EC is measured in micro-Siemens per centimetre or μS/cm.

TDS is computed based on a simple assumption that the relationship between dissolved solid concentrations and conductivity of the water is linear enough to extrapolate the relation throughout the whole operating range of the sensor which is close to 1000 ppm. Pure water shows conductivity as 0μS/cm and a water sample with higher TDS shows higher conductivity. Salinity is computed based on the fact that the major contributor of conductivity in any given liquid sample is salt or similar ions. Equations 6.1 and 6.2 describe the relationship between TDS and EC and relation between EC and salinity, respectively.

$$\text{Total Dissolved Solids (ppm)} = EC(\mu S/cm)/2 \tag{6.1}$$

$$\text{Salinity (ppm)} = EC(\mu S/cm) \times 0.55 \tag{6.2}$$

6.5.3.4 Water Level

Water level is measured using a float switch shown in Figure 6.4. A float switch is a mechanical switch that floats on top of a liquid surface. As the liquid level goes up or down, it moves vertically with the liquid level. Depending on the counterweight and preset 'trigger', the mechanical switch opens or closes allowing an electrical current through it to the connected device.

6.5.3.5 Ammonia

Aqueous ammonia concentration is calculated based on a formula developed by the United States Environmental Protection Agency (USEPA) in 2016 for freshwater ammonia analysis and the mole-fraction analysis of ammonia based on its pK_a value for a given

FIGURE 6.4
Float switch.

temperature and a given pH, both of which are obtained from temperature and pH sensors [15]. Calculation of TAN values is carried out using an empirical approach instead of using a sensor for mainly two reasons. The former being that many of the presently available sensors create the need for a much bigger housing for the final product and also the cost of the product as some use costly selective membranes or special substances and the latter being that the inclusion of colorimetric sensors or sensing methods which included usage of reagents or any other foreign substances would, at least in principle, defeat the whole point of a smart automated system as the efficiency of the sensor would depend upon the farmer refilling the reagent regularly. The TAN values are calculated using the Equation 6.3 and the toxic ammonia concentration is obtained after substituting the value obtained for f in Equation 6.5 in Equation 6.4.

$$TAN = 0.8876 \times \left(\frac{0.0278}{\left(1+10^{7.688-pH}\right)} + \frac{1.1994}{\left(1+10^{pH-7.688}\right)} \right) \times \left(2.1 \times 10^{0.028 \times (20-Max(T,7))}\right) \qquad (6.3)$$

$$\text{Ammonia} = f \times (\text{TAN} \times 2.5) \qquad (6.4)$$

$$\text{Where mole fraction, } f = \frac{1}{1+10^{pKa-pH}} \qquad (6.5)$$

$$\text{And } pK_a = 0.09018 + \frac{2729.92}{T} \qquad (6.6)$$

6.5.3.6 Dissolved Oxygen

DO is measured with an empirical approach using the formula discussed in Equations 6.7 and 6.8 which takes values of both temperature and salinity as inputs [16]. This method is used as the inclusion of a costly DO sensor would violate our aim of cost effectiveness. Equation 6.7 gives the log value for DO concentration after adjusting for temperature and salinity compensation.

Equation 6.8 gives the value of DO concentration after correcting for O_2 saturation percentage for the DO concentration being calculated. Since our test setup is close to sea level, corrections related to atmospheric pressure are not needed [13, 17].

$$\ln O_2 = l + m \times \frac{100}{K} + n.ln\frac{K}{100} + p.\frac{K}{100} + S\left\{ a + b.\frac{K}{100} + c.\frac{K}{100}^2 \right\} \qquad (6.7)$$

Where, $l = -142.4292$ $m = 249.6339$ $n = 143.3482$ $p = -21.8942$
$a = -0.033096$ $b = 0.014529$ $c = -21.8942$ & S = Salinity

$$\text{DO (ppm)} = 0.91 \times 1.429 \times e^{\ln O_2} \qquad (6.8)$$

6.5.4 Android Application and UI

Owing to recent developments in microelectronics, microcontrollers, telecommunications and information technology, mobile applications have become integral in the control and supervision of modern IoT-driven smart control systems [18]. The android app is a simple lightweight app designed with backwards compatibility for older devices using the appropriate libraries. The application UI is divided into three main parts:

1. Sensor status
2. Controls
3. Information

Sensor status retrieves all data from the cloud server and displays the data in real time. Values exceeding the threshold are highlighted in red and normal values are shown in green. The control section allows the user to give inputs to control the motors. It is also labelled and colour coded and works interactively. The info section shows all the alerts, last update information (date and time) and also the suggested actions when the values exceed threshold.

6.6 Architecture of the System

Figure 6.5 shows the initial prototype for the system which is based on IoT. It consists of a sensing part, a control part, a human interface part which is the mobile application and a server that handles all the incoming and outgoing data. In an IoT system, devices may

FIGURE 6.5
Prototype.

be connected using one of several connection protocols such as NB-IoT, LoRa, Sigfox, Wi-Fi, or even Ethernet [4, 6, 7, 19]. Our system uses Wi-Fi for operation. The system is split between two main control boards, one dedicated for sensing the parameters and the second one which serves as the bridge between the human input and the actuators. The second board is Wi-Fi enabled so that it maintains constant connection with the server. The motors to be controlled are connected to this board so that control action may be carried out quickly in real time. The android app allows the farmer to view parameters such as the temperature, pH, TDS, ammonia, salinity, electrical conductivity, DO and water level in real time as well as the current operational status of the connected motors. The parameters that are out of range will be highlighted and a suggested control action is also displayed so that the inexperienced farmers can also benefit from the system. The app also updates information regarding loss of power supply during set specific time intervals. The app also displays information such as the last update interval so that any issues such as damage or network loss can be easily identified and sorted. The system can be powered by an external source as well as the on-board battery. The on-board battery system is a lithium-polymer battery that allows for autonomous operation. The system is geared for use in outdoor conditions, mainly in commercial sized ponds with multiple motors but can also be downsized to be used for indoor tanks as well as big aquariums.

6.7 Working Principle and Flow of Control

Table 6.1 shows the parameters, their optimal ranges and the corresponding actions that will be taken by the system when a change comes into effect. The sensors are connected to a common power rail controlled by the Arduino through a relay of the 4 channel relay module. This is done to reduce power wastage by the sensors. The pH sensor is operated separately with all remaining sensors in OFF condition so as to avoid errors that may occur in pH measurement due to close proximity of an active conductivity probe. Once the sensing is complete the data is processed by the Arduino and then sent to the ESP using

TABLE 6.1

Parameters, Optimal Ranges and Associated System Actions

Parameter	Optimal Range	Action
Temperature	20–32°C	Alert given
pH	6.5–8.5	Alert given
Ammonia	<0.5 ppm	Alert given, circulation motor will be turned ON to reduce ammonia through surface exchange
Salinity	<350 ppm	Alert given and subsequent advice to change water if salinity increases over 400ppm
TDS	<400 ppm	Alert given
EC	625 μs/cm	Alert given
DO	>5 ppm	Alert given, Aerator will be turned ON
Water Level	As per pond specifications	Alert given, Water pump will turn ON to maintain water level

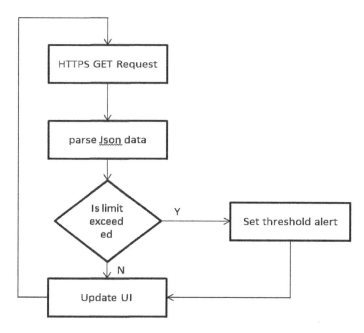

FIGURE 6.6
Application UI update flowchart.

the UART (Universal Asynchronous Receiver Transmitter) communication protocol via SoftwareSerial library. Once the values are parsed into the respective original parameter values, the ESP uploads the parsed data into the cloud server via a secure channel for data integrity. This process is initiated only if the ESP receives any data in the predefined model.

The ESP checks the operational logic of all the connected motors in the cloud server and this operation is carried out at the start of each null return loop. The cloud receives this data and stores these in the designated data fields. From Figure 6.6, we can see how the UI updates itself over the course of a single execution cycle of the full operation cycle. The android app regularly calls for updates for data by performing a simple HTTPS (Hypertext Transfer Protocol Secure) GET method and the response to the request is then parsed. The last update timeline is also extracted from the response. The app has two event listener functions that monitor the quality parameters and inputs for the motors by the farmer. Whenever a parameter exceeds the safe limit, the text becomes a red colour indicating threshold exceeded to the famer. The error message of 'parameter critical' is also displayed in the info section highlighted in red. The ESP checks the operational logic of all the connected motors in the cloud server and this operation is carried out at the start of each null return loop as discussed in Figure 6.7.

Figure 6.8 discusses the operation sequence of the UI. When a motor is turned 'ON', the UI makes the necessary changes to change the colour of the button text to green signalling the farmer that the motor is now ON.

When the motor is OFF, the OFF button text becomes red in colour. A delay of 15 seconds is given to the server app communication channel so as to protect the mechanical relays operating the motors from damage due to repeated high speed ON/OFF.

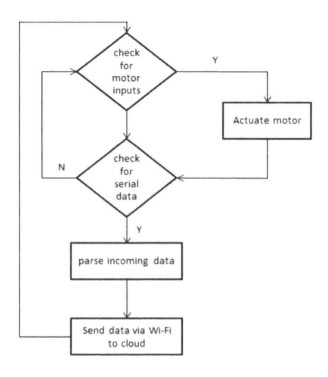

FIGURE 6.7
ESP data flowchart.

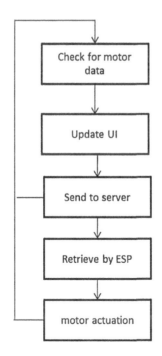

FIGURE 6.8
Actuator data control flowchart.

6.8. Results and Discussions

6.8.1 Testing of Sensors and Arduino ESP UART

All output values of the sensors are connected to the Arduino and sent to the cloud via the ESP. This forms the ex-situ heart and soul of the system. Figure 6.9 shows the serial data obtained in the serial port in ESP via UART. The values are transferred from the Arduino to the ESP using the UART connection between the two boards. Table 6.2 shows the values of a sample set obtained during testing of the system in two live ponds which were stocked with pearl spot which was being farmed using the high density aquaculture method.

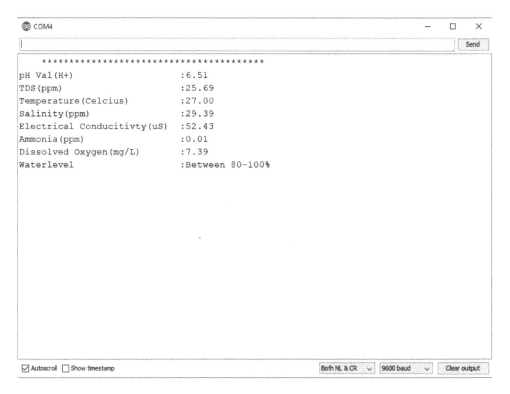

FIGURE 6.9
Sensor outputs on Arduino serial COM port.

TABLE 6.2

Sample Set of Data Received from the System for Two Ponds

	Temp	pH	NH3+	DO	TDS	Salinity	EC	W. level
Pond 1	27.87	6.91	0.02	5.47	220.27	242.3	440.54	100
Pond 2	27.64	6.86	0.02	5.7	260.4	286.44	520.8	100

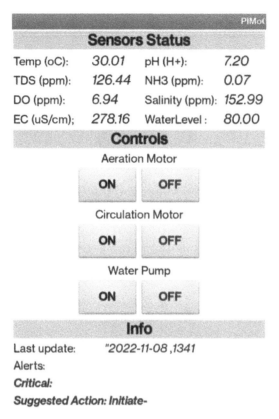

FIGURE 6.10
Application UI after receiving data.

6.8.2 Testing the Application

The app performs as expected without any visual or discernable lag or noticeable glitches. There is no visible performance difference for the app while being tested across multiple versions of android for various devices. The colour coding of both the parameter window and the control window were tested and the motors were also operated in multiple sequences and no lag was observed both in data transmission and in UI update. Figure 6.10 shows how the application looks after the data is received and updated.

6.8.3 Testing of IoT Framework

The IoT framework is designed to operate on Wi-Fi networks and has relative ease with connecting to Wi-Fi networks. The overall performance was satisfactory with no loss of functionality or speed after continuous use under various operating conditions. Figure 6.11 shows the GUI (Graphical User Interface) of the ThingSpeak server displaying the sensor data received from the ESP. There are eight individual widgets for displaying the data received. Each widget displays the readings of all the different parameters are shown in the graphs and abnormal values may indicate a sensor being faulty or disconnected from the device possibly during shifting to other ponds.

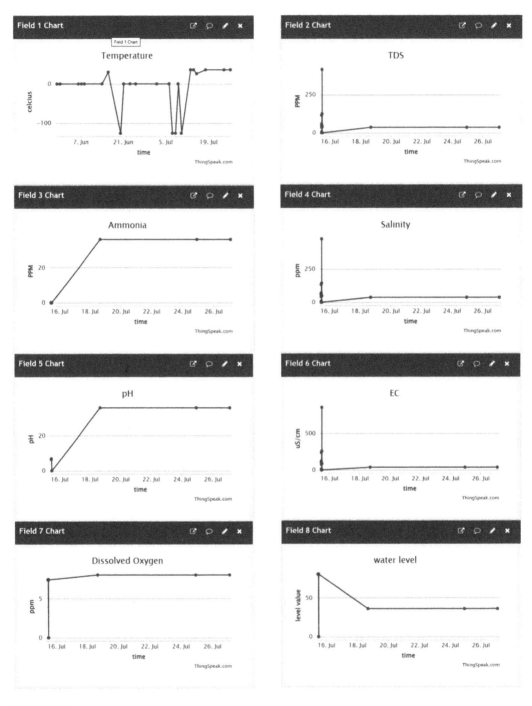

FIGURE 6.11
ThingSpeak server interface.

6.9 Conclusion

All the prior enumerated functionalities of the app are tested. Relay switching is observed for pH sensor and TDS sensor to allow for control over cross-talk between sensors. All the eight parameters are readily read by Arduino, transferred serially bit by bit to the Arduino to the ESP and parsed back to required data format by ESP. No observable lag was found during the data transmission and data integrity was maintained throughout the transmission. The ESP displays the data via SM (serial monitor) of the Arduino and also sends the data to the cloud sensor within an acceptable window. A small but detectable lag was observed while the server updated the value into the user interface but this lag did not seem to affect either the transmission of data to the app or processing of GET requests from the application. The application is tested in all the features and performs well. Colour coding and all other interactive UI components perform with ease, precision and speed. The motor control operation performs with a good accuracy and performs accordingly to each button click which has been tested in various sequences. The experimental results provide concurrent proof that our proposed system achieves all our stipulated primary and secondary objectives and helps farmers to navigate through the process of aquaculture water quality control and controlling of associated essential equipment such as motors, pumps and aerators with precision and reliability along with providing remote access feature for all the mentioned objectives.

References

[1] Dolan, 2015, *"The effects of aquarium size and temperature on colour vibrancy size and physical activity in bettasplendens"*.

[2] T. Masaharu, et al., 2014, *"Effect of temperature on survival, growth and malformation of cultured larvae and juveniles of the seven-band grouper epinephelus septemfasciatus"*, Fisheries Sci., vol. 80, no. 1, pp. 69–81.

[3] C. Dupont, P. Cousin and S. Dupont, 2018, *"IoT for aquaculture 4.0 smart and easy-to-deploy real-time water monitoring with IoT"*, in Proc. Global Internet Things Summit (GIoTS), pp. 180–184.

[4] T. I. Salim, T. Haiyunnisa, and H. S. Alam, 2016, *"Design and implementation of water quality monitoring for eel fish aquaculture an examination of microbubble aeration"*, in Proc. Int. Symp. Electron. Smart Devices (ISESD), pp. 208–213.

[5] J.-H. Chen, W.-T. Sung and G.-Y. Lin, 2015, *"Automated monitoring system for the fish farm aquaculture environment"*, in Proc. IEEE Int. Conf. Syst., Man, Cybern., pp. 1161–1166.

[6] Y. Lin and H. Tseng, 2019, *FishTalk: An IoT-Based Mini Aquarium System*. IEEE Access, 7, 35457–35469.

[7] K. R. S. R. Raju and G. H. K. Varma, 2017, *"Knowledge based real time monitoring system for aquaculture using IoT,"* in Proc. IEEE 7th Int. Adv. Comput. Conf., Jan. 2017, pp. 318–321.

[8] S.-P. Tseng, Y.-R. Li and M.-C. Wang, 2016, *"An application of Internet of Things on sustainable aquaculture system"*, in Proc. Int. Conf. Orange Technol., pp. 17–19.

[9] S. Sharpe, 2018, Aquarium Nitrogen Cycle: How an Aquarium Cycles [online] Available: https://www.thesprucepets.com/aquarium-nitrogen-cycle-1378370.

[10] J. E. Bly and W. L. Clem, 1992, *"Temperature and teleost immune functions"*, Fish Shellfish Immunol., vol. 2, no. 3, pp. 159–171.

[11] G. Farmer, 2016, *CO2: Striking the Balance* [online] Available: https://www.practicalfishkeeping.co.uk/features/articles/co2-striking-the-balance.

[12] B. Akhmetov and M. Aitimov, 2015, *"Data collection and analysis using the mobile application for environmental monitoring"*, Procedia Comput. Sci., vol. 56, pp. 532–537.

[13] Algone, 2018, The Importance of Oxygen in the Aquarium. General Aquarium & Fish Information. [Online]. Available: https://www.algone.com/oxygen-in-the-aquarium.

[14] F.-F. Ruth, 2013, *Dissolved Oxygen for Fish Production. Texas A&M AgriLife* [Online]. Available:https://agrilifecdn.tamu.edu/fisheries/files/2013/09/DissolvedOxygen-for-Fish-Production1.pdf.

[15] K. Emerson,, R. C. Russo, R. E. Lund and R. V. Thurston,, 1975, *Aqueous ammonia equilibrium calculations: effect of pH and temperature*, J. Fish. Res. Board Can., vol. 32, pp. 2379–2383.

[16] Jetajockey, 2011, Your Guide to Ammonia Toxicity. Aquarium Advice [Online]. Available: http://www.aquariumadvice.com/forums/f12/yourguide-to-ammoniatoxicity-159994.html.

[17] R. F. Weiss, 1970, *"The solubility of nitrogen, oxygen and argon in water and seawater"*, Deep-Sea Res., vol. 17, pp. 721–735.

[18] T. Sarac, 2018, Electrical Conductivity in Freshwater Aquariums, [online] Available: http://fluvalaquatics.com/ca/explore/did-you-know/equipment/155-electrical-conductivity-monitoring-system-part-two/#.XAL_hzgzZ0x.

[19] Y.-W. Lin, Y.-B. Lin, M.-T. Yang and J.-H. Lin, 2019, *"ArduTalk: An Arduino network application development platform based on IoTtalk"*, IEEE Syst. J., vol. 13, no. 1, pp. 468–476.

7

Managing Huge IoT Workloads Using Oracle Database 19c

CVSR Syavasya and Akkalakshmi Muddana

CONTENTS

DOI: 10.1201/9781003226888-7

7.1 Introduction

Over the past decade, a drastic increase has been observed in smart device implementation. The internet becomes a hub for connecting dual devices and smart meters that is connected to every phone and tablet and shares data that allows remote access, automatic software updates, error reporting and sensor transmission. Gartner estimates that, by the end of 2021, there will be more than 26 billion connected devices.

7.1.1 Internet of Things in Database Perspective

With the intervention of smart devices, it became a drastic enhancement in volume and frequency of data being written and parsed in detail. This condition is often referred to as the Internet of Things or IoT. Being able to enter and analyze data rates that are growing rapidly in an efficient and timely manner is important for businesses to maintain their competitive advantage. Determining the best data management platform is a common problem faced by many organizations in various industries. Some people think that the NoSQL database is necessary for the IoT task load because the required import rate exceeds the traditional power of relationship data. This is simply not true. The relationship database can easily surpass the performance of the NoSQL database when properly integrated (W. Ali et al., 2019).

Oracle Database is more than capable of inserting hundreds of millions of lines per second. It is the industry's leading database in terms of analytics, high availability, security and scalability, making it an excellent choice for the most important IoT performance loads. Data import performance is affected by many variables, including the method used to enter data, the schema, uniformity and the level of commitment. The same is true for analytical questions. This chapter describes the best ways to ensure efficiency in installing and analyzing large amounts of real-time data with Oracle Databases (H. Albreiki et al., 2019).

7.1.2 Scalability

Scalable feature is a capable option in a system to provide throughput equally and is restricted only by the available hardware resources. Oracle Database provides the ability to measure (increase hardware capacity within a single server) or scale (increase the number of servers in a collection). The consensus is that the measurement solution is preferred for IoT projects as it allows for a lower cost. Oracle Database offers two options for building limited architectures: Real Application Cluster (RAC) and Oracle Sharding (C. Asiminidis et al., 2018).

7.1.3 Flexibility

IoT is currently on inception that utilizes the latest features that come on each latest tool. Being able to quickly become accustomed to modifications in formats of data and efficiently analyze and manage large volumes of data is critical. We will showcase the different aspects of Oracle Database that make it possible to handle large volumes of data while still providing a very flexible schema.

7.1.4 Real-Time Analysis

The time analysis of the data captured in an IoT scenario can seriously affect actual business outcomes. It has the potential to

- optimize the business handling and minimize functioning costs;
- forecast equipment failure;
- establish new product contributions or services;
- recommend differentiated client experience.

7.2 Scalability and Flexibility Techniques

7.2.1 Scalability Techniques

7.2.1.1 Real Application Clusters

RAC is a customized and integrated application that works without glitches with a group of interconnected nodes to the shared storage. If the cluster server fails, the database continues to run on the remaining nodes, and in case we require the additional capacity of processing, then we add another node to the cluster without any impact by downtime.

7.2.1.2 Oracle Sharding

Oracle Sharding is another custom-integrated application that enables the distribution and duplication of data in an Oracle data pool that does not have sharable software and hardware. The group of instances or databases is deployed in the application as a single logical database. Sharding divides the database into an independent database of data, thus avoiding failure or retrieval of cases at the edge of a single database. Data is still distributed across all shards using horizontal partitions. Space management is managed at the object level with the help of Oracle Database and taken from the table area at which the object sits. As per the recommendation from Oracle, the usage of bigfile table locations minimizes the number of data files that needs to be manageable in nature. The bigfile tablespaces are localized table spaces that use segment space management with the AUTO option. While creating a bigfile tablespace, the original data file is formatted. Each time the datacenter is expanded, the extended component must also be formatted. Extending and formatting data files is a costly task that has to be minimized (wait event: Data Init write). In addition, formatting is done sequentially (S. Alapati et al., 2009).

For good performing capability, Oracle recommends reducing space allocation tasks during loads by defining the size of the automatic extension in a large table area. The AUTOEXTEND parameter controls how much extra space can be added to the bigfile table area when it runs out of space.

7.2.1.3 Data Loading Mechanisms

So far, we have focused on building a data database. Now let's change our focus on data import. With Oracle Database, data can be grouped or categorized in two ways: standard input or direct input. You can think of data entry as putting things in your cart and paying for them at the store. You can never pick one item at a time and pay for it before choosing the next item on your list (inserting one line followed by a commitment). You can go to the store, collect all the items on your list and go check once (many lists followed by commitment). It is the same when you want to insert data properly into a database (J. Dizdarević et al., 2019).

7.2.1.4 Conventional Inserts

Conventional installation uses the SQL INSERT statement to add new lines to a table or partition. Oracle Database automatically keeps the track of all issues that reflect integrity and other indicators in the table. The logical storage space within the data blocks that already form the table. All aspects of the standard INSTALL statement are recorded in the refresh logs in the event of a failure. Normally, an INSERT command adds one line at a time and is followed by a COMMIT, although it is possible to add multiple lines with an INSERT command using INSERT ALL.

7.2.1.5 Locking during Load

At the time of direct path load operation or at the parallel data manipulation language (DML), Oracle internally locks the whole target table exclusively. This kind of locking prevents the other DML or data definition language (DDL) execution from happening against the table or its partitions, but the table's data is totally accessible for queries from other sessions. We may avoid acquiring a table-level lock by using the partition extended syntax, which locks only the specified partition.

```
INSERT /*+ APPEND */ INTO emp_table PARTITION FOR (to_date('15-JAN-2012',
'DD-MON-YY')) SELECT * FROM exp_tab_ht_dec_25;
```

7.2.1.6 Memoptimized Rowstore for Loading Streaming Data

With multiple IoT operating loads, data is continuously transferred to a database directly from a device or smart device. Oracle Database 19c provides an effective way to enter streaming data through the Intelligent Line Store. With Memoptimized Rowstore – Fast Ingest, Oracle's standard trading methods are over, and data is loaded into a temporary chunk in a large pool. Since the app does not need to hold waiting to get the data to be written to disk, the installation statement returns very quickly. Note, we cannot ask for data until it writes to disk, and we may lose data if the database goes down before the inserted data is moved to disk. This behavior differs from how the transaction is traditionally performed on the Oracle Database, where the data is entered and not lost once it is written/dedicated to the database. However, many IoT applications can easily tolerate lost data as they are only interested in the difference between prices over time (B. Diene et al., 2020; D. J. Hand, 2018).

7.2.1.6.1 Database

Figure 7.1 depicts the mechanism of memory-optimized flow of inserting data into a database. Here, the rows are cached in memory and asynchronously drained in to disk. An API allows developers to check on the durability of their insert operations.

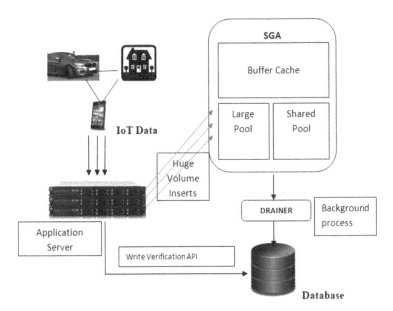

FIGURE 7.1
Diagrammatic representation of Memoptimized Rowstore: Fast Ingest.

7.2.2 Flexibility

The IoT is currently at its beginning stage with additional utilization added up with each new tool or device. It has a capability to adapt to changes quickly in the formats of data and to properly analyze as managing large amounts of data is essential.

7.3 Real-Time Analysis

7.3.1 Parallel Execution

Analytics in the IoT workload typically require queries to be done on billions of data records in real time. The key to getting real-time statistics is to use all available hardware resources effectively. As mentioned earlier, the same implementation is the most widely used way to speed up performance within data. It enables to split tasks into multiple sub-tasks performed simultaneously. Oracle website supports the same performance out of the box. You can also use Automatic Degree of Parallelism (Auto DOP) to control how and when parallels are applied to each SQL statement. Similarity is an important factor in the widespread use of IoT and is always recommended.

7.3.2 Indexing

The most common method for improving the speed and performance of archives is done by creating references to the tables involved in the query, as it provides a faster way to access data. Oracle Database offers a variety of index types, including Reverse Key,

Linguistic, Function-based, and B-Tree. Separated tables may contain local or geographical indications. The location index 'inherits' the strategy of separating from the table. As a result, each spatial index is based on the corresponding subdivision of the sub-table. With IoT workloads of highly environment-friendly IoT functions, Oracle recommends making the best use of local indicators.

7.3.3 Time-Series Analysis

Often with IoT workload, the business benefit comes from seeing a pattern or unusual rather than a review of each entry. Oracle offers a rich set of analytics features designed for SQL to support real-time analysis (RTA) of IoT data. For example, windows' functions can be used to calculate moving and collecting types of SUM, AVERAGE, COUNT, MAX, MIN and many other functions. They offer access to more than one row of tables without the need for integration. This makes it easy to compare multiple values from the same device. In the example below, Oracle's built-in LAG function compares current and previous meter readings and calculates the difference (A. Celesti et al., 2018).

7.3.4 Oracle Database In-Memory

If more IoT data analysis is required, consider using Oracle Database In-Memory (Database In-Memory). With this method, IoT data can be embedded in the memory in a new columnar format designed for memory to enhance the performance of ad-hoc analytic queries. The database maintains complete transaction compatibility between the traditional line format and the new column format, just as it maintains similarity between tables and indices. Oracle Optimizer knows exactly what data is available in column format and automatically submits column format analysis questions and online transactional processing (OLTP) performance to line format, ensuring outstanding performance and complete data compatibility for all tasks without application modifications. There is only one copy of the data left in storage (in line format), so there are no additional storage costs or implications for uploading data, as no other transactions or reversals are performed (Z. Daher and H. Hajjdiab, 2018).

Unlike other In-Memory column solutions, not all data in a database needs to be stored in memory in column format. With In-Memory Database, only critical performance tables or partitions should be stored in memory. This allows businesses to send real-time analytics of interested data while keeping historical data well on disk, at a minimal cost. For queries accessing data in the queue and in column format, the database will use its extensive functionality for all memory, flash and disk access and data integration, above the Keeping IM Column Store Compatible Store.

7.4 Comparative Study of the Techniques

7.4.1 Limitations of Managing Data in Previous Oracle Database Versions

Following are the limitations of the existing mechanisms for managing the data in previous database versions and how Oracle 19c overcomes it.

7.4.1.1 Limitation 1: Parallel DML

Parallel Inserts – Resource contention – Data loading Mechanism-High Resource consumption in previous versions, with the presence of huge IoT workload, whenever multiple users tried to execute the same query at the same time, there was resource level contention that led to high CPU utilizations and high I/O wait time. This has degraded the database and server performance. To overcome this problem, in Oracle 19c, a new feature was introduced to manage the resources whenever a huge IoT workload query got executed at the same time from multiple users' sessions. If the redundant query takes the same CPU time and the same elapsed time, then the redundant query is blacklisted/prevented from execution. This concept is known as SQL Quarantine. Whenever a particular SQL statement exceeds the specified resource limit, then the execution of that query will be halted by Resource Manager and it 'quarantines' that query plan. The explained plan is then placed on a 'blacklist' of plans that the database will not execute. This SQL Quarantine feature in turn helps the performance as it prevents the future execution of a costly SQL statement which has now been quarantined.

7.4.1.1.1 Demonstration of Limitation

In this scenario, User-1 and User-2 tried to load huge amounts of data simultaneously. Figure 7.2 shows User-1 connected to the database, and Figure 7.3 shows database connected to User-1, and Figures 7.4 and 7.5 show the database connected to User-2 and show the top process IDs with their CPU utilizations before parallel inserts.

CPU Usage: Initially CPU Usage is 2.6%.

While parallel inserts operations are in progress, CPU usage is drastically increased from 36% up to 50%.

With this limitation of previous versions, Oracle Database 19 cloud version mitigates the difficulty of bulk server resources at the requests from query.

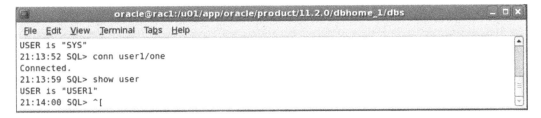

FIGURE 7.2
Database connection to user1.

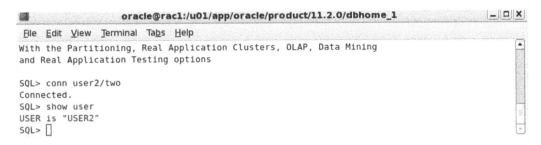

FIGURE 7.3
Database connection by user2.

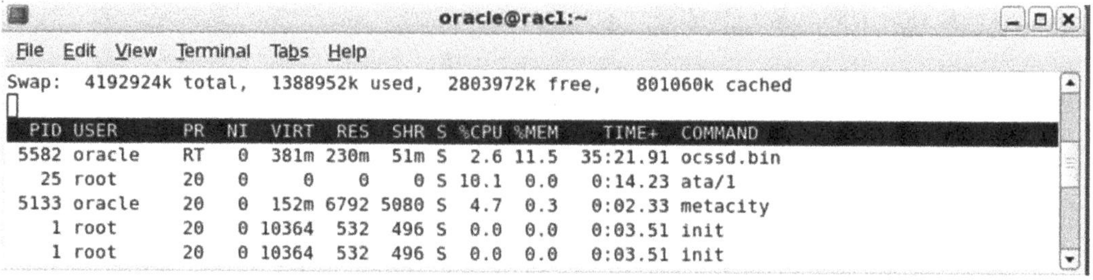

FIGURE 7.4
This shows the top process IDs with their CPU utilizations before parallel inserts.

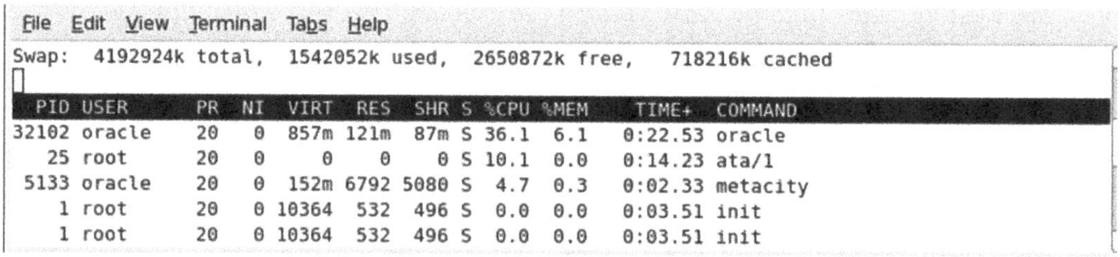

FIGURE 7.5
This shows the top process IDs with CPU usage while parallel inserts.

DEMONSTRATION OF SQL QUARANTINE FEATURE:

```
SQL> create table problem_table (id number, code number, name
varchar2(42));
Table created.
SQL> insert into problem_table select rownum,  mod(rownum,100)+1,
'CVSR Syavasya' from dual connect by level <=20000;
20000 rows created.
SQL> commit;
Commit complete.
SQL> exec dbms_stats.gather_table_stats (ownname =>null, tabname
=>'PROBLEM_TABLE');SQL>
PL/SQL procedure successfully completed.
SQL> select a.* from problem_table a, problem_table b; -- This take
long elapsed time
        283    84 CVSR Syavasya
        283    84 CVSR Syavasya
        283    84 CVSR Syavasya
1000000 rows selected.
Total execution time: 26.54 seconds
SQL> begin
dbms_resource_manager.create_pending_area;
dbms_resource_manager.create_consumer_group(CONSUMER_GROUP=>
'TABLE_LIMIT_TIME');
```

```
dbms_resource_manager.set_consumer_group_mapping(attribute =>
'ORACLE_USER', value => 'TABLE', consumer_group =>'TABLE_
LIMIT_TIME');
dbms_resource_manager.create_plan(PLAN=> 'LIMIT_TIME');
dbms_resource_manager.create_plan_directive(PLAN=>'LIMIT_TIME',
GROUP_OR_SUBPLAN=>'TABLE_LIMIT_TIME', SWITCH_GROUP=>'CANCEL_SQL',
SWITCH_TIME=>30);
dbms_resource_manager.create_plan_directive(PLAN=>'LIMIT_TIME',GROUP_
OR_SUBPLAN=>'OTHER_GROUPS', CPU_P1=>100);
dbms_resource_manager.validate_pending_area;
dbms_resource_manager.submit_pending_area;
end;
/  2    3    4    5    6    7    8    9    10   11
PL/SQL procedure successfully completed.
SQL> select a.* from problem_table a, problem_table b;
select a.* from problem_table a, problem_table b
                 *
ERROR at line 1:
ORA-56955: quarantined plan used
Elapsed: 00:00:00.00
SQL> select sql_id,  sql_quarantine,  avoided_executions from v$sql
where sql_id ='awg3wwn44jf3f';
SQL_ID          SQL_QUARANTINE                    AVOIDED_EXECUTIONS
----------------------------------------------------------------------
awg3wwn44jf3f SQL_QUARANTINE_1tcgjr28h8qd1483de993      2
```

7.4.1.2 Limitation 2: JSON Sustainability

Previous versions do not have its support on Node.js with SODA APIs, C, Java and Python. But coming to Oracle Database 19c version, it has easier syntax for the functionality of JSON that allows users to perform partial updates of JSON. Many new SQL features in version 19c are related to JSON. The first type of these JSON extensions is related to standard SQL functions that were already based on previous releases.

7.4.1.3 Limitation 3: Automatic Indexing

In previous database versions, whenever we create the indices, a DBA needs to manually test the benefit and make use of indexing using hints or other related methods to make the performance improve. To overcome this issue, automatic indexing functionality works as a DBA that exists like a built-in asset in the structure of database by cross-checking the requirement for new indices and the necessity for current indices. It creates new ones when required and drops them when they do not have the potential impact of improving the performance. Oracle Database 19c provides a machine learning feature of the algorithm having the functionality to provide regular index correction. The machine learning algorithm leads to improved servers by boosting the performance in addition to cost savings.

7.4.2 Building Oracle Database from Scratch by Reproducing Huge IoT Workloads

In this section, Oracle Enterprise Linux 8.2 version is installed, which built Oracle Database 19c Enterprise Edition software binaries and created Oracle Database 19c:

```
select banner  from v$version;
BANNER
-----------------------------------------------------------
Oracle Database 19c Enterprise Edition Release 19.0.0.0.0
- Production
SQL> select name,open_mode,status from v$database,v$instance;
NAME    OPEN_MODE          STATUS
--------- -------------------- ------------
ORCL    READ WRITE         OPEN
SQL>!date
Sun Aug  1 13:17:54 EDT 2021
SQL>!hostname
ol8-19.localdomain
```

To hold the huge IoT workload, bigfile tablespace is created with name iot_data with a size 5 GB. In addition to this, sga_target (database memory) is increased from 600 MB to 1200 MB (here server RAM size is 3 GB) so as to withstand the IoT workload.

```
SQL> CREATE BIGFILE TABLESPACE iot_data
DATAFILE '/u01/ts_data_bigfile.dbf' SIZE 5G AUTOEXTEND ON
;
Tablespace created.
```

User is created with name 'iot' and granted unlimited quota on tablespace 'iot_data'.

```
SQL> create user iot identified by iot default tablespace iot_data;
User created.
SQL> alter user iot quota unlimited on iot_data;
User altered.
```

With the help of the *direct path read insert* method, 7 million records are loaded onto the table with name: 'emp'. To achieve this insert operation, a procedure is created to enable direct path insert of time-series records.

```
SQL> show user
USER is "IOT"
SQL>  create table emp (empid number,emono number,salary
number,rollid number);
SQL> set timing on;
SQL> declare
 TYPE emp_array is TABLE OF emp%ROWTYPE;
 l_emp_array emp_array:=epm_array ();
 start_time number;
 elapsed number;
 begin
 for time in 1. . 100
```

```
loop
for indid in 1. . 7
loop
for insid in 1. . 1000
end loop;
start_time:=DBMS_UTILITY.GET_TIME ;
forall p in l_emp_array.first. . l_emp_array.last
insert /*+ APPEND_VALUES */ into emp
values l_emp_array(p);
elapsed := DBMS_UTILITY.GET_TIME - start_time;
dbms_output.put_line('elapsed time (seconds)=' || elapsed/100 );end;
/
PL/SQL procedure successfully completed.
Elapsed: 00:00:33.14


7 Lakh records have been inserted in 33 seconds of duration using
direct path insert method.

SQL> select count(*) from emp;
   COUNT(*)
----------
    700000
```

This recent Oracle version of the 19c has been introduced in January 2019. It has been known as the long-term release of the 12.2-oriented product family information databases. This particular version will be supported until 2023, with extended support available until 2026.

7.4.3 Data Handling Mechanism Using Real-Time Analysis, Storage and Performance Enhancement Mechanism Using Memoptimized Rowstore

Memoptimized Rowstore (MR) accelerates the performance of data query based on the frequent usage of tables of the query based on primary key variables. To use Memoptimized Rowstore – Fast Ingest, we must first enable one or more tables for fast ingest by adding the clause MEMOPTIMIZE FOR WRITE to ALTER TABLE or CREATE TABLE statement. Then the MEMOPTIMIZE_WRITE hint is used in all subsequent insert statements.

The example below explains how to utilize this Memoptimized ingest feature and is compared with the performance of normal insert with the Memoptimized ingest in terms of elapsed time:

Case-1 – Memoptimized Insert

```
SQL> create table fast_ingest (
   emp_id number primary key,
   emp_name varchar2(10))
```

```
    segment creation immediate
    memoptimize for write;
SQL> declare
    a number(10,0);
    begin
    for a in 1..10000
    loop
      insert /*+ MEMOPTIMIZE_WRITE */ into fast_ingest values
(a, 'test');
      commit;
    end loop;
    end;
   /  2    3    4    5    6    7    8    9    10
PL/SQL procedure successfully completed.

  Elapsed: 00:00:04.73
```

Case-2 – Conventional/Regular Insert

```
SQL> create table normal_ingest (
  2   emp_id number primary key,
  3   emp_name varchar2(15));
Table created.
SQL>
SQL> declare
    a number(9,0);
    begin
    for a in 1..100000
    loop
      insert /*+ normal_write */ into normal_ingest values (a, 'test');
      commit;
    end loop;
   end;
   /
PL/SQL procedure successfully completed.
  Elapsed: 00:00:32.99
```

7.4.4 Comparison of Results

By the above comparison, it is evident that the performance is faster in the case of Memoptimized ingest than the normal insert. The comparative results using our approach are shown in Table 7.1.

TABLE 7.1

Comparison of Elapsed Time between Conventional
Insert and Memoptimized Row Ingest

SL. No.	Method Name	Elapsed Time
1.	Conventional Insert	32.99 seconds
2.	Memoptimized Row ingest	4.73 seconds

Note: This functionality is applicable only in Oracle Exadata
or Oracle Cloud environments.

7.5 Open Research Problems

This section will include case studies related to Oracle Database IoT data loading mechanisms, performance optimization and future research opportunities in various domains.

Case Study 7.1: Automatic Indexing

Automatic Indexing acts as a DBA within data that assesses the necessity to create new indices and the requirement to hold the existing indices. The new indices are created based on the criticality of its requirement for any performance improvement factor and discard the indices whenever they create any signal for any performance hindrance.

```
-------------------------------------------------------------------------
| Id  | Operation   | Name | Rows  | Bytes | Cost (%CPU)| Time |
-------------------------------------------------------------------------
|   0 | SELECT STATEMENT | |    1 |    20 |    3   (0)| 00:00:01 |
|*  1 |   TABLE ACCESS FULL LOAD| EMP  |    1 |    20 |    3   (0)|
00:00:01 |
-------------------------------------------------------------------------
SQL> alter index id_emp_ix_01 visible;
Index altered.
SQL> set autotrace on;
SQL> select * from emp where ename = 'INDIA';
-------------------------------------------------------------------------
|Id| Operation.            | Name        | Rows| Bytes| Cost (%CPU)
| Time    |
| 0| SELECT STATEMENT      |             |    1|    14|   2 (0)
| 00:00:01|
| 1|   TABLE ACCESS BY INDEX ROWID BATCHED| REGIONS     |    1|    14|
2 (0  )| 00:00:01|
|*2|    INDEX RANGE SCAN       | ID_EMP_IX_01|    1|     |   1 (0)
| 00:00:01|
```

We linked to the 19c Database and started with the use of the statement below that activates the indexing to happen in an automated way.

Note: This functionality is applicable only in Oracle Exadata or Oracle Cloud environments.

Challenges:

1. Tables that have stale statistics will not be considered for auto indexing.
2. Quarantined statements of SQL will not be permitted to utilize automatic indices in future.

Case Study 7.2: Memoptimized Rowstore

Section 7.3 describes the overview of Memoptimized Rowstore with a test case scenario showcased as an example of implementation along with its performance benefits. Here, in this section, we propose below research problems in this Memoptimized Rowstore feature:

Fast ingest is much more efficient than a series of conventional single transactions. But, there are some disadvantages:

i. Data loss occurs if there is an unexpected database instance crash. This happens because, in this feature, the data is initially stored in a large pool instead of directly onto the disk.

ii. Delayed visibility of inserted data: Once the data gets inserted onto the table, the data is not visible immediately to other users because the data is not still permanently stored in the disks.

7.6 Future Research Opportunities

As part of future work, there is a need to investigate and find an alternate solution for auto indexing mechanism to pick up the tables having stale statistics. This is because there can be certain client requirements to lock the statistics, and in this case, statistics may be obviously old and cannot be chosen as potential candidates for automatic indexing.

There is a research scope in identifying solutions for preventing data loss in the case of a sudden database crash while in the process of Memoptimized Row ingest, finding a solution for this data loss might be a huge advantage.

7.7 Conclusion

The increased use of smart devices has made a huge increase in the frequency and volume of data. Oracle Database is more than capable of inserting hundreds of millions of lines per second and measuring petabytes of data. It is the best choice for the most important IoT function given its support for flexible schemes, ultra-fast In-Memory availability and leading industry availability. In order to overcome the limitations in previous versions like high CPU usage during the parallel execution of resource intensive queries, we have showcased how the new features of Oracle 19c will prevent high CPU usage with the help of a concept called SQL Quarantine. Also, to overcome the limitation of poor index creation by Database Administrator, automatic indexing feature of Oracle 19c has been highlighted. By this feature, the indices are chosen automatically by the Oracle optimizer and thereby maintain the smooth running of queries by choosing a good plan hash value.

References

S. Alapati. 2009. *Expert Oracle Database 11g Administration*, Springer Science and Business Media LLC.

H. Albreiki, L. Alqassem, K. Salah, M. H. Rehman and D. Svetinovic. 2019. Decentralized Access Control for IoT Data Using Blockchain and Trusted Oracles. IEEE International Conference on Industrial Internet (ICII), pp. 248–257.

W. Ali, M. U. Shafique, M. A. Majeed and A. Raza. 2019. "Comparison between SQL and NoSQL databases and their relationship with big data analytics." Asian J. Res. Comput. Sci., vol. 4, no. 2, pp. 1–10.

C. Asiminidis, G. Kokkonis and S. Kontogiannis. 2018. "Database systems performance evaluation for IoT applications," Int. J. Database Manage. Syst., vol. 10, no. 06, pp. 1–14.

A. Celesti, A. Galletta, L. Carnevale, M. Fazio, A. Lay-Ekuakille and M. Villari. 2018. "An IoT cloud system for traffic monitoring and vehicular accidents prevention based on mobile sensor data processing." IEEE Sensors J., vol. 18, no. 12, pp. 4795–4802.

Z. Daher and H. Hajjdiab. 2018. "Cloud storage comparative analysis Amazon simple storage vs. microsoft azure blob storage." Int. J. Mach. Learn. Comput., vol. 8, no. 1, pp. 85–89.

B. Diene, J. Rodrigues, O. Diallo, E. Ndoye and V. V. Korotaev. 2020. "Data management techniques for Internet of Things." Mech. Syst. Signal Process., vol. 138, pp. 1–19.

J. Dizdarević, F. Carpio, A. Jukan and X. Masip-Bruin. 2019. "A survey of communication protocols for Internet of Things and related challenges of fog and cloud computing integration." ACM Comput. Surv., vol. 51, no. 6, pp. 1–29.

D. J. Hand. 2018. "Statistical challenges of administrative and transaction data." J. R. Stat. Soc. A (Statist. Soc.), vol. 181, no. 3, pp. 555–605.

S. J. Hussain, T. Farooq., et al. 2013. *Expert Oracle RAC 12c*, Apress.

T. Kyte. 2005. *Expert Oracle Database Architecture*, Springer Science and Business Media LLC.

H. V. Le and A. Takasu. 2018. "G-HBase: a high performance geographical database based on HBase," IEICE Trans. Inf. Syst., vol. E101.D, no. 4, pp. 1053–1065.

Y. Liu, K. A. Hassan, M. Karlsson, Z. Pang and S. Gong. 2019. "A datacentric Internet of Things framework based on azure cloud." IEEE Access, vol. 7, pp. 53839–53858.

Oracle Corporation. 2021a. https://www.oracle.com/technetwork/database/in-memory/overview/twp-bp-for-iot-with-12c-042017-3679918.html. Accessed 25 August 2021.

Oracle Corporation. 2021b. https://www.oracle.com/a/otn/docs/19c-Oracle-QoS-Management-TWP-060121.pdf. Accessed 25 August 2021.

8

Advanced Prospective of IoT in Waste Management for Sustainable Development

Juliya V Devasia and Pinkie Cherian

CONTENTS

8.1 Introduction

Pollution is a drastic phenomenon that existed for centuries in the world. Waste treatment removes contaminants from used resources. Waste management or proper waste disposal is a major difficulty in our society. Unprecedented population growth and urbanization are the major reasons for increasing waste generation. One of the important issues noticed in the waste governance is that the garbage bin at public places gets inundated well in forge ahead before the initiation of the next cleansing job (Hasnabade et al., 2021). It in turn leads to various hazardous effects that may cause some physical ailments to mankind. Sometimes it may lead to the drastic situation like cancer. Weak institutions and rapid urbanization makes many struggles to Waste collection. Nowadays, the quantity of production of urban solid waste is increasing drastically with escalating population density, economic growth and also changes in lifestyle of urban occupants. Municipal solid waste is actually a great difficulty to concerned authorities or agencies in charge. Due to the insufficiency in waste management system, approximately 85% of the total municipal solid waste management budget is impoverished for waste assemblage, haulage and dumbing. We need an efficient waste regulating system, and it ensures green clean environment and provides refreshment to the society.

Waste treatment is mostly a complex technique as it includes different technologies and processes. Internet of Things (IoT) can provide a fruitful solution for garbage management. Intelligent transportation system enables new services with smart cities. Waste collection using surveillance system might be an assistive technology, and it provides high-quality service in waste collection. Ultrasonic pitch sensors in the besuited waste bins can automatically sense maximum limit of waste in bins. Similarly, gas sensors are also present in novel smart bins for sensing hazardous gases. This is a unique approach, and it uses cloud- and mobile application–based monitoring. The assistance of cloud server can give information on emergency situations, and it is linked with municipality or any other official web server. It helps the authorities to take immediate necessary actions. Using this advanced technology, we can track the waste bin by a unique id no, it helps to identify the exact location of the place. The amount of solid waste generated in its collection time and categorized waste bins can be framed using different sensor establishments. The host server will provide all the information interconnected with the cloud-based web information system. The current status of the waste collection and transportation are monitored by the municipal or urban bodies with the help of this advanced smart system. Remote monitoring is possible using this technology. An Android or other related application is developed, and it is linked to a web server of the municipal office, through this can monitor all the cleaning processes done by the workers, thereby reducing the manpower and saving money. The notifications are correctly sent to the Android application using Wi-Fi network (Kumar et al., 2017).

The causation and ditching of waste in large aggregate has fabricated a greater perturb over time which is resentfully affecting the human survival and our environmentally sound sustainability. A true factor is that wastes are the one that heighten with the magnification of the country. Partitioning of waste is important for proper jettisoning of vast amounts of garbage wastes, and one of the interesting factors is that proper segregation of reusable materials helps to earn money from recycling agencies. People never realize the consequences of their actions, or in other words, they are not actually bothered about what they are doing. The common method for the disposal of solid wastes is purely uncontrolled, and people commonly chose river sites and open areas for dumbing of garbage wastes. This easy method of disposing solid waste cause harms to our environment and is injurious to soil fertility, plants, animals and also human life.

8.2 Reviews on Solid Waste Management

Many IoT-built smart, efficient solid waste handling systems have been moved to hand out different classes of adversities subsisting with our present solid waste management systems in smart cities. The key factor remarked from the various literature surveys is that most critical issue facing our society is an inappropriate or inefficient solid waste management system. Nowadays, the experimenter has endorsed various routines and approaches to straighten out these issues, specifically, the solid waste conduct.

Many industries are creating bulk amount of problems for the environment and human beings. The rapid assessment matrix can analyze the positive and negative impacts of this waste and create a score which help determine the level of toxicity. Recycling and sanitary landfilling are the two systems, were associated as harmonious to all and are selected as administration practice for waste conduct. Bebortta et al. (2020) studied the smart dustbin application using cognitive IoT framework. Effective garbage managements were observed and considered big challenges for smart systems. (Tiwari et al., 2020) reported the Fuzzy-based multiple criteria decision-making on the waste collection,

TABLE 8.1

Technologies Used in IoT for Solid Waste Management

	Technology	Sources
Babalola (2018)	GIS MCDA – Geographic-information-system-based multi-criteria decision analysis	Anaerobic digestion of food
Liang et al. (2013)	Analytic network process	Waste energy recovery from engines
Tiwari and Sharma (2020)	Fuzzy-based multiple criteria decision	Waste management
Bebortta et al. (2020)	Cognitive IoT framework	Smart dust bins
Shayesteh et al. (2020)	Assessment matrix method	Industrial park

disposal and recycling methods. The study emphasized the public-private partnership with solid waste management services can make this technology to practical side. Table 8.1 explains the different technologies adopted by different areas to get rid of waste using smart technologies.

The gas collected from exhaust of engine were analyzed and utilization measures were adopted using analytic network process. This method is considered as a suitable tool for waste recovery from engine for the engineer.

8.3 Different Exemplar and Tack for Waste Disposal

The refuse spawned from disparate segments of the society can be categorized into different types based on its composition or physical properties, and it's purely on fundamental basis. The solid waste discarded by urban municipalities, generated mainly from households, office, shops, schools, hospitals and other institutions, contains a mixture of food waste, plastic waste, medical waste, metals, and glasses and also contains a small quantity of hazardous waste. Selective collection, segregation, processing and proper disposal are the basis for proper waste management.

Different sort of wastes are delineated as follows:

Organic waste: This waste is biodegradable or compostable waste that transpired from either plants or animal. Case in point with the organic waste includes green rot, paper dissipates, innocuous wood waste, manure, human waste, food waste, sewage, slaughterhouse waste, landscape and pruning waste.

Recyclable waste: This is a pointer integrant of waste curtailment and is the task of accumulating and depurating of particulars that would or else to be catapult away as waste debris and shift them into contemporary useful upshot. Recyclable materials include variant of glass, carbon-enriched paper, cardboard-embedded metals, voltaic, fabrics, batteries, plastics, and tires. Humus and other reclaim of biodegradable waste is also a form of recycling. Recycling promotes environmental sustainability by removing raw materials and reducing the need for waste disposal.

Industrial waste: The waste produced by the industrial exhaust and production activity is also a knowable source. It includes any earthly that embellish nugatory during a constructive activity. Industrial effluents contain various toxic byproducts release into the environment causing harm to humans and wildlife.

Hospital-related/biomedical waste: Any sort of waste originated in hospitals and medical clinics mostly containing potentially infectious materials that mediate malady to mankind when they come into contiguity with it. It should be served according to entrenched standards, with all viable attention and care.

Commercial waste: Commercial wastes are non-hazardous solid waste that is collected from commercial habitual, such as clothing hoard, toys, and contrivance, used mainly for the purposes of a trade or business or for the purpose of sport, recreation, education or entertainment. It usually consists of a mixture of bricks, tiles, concrete, heavy loads of timber, metal, plastic, paper etc.

Green waste: Biological waste is the any biotic/animate waste that can be nutritive for soil. It is the material that results, mainly, from refuse from gardens, such as the pruning of trees, branches, trunks, barks, leaves that fall in the streets and domestic or industrial kitchen wastes. Green waste can be used to ameliorate the attribute and unceasing of industrially reared top soils and also used for the production of organic fertilizer.

Electronic waste: It is described as repudiated electrical or electronic devices that are menacing for refurbishment, reutilize, flea fair or for disposal. They contain potentially harmful chemicals like "lead, cadmium, beryllium, brominated flame retardants" etc. that are deleterious to people and the environment.

Nuclear waste: Radioactive waste is a type of perilous waste that carries radioactive materials and that is generated from nuclear plants, fuel processing plants, hospitals and scientific laboratories etc. Because of its hazardous nature, depository and scrapping of radioactive waste are strictly regulated by the government bureaus in order to fortify human robustness and environment.

8.4 Novel Smart Waste Bin

Merits of IoT services make its application to be ideal for waste management purposes. Especially, in academia, industry and major government sectors, these technologies are wide-spreading. Illegal, indiscriminate and ignorance of waste management had created considerable loss to habitat along with environmental issues. To hand on this situation, various research studies on waste management based on IoT technology are still in performance. For this, radio frequency identification (RFID) technology provides waste management platforms and system services (Nielsen et al., 2010). Figure 8.1 discusses about the features of RFID technology and how it receives stored data.

RFID has two components, namely, tags and readers. The radio waves are used to communicate and portable device with inbuilt cabinets (Zhu et al., 2012). It enables waste weighing system and could provide the ability to measure the waste constituents. Using this novel technology, it increases the waste management efficiency through automation. It can also enhance the environmental responsibility and concern of the mankind.

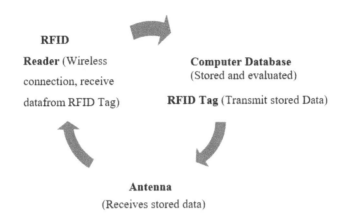

FIGURE 8.1
Features of RFID technology.

8.5 Environmental Impacts of RFID Technology

RFID has environmental potentiality that it can analyze the disposal and recycling of packing materials containing RFID tags. Rapid growth of this technology could accumulate the spent tag, antenna and readers on municipal waste streams. A huge collection of minerals like copper, silver compounds, silicon's, adhesives, plastic contained in these tags can create a municipal waste globally. These tags are considered hazardous and can pollute the water resources with potential risk. It can also disrupt the recycling process of the environment. Existence of waste and proper detectors produces favorable measures using this technology.

8.6 GSM/GPRS Technique

Interface between the transmitter and receiver in GSM (Global System of Mobile) (Singhvi et al., 2019). GPRS system complex provide the data stored in dustbin and its level of toxicity. Using this technology, ultrasonic sensors can sense the filling level of dustbin. The toxicity level can be measured using gas sensors and also give the indication of hazardous gas emissions. The level of intensity is measured through GSM module. At specific intervals data are stored with time and date in the website. Through mobile GPRS system, the municipal authority gets information regarding the filling and defiling of the dustbins (Baldo et al., 2021). GSM communication modem provides information on the data required for the authorities that the garbage reaches the threshold limit (Vasagade et al., 2017). Figure 8.2 clearly discusses about the mechanism of GSM modem and its modulating protocol in detecting the waste in dustbin.

Many research studies are currently working on to determine the accuracy on the data and the limit of generation of the waste. This kind of technology can provide a solution for the health, environmental and social issues associated with improper dustbin displacement in the city.

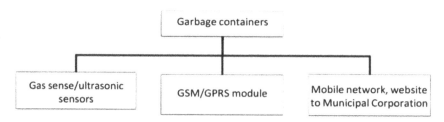

FIGURE 8.2
GSM/GPRS functioning system for dustbin.

8.7 Categorical Approach for Waste Management

Rapid growth in the rate of population in the community level result automated upgraded use of large-scale products from the markets. This surplus increase can create an evolution of waste in new urban areas and associated cities. Strong waste administration is crucial and for that a categorical application is necessary to compartmentalize the approach. Figure 8.3 clearly explains the categorical approach in collecting the waste and deriving useful product out of it.

Solid waste, including plastic, can be easily recycled to produce a better valuable and useful product. The appearance of hazardous gas can be made less toxic and can be used in industry for better economic growth. Compost obtaining through the domestic waste and agriculture output can be further refined for making fertilizers. The application of waste is vibrant, and proper management of solid waste is essential in order to provide a fruitful effect to society. Lot of cyber physical systems are changing the technology for waste transfer, and detection and categorical approaches are administered for effective delivery of technology (Pardini et al., 2019). Cloud-based waste management for this categorical technology will be useful for decision-making in waste collection. Arduino IDE and 8051 microcontroller model scrutinize the data from sensors, and this will measure the depth of waste in the stock (Nirde et al., 2017).

FIGURE 8.3
Categorical approach of waste management.

8.8 Societal Implication on Smart Technology

A critical aspect that needs to be noted is the human influence during the architect of solid waste management. The different behavior pattern of people belonging to various cultures on this technology is crucial to be undertaken. Dynamic multi-stimulation trials are applied by the researchers in order to predict the behavior of the people based on modeling agent applied in both urban and individual areas (Ochoa et al., 2017). The panic nature of people is visualized by the researcher while establishing the technology in the areas with crowd population.

Another importance finding is the battery consumption level, for the working of the sensors. Use of expensive device like actuators, microcontrollers and transmission modules are widely used in the model (Anagnostopoulos et al., 2017). Such smart devices are successfully submerged in the environment to keep track and accumulate accurate particulates or data's. Renewable energy devices like photovoltaic panel for battery can avoid the constant manual replacement function in the build devices. Sensor nodes are considered an efficient maintainer of energy levels, and computational capacities are also considered idle (Cerchecci et al., 2018). Much new advancement in preparation of novel sensors with minimum cost and minimum power consumption is in the platform.

8.9 Conclusion

Technology is the computational phase in this new era of waste management that benefits the competent authorities. A waste management system mainly engrossing on citizens prospective that can interrelate with the idle complex through mobile requisition is necessary. This will be helpful to find the bin location closer to the residence area and use it effectively. Knowing this indication, the user can discard the waste if it shows empty level detection through GPS. This strategy can make the people avoid the overflow of containers and take remedial action on it. Corporation authorities can collect the waste as per the instruction obtained from the nearby residence bin, which can reduce the cost and also low fuel consumption. Such advancement can create a better collection path with enormous profit to smart cities in the community. The successful side comes only when the people get aware about the discarding of waste in inappropriate times. Thus, to accomplish this transfiguration of conservative cities to smart cities, waste conduct becomes a censorious concern in today's world. Wielding IoT, it is workable to spoor the bearings where waste is generated, monitor the threshold limit of containers, eliminating spillover of waste and most importantly can avoid the spread of diseases. The success of the proper waste management system ensures the welfare of society.

References

Anagnostopoulos, T., Zaslavsky, A., Kolomvatsos, K., Medvedev, A., Amirian, P., Morley, J., & Hadjieftymiades, S. (2017). Challenges and opportunities of waste management in IoT-enabled smart cities: A survey. IEEE Transactions on Sustainable Computing, 2(3), 275–289.

Babalola, M. A. (2018). Application of GIS-based multi-criteria decision technique in exploration of suitable site options for anaerobic digestion of food and biodegradable waste in Oita City, Japan. Environments, 5(7), 77.

Baldo, D., Mecocci, A., Parrino, S., Peruzzi, G., & Pozzebon, A. (2021). A multi-layer LoRaWAN infrastructure for smart waste management. Sensors, 21(8), 2600.

Bebortta, S., Rajput, N. K., Pati, B., & Senapati, D. (2020). A real-time smart waste management based on cognitive IoT framework. In Advances in Electrical and Computer Technologies (pp. 407–414). Springer, Singapore.

Cerchecci, M., Luti, F., Mecocci, A., Parrino, S., Peruzzi, G., & Pozzebon, A. (2018). A low power IoT sensor node architecture for waste management within smart cities context. Sensors, 18(4), 1282.

Hasnabade, R., Hadole, V., Jangid, R., & Magar, H. (2021). IoT based garbage monitoring system using arduino. International Journal of Advanced Research in Science, Communication and Technology, 798–800.

Kumar, B. S., Varalakshmi, N., Lokeshwari, S. S., Rohit, K., & Sahana, D. N. (2017). Eco-friendly IoT based waste segregation and management. 2017 International Conference on Electrical, Electronics, Communication, Computer, and Optimization Techniques (ICEECCOT), 297–299.

Liang, X., Sun, X., Shu, G., Sun, K., Wang, X., & Wang, X. (2013). Using the analytic network process (ANP) to determine method of waste energy recovery from engine. Energy Conversion and Management, 66, 304–311.

Nielsen, I., Lim, M., & Nielsen, P. (2010). Optimizing supply chain waste management through the use of RFID technology. 2010 IEEE International Conference on RFID-Technology and Applications, 296–301. IEEE.

Nirde, K., Mulay, P. S., & Chaskar, U. M. (2017). IoT based solid waste management system for smart city. 2017 International Conference on Intelligent Computing and Control Systems (ICICCS), 666–669.

Ochoa, A., Rudomin, I., Vargas-Solar, G., Espinosa-Oviedo, J. A., Pérez, H., & Zechinelli-Martini, J. L. (2017). Humanitarian logistics and cultural diversity within crowd simulation. Computations Systems, 21(1), 7–21.

Pardini, K., Rodrigues, J. J., Kozlov, S. A., Kumar, N., & Furtado, V. (2019). IoT-based solid waste management solutions: A survey. Journal of Sensor and Actuator Networks, 8(1), 5.

Sharma, M., Joshi, S., Kannan, D., Govindan, K., Singh, R., & Purohit, H. C. (2020). Internet of Things (IoT) adoption barriers of smart cities' waste management: An Indian context. Journal of Cleaner Production, 270, 122047.

Shayesteh, A. A., Koohshekan, O., Khadivpour, F., Kian, M., Ghasemzadeh, R., & Pazoki, M. (2020). Industrial waste management using the rapid impact assessment matrix method for an industrial park. Global Journal of Environmental Science and Management, 6(2), 261–274.

Singhvi, R. K., Lohar, R. L., Kumar, A., Sharma, R., Sharma, L. D., & Saraswat, R. K. (2019). IoT based smart waste management system: India prospective. 2019 4th International Conference on Internet of Things: Smart Innovation and Usages (IoT-SIU), 1–6.

Tiwari, A., & Sharma, P. (2020). Using fuzzy based multiple criteria decision making for selecting private firm for waste management PPP contract arrangement. IOP Conference Series: Materials Science and Engineering, Vol. 955, No. 1, 012106. IOP Publishing.

Vasagade, T. S., Tamboli, S. S., & Shinde, A. D. (2017). Dynamic solid waste collection and management system based on sensors, elevator and GSM. 2017 International conference on inventive communication and computational technologies (ICICCT), 263–267. IEEE.

Zhu, X., Mukhopadhyay, S. K., & Kurata, H. (2012). A review of RFID technology and its managerial applications in different industries. Journal of Engineering and Technology Management, 29(1), 152–167.

9

IoT for Water Management: A Sustainable Solution

Shraddha Khamparia, Siddharth Jabade, Shrikaant Kulkarni,
Priya Nakade, and Dhananjay Bhatkhande

CONTENTS

9.1 Introduction

Water is a wonderful compound required for the sustenance of life on blue planet. A broad range of lifeforms relies substantially on water for carrying out their metabolic activities. An increase in the consumption of water has been observed with exponential growth in the population and overexploitation and misuse of water, which has culminated in ever-increasing concerns about the scarcity of water (Ma et al., 2020). Apart from common

DOI: 10.1201/9781003226888-9

concerns about potable water scarcity, there are growing concerns raised about the scarcity of water for agricultural purposes too (Rosa et al., 2020; Vallino et al., 2020). To tide over these challenges, conserving water resources optimally and numerous water management systems (WMSs) have been designed and adopted so far by the incorporation of numerous technologies which are however higher in cost and energy consumption. Therefore, designing a sound WMS is of pivotal importance which can monitor water level and quality in real time.

Real-time WMS is instrumental in reducing the wastage of water to abysmally low level, e.g., from tanks that are overflowing. WMS helps in diagnosing and detecting water leakages if any in a smart home by bringing about a real-time analysis of water level at different times in the day. A smart WMS (SWMS) is therefore very much required for a smarter and livable planet. A major reason for the reluctance in adopting SWMS is ascribed to its high cost. However, after the introduction of Internet of Things (IoT) (Hammi et al., 2017), the cost reduced significantly. IoT consists of a system with a host of inter-connected devices possessing tremendous capability of transmission of data. WMS driven by reduced cost of IoT has been gaining momentum over the years. Devices in an IoT ecosystem can communicate among themselves incredibly and transfer data without any human intervention and subsequently making them ideal candidates for catering to the needs of real-time WMSs. In the recent past, research initiatives have been taken to analyse water quality on real-time basis by examining factors such as pH, dissolved oxygen (DO), temperature, biochemical oxygen demand (BOD), and total dissolved solids (TDS). Such IoT-based WMSs provide real-time sustainable solutions by addressing the problems confronted by smart cities.

IoT-enabled WMSs are cost-effective solutions which are quite easily scalable. Cheap sensors provide for easy measurement of numerous contaminants, thereby leading to qualitative assessment of water. Deployment of state-of-the-art communication tools to present-day WMSs without much modification in their configuration is very much possible. Applications of IoT-enabled technologies allow smart access to ensure control, and to monitor continuously from a remote place. The IoT is considered a core technology useful both for present and future information and communication technology. The chapter addresses the need of water management and intervention of IoT for making the system more efficient, effective, and sustainable. Furthermore, latest advancements in IoT-enabled WMS have been discussed, followed by case studies of different countries. IoT being in the focal point of the Fourth Industrial Revolution, its sustainability aspect is explained with United Nations Sustainable Development Goals (SDGs). A mechanism is proposed with data security and the inclusion of innovative technologies to make it more scalable and efficient.

9.2 Water Management

It has been evident that human ambitions and race towards modernisation have brought about irresponsible consumption of water resources, which has now posed a threat to upcoming generations for their survival. According to the latest data published by United Nations on SDG 6, it is reflected that around 2.3 billion people live in water-stressed countries, of which 733 million live in high and critically water-stressed countries.

There has been a requirement to double the progress rate for the integrated water management approach since 107 countries are not on track to have sustainably managed water resources by 2030. Also, 26% of the world's population lack safely managed drinking water facilities in 2020 (UN-Water, 2021: Summary Progress Update 2021 – SDG 6 – water and sanitation for all. Version: July 2021. Geneva, Switzerland). Water is essential for living and for all economic activities; hence, efficiency attainment in managing water resources is evident. Water management deals with the effective management of water resources, their monitoring, and regulatory measures. With the intelligent use of water resources, there has been a significant risk on energy and food production front with an ever-increasing population of the world. Nonstationary supply and demand put an additive burden on the natural cycle, whereas due to rapid industrialisation and globalisation, drastic climate changes have been noticed, further deteriorating the condition. Hence, efficient and effective water management is required for the equitable supply of an essential natural resource, "Water". Creative solutions are required to check severe water management crises. From technology intervention to community participation with advocacy of water-centric policies, intelligent water management strategies are in great demand (Cosgrove and Loucks, 2015).

A wireframe is depicted in Figure 9.1, connecting all the aspects of an SWMS. What is most sought after is the existing WMS with smart technologies that make it more transparent and accessible to all stakeholders. The inclusion of one water framework in water management that addresses drinking water, wastewater treatment, recycled water, and resilient infrastructure should be at the forefront. Also, with the intervention of the state-of-the-art technologies, climate change issues can be addressed by coping with disasters or extreme conditions.

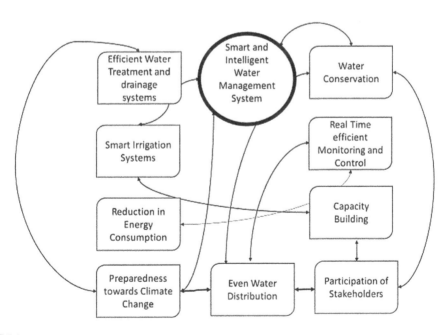

FIGURE 9.1
Smart water management framework.

9.2.1 IoT Interventions in Water Management

Momentum has been gained to adopt SWMs in this dynamic world facing several changes related to water security and natural disasters. The emergence of IoT has been the driving force for the attainment of SDGs. IoT coupled with water management addresses the problems related to freshwater scarcity, water consumption patterns, agricultural water issues, and water quality. Moving towards sustainability, the concept of smart cities and smart grams (villages) is to establish a linkage among urban, peri-urban, and rural areas, in which IoT-based WMSs are a promising technology to cater to the problems. IoT-based systems are enabled for monitoring the quality of water (surface as well as ground), flood levels accompanied by early warning systems, monitoring irrigation systems dealing with soil permeability, and optimisation of water required for crops, as depicted in Table 9.1. IoT has a broad range of applications at all levels, from households to industries and from rural to urban areas. This includes monitoring wastewater treatment facilities, pump station monitoring, the incorporation of automatic on-off IoT valves, remote metering for analysing consumption patterns of consumers, leakage detection followed by conservation activities like rainwater harvesting, drip irrigation, and recycling of water.

IoT devices can be implemented in household appliances, water distribution systems, and industries, as depicted in Figure 9.2. Applicability of IoT in household appliances can be seen with the introduction of auto on-off valves, sensors, and meters for the analysis of water quality, water wastage, and leakage detection. Also, it enables users to monitor water waste in the case of accidental unattended water dispensing devices. It assists in water conservation and guides towards responsible consumption of the most precious resource, water. On the other hand, in centralised water distribution systems through underground buried pipes for drinking and domestic use, the integration of IoT systems eases the decision-making based on real-time monitoring and provides an early warning for any potential problems.

IoT-enabled water treatment systems are amenable to maintenance work in the case of scheduled maintenance or sudden stoppage and ensure uninterrupted water to consumers. Furthermore, most industries utilising water at different stages of the process involve the release of wastewater which, if monitored using IoT devices, save time, money, and resources. In terms of cost-effectiveness, long-term economic benefits can be accrued along with environment benefits with requisite initial investment.

TABLE 9.1

Applications of IoT in Water Management Systems

Applications	Details
Water quality monitoring	Ground, aquifers, river basin, dams, in-pipe, etc.
Water level monitoring	Floods, aquifers, dams, water table
Irrigation systems monitoring	Drip irrigation, monitoring water usage, etc.
Wastewater treatment	Storm water, sewage treatment, water treatment
Water consumption monitoring	Water metering, water auditing, etc.
Groundwater monitoring	Pollutant detection, distribution pattern, etc.
Water conservation	Reusing, recycling, leak detection, judicious consumption

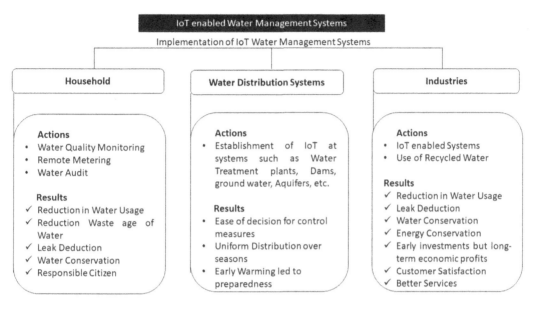

FIGURE 9.2
Implementation and advantages of IoT-enabled water management systems.

9.2.2 IoT Architecture in Water Management Systems

Integrating the coupling technology and management systems with IoT can opt for urban and rural areas in industries and household levels. Figure 9.3 shows a generalised framework of IoT-based WMS. It comprises a controller, sensors, and an application with a display

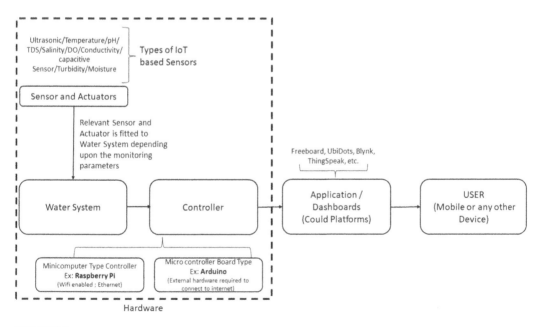

FIGURE 9.3
Framework of an IoT-enabled water management system.

screen showcasing quality parameter values. There is two-way communication between the sensors and the controller. Sensors acquire the data and pass it on to the controller. A controller is like a miniaturised processor which can connect with the network and can run programs. It is programmable and transfers it to the server to store and analyse data acquisition from sensors. Other than Raspberry Pi and Arduino, other controllers are also available such as BeagleBoard, Netduno, ZigBee, fuzzy controllers, and NodeMCU. In general, the microcontroller board type is found to be cheaper than minicomputer-type controllers.

Some low-power communication technologies such as Bluetooth Low Energy (BLE), Wi-Fi, and Narrowband IoT (NB-IoT) are implemented to maintain the efficient linkage between low-power and memory-intensive IoT devices and networks. Application is a program available on the web meant for fetching data from the controller followed by displaying it in the user interface. Automation of water services can be very well addressed by IoT tools which connect with the local network for easier associability. Traditionally, IoT framework revolves around three layers: the physical layer (hardware with sensors, IoT devices to existing systems) converting the collected data into usable form; the second layer is the network layer where the information is stored and transported; and, in contrast, the third layer is the software or an application assessed by controlling and monitoring agencies for processing data and necessary action.

9.2.3 Components of IoT in Water Management Systems

With the overview of the IoT framework in the above section, each prime component is discussed at length. Some of the examples of devices and systems used are depicted in Table 9.2.

TABLE 9.2

Components of IoT Systems Employed in Water Management Systems (García et al., 2020; AlMetwally, Hassan, and Mourad, 2020; Singh and Ahmed, 2020)

Purpose of Deployment	Microcontrollers	Embedded Programming Language	Commonly Employed Sensors	Communication Technology
Water quality control	TI CC3200; Raspberry Pi, Arduino Uno, NodeMCU V3, LPC2148	Energia IDE, Python, Arduino C, Lua scripting	Water Level, pH, YL-69 conductivity, turbidity, ultrasonic, water flow, rainfall	ZigBee, Raspberry Pi (Wi-Fi build), ESP8266, ESP8266
Smart irrigation systems	Atmega328; Mamdani fuzzy controller, Arduino Uno, Arduino Mega, Raspberry Pi 3 Model B, Raspberry Pi 1 Model B, Raspberry Zero Raspberry Pi 3	Arduino C, MATLAB	Water level, soil moisture, DHT11, YL-69, VH400, FC-28, 200SS, HA2002 SEN0114, SM300, S-XNQ-04, DHT22, LM35, TMP36	ZigBee, RFID, Z-Wave, Thread, BLE, Wi-Fi, NB-IoT, LTE-M, EC-GSM, LoRaWAN, Ethernet, GSM, Bluetooth, GPRS, IEEE 802.15.4
Water consumption monitoring	PIC16f877; Raspberry Pi , MSP 430, NodeMCU, Arduino Uno, Arduino Mega; Raspberry Pi Zero, 3B; Arduino Nano	C, Arduino C, MATLAB, Python, Lua scripting, Arduino IDE	Ultrasonic level, turbidity, water flow, pressure, solenoid valve	Wi-Fi build in MC, GSM/GPRS, CC2650, ESP8266-12E

9.2.3.1 Sensors and Actuators

Sensors are the devices in WMSs utilised to measure different parameters, such as pH, water level, water flow, turbidity, and temperature, in the prevailing environment, while actuators are the mechanical systems where the decisions will be made based on the coding from controllers. Some of the sensors and actuators with generalised features have been discussed here. Flow sensor, such as YF-S201 (5 V; temperature −25 to 80°C; 1–30 L/min @ 2.0 MPa), is a cost-effective sensor measuring water flow based on the Hall effect. pH sensors are used for monitoring the alkaline and acidic nature of water (5 V; 0–14 pH range). Temperature sensors monitor temperature variation in °C. Turbidity sensor (0–5 NTU) measures the cloudiness of water with a light scattering mechanism. Ultrasonic water level sensor (widely utilised for real-time monitoring water levels) uses sound waves to monitor water level in the system and helps to detect any possible overflow. Water flow sensor based on a rotational component of integrated pinwheel translates the activity in electrical pulses indicating the quantum of outgoing water. Actuators are classified based on the type of movement required for an action. Actuators are provided with servo motors and can move linear, angular, or a specified degree rotation. Some of the actuators are hydraulic, pneumatic, electrical, mechanical, thermal, magnetic, and so on. Hydraulic actuators are provided with cylindrical/fluid motors used for elevating or lowering the system; it is expensive and has a disadvantage in terms of frequent maintenance of maintenance. Pneumatic actuators used in robotic movements have a comparative advantage of cost-effectiveness and capability to work under varied temperature conditions. It requires a continuous working air compressor for proper functioning. Electrical actuators convert electrical to mechanical torque with high precision but are quite expensive. Thermal or magnetic actuators use shape memory alloys.

9.2.3.2 Controllers

Controllers are responsible for storing, retrieving numerical data from sensors, and give commands. Arduino (open source; runs only one program at a time) is easy-to-use hardware and software microcontroller for electronic prototyping and is classified as microcontroller board type. Raspberry Pi (Linux OS; runs multiple programs simultaneously) is pocket-sized minicomputer-type microcontrollers with a dedicated processor, USB ports, SD card slot, and an inbuilt graphic driver for outputs through HDMI. Several versions, such as Raspberry Pi 3 (1.2 GHz; 64-bit quad-core; ARMv8 CPU; 1 GB RAM), are available with built-in WLAN and Bluetooth. Some other processors are displayed in Table 9.2.

9.2.3.3 Communication/Transmission Technology

IoT devices have very little memory and have low power, which are powered by efficient transmission technologies. Several communication/transmission technologies are available right from 2G, 3G, 4G, 5G, Wi-Fi, Bluetooth, LAN, Ethernet, and others, as shown above in Table 9.2. ZigBee (low-cost, low-power wireless) is an open global standard module-to-module transmission technology that operates in the standard frequency of 2.4 GHz and an operating voltage of 2.8–3.6 V and has a range of 40–60 m. Some other types of technologies put into effect by researchers around the globe for water management include BLE, low-power Wi-Fi, NB-IoT, Long Range Radio (LoRA), etc. BLE and low-power Wi-Fi consume less energy than standard Wi-Fi. LoRA is considered a commercially adopted technology (García et al., 2020; AlMetwally, Hassan, and Mourad, 2020; Singh and Ahmed, 2020).

9.2.3.4 Cloud Platforms

For controlling and monitoring IoT devices, the cloud provides a space for accessing data and communication to users via application. The examples of such platforms are Blynk, FreeBoard, Ubidots, ThingSpeak, and Watson IoT platform (IBM).

9.2.3.5 Transmission Protocol

Transmission protocols are the connectors among the cloud, controllers, and devices. The transmission protocol is HTTP (Hypertext Transfer Protocol), MQTT (Message Queuing Telemetry Transport), or others. Generally, MQTT has been preferred over HTTP because of limitations of the latter such as inability to drive event-based communication, limited to one-to-one communication, unidirectional, and synchronous. Other advanced transmission protocols are Advanced Message Queuing Protocol (AMQP), Constrained Application Protocol (CoAP), etc. (García et al., 2020; AlMetwally, Hassan, and Mourad, 2020; Singh and Ahmed, 2020).

9.2.4 Recent Advancements in Water Management Systems with IoT

IoT has been in existence since 1999 with the emergence radio-frequency identification (RFID) and has gained momentum over the last few years in water management. In recent times, IoT has not only been limited to water metering but also analyses potable water and wastewater in-depth, including level indication. Application of IoT can be seen in industries, cities, municipalities, irrigation, and agriculture for optimisation of responses and reduction in cost.

Hadipour and his coresearchers observed that an innovative IoT-based multi-intelligent control system (MICS) has been employed in the agricultural sector and is operated via short message service (SMS) or ringtone. MICS consisted of an electro-pump controller, water level in reservoir, and alarm control system. IoT-enabled MICS resulted in satisfactory outcomes concerned with reliability and water saving (60%). One of the most important benefits of the proposed control system is simplicity and low cost (Hadipour, Derakhshandeh, and Shiran, 2020). However, technologies like Supervisory Control and Data Acquisition (SCADA), GIS, geographic information system, hydraulic models, billing services, automatic meter reading, mobile-based applications, and advanced metering infrastructure are already in place. However, with IoT intervention, more feasibility, scalability, and transparency have been achieved by SCADA coupled with IoT which reduces the reaction time (remote monitoring and real-time reporting), enhances production and operational efficiency, gives better visibility to industrial assets, and maximises performance.

NB-IoT, a novel technology, has been developed to overcome the requirements of a wide area with low-power networks. NB-IoT is better placed since it is scalable and can be applied to personal devices/gadgets (Ullah et al., 2021). According to the studies, an improved version of an intelligent water management platform is called an energy-efficient water management platform (EEWMP), which is effective in terms of energy consumption (30% less) and far more stable than the existing ones in irrigation systems. Another advancement has been noticed with the inclusion of big data analysis in data collection from deployed IoT sensors. With heavy data load and rapid processing, big data proves to be a boon for water distribution networks of domestic water and wastewater. The study revealed that big data has advantages like collection, storage, analysis, and visualisation, enabling quick strategy framing (Nie et al., 2020).

Mohammad and his coresearchers, in 2021, experimented on IoT-based architecture for the desalination of seawater. The result was encouraging in terms of optimisation of resources such as resources, solar power consumption, and response time (Alshehri et al., 2021). Thakur and the team in 2021 proposed an edge computing framework with a blockchain model for incentivising in response to domestic water saving using soft computing methodologies. A feedforward neural network (FNN) trained via symbiotic organism search (SOS) has been utilised for the effective prediction of water consumption (Thakur et al., 2021).

In one of the works, an IoT solution coupled with cat swarm optimization (CSO)-based neural network algorithm is proposed to detect the water quality and forecast when the measured parameters are lower than threshold values followed by alterations in the consumers (Mariammal, 2021). For intelligent irrigation systems, a neural network-trained IoT-based fuzzy energy-aware route has been adopted to manage agricultural files' irrigation (Rezaeipanah, 2021).

Other advancements in IoT-enabled WMSs include low-power wide-area network (LPWAN) technology, such as LoRaWAN, which are better than traditional 3G/4G and telemetry systems. Cloud technologies, such as Microsoft Azure, offer scalable data storage infrastructure, analysis, machine learning, and artificial intelligence applications. The long-range radio (LoRa) and LPWAN is one of the novel IoT communication technologies with an excellent capacity for development bringing about advancements in many fields. The benefits of this technology can be attributed to its capabilities of ultra-long-distance communication, low power consumption, and ease of deployment, among others. Wireless sensor network (WSN) technology has been widely employed with features such as feasibility and rapid establishment of communication.

Some other applications like IoT solution accelerator, a Cumulocity IoT, are used for managing water use live data and analytics to detect leakages and water losses for metered and non-metered consumption. Another IoT factory software platform integrates water meters using LoRaWAN collecting data and notifies missing data, technical issues, overconsumption, and non-consumption. Temboo analyses water quality, monitors water and soil environment, and works in stewardship. Libelium smart water solutions detect water levels, chemicals, and contaminants in water using IoT sensors and transmit data to the cloud using 4G/Wi-Fi or LoRA.

Furthermore, security is one of the concerns, which arises with IoT-embedded WMSs. Security issues involve the denial of service (DoS), data type probing, negative control, malicious operation, scan, spying, wrong setup, DoS attackers, jamming, spoofing, and privacy leakage. Intrusion to physical devices can be counteracted by installing additional passive infrared sensor (PIR) sensors and buzzers. To ensure efficient system performance and avoid any manipulation, data privacy and security become indispensable. To avoid any intentional SQL injections, flooding attacks, cloud malware injection, and ransomware, a new technique, blockchain, is applied to secure IoT systems that allows secure data storage and communication. Another approach for detecting intrusions in IoT sensors can be achieved by using machine learning. Based on the study, random forest and neural networks were found to be effective amongst others. Earlier study showed that the radio frequency (RF) classifier achieved the highest accuracy in detection attacks. Alharbi et al., in 2021, proposed a transparent, reliable, integrated system of IoT and blockchain for measuring real-time water quality and instant alert for the violation of norms leading to the penalisation of the offenders, thereby addressing the problem of point and non-point pollution (Alharbi et al., 2021). IBM Linux ONE 2020 is one of the secure platforms for IoT-based systems (Deloitte Report https://www2.deloitte.com/content/dam/Deloitte/us/Documents/about-deloitte/blockchain-iot-wastewater-management.pdf).

9.2.5 IoT and Water Conservation

Water conservation refers to policies, strategies, and activities to manage freshwater as a sustainable resource, protects the water ecosystem, and meets current and future human demands. Using IoT, smart water meters, smart water sensors, smart leak detectors, and smart irrigation systems have acquired great demand for water conservation techniques. Along with these, systems like rainwater harvesting are also used. Artificial intelligence-enabled IoT accomplishes tasks automatically and provides up-to-date information, allowing for informed and methodical decision-making using the mentioned digital systems.

Traditional water conservation measures have been used, but smart devices that use IoT technology are the answer to tackle water-related issues at the higher level, especially in the scenarios of climate change knocking at the door. Smart water meters, sensors, and irrigation systems are simple to install in houses, fields, and industries. As many countries face water depletion, water conservation is the solution to safeguard resources for future generations. According to the WRI report, surface water depletion will be occurred in 167 countries by 2030 and severe water stress by 2040 (WRI Report https://www.wri.org/insights/ranking-worlds-most-water-stressed-countries-2040).

The smart water sensor is simple to install and will alert the consumer when there is a leakage and warns of any sudden rise in temperature and humidity parameters. Water leakages are detected using cellular technology and a call centre using a smart leak detection system. From a freshwater reservoir through wastewater collection and recycling, smart water technology now delivers transparency and greater control to the whole water supply chain. This category consists of IoT water management equipment, systems, and software applications that aid in optimizing water quality monitoring, distribution, and consumption, as well as implementing smart water treatment methods. Several studies have been carried out for real-world deployment of a residential water consumption monitoring system, irrigation systems, water quality monitoring, etc. In the revolutionary wireless water monitoring systems, flow rate sensors are set at various detecting points throughout a residence to collect data. Information, education, and awareness are some non-technical measures that can affect consumer behaviour.

One of the examples is water metering systems, where a water meter with a data logger for capturing data, a communications technology for transmitting the data, and a server for processing the data are used. The smart system often allows utilities or third-party firms to continuously monitor or read water usage data in real time or at predetermined intervals. Consumers can also use mobile devices and laptops to obtain their consumption data via online portals. Utilities at times employ a right mix of communication technologies to achieve their diverse transmission objectives. A direct wire connection is appealing, dependable, and offers high bandwidth. However, the installation and maintenance expenses of wiring millions of meters are high and sometimes infeasible too. On the other hand, wireless networks are more adaptable and capable of connecting more devices at lower cost and effort. Cellular, Wi-Fi, Bluetooth, LoRa, satellite, and other wireless technologies are popular for smart metering. The maximum range, transmission rate, capacity, ability to tolerate inference, and other criteria vary among communication networks. As a result, utilities can have right balance of wired and wireless technologies to improve coverage and quality. Another critical IoT intervention that has come to the fore is water audit. Water auditing is a type of survey determining the efficiency with which water is utilised. It is a qualitative and quantitative analysis of water consumption to identify means of reducing, reusing, and recycling water. Water audit assists in finding the route of the water. A water audit is an effective management tool for minimising losses, optimising various uses, and thereby enabling considerable conservation of water. Most water schemes are dedicated to sourcing, treating, and delivering safe water to the public without reporting water loss.

The auditing process includes three steps: initial step pre-audits water use, collecting primary data from sources of water (water consumption from various utilities wastewater generated, etc.) and defining an inventory, while the intermediate phase examines the system for efficient and effective consumption. While the final step includes post-auditing measures encompassing awareness about water conservation and remedial measures (maintenance, water efficiency plan, etc.).Water audit identifies the barriers and risk areas so as to understand the course water is taking after leaving the source point. Accurate information allows for identifying the ways to enhance water efficiency, and thereby to contribute to water conservation by minimizing losses. Moreover, it leads to the reduction in water losses and in improving the reliability of the supply system.

9.3 Global Case Studies

The section deals with the relevant case studies from across various countries. The case studies discuss the implementation of IoT at different levels and share the technical aspects of the same. With the advancement from the First Industrial Revolution to the fourth, the trends have been shifted from automation to mass production to electronic and information technology, and now it is focused on smart systems and cloud computing. Real-time water quality monitoring for Krishna River in India has been discussed at length, followed by the case study of smart cities in Nepal, Spain, Australia, Korea, and others.

9.3.1 IoT for Real-Time Water Quality Monitoring – Krishna River, India

Monitoring water quality on a real-time basis is an important application of IoT. The traditional method of water quality measurement is a prolonged, costly, and time-consuming process. It requires a workforce for water sampling, connecting with the laboratory to perform sample analysis for various water parameters. The challenge was taken up to develop an IoT-enabled statistic model for the analysis of different water parameters of river Krishna on a real-time basis. Various water parameters, such as pH, temperature, DO, conductivity, TDS, and BOD, were considered to assess quality. Six different stations of river Krishna flowing from the state of Karnataka, India, were selected for water sampling. Temperature sensor, pH sensor, conductivity sensor, DO sensor, a sensor for BOD, and microcontroller were physical devices connected in IoT framework and a Wi-Fi unit to network and collaborate. Water quality parameters were successfully monitored and analysed on a real-time basis using IoT and the one-way ANOVA statistical method. The result showed that water quality strongly depends on the season and considered water parameters play an essential role in assessing the water quality season-wise. In the future, the collected data on the cloud can be used to make the IoT system smart and intelligent by integrating machine learning algorithms. The smart IoT system will take action for any abnormal change in the analysis of water parameters to maintain the quality (Pujar et al., 2020).

9.3.2 IoT for Smart City in Water Supply Management – Kathmandu Valley, Nepal

SWMSs play a vital role in developing smart cities. Parameters for smart water supply include monitoring overflow, leakage, automatic bill generation, online payment, and status of water consumption not only for the public but also for the entire city. To make Kathmandu city smart, an IoT-based framework was developed for water supply management and tested at six spots for 360 days. The architecture of IoT was developed using Raspberry Pi (central processing unit), ultrasonic sensor, relay, water pumps, routers, Cat 6 cable (for communication between the tanks), water tanks, database, smartphones, and web interface. Cloud-based technology was implemented in the developed framework for its easy scalability using Python programming.

Real-time monitoring of water consumption and leakage was recorded in selected slots. IoT framework identified the leakage and prevented water overflow. House owners were highly delighted with this IoT application installed in their homes. The central water management authority can use the big data collected from the cloud for smart water supply in the future. Automatic bills can be generated by applying simple billing formula. This developed IoT framework can be used for water management and sectors like waste management and electricity management (Gautam et al., 2021).

9.3.3 IoT for Water Resource Management in Agro-Industrial Environments, Spain

Water management of various water resources, like wells, desalination plants, and consumers with different water needs that are geographically separated, is the challenge in front of agro-industrial environments. Enabling technologies like IoT in centralised water management can be an essential solution for the optimum management of water distribution. The real facilities in Almería, Spain, were used in this study to consider agro-industrial districts composed of consumers (three greenhouses and one office building) and water resources (water public utility network and solar desalination plant). To manage the water requirement of all consumers and minimise the operating cost of the solar desalination plant, cloud IoT architecture based on FIWARE (The Open Source Platform for Smart Digital Future) standard was proposed to communicate with all consumers and model predictive controller to optimise cost. FIWARE is an IoT platform proposed by Europium Union.

Solar desalination plant consists of an array of membrane distillation (MD), and the plant was entirely IoT controlled to receive and share the information. Output water from desalination plant was collected in tank, and tank was connected to the water distribution system. Like desalination plants, greenhouses and office buildings were also totally monitored by sensors and actuators to optimise the water requirement. The proposed architecture of IoT was divided into three layers: Context Producer (comprising all physical devices of an ecosystem capable of exchanging data), Backend (all services of data analysis and Model Predictive Control (MPC) approach), and Frontend (link to the client for data visualisation).

Feeding the consumer's maximum requirement from desalination plant of water was considered the basis for optimum management. The result showed that, with an increase in water requirement and a decrease in water level in a central tank, MPC increases the number of MD modules turned on to enhance generation from the desalination plant, thereby avoiding the water requirement from public utility network. Public utility water was used only when desalination water was not sufficient to fulfil water requirements. In terms of operational cost, in manual operation, a significant number of MD modules were turned on, producing more water than they need and hence an increase in cost. In terms of economic saving, the use of IoT in water management of this agro-industrial environment decreased the optimum cost of sanitation plant by 87% and total cost by 75%. This decrease in cost is also reflected in the cost of water demanded by the consumer. It has reduced from 1.51 €/m^3 in manual non-optimum procedure to 0.44 €/m^3 using IoT (Muñoz et al., 2020).

9.3.4 IoT for Development of Smart Watering System – Cairns, Australia

Application of poor water management techniques water management techniques in irrigation is the major reason for water wastage. Water required in irrigation depends upon many factors such as earlier water content used, soil properties, live moisture level, plant characteristics, and local weather conditions. Over-irrigation leads to water wastage and also the leakage of nutrients into nearby streams. Therefore, IoT-enabled smart irrigation system was developed to predict optimum water requirement for irrigation in the park to preserve water resources and decrease the costs of irrigation.

Two parks from Cairn's city of Australia were selected for the study. Soil survey using dual electromagnetic identified three moisture zones within the park: dry zone, moderate moisture zone, and high moisture zones indicating the varied quantity of water requirement. Micro-weather stations and soil moisture sensors were deployed in all moisture zones of the park to collect weather and moisture-related data on a real-time basis. Moisture-detecting sensors were installed in 10-, 30-, 90-, and 120-cm depth to calculate unused stored water at the depth. The soil from different moisture zones was tested for other properties like soil type, water holding capacity, infiltration rate, and plant characteristics. The raw data of sensors collected from the cloud was analysed using data mining techniques. Real-time data collected from the IoT framework, along with data of lab tests, was fitted in various machine learning algorithms to predict the irrigation requirement for scheduling watering through sprinkler. The smart irrigation system was found to be quite effective in controlling and predicting the irrigation requirements of the park located in dry, semi-wet, and wet zones (Chandrappa et al., 2020).

9.3.5 IoT for Development of Smart Watering Management, Seosan, Korea

Smart water management has received significant attention in the last decades due to an increase in natural calamities attributed to climate change, decreased water quality, and increased water requirement due to urbanisation and population growth. To overcome these challenges, Korea Water Resources Corporation (K-water) introduced IoT in water management. The development of an SWMS led to reduced water leakage and improved revenue by remote metering using smart meters, which was the main purpose of this project.

K-water required initial fixed investment for facility installation and operating cost, with significant returns on investment expected in the long term. Digital meter, remote transmitter, base station, and monitoring system were installed as a part of smart devices. Real-time data measured by smart meters were transmitted to base stations using a remote transmitter. Big data from base stations were transmitted to the monitoring system to be analysed. A significant increase in water management efficiency was recorded by integrating traditional WMSs with smart IoT-based management tools. The project is expected to give a return of 1,179 million over 566 million invested with a cost-benefit ratio of 2:1. The return of investment is predicted to come within four years after installation of the system.

Therefore, to overcome water management challenges, IoT-enabled smart water management is considered the best cost-effective solution (Yi et al., 2018).

Similarly, IoT-enabled WMSs have been reported for water management of flood and drought in South Korea, and real-time water quality management is enabled in Paju, South Korea, and Paris, France. Overexploitation monitoring of groundwater enabled with IoT has been implemented in Guantao County, China; Water quality and leak detection in Mexico City, Mexico, water management for smart irrigation in Mozambique, Tanzania, Zimbabwe. Similarly, water quality, leak detection, and energy conservation are implemented in the Netherlands, Spain, France, and United Kingdom. In addition, the potential for rainwater collection and stormwater management using IoT has been tapped in Toronto, Canada (Smart Water Management Project Report, K-water Korea Water Resources Corporation & IWRA the International Water Resources Association, 2018).

9.4 IoT for Sustainable Development

Moving towards the SDGs 2030, incorporating IoT-enabled systems will assist in achieving several targets of all 17 SDGs. According to a recent report furnished by Engineering, IoT, Industry 4.0, and R&D (EIIR Trend report, 2021) Trends, water is one of the classified categories where sustainability services are in great demand. Sustainability services involve waste consumption reduction, increase in efficiency, change in utilisation pattern, etc. Measures are incorporated right from small-scale, household products to large-scale industries. The existing systems can be well coupled with IoT to save water, efficient products, recycling, sewage treatment plants, desalination plants, etc. (EIIR Trend report, 2021).

An average adult consumes around 100 gallons of water per day, which may be significant with expanding population and decreasing water sources. Water stress has been experienced because of this ever-increasing demand for water by communities and industries. Existing water resources have been under tremendous pressure because of pollution, population, irresponsible exploitation and consumption, and wastage. Much of the attention on water conservation has been given on improving the technology of water-using appliances to make them more water-efficient. However, because user engagement with water-using appliances has a significant impact on the amount of water consumed by the appliance, which is determined by the habits, rituals, and expectations of water consumption, more user-focused research is required. The IoT solutions collaborating with SDGs have been portrayed in Figure 9.4.

With its three pillars, sustainable development addresses and targets the overall development of humankind without harming nature. Furthermore, water is an entity associated with each sector; with the implementation of an intelligent WMS, not only SDG 6 can be addressed, but also IoT-enabled smart systems associate themselves with all other 16 SDGs. Social benefits of implementing SWMSs ensure rightful and equitable distribution of water by implementing advanced technology and building resilient infrastructure in extreme events addressing SDG 1, i.e., No Poverty. The food production problem is integrated with constant monitoring of irrigation systems, transcending to SDG 2, Zero Hunger. With better quality of water due to water quality monitoring, the population's health attains the target of good health and well-being, SDG 3. Inculcation of technical

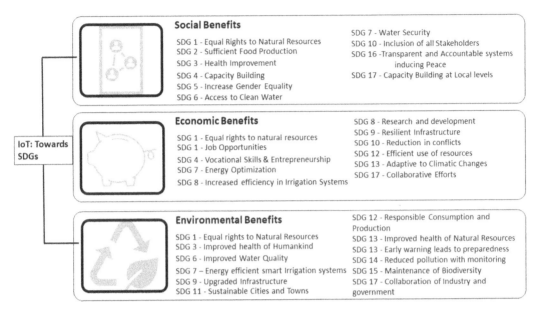

FIGURE 9.4
Internet of Things: solution towards Sustainable Development Goals.

and entrepreneurship skills and increasing opportunities for women leads to imparting quality education encompassing gender equality goals. The transparency and inclusion of all the stakeholders to save water and reduce water wastage contribute to SDGs 7, 10, 16, and 17.

With equitable, transparent, accountable technological interventions, SDGs 1, 4, 7, and 8 are addressed substantively, accruing economic benefits to society and the community. With resilient infrastructure, industry innovation targeting SDG 9 reduces inequalities by providing job opportunities to all. Sustainable consumption is one of the SDGs, which further renders economic benefits to the city, nation, and world. Collaborative efforts at local, national and international levels constitute SDGs 2030 agenda, and the cost-effectiveness of IoT systems has been examined. According to the research carried out by research group for water management, it was demonstrated that the investments made for the project would compensate within three months of instalment (Maroli et al., 2021).

9.5 Proposed Mechanism

Based on the extensive study and observations all over the globe in most of the applications of water management, advantages, risks, and control measures have been consolidated in Table 9.3. Furthermore, in this section, a mechanism is proposed incorporating the aspects of data handling, data security, and community participation.

IoT has several advantages with its feasibility in their installation in households, municipalities, commercial buildings, and industries. It helps in water conservation meeting the requirements of SDG 6. Furthermore, it is customisable in tune with the requirements;

TABLE 9.3

Advantages, Risks, and Control Measures with IoT Enables SWSMs

Advantages	Risks	Measures/Controls
• Intelligent automatic system • No manual intrusion • Adaptive • Ease in deployment • Applicable at public and private sectors • Reduces risks • Checks water loss • Increases operation efficiency • Customisable • Dedicated dashboards • Wireless connectivity over traditional • Wired connection • Cost-effective • Remote access • Cloud-based • Strong integration with stakeholders • Works on the internet as well as LAN • Optimisation of process • Improved capital planning for maintenance • In line with ISO 37122;2019	• Lack of proper planning before implementation can lead to failure • Inability to handle the large volume of data • Security issues • Unclear business objectives • Wi-Fi could be lost • Physical manipulation of devices	• Proper visualisation • Application of software • Digital infrastructure for effective integration of IoT data • Authentication ID • Incorporation of statistician • Capacity building • Incorporation of big data analysis • Incorporation of machine learning • Incorporation of Blockchain technology • Application of LoRA instead of Wi-Fi

the cloud-based approach makes it more viable while continuous monitoring reduces the operational and maintenance cost. The risk arises when it is implemented without proper knowledge and planning. Furthermore, handling extensive data remains a daunting task while security issues, like jamming and spoofing, may surface with a cloud-based system. Moreover, physical manipulation of on-site devices needs to be verified and monitored via buzzers or alert systems. Though there are certain risks involved, yet with control measures, IoT proves to be the enabling technology in smart management system at large scale.

The proposed mechanism focuses on enabling IoT-based technologies in different domains of WMSs use (i.e., water quality and water metering/auditing) with proper policy documentation dos and don'ts. After implementation, real-time monitoring with proper care data security using blockchain and machine learning approach need to be adopted as a fourth layer of IoT-enabled systems. Further analysis of transferred data needs to be adequately analysed, and predictive modelling needs to be done to employ control measures before getting any negative results. Furthermore, a statistician needs to be included in the team for proper authentication of data to check for manual manipulation. Accomplishment and acceptance of the system require community participation with technological ingestions coupled with industrial products; hence, consumer awareness of the overall benefits of the technology is of importance. In addition, the failure of sensors could be one of the issues that may go unnoticed, including a self-diagnostic system to check for the health of

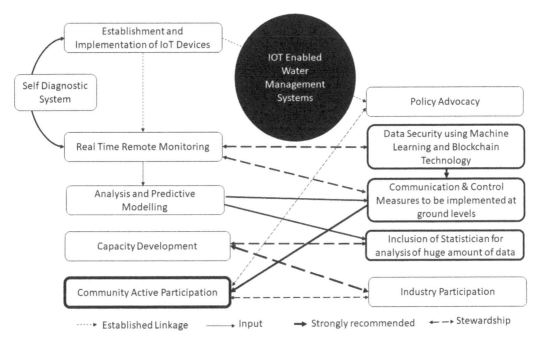

FIGURE 9.5
The mechanism for implementation of IoT in water management systems.

sensors to avoid any delayed detection. The proposed mechanism depicted in Figure 9.5 enables the IoT-embedded WMS robust in all scenarios. The proposed mechanism underlines the effective, transparent, and suitable solutions for WMSs that address all the SDGs in one or the other way.

9.6 Conclusion

An efficient SWMS is aimed at eliminating the cost towards the analysis water samples in an off-line lab. Moreover, it assures that the water quality prevents the public from getting conflicted with any of the diseases and reduces the cost of maintaining the quality of water. SWMS advocates the concept of a smart city which doesn't ask for any human interventions and thereby cut down the labour and operation costs. It also makes use of various filters applied to exacerbate the water quality efficiently.

An SWMS is the need of hour for designing and developing smart utilities in smart cities or colonies. Application of IoT in WMSs is gaining a huge momentum over the time. Cost-effective sensors linked with IoT devices have met the challenges in terms of water quality measurement. In this chapter, different parts of IoT-enabled WMSs are discussed apart from a cursory look at incumbent SWMSs. Different factors, like water level, pH, turbidity, and salinity, are identified for comparison in performance behaviour of incumbent systems. In addition, essential qualities of SWMSs are listed. Some of the challenges or risks associated lie with the manipulation of data and data security which can be well addressed by machine learning security and blockchain techniques. However, challenges of minimising real-time energy use are very much there. Primarily an SWMS driven by IoT and machine learning holds a lot much of promise and potential by employing machine learning-enabled predictions in enhancing the performance of the SWMS. Moreover, the accuracy in predictions is quite noticeable in irrigation and flood control and is in fact a big challenge. Quantitating economic water scarcity (EWS) preferentially in agriculture domain with the help of IoT technologies needs to be investigated further. IoT technologies will be deployed in various industries such as smart cities, health, environment, utility, and security. Furthermore, in the 21st century, WMSs will be groomed with advanced technologies for providing sustainable solutions to exponentially growing human population, including draught-prone and water-deprived areas. The IoT system coupled with wireless devices will be most sought after to meet the requirements of voluminous futuristic challenges. Recent studies stress upon the inclusion of IoT-based water quality monitoring, thus assisting in moving out from the status of water scarcity (Sapra, Kalra, and Sejwal, 2022). Further study reveals that water management needs to be implemented at all levels right from industries, educational institutes, and households (Siddamal et al., 2022).

9.7 Future Prospects

The design and development of the IoT-enabled WMS is capable of running in an autonomous manner. Various buildings in the city with built-in SWMSs can be connected through a single network. They can be monitored continuously for the water quality and consumption patterns in various areas other than studying the causes that alter the quality of water quality and correcting it suitably.

Essential qualities of these smart systems can be listed from such studies, which need to be incorporated in future designs. Moreover, a sound architecture of an SWMS driven by IoT and machine learning has ample scope in acquiring all necessary attributes to facilitate the use of artificial intelligence and machine learning to enable predictions which are bound to boost the efficiency of the SWMSs quite a lot.

References

Alharbi, N., Althagafi, A., Alshomrani, O., Almotiry, A. and Alhazmi, S., 2021, July. A blockchain based secure IoT solution for water quality management. In 2021 International Congress of Advanced Technology and Engineering (ICOTEN) (pp. 1–8). IEEE. https://www2.deloitte.com/content/dam/Deloitte/us/Documents/about-deloitte/blockchain-iot-wastewater-management.pdf; https://www.wri.org/insights/ranking-worlds-most-water-stressed-countries-2040

AlMetwally, S.A.H., Hassan, M.K. and Mourad, M.H., 2020. Real time Internet of Things (IoT) based water quality management system. Procedia CIRP, 91, pp. 478–485.

Alshehri, M., Bhardwaj, A., Kumar, M., Mishra, S. and Gyani, J., 2021. Cloud and IoT based smart architecture for desalination water treatment. Environmental Research, 195, pp. 812.

Chandrappa, V.Y., Ray, B., Ashwath, N. and Shrestha, P., 2020, June. Application of Internet of Things (IoT) to develop a smart watering system for cairns parklands – A case study. In 2020 IEEE Region 10 Symposium (TENSYMP) (pp. 1118–1122). IEEE.

Cosgrove, W.J. and Loucks, D.P., 2015. Water management: Current and future challenges and research directions. Water Resources Research, 51(6), pp. 4823–4839.

García, L., Parra, L., Jimenez, J.M., Lloret, J. and Lorenz, P., 2020. IoT-based smart irrigation systems: An overview on the recent trends on sensors and IoT systems for irrigation in precision agriculture. Sensors, 20(4), pp.1042.

Gautam, G., Sharma, G., Magar, B.T., Shrestha, B., Cho, S. and Seo, C., 2021. Usage of IoT framework in water supply management for smart city in Nepal. Applied Sciences, 11(12), pp. 56–62.

Hadipour, M., Derakhshandeh, J.F. and Shiran, M.A., 2020. An experimental setup of multi-intelligent control system (MICS) of water management using the Internet of Things (IoT). ISA Transactions, 96, pp. 309–326.

Hammi, B., Khatoun, R., Zeadally, S., Fayad, A. and Khoukhi, L., 2017. IoT technologies for smart cities. IET Networks, 7(1), pp. 1–13.

Ma, T., Sun, S., Fu, G., Hall, J.W., Ni, Y., He, L., Yi, J., Zhao, N., Du, Y., Pei, T. and Cheng, W., 2020. Pollution exacerbates China's water scarcity and its regional inequality. Nature Communications, 11(1), pp. 1–9.

Mariammal, M.G., 2021. Efficient IoT based water quality prediction using cat swarm optimized neural network classification. Psychology and Education Journal, 58(1), pp. 4279–4282.

Maroli, A.A., Narwane, V.S., Raut, R.D. and Narkhede, B.E., 2021. Framework for the implementation of an Internet of Things (IoT)-based water distribution and management system. Clean Technologies and Environmental Policy, 23(1), pp. 271–283.

Muñoz, M., Gil, J.D., Roca, L., Rodríguez, F. and Berenguel, M., 2020. An IoT architecture for water resource management in agroindustrial environments: A case study in Almería (Spain). Sensors, 20(3), pp. 596.

Nie, X., Fan, T., Wang, B., Li, Z., Shankar, A. and Manickam, A., 2020. Big data analytics and IoT in operation safety management in under water management. Computer Communications, 154, pp. 188–196.

Pareekh Jain, CEO and Lead Analyst, EIIR Trend, 2021. Sustainability engineering services. https://eiirtrend.com/static/wp-content/uploads/2021/06/pov-sustainability-engineering-services.pdf

Pujar, P.M., Kenchannavar, H.H., Kulkarni, R.M. and Kulkarni, U.P., 2020. Real-time water quality monitoring through Internet of Things and ANOVA-based analysis: A case study on river Krishna. Applied Water Science, 10(1), pp.1–16.

Rezaeipanah, A., 2021. An IoT Fast and Low Cost Based Smart Irrigation Intelligent System Using a Fuzzy Energy-Aware Routing Approach.

Rosa, L., Chiarelli, D.D., Rulli, M.C., Dell'Angelo, J. and D'Odorico, P., 2020. Global agricultural economic water scarcity. Science Advances, 6(18), pp. 6031.

Sapra, P., Kalra, V. and Sejwal, S., 2022. Blockchain and IoT for Auto Leak Unearthing. In Cyber Security and Digital Forensics, pp. 381–390. Springer, Singapore.

Siddamal, S.V., Talikoti, V., Umrani, P., Uppin, S.S., Kulkarni, V. and Hiremath, S., 2022. Framework for a Green Campus-LoRa™-Based Low-Power Smart Water Management for Campus. In Information and Communication Technology for Competitive Strategies (ICTCS 2020), pp. 363–371. Springer, Singapore.

Singh, M. and Ahmed, S., 2020. IoT based smart water management systems: A systematic review. Materials Today: Proceedings. 46(11), 2021, pp. 5211–5218. https://doi.org/10.1016/j.matpr.2020.08.588.

SMART WATER MANAGEMENT Case Study Report Executive Summary, K-water (Korea Water Resources Corporation) & IWRA (the International Water Resources Association)- Smart Water Management Project, pp. 1–32, 2018.

Thakur, T., Mehra, A., Hassija, V., Chamola, V., Srinivas, R., Gupta, K.K. and Singh, A.P., 2021. Smart water conservation through a machine learning and blockchain-enabled decentralized edge computing network. Applied Soft Computing, 106, pp. 274.

Ullah, R., Abbas, A.W., Ullah, M., Khan, R.U., Khan, I.U., Aslam, N. and Aljameel, S.S., 2021. EEWMP: An IoT-based energy-efficient water management platform for smart irrigation. Scientific Programming, 2021, pp. 1–9.

UN-Water, 2021. Summary Progress Update 2021 – SDG 6 – Water and Sanitation for All. Version: July 2021. Geneva, Switzerland

Vallino, E., Ridolfi, L. and Laio, F., 2020. Measuring economic water scarcity in agriculture: A cross-country empirical investigation. Environmental Science & Policy, 114, pp.73–85.

Yi, S., Ryu, M., Suh, J., Kim, S., Seo, S., Kim, S., 2018. "Case Study of Seosan Smart Water Management", K-water (Korea Water Resources Corporation) & IWRA (the International Water Resources Association) - Smart Water Management Project, pp. 74–109.

10

Smart Water Management System Powered by the Internet of Things (IoT) for Real-World Applications

Fantin Irudaya Raj E and Appadurai Mangalraj

CONTENTS

10.1 Introduction

From smart cities to smart homes, traffic management systems to transportation, and a variety of other industries, the Internet of Things (IoT) is intertwined with almost every aspect of our lives [1]. The IoT has a significant impact on the subject of water management systems. Although ensuring proper water usage is difficult, proper adoption of IoT technology in water management systems would undoubtedly make our lives easier and conserve our vital resources. Water scarcity is mostly caused by poor resource management, according to the United Nations Development Program. Water scarcity is anticipated to impact more than 50 percent of the world's population by 2025, indicating that water will become a valuable resource in the near future [2]. The IoT has exploded in popularity since its conception. IoT is defined as the concept of connecting things using wireless technology. Numerous sensors are specially designed for a particular application that can be used to extract real-time information and share the information through means of interconnection. The IoT is a network of things, homes, gadgets, automobiles, and other items that have electronic systems and are connected to communicate and perform operations. IoT is rapidly evolving in tandem with the newest advancements in embedded and wireless

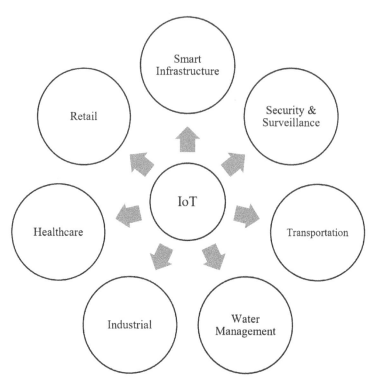

FIGURE 10.1
Different applications of IoT in the present environment.

technologies. IoT devices may now be implanted even in remote regions thanks to the development of low-power microcontrollers and sensors. IoT devices are built to function with a wide range of embedded controllers and wireless technologies. IoT is progressing, with millions of devices connecting every day to generate vast amounts of data that can be used to take action in the future [3]. The different applications of IoT in the present environment are depicted in Figure 10.1.

The present works focus on IoT-enabled water management in modern agriculture, urban areas like smart cities, and industries. Water is valuable, and its supply must be regulated. With the increase in urban population and industrialization, water demand is increasing at an exponential rate. Therefore, it is critical to have mechanisms in place to prevent water loss and use water efficiently to maintain a proper supply-demand ratio. Proper water management and conservation lead to a sustainable environment. A simplified IoT-based water management system is depicted in Figure 10.2. Any water reservoir or overhead tank used in home applications can be used with it. It typically consists of a web-based application for a data display, sensors, and controllers. Sensors are devices that are linked to the controller and used to record values such as turbidity, water level, temperature, and pH value. Sensors collect actual physical data and send it to the controller. A controller is a microprocessor or microcontroller unit that receives the sensors' actual physical data and executes the programs. Finally, store those values into a cloud database for future analysis. A web-based application is basically an internet-based program that gets data from the controller and displays it in the user interface [4, 5].

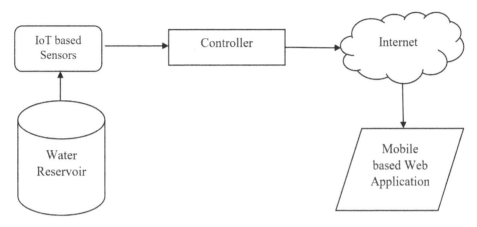

FIGURE 10.2
A simplified IoT-based water management system used in smart buildings.

Water management systems based on IoT are low-cost and scalable solutions. Water quality may be easily tested for the presence of numerous contaminants, thanks to low-cost sensors. Because widely utilized communication technologies are generally available, they can be easily integrated into existing systems. In addition, the adoption of IoT platforms enables simple control and monitoring from remote locations.

10.2 Architecture of IoT-Powered Water Monitoring System

Sensors of various types, advanced communication technologies, embedded-based modern controllers, and various cloud platforms all contribute to an effective IoT depends on water management system. The various elements of an IoT-powered water management system are depicted in Figure 10.3.

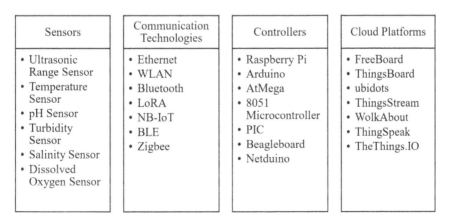

FIGURE 10.3
The various elements of an IoT-powered water management system.

10.2.1 Parameters of Water Quality

The task of determining the drinking water quality is challenging and involves a lot of parameters. While certain quality characteristics are simple to monitor, others necessitate the use of specialized machinery and knowledge [6]. The following are some of the most commonly used water quality parameters.

a. Salinity: It's a measurement of how much salt is dissolved in water. Higher salinity levels are harmful to the human body. Drinking water should have a salinity of less than 200 ppm.

b. Temperature: Temperature is another important parameter that has a significant impact on the quality of water. The WHO recommends that the normal drinking water temperature must be lesser than 30°C in the reservoir [7].

c. Total dissolved solids (TDS): It's a measurement of how much inorganic and organic matter is dissolved in drinking water. High TDS levels represent the existence of a substantial number of minerals in the water. The TDS of the drinking water must be lesser than 500 mg/L. If the TDS level is getting higher than 1000 mg/L, that water is unfitted to drink.

d. Conductivity: It's a way to see what's dissolved in water by measuring its ability to conduct electricity. For drinking water, the conductivity value must be lesser than 400 μS/cm.

e. Turbidity: It is a metric for determining the clarity of the drinking water. Therefore, it's a crucial indicator of the quality of water. Normally, it is measured in Nephelometric Turbidity Units (NTU) or Formazin Turbidity Units (FTU). The drinking water's turbidity must be lesser than 5 NTU as per the WHO guidelines [8].

f. Dissolved oxygen: It refers to the amount of dissolved oxygen (O_2) in water. The percentage of dissolved oxygen in water might indicate the water's quality. The concentration of dissolved oxygen in moving water, such as a stream or river, is higher, but stagnant water has a lower concentration. Although a higher dissolved oxygen value improves the flavor of the water, it also causes pipe corrosion.

g. pH: It is a measurement of a water-based solution's acidic and basic properties. The pH of a basic solution is greater, whereas the pH of an acidic solution is lower. The pH level should be between 6.5 and 9.5 for the water, according to the WHO [9].

10.2.2 IoT-Based Sensors

In an IoT-based water quality monitoring system, several sensors for detecting factors such as range, temperature, and humidity are available on the market. For example, pH, temperature, and ultrasonic sensors are all common sensors used in water management systems powered by IoT.

a. pH sensor: It is used to determine the basic and acidic characteristics of a water-based solution. The pH of a basic solution is greater, whereas the pH of an acidic solution is lower. As already mentioned, the WHO recommended optimal pH value is around 6.5–9.5. Irritation of the eyes, skin, and mucous membranes occurs when too high pH levels [10].

b. Temperature sensor: As per WHO guidelines, to prevent the organism from growing, water temperatures should be kept outside the range of 20°C–50°C. The temperature is an essential component in determining water quality. Various sensors for measuring temperature in a larger range (50°C–125°C) are available on the market [11].

c. Ultrasonic sensor: The water level in a reservoir or a tank can be measured using an ultrasonic range sensor. This sensor is commonly utilized to monitor the level of water in a water tank in real time. It is a distance measuring sensor that may be connected to a variety of controllers on the market.

10.2.3 Low-Power IoT Devices

Many low-power communication methods have been created to fulfill the resource-constrained, memory-intensive, and low-power IoT devices. Low range (LoRA), Narrowband IoT (NB-IoT), low-power Wi-Fi, ZigBee, Bluetooth Low Energy (BLE), and others are examples of these technologies. LoRA and NB-IoT are communication technologies based on low-power wide-area networks (LPWAN). LoRA is the first low-cost communication technology to be commercially available. It allows for long-distance communication at a low data transfer rate of up to 40–50 kbps. On the other hand, NB-IoT has a higher data rate than LoRA but uses less power and has a higher cost per device. ZigBee is a low-data-rate short-range communication protocol based on the IEEE 802.15.4 standard used in automation, industry, and other applications. Low-power Wi-Fi is based on the IEEE 802.11ah standard and requires less power while achieving a longer transmission range than conventional Wi-Fi. In addition, the peripheral devices go into sleep mode and then wake up whenever a central node sends a packet. It helps to reduce the overall energy usage of the network.

10.2.4 Controllers

Microcontroller boards and minicomputers are the two types of controllers for IoT-based water management systems. Arduino is an example of a microcontroller that repeatedly executes the same program [12]. When compared to minicomputer controllers, these are comparatively inexpensive. A single-board pocket-sized computer controller like the Raspberry Pi [13] is an example. These are full-fledged computers capable of running many programs in a parallel manner. The Raspberry Pi has an integrated Wi-Fi and Ethernet network interface and the Arduino board requires additional hardware setup for connecting to the internet.

10.2.5 Application Platform

A plethora of IoT platforms, sometimes known as dashboards, have arisen as a result of the rapid adoption of IoT devices. Companies such as Blynk [14], ThingSpeak, Ubidots, FreeBoard, and others create applications for administering [15] and monitoring IoT devices [16] via mobile devices.

10.3 Water Conservation in IoT-Based Modern Agriculture

Agriculture is a developing country's primary source of revenue. Agriculture's primary resource is water. We currently see a significant quantity of water being lost in the irrigation process. It is due to the fact that irrigation is automatically planned at a specific time, regardless of the weather or the amount of moisture in the soil. The adoption of IoT can help solve the problem of water waste. IoT sensors can detect weather conditions and soil moisture, allowing the proper amount of water to be delivered to the right location at the right time. The production of agriculture is increasing as a result of this smart farming method. Farmers may also monitor and water their crops using IoT-equipped smart devices from remote areas [17]. Figure 10.4 illustrates the IoT-based modern monitoring and watering system.

In the system mentioned above, various sensors have been used, and they are deployed in various places of the agricultural field. The important sensors used in the present system are humidity sensor, temperature sensor, moisture sensor, and rain detection sensor. The ultrasonic sensor is also used as a water tank level indicating sensor. These sensors sensed the actual status of the field where it is placed. The sensed information is passed

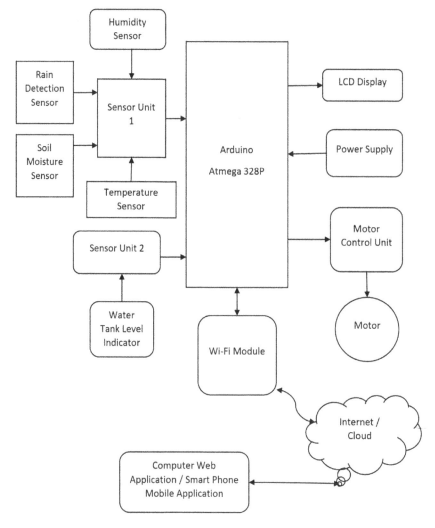

FIGURE 10.4
IoT-based smart agriculture monitoring and watering system.

to the sensor unit. The sensor unit transmits that information to the controller. Here, the low-cost Arduino processor is utilized. The processor has a Wi-Fi module. Through that module, the information received has been made available in the cloud platform. This information can be viewed using any web-based application by the observer or farmer from remote locations even. The farmer or observer can make corrective decisions based on the field's actual needs, atmospheric, and weather conditions. The same process can be automated with a microcontroller even. From this, a huge amount of water wastage can be eliminated. The productivity is also getting increased. It will lead to water conservation and sustainable development.

10.4 Water Conservation in Residential Buildings

Water is one of the essential natural resources for all living beings to survive. In the world, more than 75 percent of space is enclosed by water. Most of the water is salty; only 3 percent of water is freshwater [18]. Freshwater is only potable for several applications and so freshwater usage is gradually increasing day by day. An increase in population and comfort living style further enhanced the freshwater demand. Clean water is used in major industrial, commercial, and residential requirements. Water is used in every routine activity in every home. The freshwater is spent for bathing, cleaning, cooking, and drinking purposes. The wastewater from the bath hub and vessel cleaning tub is directly sent to the drainage system. The wastewater from each house continuously accumulates and forms a huge dirty water pond in each developed city. The water usage in the city is properly managed in the smart city project. The smart metering system is erected in each building or house to gather information about water consumption and water drain levels. Figure 10.5

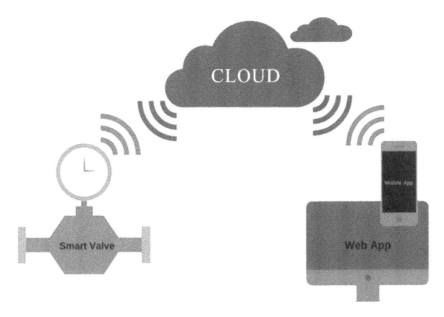

FIGURE 10.5
IoT device for water metering system.

shows the smart metering system of the smart city project where the information is shared to the cloud storage. Each person can read the central store data through a smart mobile app. The average, as well as peak water consumption of the entire city, is monitored and recorded. The provision for water conservation to meet the growing demand in each city is analyzed. The surrounding water resources survive, and a project plan is developed to transfer the nearby water resource to the city's heart [19].

It is one side of the smart city project to comfort the people in the inner city with all facilities. On the other hand, electronic sensors and IoT devices recorded the dirty water drained out from each house and street. The number of impurities available in the drainage water is sensed, measured, and stored. Several factors of the dirty water such as pH value, dissolved chemical solvent are observed. The well-known gem concept such as reuse, reduce, and recycle is implemented in the municipal drainage management system. For example, the water with low dissolved particles from the bathtub is reused to clean the restroom. The vessel cleaning water is purified by a simple filter and sent to the garden watering system. It reduces the overall water consumption from a municipal water supply. The modern purification system and resupply recycle the accumulated city drainage water to the city for usage. The groundwater level is the factor to be monitored in densely populated cities. The groundwater level goes down each year due to the enormous water consumption in metropolitan cities. The major reason for groundwater depletion is the rapid pumping of groundwater from greater depth. But the underground water recharge amount by rainfall is less than groundwater pumping out. Therefore, rainwater harvesting is one of the best solutions for groundwater recharge. Figure 10.6 illustrates the rainwater harvesting system in the residential buildings. The water is recharged underground through the sand filters to remove the impurities. It enhances the water level in the well and bore of the residential houses.

Another most feasible method of rainwater utilization is a smart rain container. Normally in the rainwater harvesting method, the freshwater is recharged to the underground. For the usage, the water is pumped from the bore or well. The groundwater also gets salty and, in some regions, the TDS level is increased too much. And so, the rainwater is stored in the small barrel and efficiently used for the daily routines. The IoT-based smart

FIGURE 10.6
Water collection through the rainwater collection system.

rainwater storage barrel gives real-time information for the water usage in the required process. Electronic sensors monitor the water level in each barrel. The advantages of this innovative concept are to decentralize the water stored underground instead of the water stored in the barrel. The stored water is used in toilet cleaning or irrigation. The alternative advantage of the water storage concept is the possibility of flooded flow in the drainage is reduced. Instead, the rainwater is stored for real-time usage. Big data analysis with IoT sensor technology is another recent technique in the smart management of several projects. A huge amount of information is gathered through several IoT devices installed in the required locations. The quality of water, water consumption rate, wastewater release amount from each residential house, leak amount detection to alert the municipal water suppliers, contamination amount of outlet drainage water is the information collected through the modern IoT sensor technologies. The gathered information is filtered to segregate the garbage information from useful data through software tools. Then the relevant information is used to predict the physical nature of the water. Thus, the sustainable water administration in the smart city project is feasible from this precise information. Thus, the smart city project gives the sustainable usage of natural resources and creates less impact on the environment.

10.5 Water Conservation in a Home Garden

The watering requirement of plants depends on several environmental aspects. Three factors determine the quantity of water delivered to the garden: collected from external resources, user input, or data gathered from the surrounding environment. The plant species category, air humidity, soil type, soil moisture level, solar intensity, and rainfall are the environmental factors that defined the water requirement for irrigation on a particular day. The IoT devices are fitted and linked with the central server to gather the surrounding information. The sensing element undergoes surveillance about the soil humidity and moisture requirement. From this actual amount of supply to the garden is calculated. The time for watering the garden is done in low temperature and humid periods. Thus, the water wastage due to evaporation is controlled. The temperature and relative humidity measurement sensor play an active role in finding the garden's water requirement. The water saturation level of the land is calculated to avoid excess watering of the garden. The nutrition demand for the plant growth is also analyzed and provided through the watering system. For some species, the shade level is adjusted with assistance from radiation intensity measurement. The light sensors provide the incident radiation value. Depending on the soil type, either may be the loose or clay variety soil, a watering method must be varied. The waterlogging has occurred in clay-type soil so that the quantity of water delivered to the garden is at a minimal level. If the excess water supply is in the garden, root decay is happened due to waterlogging. For loose kinds of soil, the watering is done for the longest time due to the porosity of the soil. The water is immediately drained out into the earth. The plant takes the water from the soil for a shorter duration only. This type of information is gathered through a proper sensor module. The vertical soil sensor is mainly used to measure this soil moisture level and the rate of water penetrated through the soil. Apart from the soil factors, the external parameter is also collected through IoT sensor modules. The amount of rainfall in that garden for the past few days is also accounted for deciding the amount of water irrigated into the garden. The weather forecast is also taken into account to eliminate water wastage by utilizing natural rainfall. The watering schedule is changed based on the anticipated weather conditions. A complete sensor and IoT device integrated control system is implemented to monitor, analyze, and decide on the watering system.

Similarly, the chemical fertilizer requirement is also provided through a proper electronic management system for sustainable water utilization. Another parameter to calculate the water requirement is transpiration and evaporation type of water loss. Several types of factors are taken into account for predicting this type of water loss. The efficient control system connected with several IoT and sensor modules supplies the data to predict the optimum amount of water required for the garden.

10.6 Sustainable Urban Water Management

The urban area needs a major amount of water resources for day-to-day activities. The main factors considered for developing a water management system in a sustainable form are surrounding rainfall, total population, drought, weather conditions, and consolidation of all resources. The sustainable management of water resources is attained by providing the proper knowledge about their water usage for a certain period. The water flow pipe design is checked with the help of finite element software packages [20–27]. The education is to focus on the efficient way of using water for their needs inside the home and also provide awareness about unintelligent water utilization in the outdoors. People must have a deeper understanding of the hazards of excessive water handling and their side effects. Thus, consumer awareness is one of the key options to minimize extreme water usage. The efficient devices must be erected in every node. The motivation to reuse the effluent water by required treatment is encouraged. For example, the dirty water from the bathtub is used to water the garden plants by a simple filtration process [28, 29]. Figure 10.7 illustrates the pictorial representation of possible ways to avoid excess water usage in daily routine.

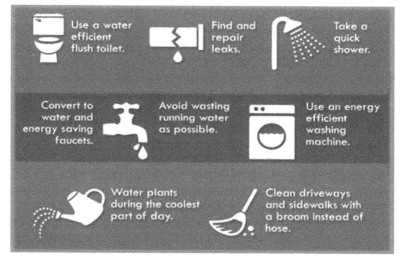

FIGURE 10.7
Efficient water utilization techniques.

Industries also consume plenty of water resources for several processes, and the wastewater is not recycled. The cheap faders available in the market are used to handle the huge quantity of wastewater. The smart solution is to control the water consumption in residences and industries by the automated metering system [30, 31]. The daily usage of water is measured and informed to the end-users. The water consumption charges are allotted based on their monthly usage. For sustainable water utilization, the single point of water metering system is not sufficient. Some monetary benefits are given to the good end-users based on the gathered information from the metering system. People are encouraged by fiscal context on their water usage. Outdoor water utilization is also taken into account [32, 33]. The gardens are installed with a sprinkler for efficient watering the plant. The sprinkler must be placed in the proper position and direction. Figure 10.8 shows the reduce reuse and recycle concept about natural resource utilization for an efficient water management system. The watering of garden plants is automated with the help of intelligent water quantifying system. Based on the soil humidity and weather conditions, the intelligent watering system can take the amount of water given to plants. The intelligent system stores information about water usage.

Further, the water management system is improved by smart electronic devices. The sensors and IoT devices are installed for smart water metering across the city. The water consumption data of each residential is transferred to the central server through a wireless data transmission system. The daily, weekly, monthly, and yearly water consumption information is stored in the central server and reported to the end-users. In the smart app, the residents can know the average water consumption throughout the year. From this, excess water usage is compared with nearby residents, and the people make the possible water usage reduction.

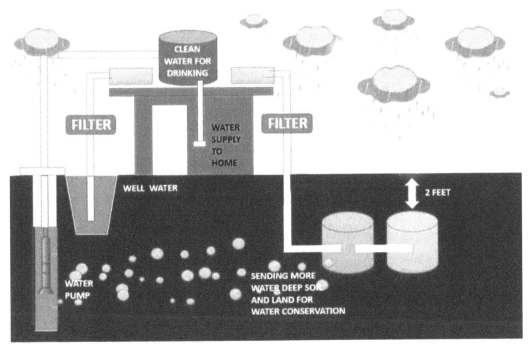

FIGURE 10.8
Water conservation techniques for sustainable management.

10.7 Industrial Water Management

Industrial is also one of the big consumers of freshwater resources. The different industries such as the power sector, manufacturing and processing industries need huge amounts of water for their function. The water is stored in the reservoirs and overhead tanks for regular running of industry without water storage. The large reservoirs and huge overhead tanks that human workers cannot monitor every minute are not feasible. The IoT devices are installed in each storage element to monitor and alert the real-time statistics about the water storage reservoirs. The data is automatically updated in the central servers for efficient handling of several input and output resources. Especially in water handling systems, water quantity available in stock, electrical conductivity, chlorine, and TDS level of water is examined in real-time for dynamic situation handling. This gathered information helps to run the system without any obstacles to any shortage of water. The information about everyday water consumption of the industries, water shortage level in reservoirs, water quality range is continuously updated in the database. It is used for further forecast in industrial scheduling. For example, in the industry, all processes need fresh water and clean water. The water input to the boiler must be in every TDS level, but the water required for the cooling tower may be higher or lower TDS amount. And so, the boiler input water for steam generation is filtered and desalinated properly. But the drainage output from the desalination or de-chlorination process is fed to the cooling tower. It may opt-in industrial practice through efficient data collection and handling through smart devices.

10.8 Conclusions

The present work discussed IoT-powered smart water management systems for urban, agricultural, and industrial applications. The architecture of IoT-based water monitoring systems and the different parameters used to decide the quality of drinking water; different sensors can get deployed in a water management system. It also discussed different communication technologies, controllers, and application platforms used in recent times. Water conservations in IoT-based modern agriculture, residential buildings, and a home garden are also discussed. The water management in urban areas and industries with the help of IoT is also explained briefly. Through adopting the IoT-based smart water management system, water conservation and resource sharing become easier. Compared with other conventional methods, the IoT-powered water management system shows high performance, less implementation cost, and superior quality. Thus, the system presented is more suited for sustainable development and effective water conservation.

References

1. Hajjaji, Y., Boulila, W., Farah, I. R., Romdhani, I., & Hussain, A. (2021). Big data and IoT-based applications in smart environments: A systematic review. Computer Science Review, 39, 100318.

2. Young, S. L., Frongillo, E. A., Jamaluddine, Z., Melgar-Quiñonez, H., Pérez-Escamilla, R., Ringler, C., & Rosinger, A. Y. (2021). Perspective: The importance of water security for ensuring food security, good nutrition, and well-being. Advances in Nutrition, 12(4), 1058–1073.

3. Makhdoom, I., Abolhasan, M., Abbas, H., & Ni, W. (2019). Blockchain's adoption in IoT: The challenges, and a way forward. Journal of Network and Computer Applications, 125, 251–279.

4. Lee, H. C., & Ke, K. H. (2018). Monitoring of large-area IoT sensors using a LoRa wireless mesh network system: Design and evaluation. IEEE Transactions on Instrumentation and Measurement, 67(9), 2177–2187.

5. Bedi, P., Mewada, S., Vatti, R. A., Singh, C., Dhindsa, K. S., Ponnusamy, M., & Sikarwar, R. (2021). Detection of attacks in IoT sensors networks using machine learning algorithm. Microprocessors and Microsystems, 82, 103814.

6. Meride, Y., & Ayenew, B. (2016). Drinking water quality assessment and its effects on residents' health in Wondo genet campus, Ethiopia. Environmental Systems Research, 5(1), 1–7.

7. Singh, M., & Ahmed, S. (2020). IoT based smart water management systems: A systematic review. Materials Today: Proceedings, 46(11), 5211–5218.

8. Edition, F. (2011). Guidelines for drinking-water quality. WHO Chronicle, 38(4), 104–108.

9. Vallino, E., Ridolfi, L., & Laio, F. (2020). Measuring economic water scarcity in agriculture: A cross-country empirical investigation. Environmental Science & Policy, 114, 73–85.

10. Vasseghian, Y., Almomani, F., & Dragoi, E. N. (2021). Health risk assessment induced by trace toxic metals in tap drinking water: Condorcet principle development. Chemosphere, 286(Pt 2), 131821.

11. Mian, H. R., Hu, G., Hewage, K., Rodriguez, M. J., & Sadiq, R. (2021). Drinking water quality assessment in distribution networks: A water footprint approach. Science of the Total Environment, 775, 145844.

12. Vallejo, W., Diaz-Uribe, C., & Fajardo, C. (2020). Do-it-yourself methodology for calorimeter construction based in Arduino data acquisition device for introductory chemical laboratories. Heliyon, 6(3), e03591.

13. Upton, E., & Halfacree, G. (2014). Raspberry Pi User Guide. John Wiley & Sons, The Atrium, Southern Gate, Chichester, West Sussex, PO19 8SQ, United Kingdom.

14. Media's, E., Syufrijal, & Rif'an, M. (2019). Internet of things (IoT): Blynk framework for smart home. KnE Social Sciences, 3(12), 579–586.

15. Sijini, A. C., Fantin, E., & Ranjit, L. P. (2016). Switched reluctance motor for hybrid electric vehicle. Middle-East Journal of Scientific Research, 24(3), 734–739.

16. Chouhan, A. S., Purohit, N., Annaiah, H., Saravanan, D., Raj, E. F. I., & David, D. S. (2021). A real-time gesture based image classification system with FPGA and convolutional neural network. International Journal of Modern Agriculture, 10(2), 2565–2576.

17. Wang, P., Hafshejani, B. A., & Wang, D. (2021). An improved multilayer perceptron approach for detecting sugarcane yield production in IoT based smart agriculture. Microprocessors and Microsystems, 82, 103822.

18. Thakur, T., et al. (2021). "Smart water conservation through a machine learning and blockchain-enabled decentralized edge computing network." Applied Soft Computing, 106, 107274.

19. Inman, D., & Jeffrey, P. (2006). A review of residential water conservation tool performance and influences on implementation effectiveness. Urban Water Journal, 3(3), 127–143.

20. Appadurai, M., Raj, E. F. I., & Venkadeshwaran, K. (2021). Finite element design and thermal analysis of an induction motor used for a hydraulic pumping system. Materials Today: Proceedings, 45, 7100–7106.

21. Fantin Irudaya Raj, E., & Appadurai, M. (2021). Minimization of Torque Ripple and Incremental of Power Factor in Switched Reluctance Motor Drive. In Recent Trends in Communication and Intelligent Systems: Proceedings of ICRTCIS 2020 (pp. 125–133). Springer, Singapore.

22. Appadurai, M., & Raj, E. (2021). Epoxy/silicon carbide (sic) nanocomposites based small scale wind turbines for urban applications. International Journal of Energy and Environmental Engineering, 13, 191–206.

23. Priyadarsini, K., Raj, E. F. I., Begum, A. Y., & Shanmugasundaram, V. (2020). Comparing DevOps procedures from the context of a systems engineer. Materials Today: Proceedings.

24. Appadurai, M., & Fantin Irudaya Raj, E. (2022). Finite Element Analysis of Lightweight Robot Fingers Actuated by Pneumatic Pressure. In Recent Advances in Manufacturing, Automation, Design and Energy Technologies (pp. 379–385). Springer, Singapore.

25. Raj, E. F. I., & Balaji, M. (2021). Analysis and classification of faults in switched reluctance motors using deep learning neural networks. Arabian Journal for Science and Engineering, 46(2), 1313–1332.

26. Appadurai, M., Raj, E., & Jenish, I. (2021). Application of aluminium oxide–water nanofluids to augment the performance of shallow pond: A numerical study. Process Integration and Optimization for Sustainability, 6, 211–222.

27. Appadurai, M., & Raj, E. F. I. (2021, February). Finite Element Analysis of Composite Wind Turbine Blades. In 2021 7th International Conference on Electrical Energy Systems (ICEES) (pp. 585–589). IEEE.

28. Nguyen, T. T., Ngo, H. H., Guo, W., Wang, X. C., Ren, N., Li, G., & Liang, H. (2019). Implementation of a specific urban water management – Sponge City. Science of the Total Environment, 652, 147–162.

29. Neelakandan, S., Rene Beulah, J., Prathiba, L., Murthy, G. L. N., Irudaya Raj, E. F., & Arulkumar, N. (2022). Blockchain with deep learning-enabled secure healthcare data transmission and diagnostic model. International Journal of Modeling, Simulation, and Scientific Computing, 13(04), 2241006.

30. Koufos, D., & Retsina, T. (2001). Practical energy and water management through pinch analysis for the pulp and paper industry. Water Science and Technology, 43(2), 327–332.

31. Chandrika, V. S., Isaac, J. S., Daniel, J., Kathiresan, K., Muthiah, C. T., Raj, E. F. I., & Subbiah, R. (2021). Experimental investigation of the solar distiller using nano-black paint for different water depths. Materials Today: Proceedings, 56(3), 1406–1410.

32. Sikka, A. K., Islam, A., & Rao, K. V. (2018). Climate-smart land and water management for sustainable agriculture. Irrigation and Drainage, 67(1), 72–81.

33. Raj, E., Appadurai, M., & Athiappan, K. (2021). Precision Farming in Modern Agriculture. In Smart Agriculture Automation Using Advanced Technologies (pp. 61–87). Springer, Singapore.

11

Internet of Things Based on Field Soil Property Prediction System: For Optimally Monitoring the Soil Fertility Status

Aarthi R and Sivakumar D

CONTENTS

11.1 Introduction

The agriculture industry in India needs to increase profitability. Our population growth will exceed 1.7 billion in 2050. Currently, agriculture accounts for about 16 percent of GDP in 2019–2020 and employs 44 percent of the country's workforce closely. Nearly ~300 MT of food grain and horticulture crop output produced in 2019–2020. Despite this, India's agriculture sector suffers from limited land-labor resources, post-harvest losses and lower income [1]. Successful management practices are required to handle agriculture-related issues. Indian agriculture sector needs to concentrate on efficient government policies, farm mechanization and adoption of smart techniques in agro-industries.

IoT concept emerged in different domains, including health monitoring, transport and logistics, digital cities and buildings, industrial applications, consumer wearables, environment and agriculture applications [2]. IoT techniques utilized different fields in agriculture like soil health monitoring, climate monitoring, irrigation control, disease and pest identification, machinery ext. Smart agricultural solutions using IoT are still in the beginning stage of development [3]. This chapter focused on IoT application in soil fertility monitoring. Soil fertility prediction practices help to receive and transfer the energy resources from soil to crop. The soil health status is severely affected in the green revolution era. Our green revolution practices focused on boosting crop yield and production via using agrochemical fertilizers. Overdosage of fertilizer affects the soil's natural balance, and this leads the several environmental degradations. Therefore, soil fertility management practices are required for increasing productivity and maintaining soil balance. The soil fertility prediction helps optimize the fertilizers dosage and minimize nutrient losses. Conventionally, the soil health status is monitored through laboratory soil analysis procedures. Over the decades, wide ranges of Morden technologies developed to predict the soil status and assist farmers for balanced fertilization [4]. IoT technology adopted to construct soil fertility prediction systems in this chapter provides detailed information on each IoT layer for measuring soil properties.

Finally, measured data was monitored through the android mobile phone and tablet. This low-cost prototyping system helps the cultivators and gardeners with crop recommendations for on-field monitoring. The sections are organized as follows: Section 11.2 discusses the related works presenting IoT adoption in the agro-industries. Section 11.3 provides the soil property prediction system with an IoT architecture. Section 11.4 discusses real-time implementation. The final section represents the conclusion and references.

11.2 Relevant Works

The following section examines the literature survey of IoT techniques implementation in various agricultural applications. Tzounis et al. proposed the literature regarding IoT adoption in agriculture sectors and identified potential IoT farming opportunities and obstacles to agricultural prospects and challenges [5]. Kaloxylos et al. discuss a farm management system and address methods for making the architecture a reality and analyzing the Internet in future farming [6]. Muangprathub et al. developed the optimal irrigation management system adopting the WSN. And field data is managed and controlled via smartphone. The final method demonstrates that the soil wetness was correctly maintained for vegetable development, lowering expenses and enhancing agricultural productivity [7]. Zhang et al. developed the IoT-based soil humidity and nutrient measurement prototype to estimate the citrus orchard nutrient status. The resulting prototype boosts citrus yield while lowering labor costs and minimizing environmental pollution [8]. Singh et al. built the Agri-info system to deliver agriculture-related information through a cloud server and smart technologies. The author has created a webpage and phone application to track the small-scale agriculture application and conduct the field implementation in Indian villages [9]. Shabandri et al. upgrade a smart tree management system for densely populated areas and metropolitan areas. The system tracks the important tree attributes like air quality, sunlight level and sound pollution level. This application result helps to increase urban afforestation [10]. Bartlett et al. designed the water irrigation scheduling for efficient application (WISE) for irrigation management. A digital phone application helps to keep records of the soil moisture deficit, meteorological measurements and required irrigation volume [11]. Angelopoulos et al. implement optimized irrigation management practices in the strawberry greenhouse environment in Greece. The smart strawberry irrigation system outperforms the regular strawberry irrigation system regarding soil humidity, water usage and performance. Sensor devices are the prime component for any

IoT project [12]. This study report explored the numerous IoT sensors for agriculture applications and the benefits and drawbacks of using sensors technologies in agriculture industries [13]. Ajith et al. designed an intelligent polyhouse-based irrigation system employing the Intel Galileo board. It helps to record the polyhouse environment's temperature, moisture, humidity and light intensity [14].

11.3 System Architecture

Farmers avoid financial losses by maintaining a balanced soil fertility state. Soil testing helps to identify soil fertility status and predicts the nutrient as stated by the crop requirement. The soil fertility prediction system is built using a four-layer IoT architecture. They are named as (i) Agro sensor module (sensing layer), (ii) Agro gateway module (communication layer), (iii) Smart analyzing and monitoring server (service layer) and (iv) Graphical user remote view application (application layer). The soil fertility prediction system predicts soil pH, electrical conductivity (salinity), soil temperature and soil moisture (humidity) content. Figure 11.1 depicts the IoT architecture of the soil fertility prediction system.

11.3.1 Agro Sensor Module

The agro sensor unit is a segment of the sensing layer in IoT architecture, it includes the sensors and controllers. The important soil properties used for soil fertility prediction are soil pH, EC, humidity and temperature. Multiple sensors include DFRobote analog pH sensor, DFRobote analog EC sensor and SHT10 sensors adopted for prototyping implementation. The Arduino UNO R3 microcontroller is adopted to integrate these sensors.

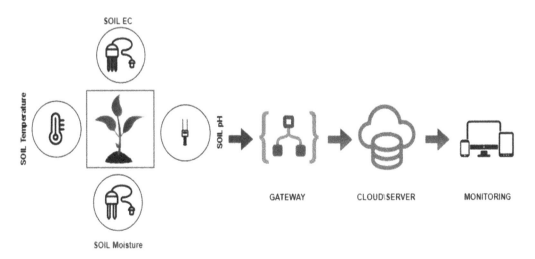

FIGURE 11.1
IoT architecture for soil fertility prediction system.

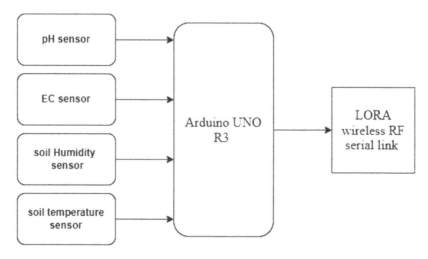

FIGURE 11.2
Sensing unit block diagram.

For data transmission, the LoRa (Long Range) wireless radio frequency serial link is employed. The block diagram of the sensing unit is illustrated in Figure 11.2.

The calibration process provides the accurate analysis of sensors. Soil pH and EC sensors are tested via a soil sampling procedure, and SHT10 sensors are analyzed through direct field measurement. Figure 11.3 represents the photograph of the sensing unit.

Figure 11.4 depicts the flowchart of a soil properties prediction system. The controller read the value from pH, EC, SHT10 sensors. The received soil ranges subsequently forwarded to the gateway module through the LoRa transceiver. The same process is continuous at every sensing process.

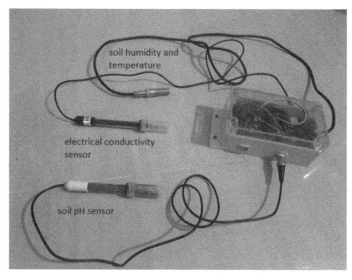

FIGURE 11.3
Prototype of sensing unit.

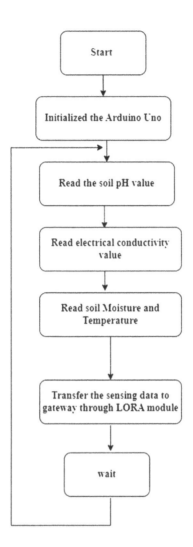

FIGURE 11.4
Sensing unit block diagram.

11.3.2 Agro Sensor Gateway Module

The gateway module provides a connection between the sensor and service layers. A wired or wireless network used as communication medium [15]. Figure 11.5 represents the working processes of the gateway unit. The primary advantages of utilizing the IoT gateway are that it extends battery life, filters and pre-processes the raw sensor data, security to a sensor, increasing the processing speed ext [16].

For the soil fertility prediction system, the Raspberry Pi 4 has been chosen as the gateway device. WIR-1286 LoRa module provides wireless communication between the sensing and gateway module. Python language used as programing unit in Raspberry Pi 4 module. Figure 11.6 represents the photograph of the gateway unit. The WIR-2186 transceiver module receives the signal from the physical layer. Then the collected dataset is forwarded to the server through the wife dongle. The gateway unit pushes the received data to the cloud by MQTT protocol using the Wi-Fi dongle. A cloudMQTT server helps to store the data.

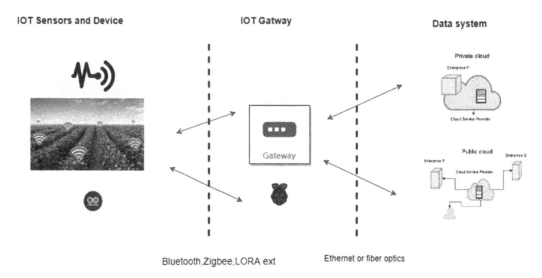

FIGURE 11.5
IoT gateway unit.

FIGURE 11.6
Gateway unit.

11.3.3 Smart Analyzing and Monitoring Server

The middleware layer is monitoring the server in IoT design. This unit receives the information from the gateway and stores received data in the server. It ensures that legitimate users send information and provide security from threats. It ensures that only authorized users submit data, provide security, and are stored on a cloud server. Figure 11.7 illustrates the MQTT protocol working for soil fertility prediction.

CloudMQTT is adopted for soil property prediction system. The cloudMQTT is managed by a mosquito platform. And cloudMQTT is a popular MQTT broker that provides multiple security measures. The user must create a customer account for utilizing the cloudMQTT. Keen Koala plan used for proposed work, it's a popular plan for small-scale IoT project. The publisher sends the massage by a topic to the broker. Subscribers also send a topic to the broker when they are interested. Using the client publish/subscribe request, the broker sends corresponding information.

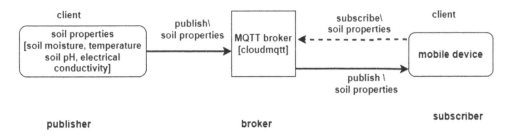

FIGURE 11.7
MQTT protocol for soil fertility prediction.

11.3.4 User Application

Mobile technologies upgraded rapidly and were adopted in healthcare, education, agriculture because of simplicity and budget-friendly. The soil fertility is monitored using a mobile application called "soil monitoring." The application was analyzed on android phones and tablets. Figure 11.8 illustrates the screen short of application screen. The soil monitoring application provides the temperature, pH, moisture and salinity details. The application gives suitable crop recommendations and salinity information using the measured ranges.

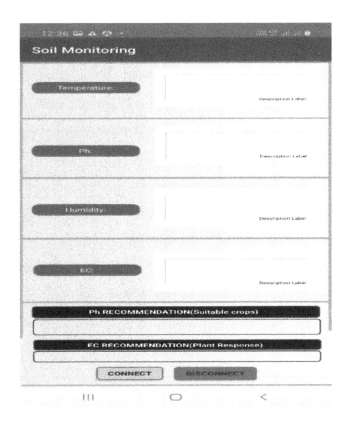

FIGURE 11.8
Soil monitoring application in android phone.

11.4 Result and Analysis

The soil fertility prediction prototype is analyzed on different agriculture fields in jayankondam block, Ariyular district. For on-field soil analysis, a USB power supply powers the Arduino controller. The measured data is carried to the Arduino controller to the agro-gateway unit using the WIR-1286 LoRa wireless transmitter. The prototype was installed and tested in the field, as represented in Figure 11.9.

The Wi-Fi (Wireless Fidelity) dongle was employed for data transfer to a cloud server. The gateway module transfers information to the cloudMQTT. Python language establishes an MQTT connection in Raspberry Pi and the cloudMQTT platform. Within a minute, the data is forwarded to the cloudMQTT platform. Figure 11.10 illustrates the cloudMQTT server receiving the data.

FIGURE 11.9
Direct field soil monitoring and analysis.

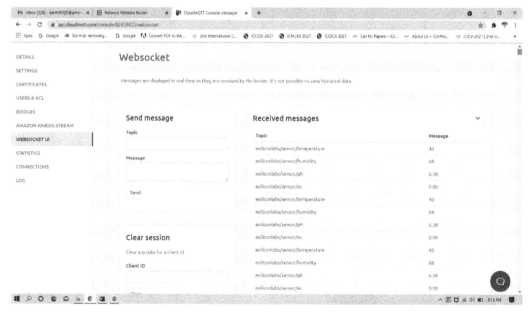

FIGURE 11.10
Sensed data monitor through cloudMQTT server.

For a non-technical person, monitoring the collected information via a cloudMQTT server is a complex task. Hence, the mobile application was created to obtain the soil property easily. The "soil monitoring" android application also makes specific recommendations, such as crop recommendation and soil salinity status based on sensed data. Figure 11.11 illustrates the mobile application view corresponding soil field testing. The soil monitoring mobile application recommends the crop and provides soil salinity details using the soil EC ranges.

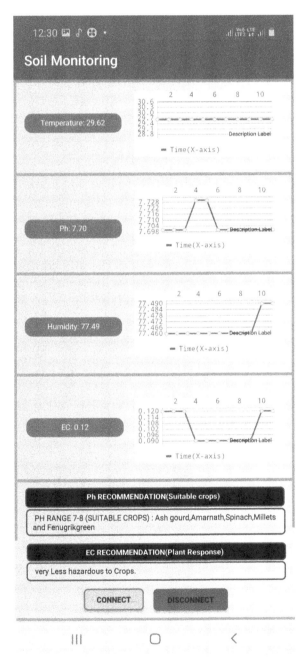

FIGURE 11.11
Android application view for corresponding field testing.

TABLE 11.1

On-Field Soil Sample Measurement

| S. No. | Sensor Value | | Crop Recommendation | Crop Response |
	EC (dsm⁻¹)	pH		
1	0.15	7.3	Most of veggies and greens, sugarcane, paddy	Very low hazardous
2	0.60	6.2	Most of veggies and greens, sugarcane, paddy	Very low hazardous
3	0.15	7.4	Most of veggies and greens, sugarcane, paddy	Very low hazardous
4	0.59	7.2	Most of veggies and greens, sugarcane, paddy	Very low hazardous
5	0.31	6.9	Most of veggies and greens, sugarcane, paddy	Very low hazardous
6	0.34	7.5	Most of veggies and greens, sugarcane, paddy	Very low hazardous
7	0.30	7.9	Most of veggies and greens, sugarcane, paddy	Very low hazardous
8	2.18	8.5	Pineapple, cabbage, beets, flowers, spices	Medium hazardous
9	0.46	7.7	Most of veggies and greens, sugarcane, paddy, peanuts	Very low hazardous
10	1.04	6.1	Sweet potato, corn cotton, peanuts, soybean	Low hazardous

Around ten different spots are predicted in 1 ha of agriculture field, and bare soil samples analyzed. Table 11.1 represents the on-field soil sample collection and analysis.

To check prototype accuracy, the collected sample was analyzed in an authorized soil testing laboratory. Comparison between laboratory analysis and sensor value for soil pH is represented in Figure 11.12. Similarly, Figure 11.13 represents the comparison between the laboratory analysis and sensor values for soil electrical conductivity.

Further, the temperature and wetness parameter help the fertigation and irrigation practices. The dataset is applied for gardening applications. This proposed site-specific

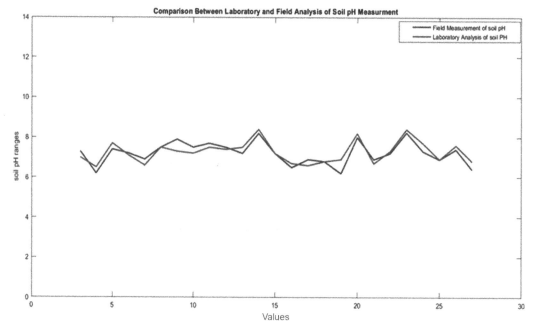

FIGURE 11.12

Comparison between laboratory and field analysis of soil pH.

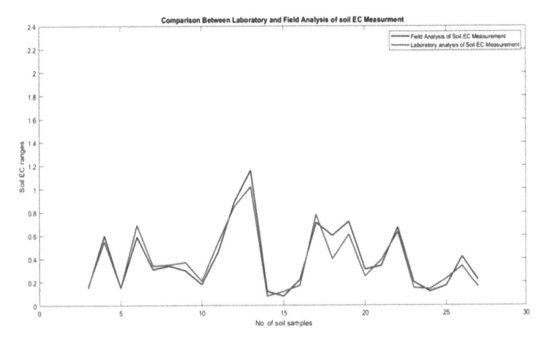

FIGURE 11.13
Comparison between laboratory and field analysis of soil EC.

soil property prediction model is efficient than the small-scale meters. And the one-time initial investment is only required. The production cost for a portable soil fertility prediction system is around 38,000 Indian rupees.

11.5 Conclusion

For real-time analysis, an IoT-based soil fertility prediction system is created and implemented. By utilizing this prototype, farmers and gardeners can predict the soil fertility level by directly analyzing the soil status through remote view applications. This proposed prototype predicts the essential soil properties. The final experimental result is applicable for gardening and field analysis monitoring to obtain the balanced soil fertility status and reduce soil contamination. The prototype can be expanded to monitor additional soil properties like soil texture and nutrient measurement, climate prediction in future analysis. The additional implementation is implemented mobile applications like fertilizer recommendation and fertigation control.

References

1. **2021**. IoT Adoption in Indian Agriculture: A **2020** Landscape. https://nasscom.in/iot-adoption-Indian-agriculture-2020-landscape.
2. Khanna, A., & Kaur, S., **2020**. Internet of Things (IoT), Applications and Challenges: A Comprehensive Review. Wireless Personal Communications, 114 (2). https://doi.org/10.1007/s11277-020-07446-4.

3. Ayaz, M., Ammad-Uddin, M., Sharif, Z., Mansour, A., & Aggoune, E.-H. M., **2019**. Internet-of-Things (IoT)-Based Smart Agriculture: Toward Making the Fields Talk. IEEE Access, 7, pp. 129551–129583. https://doi.org/10.1109/ACCESS.2019.2932609.

4. Havlin, J., & Heiniger, R., **2020**. Soil Fertility Management for Better Crop Production. Agronomy, 10(9). https://doi.org/10.3390/agronomy10091349.

5. Tzounis, A., Katsoulas, N., Bartzanas, T., & Kittas, C., **2017**. Internet of Things in Agriculture, Recent Advances and Future Challenges. Biosystems Engineering, 164. https://doi.org/10.1016/j.biosystemseng.2017.09.007.

6. Kaloxylos, A., Eigenmann, R., Teye, F., Politopoulou, Z., Wolfert, S., Shrank, C., Dillinger, M., Lampropoulou, I., Antoniou, E., Pesonen, L., Nicole, H., Thomas, F., Alonistioti, N., & Kormentzas, G., **2012**. Farm Management Systems and the Future Internet Era. Computers and Electronics in Agriculture, 89, pp. 130–144. https://doi.org/10.1016/j.compag.2012.09.002.

7. Muangprathub, J., Boonnam, N., Kajornkasirat, S., Lekbangpong, N., Wanichsombat, A., & Nillaor, P., **2019**. IoT and Agriculture Data Analysis for Smart Farm. Computers and Electronics in Agriculture, 156 (January), pp. 467–74. https://doi.org/10.1016/j.compag.2018.12.011.

8. Zhang, X., Zhang, J., Li, L., Zhang, Y., & Yang, G., **2017**. Monitoring CitrusSoil Moisture and Nutrients Using an IoT Based System. Sensors (Switzerland) 17 (3). https://doi.org/10.3390/s17030447.

9. Singh, S., Chana, I., & Buyya, R., **2020**. Agri-Info: Cloud Based Autonomic System for Delivering Agriculture as a Service. Internet of Things, 9. https://doi.org/10.1016/j.iot.2019.100131.

10. Shabandri, B., Reddy Madara, S., & Maheshwari, P., **2020**. IoT-Based Smart Tree Management Solution for Green Cities. In Internet of Things and Analytics for Agriculture, 2, pp. 181–199. https://doi.org/10.1007/978-981-15-0663-5_9.

11. Bartlett, A.C., Andales, A.A., Arabi, M., & Bauder, T.A., **2015**. A Smartphone App to Extend Use of a Cloud-Based Irrigation Scheduling Tool. Computers and Electronics in Agriculture, 111 (February), pp. 127–130. https://doi.org/10.1016/j.compag.2014.12.021.

12. Angelopoulos, C.M., Filios, G., Nikoletseas, S., & Raptis, T.P., **2020**. Keeping Data at the Edge of Smart Irrigation Networks: A Case Study in Strawberry Greenhouses. Computer Networks, 167 (2020), p. 107039.

13. Ratnaparkhi, S., Khan, S., Arya, C., Khapre, S., Singh, P., Diwakar, M., & Shankar, A. **2020**. Smart Agriculture Sensors in IOT: A Review. Materials Today: Proceedings. https://doi.org/10.1016/j.matpr.2020.11.138.

14. Ajith, G.S., Girija, M.G., & Devis, J., **2020**. Poly House Environment Monitoring System Using Intel Galileo and Sensor Network Based on IoT. Materials Today: Proceedings, 24(3), pp. 1898–1902. https://doi.org/10.1016/j.matpr.2020.03.615.

15. Glória, A., Cercas, F., & Souto, N., **2017**. Design and Implementation of an IoT Gateway to Create Smart Environments. Procedia Computer Science, 109, pp. 568–575.

16. Guoqiang, S., Yanming, C., Chao, Z., & Yanxu, Z., **2013**. Design and Implementation of a Smart IoT Gateway. In 2013 IEEE International Conference on Green Computing and Communications and IEEE Internet of Things and IEEE Cyber, Physical and Social Computing. IEEE. pp. 720–723.

12

Sanjaya: An Internet of Things-Based Wireless Performance Testing of Photovoltaic Module

Harshil Sathwara and Smita Joshi

CONTENTS

12.1 Introduction

Modern industry mostly uses traditional sources of energy, such as coal, oil, natural gas, and uranium. All these can threaten human life by not treating air pollution, climate change, or nuclear waste. Solar power, among renewable energy sources, is regarded as the most intriguing source for balancing production and consumption. India has a plentiful amount of solar energy, getting over 5,000 trillion kWh per year, with most areas receiving 4–7 kWh per sq. m on a daily basis. India can successfully utilise solar photovoltaic (PV) electricity, enabling tremendous scalability ("Ministry of New and Renewable Energy, Government of India, Overview," n.d.). PV systems are the major application of solar energy. This system comprises solar panels that directly transform solar energy into electricity (*Springer Handbook of Electronic and Photonic Materials* 2007). PV is one of the best possible renewable energy sources because of its unique properties, such as ease of installation, high reliability, minimal maintenance expenses, and zero fuel expenditures (Chine et al. 2014). However, because of the variable nature of solar radiation, the quantity of energy generated by the system is sometimes uncertain. The PV systems' generated

DOI: 10.1201/9781003226888-12

energy relies on ambient circumstances, such as temperature, solar irradiation, sunlight direction, and spectrum (Singh 2013). The PV panel features are delivered by the manufacturers under standard test conditions (Eltawil and Zhao 2010). However, under normal test circumstances, the PV properties are unknown. Therefore, it is necessary to measure the PV properties, which is why several typical types of equipment like multimeters, pyranometers, and anemometers are employed in this context. It is difficult to interpret correctly by humans when the temperature or sunlight is changing quickly. A few samples can thus be recorded, and hence not enough information about the status of the PV systems may be found and traced manually. As more rooftop solar PV systems are linked into the current grid, there is an increasing demand for real-time generating data from solar PV plants to be monitored in order to improve their overall performance. Continuous real-time monitoring of the solar system's output power is critical. It aids in the acquisition of previously unseen insights regarding dynamic behaviour and interactions. Furthermore, it can avoid the costly and time-consuming field testing required to analyse the dynamic parameters of a PV system (Syafaruddin, Karatepe, and Hiyama 2009). To increase the total energy produced by a PV system, precautions must be taken during installation. There is still a danger of failure or maintenance when a solar system is installed at a distance or at a high height. A suitable frequent monitoring mechanism is necessary if the power output from the panel is to be effective. Manual inquiry and remote wired surveillance are the most common methods of system monitoring. The disadvantages of these techniques, such as overtime and cable complexity, are noted (Raza and Ikram 2016). The PV system may potentially be poorly performing due to dust build-up and other environmental factors. It is extremely tough to monitor such failures for people since they often need to visit the location and keep operational data records. The errors can sometimes not be corrected if the system is not adequately educated or poorly functional. In addition to the PV system, a continuous monitoring system must be installed so that the system parameters may be monitored and stored in the cloud. This makes it possible to resolve problems and to undertake maintenance when the performance is poor due to certain failures. The simplest solution to resolve such a problem is to use the "Internet of Things," often known as the "IoT," for remote system monitoring. The Internet of Things (IoT) is important in people's daily lives because it allows them to link a variety of physical items to the internet. It allows things to be identified and controlled from a distance using current network infrastructure. Furthermore, IoT applications allow machines or devices to communicate without the need for human intervention, enhancing efficiency, accuracy, and economic value.

12.2 Literature Review

The study has been done to dynamically resize the renewable energy load in a sophisticated solar power management system. It accommodates solar PV power fluctuations throughout time, as well as automated load switching, advanced remote control, and priority-based system switching (Tiwari and Patel 2016). An IoT-based project solution is meant to achieve optimal power production during the accumulation of dust from solar panels. The monitoring system is meant to ensure that the solar panels are failing, and it is also possible to obtain information as to whether the solar or battery is linked to the cargo. It also shows those parameters to the user via an effective Graphical User Interface (GUI) and notifies the user of certain output limitations (Babu et al. 2018). There are systems available for the measurement of voltage, current, temperature, and solar radiation values. The Arduino ATMega2560 microcontroller recorded the data, which was then posted to the internet using the NodeMCU ESP8266 wireless transmitter. The ThinkSpeak open-source IoT cloud platform is used to store and display all sensor data so that the user may watch it remotely whenever an internet connection is available. Monitoring may be done using the ThinkSpeak website or through the MIT App Inventor smartphone app (Priharti, Rosmawati, and Wibawa 2019). Effective modelling of solar systems has been an essential method of monitoring output behaviour. The modelling of a 30 kW PV facility in China was suggested as an iterative technique for the time variables (Wang, Li, and Li 2012). The Macau real-time power and energy prediction model for a grid PV system is provided, based upon the projected power/irradiance ratio (Su et al. 2012). Using cloud data recording with LabVIEW-based monitoring system, PV performance indicators were tracked and processed ubiquitously in several research projects (Chouder et al. 2013). The use of Arduino and Excel to create a low-cost virtual instrumentation system for PV panel attributes is explained. The proposed system may track and save data from the PV system in real time. This tool is also confirmed in the study by comparing experimental data with data from a Physical Security Information Management (PSIM) PV model that has been verified by other researchers in their investigations (Hammoumi et al. 2018). Moreover, a cost-efficient IoT technology has been proposed to remotely monitor a solar system's maximum power point (MPP) (Rouibah et al. 2019). Research has been done on the measurement of incident solar irradiation with the help of silicon solar cells (Bonner and Sapsford 1966). Because PV panels are sensitive to environmental conditions, such as irradiance and temperature, electrical data and meteorological information are considered critical for the testing of PV stations. As a result, it is critical to closely monitor the operation of all PV systems, to handle concerns promptly, and to maintain them if performance is poor owing to certain flaws.

12.3 Methodology

12.3.1 Hardware Assembly and Explanation

Figures 12.1 and 12.2 show the circuit diagram and experimental set-up, respectively. The required components have been tabulated as shown in Table 12.1. The conversion from INR to USD was done as per the rate on July 12, 2021. Hence, one can see that the design is quite affordable not only for the common man and other PV module owners, but also useful for various start-ups and innovators too, since all the required primary data can be obtained from the same. The set-up uses a 20-W multi-crystalline solar panel for the experiment apart from two INA219 current-voltage sensors, a DHT11 sensor, a solar cell (4 V, 100 mA), a 10k ohm rotary potentiometer, and NodeMCU. Both the INA219 sensors, the DHT-11 sensor and the NodeMCU, are given a 5V external supply. As shown in Figure 12.1, the data pin of the DHT11 sensor is connected to the D5 pin of the NodeMCU for communication between the sensor and the microcontroller. INA219 communicates with NodeMCU through I2C; hence, the SCL and SDA pins of INA219 are connected to D1 and D2 of NodeMCU, respectively. The other INA219 sensor has an I2C address (0×41) that is connected to the solar cell for measuring irradiation, while the other INA219 sensor has an I2C address (0×40) that has its positive Vin pin connected to the positive terminal of the solar panel, and the negative

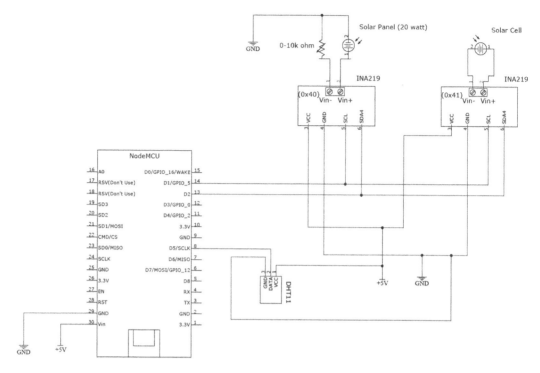

FIGURE 12.1
Circuit diagram of the Sanjaya.

FIGURE 12.2
Experimental set-up of Sanjaya.

TABLE 12.1

Costing of Components Used in Sanjaya

Serial Number	Component	Cost in INR	Cost in USD
1	Solar Panel (20 W multicrystalline)	710.00	9.53
2	NodeMCU (ESP8266)	250.00	3.36
3	Solar Cell	150.00	2.01
4	INA219 (0×40)	150.00	2.01
5	INA219 (0×41)	150.00	2.01
6	DHT11	110.00	1.48
7	Breadboard, Jumper Wires	100.00	1.34
	5V, 1A adapter and rotary potentiometer	100.00	1.34
	Total	1720.00	23.09

Vin pin is connected to one of the fixed ends of the 10k ohm rotary potentiometer, which is used as a rheostat. This rotary potentiometer is used as a rheostat and has its angle varied from 0 to 300 degrees, thus varying its resistance from 0 ohms to 10k ohms, respectively. Hence, by varying the rheostat/load, various parameters can be plotted. All the data from the sensors is given to NodeMCU. This NodeMCU is connected to the Wi-Fi, thus connecting with the Adafruit IO cloud too. Here, the Adafruit IO cloud service has been used. The dashboard is created in the service, and a live chart widget is linked with voltage, current, insolation, temperature, and humidity feeds. The Wi-Fi module sends the data to Adafruit IO from NodeMCU, which will allow the user to monitor various parameters. One can draw I-V and P-V characteristics with the presented design with the pre-defined procedure as well as connect the load which is required to be monitored by simply replacing the rotary potentiometer with the load. Figure 12.3 shows a block diagram of the presented set-up.

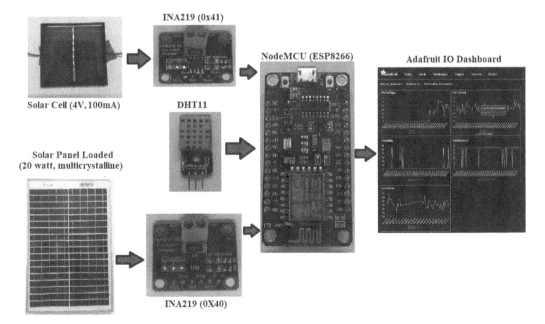

FIGURE 12.3
Block diagram of Sanjaya.

12.3.2 Working Procedure

Figure 12.4 shows the flow chart of the presented system, explaining the working procedure. Initially, a 5V external supply is given to the sensors and NodeMCU to begin the process. NodeMCU is trying to connect with Wi-Fi. If it is not connected, then it will continue trying, and if connected, then it will proceed further. Later, the MQTT client class is set up, followed by the initialization of both INA219 sensors. Through Wi-Fi, Adafruit IO services

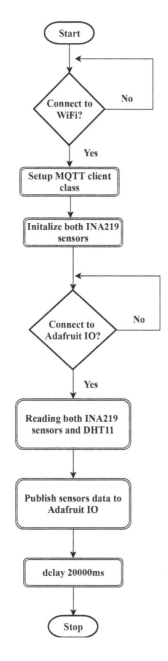

FIGURE 12.4
Flowchart of Sanjaya.

are trying to connect, and if it gets connected, it performs the next iteration or else it will continue connecting to Wi-Fi. The temperature and humidity readings from the DHT11 sensor, voltage and current reading from INA219 (0 × 40) sensor and insolation reading from the INA219 (0 × 41) sensor, after successful communication with NodeMCU, are published to Adafruit IO cloud service through the established connection. The published data are then visible on the dashboard created in Adafruit. Then a delay of 20,000 ms has been given after which it will stop and repeat the procedure. Thus, after each 20,000 ms, individual feeds are refreshed, and the chart starts updating. The uploaded data can be downloaded in either JSON or Excel format, and the analysis can be done.

12.4 Results and Discussion

12.4.1 Solar Cell Calibration

Figures 12.5 and 12.6 give a graphical representation of the I-V and P-V characteristics of the solar cell, whereas Figure 12.7 shows the experimental set-up for determining solar cell characteristics. The data was plotted using MATLAB®. Here, the solar cell is calibrated to work as a pyranometer to measure solar irradiance (Tan, Tai, and Mok 2013). The short circuit current of the solar cell is measured using an INA219 sensor with an I2C address (0 × 41) and solar irradiance is estimated with acceptable accuracy. Thus, the installation of an expensive pyranometer is avoided, bringing down the cost of the overall system. With the help of the linear regression analysis facility in MATLAB (Jiang 2013), a linear equation was found between the short circuit current of the solar cell and irradiance. Figure 12.8 shows the linear regression graph between the short circuit current of solar cells and irradiance measured using a pyranometer. The derived linear equation is then entered into the programme

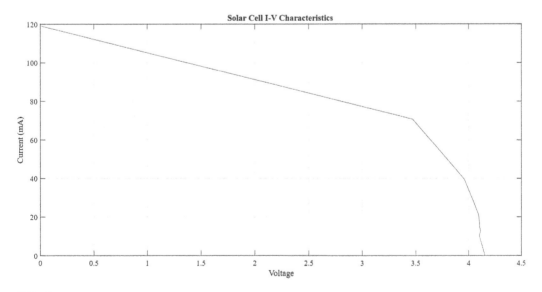

FIGURE 12.5
I-V characteristic of solar cell.

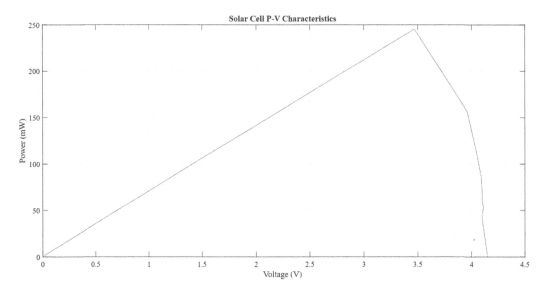

FIGURE 12.6
P-V characteristic of solar cell.

such that the short circuit current of a solar cell measured using the INA219 sensor with an I2C address (0×41) gives solar irradiance.

Table 12.2 gives information about the short circuit current from the solar cell, the actual insolation measured using a pyranometer, the estimated insolation with the help of a calibrated solar cell, and the error (%). From Table 12.2, it can be observed that the derived results are in good agreement up to the acceptable limit. With the consideration of the

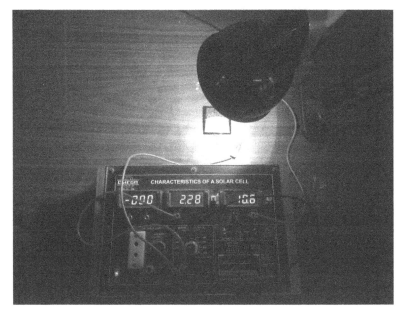

FIGURE 12.7
Experimental set-up to determine characteristics of solar cell.

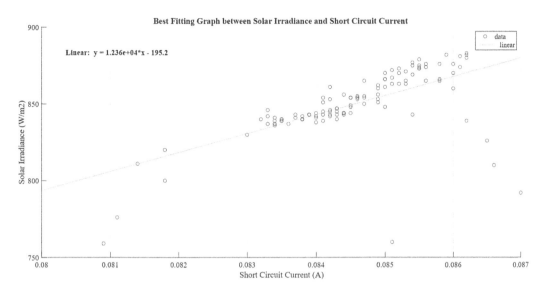

FIGURE 12.8
Linear regression graph with equation for calibrating solar cell.

TABLE 12.2

Comparison Table of Readings of Solar Cell and Pyranometer

Short Circuit Current of Solar Cell (A)	Actual Insolation (W/m²)	Estimated Insolation (W/m²)	Error (%)
0.0849	866	856.95	1.05
0.0851	867	859.42	0.87
0.0851	866	859.42	0.76
0.0856	873	865.60	0.85
0.0853	878	861.89	1.83
0.0854	877	863.13	1.58
0.0854	879	863.13	1.81
0.0858	880	868.07	1.36
0.0858	882	868.07	1.58
0.0857	884	866.84	1.94
0.0861	889	871.78	1.94

temperature coefficients and other atmospheric parameters in the solar cell, the suggested solar irradiance estimating process accuracy may be further enhanced.

12.4.2 Results of Monitored Solar Panel Parameters and Ambient Environment

Figures 12.9–12.13 give the graphical representation of monitored voltage, current, insolation, ambient temperature, and humidity, respectively. The data collection was done on June 26, 2021, at Anand Agricultural University with coordinates of 22.53° North and 72.98° East from 10:00 hours to 18:30 hours (IST). Here, the 10k ohm load was fixed with a rotary potentiometer (Figure 12.1) that has been used for monitoring purposes. The data was sent to the Adafruit IO cloud every 20 seconds and was then downloaded in Excel file format for analysis (Elliott et al. 2006). The prepared data was then imported into MATLAB and graphs were plotted.

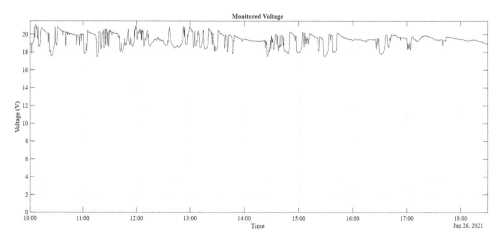

FIGURE 12.9
Voltage graph monitored using Sanjaya.

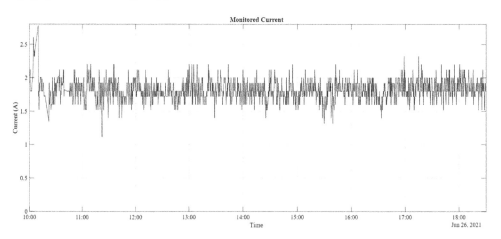

FIGURE 12.10
Current graph monitored using Sanjaya.

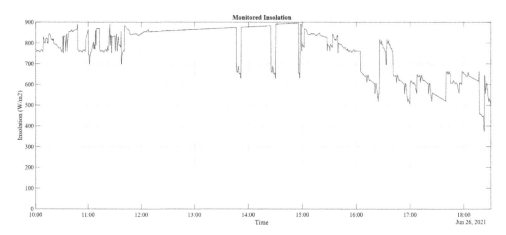

FIGURE 12.11
Insolation graph monitored using Sanjaya.

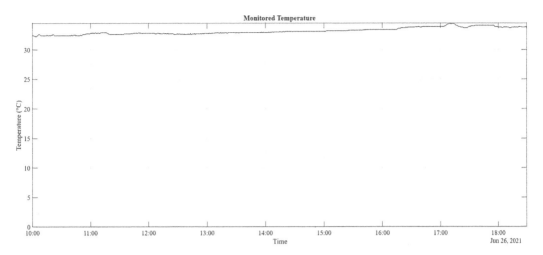

FIGURE 12.12
Temperature graph monitored using Sanjaya.

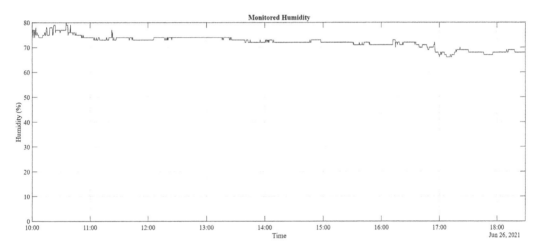

FIGURE 12.13
Humidity graph monitored using Sanjaya.

12.4.3 Solar Panel I-V and P-V Characteristics

Figures 12.14 and 12.15 show the I-V and P-V characteristics of the 20-W multi-crystal-line solar panel. The conversion efficiency is calculated by multiplying the cell-generated power (W) by the input light irradiance (W/m²) and solar cell surface area under standard test conditions (STC: 1000 W/m² at 25°C) (m²). As a result, the efficiency of conversion is dependent on a number of factors, including irradiation and temperature. Even with the same type of cell, the manufacturing process might cause electrical parameter variances. Furthermore, if losses due to cell connections are considered in a module, it is unusual to find two identical PV modules. STC is a rating system used by PV module manufacturers to assess their products. On the ground, though, such occurrences are rare. The evaluation of a module's electrical properties necessitates the transfer of these qualities to external settings, the behaviour of which cannot be predicted properly in real-world operation (i.e., the actual production of the PV facility). Finally, the actual temporal deterioration of a PV

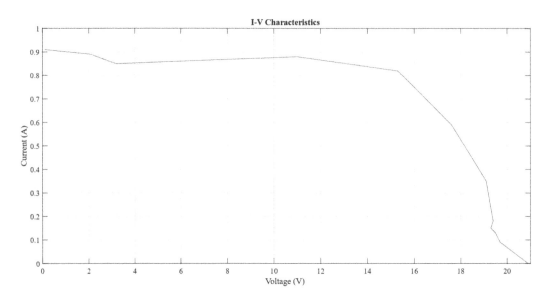

FIGURE 12.14
I-V characteristics of solar panel.

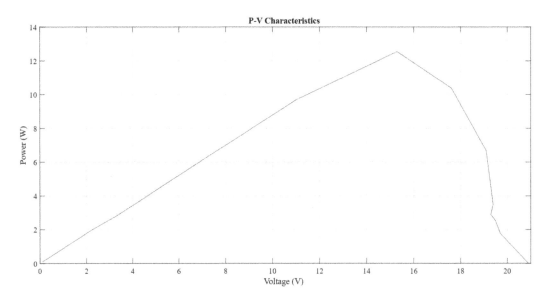

FIGURE 12.15
P-V characteristics of solar panel.

plant module allows for accurate output projections and even claims for overly uncovered damage, all of which can be examined over time. In light of this, the only way to accurately determine the electrical characteristics of a PV cell, module, or array is to measure the I-V and P-V curves experimentally (Durán et al. 2012). At 70% humidity and 33°C ambient temperature, the data was collected on June 24, 2021, at 13:00 hours on the same coordinates. Thus, in this manner, the data can be collected, plotted, and analysis can be done using MATLAB (Wang and Shen 2018).

TABLE 12.3

Readings to Determine Characteristics of Solar Panel

Time	Voltage (V)	Current (A)	Insolation (W/m²)	Output Power (W)
13:00:00	20.9	0	860	0.00
13:00:20	19.7	0.09	865	1.77
13:00:40	19.6	0.11	866	2.16
13:01:00	19.5	0.13	866	2.54
13:00:20	19.4	0.14	870	2.72
13:00:40	19.3	0.15	874	2.90
13:02:00	19.4	0.18	875	3.49
13:00:00	19.1	0.35	876	6.69
13:00:20	17.6	0.59	876	10.38
13:00:40	15.3	0.82	875	12.55
13:03:00	11	0.88	874	9.68
13:00:00	3.2	0.85	873	2.72
13:00:20	2.1	0.89	870	1.87
13:00:40	0.1	0.91	872	0.09

Table 12.3 shows the data collected from the presented system, which includes voltage, current, and insolation measured with a calibrated solar cell, the output power of the solar panel, and the efficiency. From Table 12.2, it shall be noted that the open-circuit voltage is found to be 20.9 V, the short circuit current to be 0.91 A, the maximum power output to be 12.55 W, and maximum efficiency was found to be 10.24% at MPP. Thus, from the collected data, one can calculate various other solar panel parameters too. The max voltage is found to be 19.7 V and the max current to be 0.89 apere. Thus, from these, the fill factor is found to be 95% (Rusirawan and Farkas 2014).

12.5 Applications

1. Data scientists and other enthusiasts can use the collected data for forecasting applications.

2. Direct or wireless transfer of PV characteristic experiment data, thus reducing chances of errors, manpower utilised to perform the same task, and hence proper utilisation of time and energy.

3. One can get information about voltage, current, output power (a multiplication product of measured voltage and current), solar radiation, temperature, and humidity of that particular latitude. As a result, it is possible to conduct research on the effects of various parameters on the performance of solar panels.

4. To analyse for forecasting and foresight of future generating options, revenue, etc. IoT allows for continuous recording of performance.

5. The installation minimises the difficult task of often visiting the site, collecting the performance data and troubleshooting. Therefore, it reduces interactions between users and computers when monitoring the PV system.

12.6 Future Scope

This technology could be improved and expanded to allow PV systems to detect faults and include dust sensors that trigger the robot to clean the panel, a solar charge controller with Maximum Power Point Tracking (MPPT) for low-power solar applications, and the use of wireless sensing for solar power systems to improve system accuracy (Hashim et al. 2019) (Abuzairi, Ramadhan, and Devara 2019) (Kyi and Taparugssanagorn 2019). During the display, indicating any issue that might arise on PV systems, several thresholds and message systems can be combined with it. Various pressure and airflow sensors can be integrated in order to study the effects of pressure and airflow on the performance of PV parameters.

12.7 Conclusion

Monitoring the solar module with IoT is an important step in the daily integration of renewable energy sources into the grid. This will aid future decision-making for large-scale solar power plants and solar module grid integration. This article discusses a solar panel remote monitoring system based on the IoT. A system for transferring remote data to a server for supervision has been explored, developed, and implemented. The Adafruit IO cloud service interface will drastically reduce manual monitoring time. The results of the tests demonstrate that the developed monitoring system provides a web-based interface through which users may navigate PV array data in real-time, such as PV array current and voltages, ambient temperature, humidity, and solar radiation at these exact coordinates. The short circuit current from the solar cell can also be used to estimate the sun's irradiance with reasonable accuracy. Due to the installation of a costly pyranometer to watch solar radiation, this leads to the elimination of PV system performance monitoring and efficiency assessment. The project's main benefits are reduced human involvement, real-time monitoring and historical data processing, low costs, and ease of implementation. Substitute human interaction with multimeter data readings to reduce errors and save time, energy, and money. As a result, the proposed method can make the assimilation and recording of data, as well as the production and customization of reports, easier to improve the performance of solar systems.

Acknowledgement

The authors wish to thank Dr. H. B. Soni, principal GCET, and Dr. Ritesh Patel, HOD Electrical Department. The authors also wish to thank IIT Bombay and MNRE for providing the solar panel kit. The G.H. Patel College of Engineering and Technology's Student Start-Up Innovation Program (SSIP) Cell is grateful for providing a grant of INR 35,000/- (ID-GCETSSIP2021-22EE02) to set up the project and conduct the experiment.

References

Abuzairi, T., W. W. A. Ramadhan, and K. Devara. 2019. "Solar Charge Controller with Maximum Power Point Tracking for Low-Power Solar Applications." *International Journal of Photoenergy* 2019. doi:10.1155/2019/5026464.

Babu, R., L. R. Lokesh, D. Rambabu, A. R. Naidu, R. D. Prasad, and P. Gopi Krishna. 2018. "IoT Enabled Solar Power Monitoring System." *International Journal of Engineering and Technology(UAE)* 7 (3.12 Special Issue 12): 526–30. doi:10.14419/ijet.v7i3.12.16172.

Bonner, M. G., and C. M. Sapsford. 1966. "Measurement of Solar Radiation by Silicon Solar Cell." *Solar Energy* 10 (4): 195–202. doi:10.1016/0038-092X(66)90013-2.

Chine, W., A. Mellit, A. Massi Pavan, and S. A. Kalogirou. 2014. "Fault Detection Method for Grid-Connected Photovoltaic Plants." *Renewable Energy* 66. Elsevier Ltd: 99–110. doi:10.1016/j.renene.2013.11.073.

Chouder, A., S. Silvestre, B. Taghezouit, and E. Karatepe. 2013. "Monitoring, Modelling and Simulation of PV Systems Using LabVIEW." *Solar Energy* 91. Elsevier Ltd: 337–49. doi:10.1016/j.solener.2012.09.016.

Durán, E., J. M. Andújar, J. M. Enrique, and J. M. Pérez-Oria. 2012. "Determination of PV Generator I-V/P-V Characteristic Curves Using a DC-DC Converter Controlled by a Virtual Instrument." *International Journal of Photoenergy*. doi:10.1155/2012/843185.

Elliott, A. C., L. S. Hynan, J. S. Reisch, and J. P. Smith. 2006. "Preparing Data for Analysis Using Microsoft Excel." *Journal of Investigative Medicine* 54 (6): 334–41. doi:10.2310/6650.2006.05038.

Eltawil, M. A., and Z. Zhao. 2010. "Grid-Connected Photovoltaic Power Systems: Technical and Potential Problems-A Review." *Renewable and Sustainable Energy Reviews* 14 (1): 112–29. doi:10.1016/j.rser.2009.07.015.

Hammoumi, A. E., S. Motahhir, A. Chalh, A. E. Ghzizal, and A. Derouich. 2018. "Low-Cost Virtual Instrumentation of PV Panel Characteristics Using Excel and Arduino in Comparison with Traditional Instrumentation." *Renewables: Wind, Water, and Solar* 5 (1). Springer Singapore. doi:10.1186/s40807-018-0049-0.

Hashim, N., M. N. Mohammed, R. Al Selvarajan, S. Al-Zubaidi, and S. Mohammed. 2019. "Study on Solar Panel Cleaning Robot." *2019 IEEE International Conference on Automatic Control and Intelligent Systems, I2CACIS 2019 – Proceedings*, no. June. IEEE: 56–61. doi:10.1109/I2CACIS.2019.8825028.

Jiang, L. 2013. "Application of MATLAB-Based Regression Analysis Model in Enterprises." *Applied Mechanics and Materials* 328: 239–43. doi:10.4028/www.scientific.net/AMM.328.239.

Kyi, S., and A. Taparugssanagorn. 2019. "Wireless Sensing for a Solar Power System." *Digital Communications and Networks*. Chongqing University of Posts and Telecommuniocations. doi:10.1016/j.dcan.2018.11.002.

"Ministry of New and Renewable Energy, Government of India, Overview." n.d. https://mnre.gov.in/solar/current-status/.

Priharti, W., A. F.K. Rosmawati, and I. P.D. Wibawa. 2019. "IoT Based Photovoltaic Monitoring System Application." *Journal of Physics: Conference Series* 1367 (1). doi:10.1088/1742-6596/1367/1/012069.

Raza, A., and A. J. Ikram. 2016. "A Review of Low Cost and Power Efficient Development Boards for IoT Applications," no. December: 786–90.

Rouibah, N., L. Barazane, A. Mellit, B. Hajji, and A. Rabhi. 2019. "A Low-Cost Monitoring System for Maximum Power Point of a Photovoltaic System Using IoT Technique." *2019 International Conference on Wireless Technologies, Embedded and Intelligent Systems, WITS 2019*. IEEE, 1–5. doi:10.1109/WITS.2019.8723724.

Rusirawan, D., and I. Farkas. 2014. "Identification of Model Parameters of the Photovoltaic Solar Cells." *Energy Procedia* 57. Elsevier B.V.: 39–46. doi:10.1016/j.egypro.2014.10.006.

Singh, G. K. 2013. "Solar Power Generation by PV (Photovoltaic) Technology: A Review." *Energy* 53. Elsevier Ltd: 1–13. doi:10.1016/j.energy.2013.02.057.

Springer Handbook of Electronic and Photonic Materials. 2007. *Springer Handbook of Electronic and Photonic Materials.* doi:10.1007/978-0-387-29185-7.

Su, Y., L. C. Chan, L. Shu, and K. L. Tsui. 2012. "Real-Time Prediction Models for Output Power and Efficiency of Grid-Connected Solar Photovoltaic Systems." *Applied Energy* 93. Elsevier Ltd: 319–26. doi:10.1016/j.apenergy.2011.12.052.

Syafaruddin, E. Karatepe, and T. Hiyama. 2009. "Polar Coordinated Fuzzy Controller Based Real-Time Maximum-Power Point Control of Photovoltaic System." *Renewable Energy* 34 (12). Elsevier Ltd: 2597–2606. doi:10.1016/j.renene.2009.04.022.

Tan, R. H. G., P. L. J. Tai, and V. H. Mok. 2013. "Solar Irradiance Estimation Based on Photovoltaic Module Short Circuit Current Measurement." *2013 IEEE International Conference on Smart Instrumentation, Measurement and Applications, ICSIMA 2013*, no. November: 26–27. doi:10.1109/ICSIMA.2013.6717943.

Tiwari, S., and R. N. Patel. 2016. "Real Time Monitoring of Solar Power Plant and Automatic Load Control." *4th Students Conference on Engineering and Systems, SCES 2015.* doi:10.1109/SCES.2015.7506453.

Wang, H., and J. Shen. 2018. "Analysis of the Characteristics of Solar Cell Array Based on MATLAB/Simulink in Solar Unmanned Aerial Vehicle." *IEEE Access* 6 (c): 21195–201. doi:10.1109/ACCESS.2018.2802927.

Wang, W., N. Li, and S. Li. 2012. "A Real-Time Modeling of Photovoltaic Array." *Chinese Journal of Chemical Engineering* 20 (6). Chemical Industry and Engineering Society of China (CIESC) and Chemical Industry Press (CIP): 1154–60. doi:10.1016/S1004-9541(12)60601-6.

13

IoT-Based Designing of Single Bit Six-Transistor Static Random Access Memory Cell Architecture for Industrial Applications

Reeya Agrawal and Sangeeta Singh

CONTENTS

DOI: 10.1201/9781003226888-13

13.1 Introduction

A changeable entrance is a pathway that does not lose any data. The adaptable route has gained popularity due to its lack of adiabatic setbacks, which will reduce glow scrambling. The very large-scale integrated (VLSI) circuit system architecture has attracted interest in recent years thanks to its wide variety of applications [1]. Due to progress in collecting, the mapping of low-power recall cells has attracted interest in recent years. Fixed memories are a form of memory consisting of circuits that may store the length of their vitality. Because of its speed, static discretionary get to recollection stands out among other recollection cells. 6TSRAMC employs a primary bistable circuit to store a file's bit. In the typical 6T cell, two cross-attached inverters form a bolt to stock the files. Past data must be deleted whenever necessary to secure other data in a comparable cell, demonstrating the irreversibility functioning of the remembrance cell and achieving the glow fading. The estimations are irreversible suggested 6TSRAMC design utilizing reversible route project, stored in the standard remembrance [2]. Waste yield refers to any time-consuming entryway yield. The usual test for reversible circuit architecture is to reduce the decreasing gain.

Electronic memory is a critical component of new applications in the age of sophisticated technology. Memory devices are often classified into two types based on the amount of power required to memories the recorded data. Non-volatile (NV) memory (NVM), on the other hand, is capable of storing data without consuming any power [3]. Emerging NVMs have been presented as a solution to the critical system performance bottleneck and basic restrictions associated with reducing device size and growing process complexity. High-performance computing fuels the advancement of semiconductor technology. Consumer electronics is evolving toward data-centric applications in the internet of things (IoT) era, with new criteria like ultra-low-power operation, low-cost design, high density, high reliability, and increased data storage capabilities, among others [4]. Sensor nodes reduce data rates and power usage. Serial buses like SPI or I2C transfer data between system components [5]. The microcontroller unit (MCU) handles IoT node transactions as the "master controller." The gateway sends sensor data to the wireless device and receives control instructions. Typical IoT sensor nodes are shown in the Figure 13.1.

13.1.1 6TSRAMC-Based Microcontroller Optimizes Security

NV 6TSRAMC encryption of memory using data encryption standard (DES) or triple DES is a proven secure memory storage device that establishes a cryptographer's barrier preventing unwanted access to sensitive data [6]. The volatile nature of 6TSRAMC can further be protected by integrating tamper-reactive sensors, which, if interfered with, destroy encryption keys. Automatic programs and data memory encryption capabilities safeguard data in financial applications such as personal identification numbers (PINs) pads. Financial services have several rules and processes to maintain the security of both hardware and software. Even if the microcontroller is covered by a protective housing

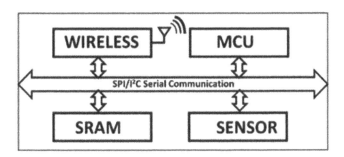

FIGURE 13.1
Typical IoT sensor node.

and a burglar alarm is placed, a specific aggressor can disable the power and disable the alarm system. The manipulative cryptographic barrier of the microcontroller provides a safe cocoon for encrypted data even if an enclosure is available [7]. The gadget that calculates the invaders by quickly deleting the secret key, software, and data memory protects itself.

13.1.2 Physical Memory with Building Trust

Most embedded systems are built on general-purpose computers, selected for diversity and simplicity [8]. On the other side, these advantages may become liabilities if security breaches occur. Because a hacker's first target is usually the physical memory of the microcontroller, choosing the best memory technologies for payment terminals is crucial. In the lack of power, the two significant countermeasures to avoid this scampering are establishing robust encryption in the memory bus and selecting memory technology. Embedded systems include built-in floating gate memory microcontrollers for security, such as erasable programmable read only memory (EPROM) and flash memory [9]. The most sophisticated memory technology, on the other hand, erases content instead of trying to hide it. If a UV-erasable EPROM does not require power to delete, it is more sensitive to the time-consuming nature of UV light for minutes. To delete a flash memory or electrically erasable programmable read-only memory (EEPROM), the processor must be switched on and supply voltage within the specified range. Subjects like 6TSRAMC favor the memory technologies if power is switched off or when the tamper detection circuit is engaged because it operates as one way:

- The memory is reset to zeros when the battery is removed, and the circuit of manipulation erases the internal memory and encryption keys in nanoseconds.
- Under application software control, the external memory can be cleaned if write times are below 100 ns.

After programming, the final step is to set one or more internal lock bits for specific systems. In practice, all the memory can be wiped out only by removing the lock bit, which can reprogram the device but destroy the memory content of the software [10]. A unique security feature is provided as an internal memory encryption array, which encrypts the result of the memory array when a hardware programmer tries to validate or dump its contents. The lock-bit strategy might be defeated, on the other hand. According to sure device makers, one-time-programmable devices in a solid plastic container give security against lock-bit hacking [1].

13.1.3 6TSRAMC Speed

All safe applications demand quick read/write cycle rates for the best level of security. 6TSRAMC is presently the fastest accessible memory technology. It can be washed or "zeroed" instantly as part of a tamper reaction. 6TSRAMC is also straightforward, cheap, and has unique data security capabilities [11].

- **Authenticating the transaction**

This module needs a secure onboard software-based microcontroller, including keypad device drivers, magnetic card readers, smart card readers, and LCDs, as well as the approvals of financial authorities and issuers of credit cards [12]. Since the PIN pad microcontroller's memory footprint can be hundreds of Kbytes, additional storage is needed, extending beyond a single chip's economic size. Unless the microcontroller and external memory communicate using strong encryption, as stated previously, external memory is subject to eavesdropping. For such an encryption system to work, some requirements must be met: Encryption and decryption must take place at the same time as instructions are being implemented [13]. Every software fetch or a specific number of bytes has to be used for cryptographic techniques, such as the DES. Strong, quick, and hardware-based encryption techniques are needed. To support the cryptographic engine's fast data transfer speeds, external memory must be 6TSRAMC. A battery-powered 6TSRAMC is also required in the event of tampering so that memory may be wiped rapidly [14]. Encryption keys and other data critical to the cryptographic operation should never be viewed outside the processor. At least a portion of the encryption keys must be generated and securely stored by the processor. These keys are deleted as part of the tamper response, leaving the external memory unreadable. A bootloader built into the CPU is responsible for initial software and data loading and encryption [15].

13.1.4 What Is IoT?

For an intelligent lifestyle, connected and intellectual functioning is necessary. More RAM is required for all these activities. More RAM is required for all these activities [16]. Designers have seen many new opportunities and problems as the IoT proliferates. Although the number of available memory choices is presently not equal to the number of IoT devices available, it may look like this when it is decided what it needs to contain [17].

13.1.4.1 Cost

The costs are considered; the costlier the memory, the more costly the end output. The investigator must evaluate the market-dependent cost vs performance alternatives.

13.1.4.2 Power Consumption

Most IoT equipment is powered by tiny batteries or refilled with environmental energy. In this way, it is necessary to think about the energy consumption of the memory and select to use the most nominal voltage and power when in operation.

13.1.4.3 Start-Up Time

Users want high-quality gadget performance; sufficient RAM is necessary for rapid start-up. Since on-chip storage is extensive, it offers a code-in-place option that allows the device to run code without copying operational code from a separate EEPROM chip, reducing boot time and the cost of the chip.

13.1.4.4 Size

As most IoT equipment is tiny, embedded technology must also be compact. Since the more silicon wafer area is needed, the higher the cost, keeping the amount of memory processing space necessary to a minimum is also required.

13.1.5 IoT Memory Types

Embedded technology developers often choose a memory from one of the following categories.

13.1.5.1 Traditional External Flash Memory

This form of memory is used for many consumer items, as it is cost-effective, robust, and flexible, has a high density, and is capable of running in situ without excessive power. The perfect NOT-AND (NAND) flash for high-capacity, low-cost applications like wearable devices, whereas NOT-OR (NOR) Flash is excellent for low-memory devices, including global positioning system (GPS) and e-readers [18].

13.1.5.2 Embedded Flash Memory

It is becoming more common for IoT devices to use embedded flash memory (eFlash) for data and code storage. eFlash is expected to become the most common form of IoT storage due to its high performance and density [19]. Memory that can be programmed in real time is very adaptive using this form. IoT devices are increasingly using eFlash to store data and code. Several analysts believe that eFlash will become the most popular kind of IoT storage because of its excellent performance and density.

13.1.6 Techniques of Power Reduction

The primary operational approach for power reduction methods such as the power reduction dual sleep technique (PRDST) shown in Figure 13.2, power reduction sleep transistor technique (PRSTT) shown in Figure 13.3, power reduction forced stack technique (PRFST), and power reduction sleep stack technique, which has been used to evaluate various parameters in the 6TSRAMC circuit, is explained in this section [20]:

i. State saving
ii. State destructive

13.1.6.1 Power Reduction Dual Sleep Technique (PRDST)

The area criteria for this approach are improved by adding four transistors, PM0, PM1, NM0, and NM1. In the PRDST, two additional pull-up and pull-down transistors in either an OFF/ON state were used in sleep mode [21].

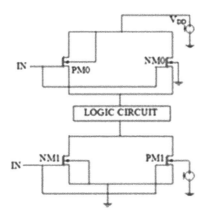

FIGURE 13.2
Power reduction sleep stack technique.

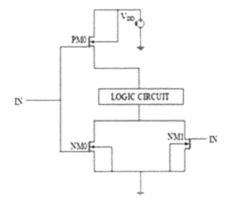

FIGURE 13.3
Power reduction forced stack technique.

13.1.6.2 *Power Reduction Sleepy Stack Technique (PRSST)*

Another alternative for reducing power consumption is the "stacking" strategy, in which a current transistor is broken down into two half-sized transistors. A shortened inversion distance between the two transistors is formed when both transistors are turned off simultaneously [22].

13.1.6.3 *Power Reduction Sleep Transistor Technique (PRSTT) and Power Reduction Forced Stack Technique (PRFST)*

In PRSTT and PRFST (i) between a supply voltage and the pull-up network in a circuit, P_{MOS} is placed, whereas (ii) between pull-down network and G_{ND} in-circuit, N_{MOS} is placed [23, 24].

13.1.7 Related Work/Background

Habeeb et al. [25] describe many VLSI chips now have 6TSRAMCs, which are fast and low-power. Simultaneously, increasing integration and operation speeds have made power dissipation essential. As a result, a lot of work has gone into employing circuit and architectural approaches to reduce the power consumption of complementary metal-oxide-semiconductor (CMOS) RAM chips.

Zhang et al. [26] describe that 6TSRAMC has a few benefits over dynamic random access memory (DRAM). That is why SRAM is commonly chosen. The significant advantage is that 6TSRAMC does not require regular periodic refreshing, meaning that whatever is stored in a 6TSRAMC will last until the power is turned on. However, in the case of DRAM, it is necessary to refresh it regularly. As a result, 6TSRAMC is commonly used. Again, 6TSRAMC is divided into many categories, such as 4TSRAMC, 6TSRAMC, 8TSRAMC, and so on, based on the number of Metal-oxide-semiconductor field-effect transistors (MOSFET) it includes, i.e., 4TSRAMC contains four MOSFETs, 6TSRAMC contains six MOSFETs, 8TSRAMC contains eight MOSFETs, and so on. 6TSRAMC is the most commonly utilized due to its benefits over the others. Because there are fewer MOSFETs in 4TSRAMC, it takes up less chip space, but the voltage swing is significant.

Lokesh et al. [27] describe that 6TSRAMC is a critical component of the embedded cache memory found in portable digital devices. The 6TSRAMC has become a popular data storage device due to its high storage density and quick access time. The need for low voltage, low-power 6TSRAMC has increased because of the exponential rise of low-power digital devices. 6TSRAMC's performance has been assessed in latency, power, and static noise margin (SNM).

Shubham et al. [28] describe that memory is a critical component in the current VLSI system design. Before manufacturing, it must be extensively examined in space, power, and performance. Due to the ever increasing need for data processing, 6TSRAMC is a critical contender in-memory design, and it is receiving a lot of attention. Submicron scaling degrades the performance of traditional CMOS devices due to short channel effects, and circuits become unstable.

Shukla et al. [29] explain that researchers have been shrinking CMOS circuits for the last five decades to achieve successful execution in terms of speed, power blow-out, size, and unchanging quality. Our goal is to make everyday electronics, such as computers, smaller in size, faster, and consume less power. The scaling of CMOS is done to achieve speed and reduce memory size. 6TSRAMC is a data storage format that may be utilized in various devices. 6TSRAMC is now preferred over 8T and 9TSRAMC because it has a very low latency compared to 8T and 9TSRAMC, and its power dissipation is half that of 8T and 9TSRAMC.

Lakshmi et al. [13] describe that nowadays, every gadget has a high-capacity memory to meet all of the demands of clients. Power consumption and latency are two more characteristics that play a vital part in determining the device's performance. Memory is an essential component of many widgets, and its size shrinks as the device's size shrinks. In today's environment, 6TSRAMC is frequently utilized for 6TSRAMC-based memory architectures since it is more beneficial than other cells. Low-power consumption is a crucial problem in today's electronics industry, with static and dynamic power dissipation being the two essential characteristics to consider.

Shukla et al. [29] describe that 6TSRAMC takes up 60 percent of the space of system on a chip (SoCs). The MOSFET experiences numerous short channel effects under nanoscale CMOS technology at lower supply voltages and technology nodes. The static random-access memory (SRAM) cell design became increasingly complex due to higher leakage power consumption and decreased data stability. As a result, overcoming those restrictions and improving its performance is critical.

The chapter is divided into six sections. Section 13.1 describes an introduction related to IoT, IoT and cache memory relation, IoT memory types, power reduction techniques, and related work/background. Section 13.2 describes a single bit 6TSRAMC (six-transistor static random access memory cell) sense amplifiers architecture functional block diagram, which comprises a circuit of write driver, 6TSRAMC, and sense amplifiers. In contrast, Section 13.3 describes the proposed design, such as single bit 6TSRAMC CMDSA (current differential sense amplifier) architecture, single bit 6TSRAMC CTMDSA (charge transfer mode differential sense amplifier) architecture, single bit 6TSRAMC VMLSA (voltage mode latch sense amplifier) architecture, single bit 6TSRAMC CMLSA (current mode latch sense amplifier) architecture. Section 13.4 describes simulated results and discussion, such as the output waveform of command for writing data (CWD), the output waveform of 6TSRAMC, and the output waveform of single bit 6TSRAMC SA architectures of different amplifiers. Section 13.5 describes a comparison Table of simulated waveform results. Different power reduction techniques are applied over other blocks of architecture, such as 6TSRAMC and SA, to optimize power consumption. Section 13.6 describes the conclusion and future scope of the chapter.

13.2 Single Bit 6TSRAMC SA Architecture Functional Block Diagram

Each memory cell has a unique address corresponding to a data input/output pin [30]. Readability and write stability are necessary for the 6TSRAMC to operate in reading and writing modes. CWD, 6TSRAMC, and SAs designed and integrated with cadence software include CMDSA, CTMDSA, VMLSA, and CMLSA (Figure 13.4).

13.2.1 Circuit of Write Driver

CWD is a command for writing data into a memory cell. CWD refers to an integrated circuit device memory array that uses just one write enable signal to couple complementary data signals between global and local write data lines, obviating the need for complementary write enable signals in previous implementations [31]. Because a second complementary write allows signal line is no longer required. The signal path requires less on-chip

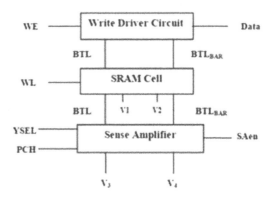

FIGURE 13.4
Single bit 6TSRAMC SA architecture functional block diagram.

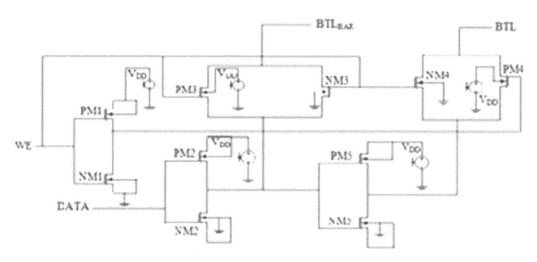

FIGURE 13.5
Circuit of write driver schematic.

device area, and power consumption decreases due to fewer line switching during a write cycle (Figure 13.5).

13.2.2 6TSRAMC Working and Schematic

Embedded devices, computers, mobile communication devices, and IC memory cards are all higher demand. In the worst case situation, this capability should be maintained for each cell. 6TSRAMC has been built for read and write stability. String inverters often strengthen cell stability during the reading operation, while passing gates are often weakened. The reverse is typically true about cell write capabilities when the storage inverter is weak and the passport doors powerful [32]. The 6TSRAMC voltage does not extend to technology in this situation and can even be raised with greater unpredictability. Installed with 6TSRAMC arrays, which can be pulsed to various levels when a reading or writing event takes place, can be utilized instead of tied to a given higher supply. In some way, this allows read and write events to be segregated from the standby state and provides for optimal distortion in each case. While such approaches might make the design more complex, they can contribute to cell stability, writing ability, and standby leakage. A 6TSRAMC can do this by changing itself, analogous to how a dynamically regulated power supply can split reading and writing needs [33] (Figure 13.6).

13.2.3 Sense Amplifier

It has been around since 1947, when it was first used to describe magnetic core memory. A sense amplifier reads data from memory by sensing and amplifying low-power signals that represent data bits contained in memory cells [34]. Current memory chips include hundreds or thousands of identical sensing amplifiers per column of memory cells. A sense amplifier is of two types:

- Differential sense amplifier
- Latch sense amplifier

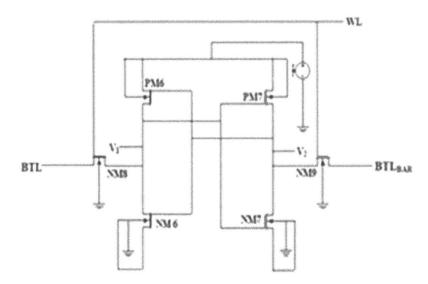

FIGURE 13.6
6TSRAMC schematic.

13.2.3.1 CMDSA Working and Schematic

CMDSA detects the current in the bit cell almost instantly. There is no need to create a differential voltage across the bit-lines for the system to work. Because the low-going bit-line may be clamped at a higher voltage than a voltage detecting amplifier can handle, bit-line pre-charge power is reduced [35]. A current conveying circuit with unity gains contemporary transfer properties, and a differential current sensor circuit is included in the CMDSA. It is made up of a variety of concepts. The current conveyor, also known as the current transportation circuit, comprises four similar-sized positive feedback P_{MOS} transistors. Because their currents are the same, their sizes are the same, and both transistors are saturated, the gate-source voltage for PM8 and PM10 will be the same. Figure 13.7 shows the current differential sense amplifier Schematic with working.

13.2.3.2 CTMDSA Working and Schematic

CTMDSA redirects a charge from high capacitance bit-lines to low capacitance sense amplifier output nodes. This results in high-speed operation and low-power consumption due to the limited voltage swing on the bit-lines [36].

Charge transfer theory: Charge is rerouted from high capacitance bit-lines to low capacitance sense amplifier output nodes when CTMDSA is used. Due to the low voltage swing on the bit-lines, this results in high-speed operation and low-power consumption.

$$Q = C_{large}\ V_{large} = C_{small}\ V_{small}$$

Voltage gain occurs when a slight change in voltage across the more significant capacitive element causes a more noticeable difference across the less capacitive component.

CTMDSA operation: The working of the CTMDSA is shown in Figure 13.8. The CTMDSA circuit is based on charge redistribution from high bit-line capacitance to a

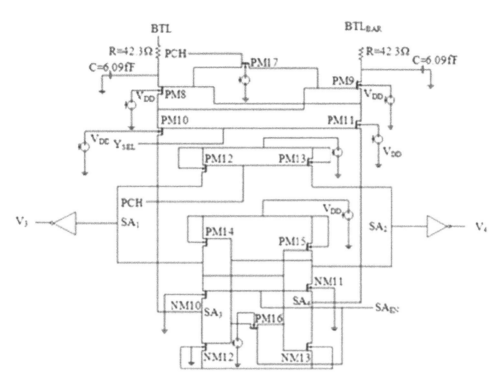

FIGURE 13.7
CMDSA schematic.

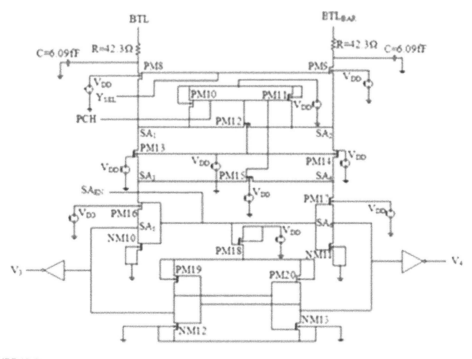

FIGURE 13.8
CTMDSA schematic.

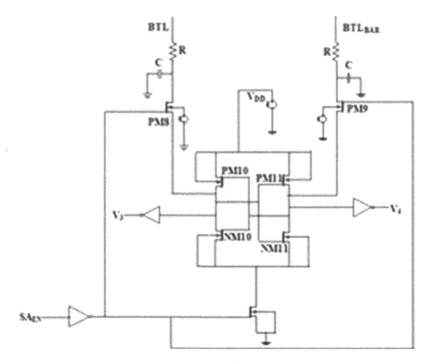

FIGURE 13.9
VMLSA schematic.

low capacitance of sensing nodes V_3 and V_4. This charge redistribution results in high-speed operation and minimal bit-line swing [37]. The circuit is made up of two parts. The gate cascades PM13, PM16, and NM10 (along with PM14, PM17, and NM11) are identical, with PM13 and PM14 biassed at V_b. Second, the cross-coupled inverters created by PM18, PM19, PM20, NM12, and NM13 control the output of the common gate amplifier (V_3 and V_4). The typical gate amplifier (V_3 and V_4) production is pre-discharged low by keeping S_{AEN} high. S_{APCH} is set too high during the assessment phase, and Y_{SEL} is charged at the bottom to select a column. CTMDSA is activated when S_{AEN} is reduced [38].

13.2.3.3 VLMSA Working and Schematic

The output nodes are formed by PM10, PM11, NM10, and NM11. There is no current flow from bit-lines to output nodes [39]. The working of the VMLSA is shown in Figure 13.9. When the sensing signal S_{AEN} is set to logic 0, the output node is connected to G_{ND}, and the output nodes are charged to high by the pre-charge transistors PM8, PM9. The transistors PM10 and PM11 are in the cut-off zone, whereas NM10 and NM11 are in the saturation zone since the output nodes V_3 and V_4 are pre-charged to high. NM12 is switched on, and node V_3 is pushed to G_{ND} when the S_{AEN} sensor switches to logic 1 [40].

13.2.3.4 CLMSA Working and Schematic

The working of CMLSA is depicted in Figure 13.10 schematic. The circuit's functioning is as follows: The CMLSA's SA_{IN} and SA_{INB} inputs receive the differential voltage on bit-lines.

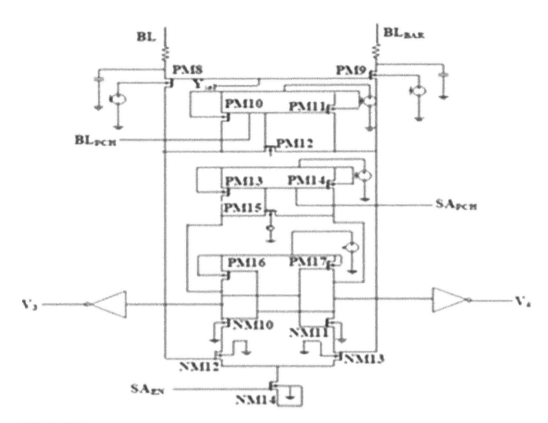

FIGURE 13.10
CMLSA schematic.

When S_{AEN} is pushed high, both V_3 and V_4 outputs discharge [41]. As a result of its greater V_{gs}, NM12 has a higher current than NM13. As a result, output V_3 releases quicker than output V_4. When V_3 drops low enough to activate PM17, V_4 is re-charged, and V_3 falls to V_{SS} [42].

13.3 Proposed Design

The proposed design Architecture of our study for Single bit 6TSRAMC CMDSA (Comprised of six input pins- WE, Data, BTL, BTL_{BAR}, W_L, and S_{AEN}, Four output pins-V_1, V_2, V_3, and V_4), Single bit 6TSRAMC CTMDSA (Comprised of eight input pins- WE, Data, BTL, BTL_{BAR}, W_L, Y_{SEL}, P_{CH}, S_{AEN}, and four output pins-V_1, V_2, V_3, and V_4), Single bit 6TSRAMC VMLSA (Comprised of six input pins, i.e., WE, Data, BTL, BTL_{BAR}, W_L, and S_{AEN}. Four output pins-V_1, V_2, V_3, and V_4.]) and Single bit 6TSRAMC CMLSA (Comprised six input pins, i.e., WE, Data, BTL, BTL_{BAR}, W_L, and S_{AEN}. Four output pins, i.e., V_1, V_2, V_3, and V_4) are depicted in Figure 13.11, Figure 13.12, Figure 13.13, and Figure 13.14, respectively.

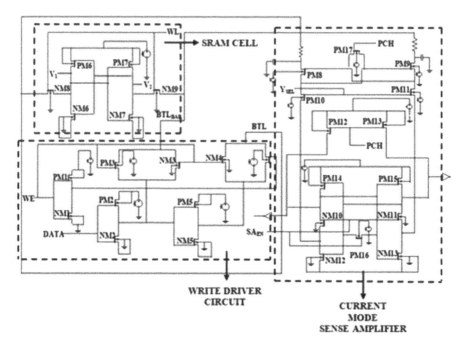

FIGURE 13.11
Single bit 6TSRAMC CMDSA architecture schematic.

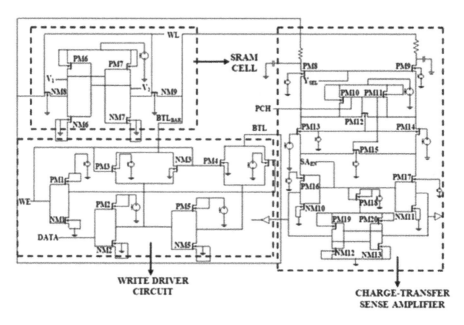

FIGURE 13.12
Single bit 6TSRAMC CTMDSA architecture schematic.

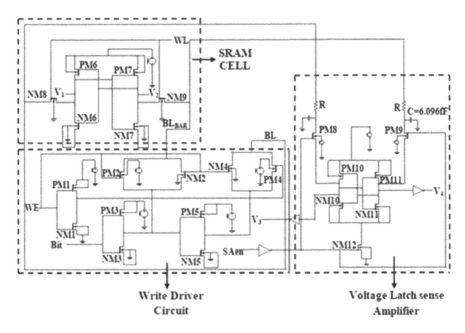

FIGURE 13.13
Single bit 6TSRAMC VMLSA architecture schematic.

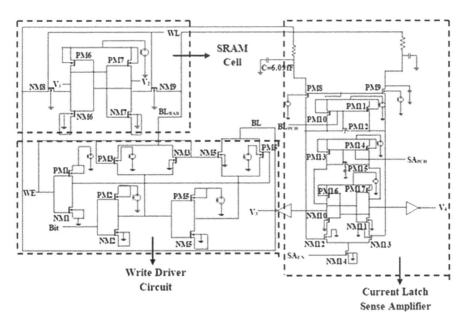

FIGURE 13.14
Single bit 6TSRAMC CMLSA architecture schematic.

13.4 Simulated Results and Discussion

In this chapter, a discussion on methodology and results has been done. As the feature size of technology decreases, the threshold voltage of MOS decreases. Because of the scale down, the threshold voltage metal-oxide-semiconductor (MOS) transistor is turned on at a lower voltage. Hence, the circuit's delay reduces, and the power dissipation as the supply voltage decreases. The output waveforms of the Circuit of write driver, 6TSRAMC, Single bit 6TSRAMC CMDSA, Single bit 6TSRAMC CTMDSA, Single bit 6TSRAMC VMLSA and Single bit 6TSRAMC CMLSA are depicted in Figure 13.15 to Figure 13.20.

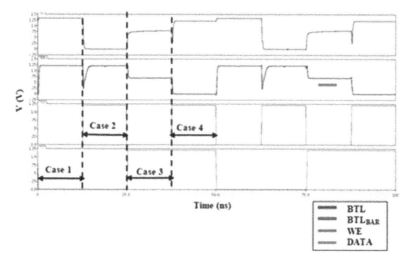

FIGURE 13.15
Circuit of write driver output waveform.

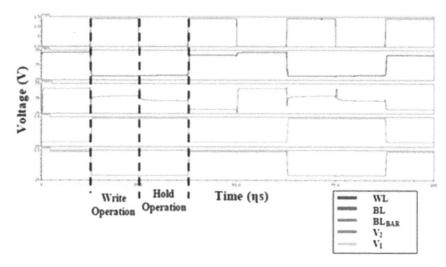

FIGURE 13.16
6TSRAMC output waveform.

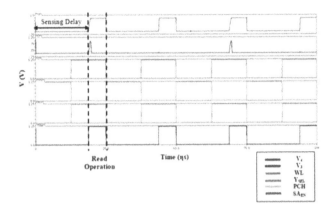

FIGURE 13.17
Single bit 6TSRAMC CMDSA architecture output waveform.

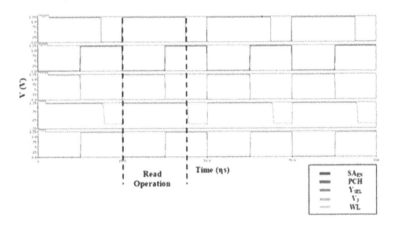

FIGURE 13.18
Single bit 6TSRAMC CTMDSA architecture output waveform.

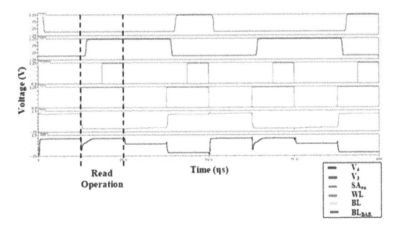

FIGURE 13.19
Single bit 6TSRAMC VMLSA architecture output waveform.

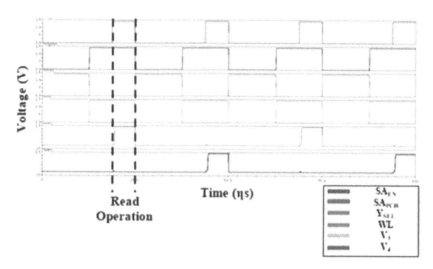

FIGURE 13.20
Single bit 6TSRAMC CMLSA architecture output waveform.

13.5 Comparison Table of Simulated Waveform Results

The power consumption of all the circuits has been analyzed in this section. Table 13.1 describes the number of transistors, delay in sensing, and consumption of power for single bit 6TSRAMC SA architecture with different types of SAs such as CMDSA, CTMDSA, VMLSA, and CMLSA at R = 42.3 Ω. The conclusion arises that single bit 6TSRAMC CMDSA architecture with 14.87 μW with 34 transistors and 18.81 ηs delay in sensing has been analyzed.

Table 13.2 shows that the single bit 6TSRAMC CMDSA architecture uses the least power of all the architectures, at 13.96 μW. TPR (techniques of power reduction) has been used to optimize power in various single bit 6TSRAMC SA architecture blocks, but there is always a trade-off between power and area.

The single bit 6TSRAMC CMDSA architecture is described in Table 13.3. When TPR is applied to CMDSA, the single bit 6TSRAMC CMDSA PRDST emerges. With 38 transistors, the architecture consumes 13.63 μW of power. As the number of transistors increases as the power decreases, so does the area.

TABLE 13.1

Cache Memory Design for Single Bit Architecture Different Parameters when R = 42.3 Ω

S. No.	Architecture	Parameters Consumption of Power	Delay in Sensing	Number of Transistors
1.	Single Bit 6TSRAMC CMDSA Architecture	14.87 μW	18.81 ηs	34
2.	Single Bit 6TSRAMC CTMDSA Architecture	46.35 μW	18.95 ηs	37
3.	Single Bit 6TSRAMC VMLSA Architecture	36.57 μW	13.50 ηs	29
4.	Single Bit 6TSRAMC CMLSA Architecture	73.92 μW	18.68 ηs	35

TABLE 13.2

Cache Memory Design for Single Bit Architecture Different Parameters when R = 42.3 Ω

S. No.	Architecture ⟍ Parameters	Consumption of Power	Delay in Sensing	No. of Transistors
1.	Single Bit 6TSRAMC CMDSA Architecture	13.96 µW	18.81 ηs	34
2.	Single Bit 6TSRAMC CTMDSA Architecture	44.32 µW	18.95 ηs	37
3.	Single Bit 6TSRAMC VMLSA Architecture	14.32 µW	13.50 ηs	29
4.	Single Bit 6TSRAMC CMLSA Architecture	26.78 µW	18.68 ηs	35

TABLE 13.3

Cache Memory Design Different Parameter Analysis when C = 6.09 fF and R = 42.3 kΩ on Applying Techniques of Power Reduction over CMDSA

S. No.	Techniques Applied Over CMDSA in Architecture	Single Bit 6TSRAMC CMDSA Architecture		
		Power Consumption	Sensing Delay	Number of Transistors
1.	PRSTT	13.82 µW	13.51 ηs	36
2.	PRFST	13.75 µW	13.70 ηs	36
3.	PRSST	13.90 µW	13.50 ηs	37
4.	PRDST	13.63 µW	13.66 ηs	38

TABLE 13.4

Cache Memory Design Different Parameter Analysis when C = 6.09 fF and R = 42.3 kΩ on Applying Techniques of Power Reduction over 6TSRAMC

S. No.	Techniques Applied over 6TSRAMC in Architecture	Single Bit 6TSRAMC CMDSA Architecture		
		Power Consumption	Sensing Delay	Number of Transistors
1.	PRSTT	12.84 µW	13.12 ηs	36
2.	PRFST	12.10 µW	13.64 ηs	36
3.	PRSST	14.14 µW	13.36 ηs	37
4.	PRDST	13.05 µW	13.51 ηs	38

Table 13.4 shows that when TPR is applied to a 6TSRAMC, the result is that a single-bit 6TSRAMC with a PRFST CMDSA architecture consumes 12.10 µW of power with 36 transistors.

Table 13.5 shows the single bit 6TSRAMC CMDSA architecture that results from using TPR on 6TSRAMC and the CMDSA conclusion that single bit 6TSRAMC with PRFST. With 38 transistors, CMDSA with PRFST architecture consumes 12.52 µW of power.

TABLE 13.5

Cache Memory Design Different Parameter Analysis when C = 6.09 fF and R = 42.3 kΩ on Applying Techniques of Power Reduction over 6TSRAMC and CMDSA

S. No.	Techniques Applied over 6TSRAMC and CMDSA in Architecture	Single Bit 6TSRAMC CMDSA Architecture		
		Power Consumption	Sensing Delay	Number of Transistors
1.	PRSTT	13.05 μW	12.75 ηs	38
2.	PRFST	12.52 μW	13.14 ηs	38
3.	PRSST	14.13 μW	12.75 ηs	40
4.	PRDST	13.52 μW	13.34 ηs	42

13.6 Conclusion and Future Scope

This chapter describes an IoT-based cache memory architecture composed of CWD, 6TSRAMC, and various types of sense amplifiers such as CMDSA, CTMDSA VMLSA, and CMLSA, as well as all architectures with other SA's implemented over cadence tool and various parameters such as a number of transistors, sensing delay, and power consumption of all architectures. This chapter examines cache memory design at different resistance (R) levels, as well as other characteristics such as the number of transistors, sensing delay, and power consumption. At R = 42.3 kΩ, the single bit 6TSRAMC CMDSA architecture consumes 13.96 μW of power, has 34 transistors, and has an 18.81 ηs sensing delay. Furthermore, TPR such as PRDST, PRSST, PRFST, and PRSTT are used to optimize the power consumption of various parts of the cache memory architecture. The results showed that a single bit 6TSRAMC architecture with power reduction forced stack approach CMDSA consumes 12.52 μW of power with 38 transistors and a sensing latency of 13.14 ηs, which is the shortest when compared to others.

References

1. Eslami, Nima, Behzad Ebrahimi, Erfan Shakouri, and Deniz Najafi. "A single-ended low leakage and low voltage 10T SRAM cell with high yield." *Analog Integrated Circuits and Signal Processing* 105 (2020): 263–274.
2. Roy, Chandramauleshwar, and Aminul Islam. "Design of low power, variation tolerant single bitline 9T SRAM cell in 16-nm technology in subthreshold region." *Microelectronics Reliability* 120 (2021): 114126.
3. Saha, Rajesh, Yogendra Pratap Pundir, and Pankaj Kumar Pal. "Design of an area and energy-efficient last-level cache memory using STT-MRAM." *Journal of Magnetism and Magnetic Materials* 529 (2021): 167882.
4. Gupta, Neha, Ambika Prasad Shah, and Santosh Kumar Vishvakarma. "BTI and soft-error tolerant voltage bootstrapped Schmitt trigger circuit." *IEEE Transactions on Device and Materials Reliability* 21, no. 1 (2021): 153–155.
5. Abbasian, Erfan, and Morteza Gholipour. "Design of a Schmitt-trigger-based 7T SRAM cell for variation resilient low-energy consumption and reliable Internet of Things applications." *AEU – International Journal of Electronics and Communications* 138 (2021): 153899.

6. Gordon, Holden, Jack Edmonds, Soroor Ghandali, Wei Yan, Nima Karimian, and Fatemeh Tehranipoor. "Flash-based security primitives: evolution, challenges, and future directions." *Cryptography* 5, no. 1 (2021): 7.

7. Bazzi, Hussein, Adnan Harb, Hassen Aziza, Mathieu Moreau, and Abdallah Kassem. "RRAM-based non-volatile SRAM cell architectures for ultra-low-power applications." *Analog Integrated Circuits and Signal Processing* 106, no. 2 (2021): 351–361.

8. Kumar, Hemant, Subodh Srivastava, and Balwinder Singh. "Low power, high-performance reversible logic enabled CNTFET SRAM cell with improved stability." *Materials Today: Proceedings* 42 (2021): 1617–1623.

9. Garzón, Esteban, Raffaele De Rose, Felice Crupi, Adam Teman, and Marco Lanuzza. "Exploiting STT-MRAMs for cryogenic non-volatile cache applications." *IEEE Transactions on Nanotechnology* 20 (2021): 123–128.

10. Shakouri, Erfan, Behzad Ebrahimi, Nima Eslami, and Mohammad Chahardori. "Single-ended 10T SRAM cell with high yield and low standby power." *Circuits, Systems, and Signal Processing* 40 (2021): 3479–3499.

11. Aparna, Chauhan RCS. "Low power PPN inverter-based 10T SRAM cell." *Indian Journal of Science and Technology* 14, no. 20 (2021): 1699–1710.

12. Agrawal, Reeya, and Vishal Goyal. "Analysis of MTCMOS Cache Memory Architecture for Processor." In *Proceedings of International Conference on Communication and Artificial Intelligence*, pp. 81–91. Springer, 2021.

13. Mishra, Jitendra Kumar, Lakshmi Likhitha Mankali, Kavindra Kandpal, Prasanna Kumar Misra, and Manish Goswami. "Design and analysis of SRAM cell using negative bit-line write assist technique and separate read port for high-speed applications." *Journal of Circuits, Systems, and Computers* 30, no. 15 (2021): 2150270.

14. Agrawal, Reeya, Manish Kumar, Manish Gupta, and Vinay Kumar Deolia. "FPGA-based power optimized CAM design using LVCMOS18 and high-speed low voltage digitally controlled impedance." *Intelligent Communication, Control, and Devices* vol 1341 (2021): 177–184.

15. Agrawal, Reeya, Neetu Faujdar, and Aditi Saxena. "Low Power Single-Bit Cache Memory Architecture." In *IOP Conference Series: Materials Science and Engineering*, vol. 1116, no. 1, p. 012136. IOP Publishing, 2021.

16. Agrawal, Reeya, and Manish Kumar. "Low power single bit cache memory architecture." *Materials Today: Proceedings* 1116 (2021).

17. Agrawal, Reeya, and V. K. Tomar. "Analysis of Cache (SRAM) Memory for Core I™ 7 Processor." In *2018 9th International Conference on Computing, Communication and Networking Technologies (ICCCNT)*, pp. 1–8. IEEE, 2018.

18. Agrawal, Reeya, and V. K. Tomar. "Implementation and Analysis of Low Power Reduction Techniques in Sense Amplifier." In *2018 Second International Conference on Electronics, Communication and Aerospace Technology (ICECA)*, pp. 439–444. IEEE, 2018.

19. Agrawal, Reeya, and Vinay Kumar Tomar. "Analysis of Low Power Reduction Techniques on Cache (SRAM) Memory." In *2018 9th International Conference on Computing, Communication and Networking Technologies (ICCCNT)*, pp. 1–7. IEEE, 2018.

20. Naga Raghuram, Ch., Bharat Gupta, and Gaurav Kaushal. "Single-event multiple effect tolerant RHBD14T SRAM cell design for space applications." *IEEE Transactions on Device and Materials Reliability* 21, no. 1 (2021): 48–56.

21. Singh, Ritu, and Sakshi Jain. "Efficient Deblocking Filter with SRAM Using 22nm FinFET Technology." In *2021 International Conference on Artificial Intelligence and Smart Systems (ICAIS)*, pp. 1470–1473. IEEE, 2021.

22. Sarmiento, Marco, Khai-Duy Nguyen, Ckristian Duran, Trong-Thuc Hoang, Ronaldo Serrano, Van-Phuc Hoang, Xuan-Tu Tran, Koichiro Ishibashi, and Cong-Kha Pham. "A sub-µW reversed-body-bias 8-bit processor on 65-nm silicon-on-thin-box (SOTB) for IoT applications." *IEEE Transactions on Circuits and Systems II: Express Briefs* 68, no. 9 (2021): 3182–3186.

23. Sharif, Adeeba, Sayeed Ahmad, and Naushad Alam. "Low-Power Memory Design for IoT-Enabled Systems: Part 1." In *Electrical and Electronic Devices, Circuits and Materials*, pp. 43–62. CRC Press, 2021.

24. Oh, Ji Sang, Juhyun Park, Keonhee Cho, Tae Woo Oh, and Seong-Ook Jung. "Differential read/write 7T SRAM with bit-interleaved structure for near-threshold operation." *IEEE Access* 9 (2021): 64105–64115.

25. Habeeb, Mohd Sayeeduddin, and Md. Salahuddin. "Design of Low Power SRAM using Hierarchical Divided Bit-line Approach in 180-nm Technology, *International Journal of Engineering Research & Technology (IJERT)* 5, no. 02 (February 2016).

26. Zhang, Jintao, Zhuo Wang, and Naveen Verma. "In-memory computation of a machine-learning classifier in a standard 6T SRAM array." *IEEE Journal of Solid-State Circuits* 52, no. 4 (2017): 915–924.

27. Lokesh, S. B., K. MeghaChandana, V. Niharika, A. Prathyusha, and G. Rohitha. "Design of reading and write operations for 6T SRAM cell." *IOSR Journal of VLSI and Signal Processing (IOSR-JVSP)* 8, no. 1, 2018 (2018): 43–46.

28. Sanjana, S. R., Roohila Banu, and Prateek Shubham. "Design and Performance Analysis of 6T SRAM Cell in 22nm CMOS and FinFET Technology Nodes." In *2017 International Conference on Recent Advances in Electronics and Communication Technology (ICRAECT)*, pp. 38–42. IEEE, 2017.

29. Shukla, Sphurti, Surbhi Singh, Khushbu Bansal, Pallavie Tyagi, and Sanjay Kumar Singh. "Design of 6T SRAM Cells on Different Technology Nodes." In *Smart Computing*, pp. 599–605. CRC Press, 2021.

30. Rawat, Bhawna, and Poornima Mittal. "Single bit line accessed high-performance ultra-low-voltage operating 7T static random access memory cell with improved read stability." *International Journal of Circuit Theory and Applications* 49, no. 5 (2021): 1435–1449.

31. Sargunam, T. G., Chinnaraj Munirathina Prabhu, and Way Soong Lim. "Design of novel low power (NLP) SRAM cell for wireless sensor network applications." *ARPN Journal of Engineering and Applied Sciences* 16, no. 7 (2021): 762–770.

32. Gavaskar, K., M. Sankara Narayanan, M. Sreenidhi Nachammal, and K. Vignesh. "Design and comparative analysis of SRAM array using low leakage-controlled transistor technique with improved delay." *Journal of Ambient Intelligence and Humanized Computing*, 13 (2021): 4559–4568.

33. Yang, Jia-Qin, Ye Zhou, and Su-Ting Han. "Functional applications of future data storage devices." *Advanced Electronic Materials* 7, no. 5 (2021): 2001181.

34. Sargunam, T. G., Lim Way Soong, C. M. R. Prabhu, and Ajay Kumar Singh. "Design and Performance Analysis of Energy Efficient 11T SRAM (E2S11T) Cell for High Performance and Low Power Applications." In *2021 IEEE International Workshop of Electronics, Control, Measurement, Signals and their application to Mechatronics (ECMSM)*, pp. 1–7. IEEE, 2021.

35. Karthi, S. P., K. Kavitha, Ganesh Babu, JR Dinesh Kumar, C. Visvesvaran, and N. Girinath. "Ultra-Low Power Memory Circuit Unit for Space Application." In *IOP Conference Series: Materials Science and Engineering*, vol. 1084, no. 1, p. 012059. IOP Publishing, 2021.

36. Bian, Zhongjian, Xiaofeng Hong, Yanan Guo, Lirida Naviner, Wei Ge, and Hao Cai. "Investigation of PVT-Aware STT-MRAM sensing circuits for low-VDD scenario." *Micromachines* 12, no. 5 (2021): 551.

37. Ahr, Pascal, Christoph Lipps, and Hans Dieter Schotten. "The PUF Commitment: Evaluating the Stability of SRAM-Cells." In *European Conference on Cyber Warfare and Security*, pp. 1–XIII. Academic Conferences International Limited, 2021.

38. Suzuki, Daisuke, Takahiro Oka, and Takahiro Hanyu. "Design of an energy-efficient binarized convolutional neural network accelerator using a non-volatile field-programmable gate array with only-once-write shifting." *Japanese Journal of Applied Physics* 60, no. SB (2021): SBBB07.

39. Talukder, B. M. S., Farah Ferdaus, and Md Tauhidur Rahman. "A Non-invasive Technique to Detect Authentic/Counterfeit SRAM Chips." *arXiv preprint arXiv:2107.09199* (2021).

40. Gangadhar, A., and K. Babulu. "Design low-power and high-speed CNTFET-based TCAM cell for future generation networks." *The Journal of Supercomputing* 77 (2021): 10012–10022.

41. Wu, Y. C., Kevin Garello, W. Kim, M. Gupta, M. Perumkunnil, V. Kateel, S. Couet, et al. "Voltage-gated assisted spin-orbit torque magnetic random-access memory for high-density and low-power embedded application." *arXiv preprint arXiv:2104.09599* (2021).

42. Khosla, Robin, and Satinder K. Sharma. "Integration of ferroelectric materials: an ultimate solution for next-generation computing and storage devices." *ACS Applied Electronic Materials* 3, no. 7 (2021): 2862–289.

14

IoT Application in Agriculture for Smart Farming: Issues and Solutions

Manmohan Sharma, Niranjan Lal, Priya Gupta, and Rahul Dandautiya

CONTENTS

14.1 Introduction

Every time you look at your smartwatch to count calories or ask Alexa or Siri to calculate the value of the pie, you are using what IoT tech is. By the simplest of definitions, IoT is the internet-controlling things. IoT devices are 'smart' devices that can transfer data over a network. The term Internet of Things (IoT) was coined in 1999 by Kevin Ashton, co-founder and executive director of the MIT Auto-ID center while presenting at Procter and Gamble as its brand manager.

The interest in developing the populace can be effectively met with IoT. Notwithstanding a developing crowd, presently anticipated to arrive at 9.6 billion by 2050, the farming business should ascend to fulfill needs, paying little heed to ecological difficulties like troublesome climate conditions and environmental change. To address the issues of that developing populace, the farming business should receive innovations to acquire a vital edge. New rural applications in savvy cultivating and exactness cultivating through IoT will empower the company to increment operational productivity, lower costs, lessen squandering, and improve the nature of their yield.

DOI: 10.1201/9781003226888-14

So, what is smart farming? Smart farming is a capital-intensive and hi-tech system of growing food cleanly and sustainably for the masses. It applies modern ICT (Information and Communication Technologies) in agriculture (Vineela et al., 2018). In IoT-based keen cultivating, a framework is worked for observing the harvest field with sensors (light, dampness, temperature, soil dampness, and so on) and mechanizing the water system framework. The ranchers can screen the field conditions from any place. IoT-based savvy cultivation is more productive than the standard methodology (ADB.org,2020).

The utilization of IoT-based keen cultivating objective daily, enormous cultivating activities, yet could likewise be new switches to elevate other developing or standard patterns in agrarian like natural cultivating, family cultivating (unpredictable or little spaces, specific dairy cattle as well as societies, safeguarding of distinctive or excellent assortments, and so forth), and improve profoundly straightforward cultivating. Regarding natural issues, IoT-based keen cultivating can give extraordinary advantages, including more proficient water utilization or streamlining information sources and medicines.

Agriculture is the backbone of the human race, and technology-supported agriculture raises vast opportunities to improve contemporary techniques (Mooney, 2020). In this chapter, a detailed and systematic review will highlight various technological domains in agriculture technologies. This chapter will mainly focus on the roles and responsibilities of the IoT, fog computing, and blockchain technologies in agriculture. In continuation, various components of discussing technologies such as sensors, microcontrollers, security algorithms, cloud servers, big data analytics (Tu et al., 2020), data mining, robotics, and virtual reality and their present applications in agriculture will also be discussed. Further technology-wise and era-wise comparative analysis will be conducted to identify features of current technologies. By performing mentioned comparative analysis, an efficient technological architecture will be discussed to improve the agriculture scenario. In the end, other advanced technologies, such as deep learning, quantum computing, and advanced Sensors, will be related to futuristic concerns.

The usage of smart and IoT-based farming will boost the productivity of any country and, at the same time, improve farmers' standards. Modern technologies like machine learning (ML) and the IoT help farmers to complete their work more efficiently.

14.2 Applications of IoT in Agriculture

14.2.1 Monitoring of Climate Conditions

Likely the most mainstream shrewd agribusiness devices are climate stations, joining different savvy cultivating sensors. Situated across the field, they gather additional information from the climate and send it to the cloud. The given estimations can be utilized to plan the environmental conditions, pick the good harvests, and take the necessary measures to improve their ability (for example, accuracy cultivating). Figure 14.1 shows the estimation for cultivating. Some examples of such agriculture IoT devices are Almeta and Smart Elements.

14.2.2 Crop Management

One more kind of IoT item in horticulture and another component of accuracy cultivating are crop executives' gadgets. Like climate stations, they ought to be set in the field to

FIGURE 14.1
Smart cultivation using IoT devices.

gather information about editing cultivating, from temperature and precipitation to leaf water potential and, by and significant harvest well-being. In this way, you can screen your harvest development and any abnormalities to adequately forestall any illnesses or pervasions that can hurt your yield. Arable and Semios can fill in as excellent portrayals of how this utilization case can be applied.

14.2.3 Precision Farming

Exactness agriculture/precision farming is perhaps the most popular use of IoT in agriculture (Chen et al., 2019). It makes the cultivating practice more exact and constrained by acknowledging sensitive cultivating applications, for example, animal checking, vehicle following, field perception, and stock observing. The objective of exactness cultivation is to break down the information created using sensors and respond as needed. Exactness farming assists ranchers in generating information with sensors and examining that data to make insightful and fast choices (Nayyar and Puri, 2016). There are various accuracy cultivating procedures like water systems, the board, domesticated animals, the executives, vehicle following, and a lot more which assume a fundamental part in expanding productivity and adequacy. With the assistance of precision cultivating, you can examine soil conditions and other related boundaries to broaden the operational effectiveness. Not just this, you can likewise identify the continuous working states of the associated gadgets to distinguish water and supplement levels. Figure 14.2 shows the devices used for precision farming (agrocares, 2021).

14.2.4 Smart Greenhouse

To make our nurseries shrewd, IoT has empowered climate stations to change the environmental conditions as indicated by a specific arrangement of guidelines. The reception of IoT in greenhouses has killed human mediation, accordingly making the whole cycle savvy and expanding precision simultaneously. For instance, sun-based fueled IoT sensors construct present-day and suitable nurseries. These sensors gather and communicate constant information, which helps progressively check the nursery state. With the assistance of the sensors, the water utilization and nursery state can be observed using messages or SMS alarms. A programmed and shrewd water system is done with the assistance of IoT.

FIGURE 14.2
IoT agriculture technology used for *precision farming.*

These sensors help to give data on the critical factor, stickiness, temperature, and light levels.

14.2.5 Predictive Analytics for Smart Farming

Exactness agribusiness and prescient information examination go connected at the hip. While IoT and keen sensor innovation are a goldmine for profoundly applicable continuous information, the utilization of information investigation assists ranchers with sorting out it and thinking of significant forecasts: crop collecting time, the dangers of sicknesses and pervasions, yield volume, and so forth. Information examination apparatuses help make cultivating, which is intrinsically profoundly reliant upon climate conditions, more sensible, and unsurprising.

For example, the crop performance platform helps farmers access the volume and quality of yields in advance and their vulnerability to unfavorable weather conditions, such as floods and drought. It also enables farmers to optimize the supply of water and nutrients for each crop and even select yield traits to improve quality. Applied in agriculture, solutions like Soil Scout would allow farmers to save up to 50% of irrigation water, reduce the loss of fertilizers caused by overwatering, and deliver actionable insights regardless of season or weather conditions (Gaur, 2021); IoT in agriculture for smart farming is depicted in Figure 14.3.

14.3 Issues and Challenges Related to IoT Applications in Smart Farming

14.3.1 Interoperability of Different Standards

With increasingly more OEMs concocting new and creative farming IoT apparatuses and stages, interoperability is quickly turning into a state of concern. The different accessible devices and advancements frequently don't keep similar innovation norms/stages – because

FIGURE 14.3
IoT in smart farming with connected devices.

of which there is an absence of consistency in the last examination done by end clients. On numerous occasions, the different gateway(s) production is fundamental for interpreting and moving information across guidelines. The test lies in changing the savvy, independent gadgets and doors to all-encompassing, rancher-agreeable stages.

14.3.2 Connectivity in Rural Areas

In numerous far-off rustic areas across the world (especially in the agricultural nations, albeit a few places in the US experience this also), a solid, dependable web network isn't accessible. That, like this, ruins the endeavors to apply savvy horticulture strategies at such places. Unless the organization's exhibitions and data transmission speeds are fundamentally improved, executing computerized cultivating will stay hazardous. Since numerous agro-sensors/entryways rely upon cloud administrations for information transmission/ stockpiling, cloud-based registering needs to get more grounded. Furthermore, in farmlands that have tall, thick trees and additionally sloping landscapes, gathering GPS signals turns into a significant issue.

14.3.3 Barriers to Entry for New Firms

Even though exactness cultivating has been a subject of extensive interest for quite a long while, the idea is still moderately 'new.' Like this, the vast equipment/programming makers that entered this market at the beginning have a particular first-mover advantage. The modest seriousness of the market can keep new firms from entering this area – with the current large firms holding a stranglehold. Ranchers can likewise deal with issues while attempting to move information streams from a more established stage to a fresher one, and there are dangers of information misfortune. The assets and steps given by a significant part in the agro-IoT area probably won't be viable with those provided by a more modest OEM – and that may keep the last from having enough customers.

14.3.4 Challenge for Indoor Farming

Most exact horticulture techniques and assets are streamlined for regular open-air cultivating. With the worth of the worldwide vertical cultivating industry projected to go past $4 billion by 2021, more consideration must be given to innovation support for indoor cultivating. The shortfall of everyday climatic variances and regular seasons must be considered while thinking of clever indoor cultivating techniques. The yield's dietary benefit should not be unfavorably influenced at all things considered. Ranchers should have the option to depend on innovation to establish the ideal developing climate (light, temperature, water accessibility) for indoor plants.

14.3.5 Technical Failures and Resultant Damages

The developing reliance of horticulture (or whatever else, besides!) on innovation accompanies a possibly genuine disadvantage. On the off chance of a mechanical breakdown in the equipment or cultivating IoT unit/sensor glitches – real yield harm can be the outcome. For instance, if the intelligent water system sensors are down, plants will probably be underwatered or overwatered. Food handling can be undermined if the mechanical assets in the capacity area(s) are not working. Indeed, even a couple of vacation moments because of a forced disappointment can have actual results – especially when reinforcement power isn't free.

14.4 Conclusion

The concept of precision agriculture is based on four pillars – right place, right source, right quantity, and right time. It has already made a difference to agriculture and farm yield performance worldwide, and once the challenges above are overcome, its benefits will become more evident and sustainable. Smart farming based on IoT technologies enables growers and farmers to reduce waste and enhance productivity ranging from the quantity of fertilizer utilized to the number of journeys the farm vehicles have made and enabling efficient utilization of resources such as water and electricity. In this chapter, we discussed the opportunities got from utilizing IoT in agriculture, followed by challenges in the application of those IoT gadgets in intelligent farming. Various types of IoT devices will be required to integrate with agriculture, and, in this case, the main problem will be related to connectivity with agriculture due to poor internet signals. The next challenges are how information will be shared with the framers, there will be difficulty in the interoperability between IoT systems and devices, and the final challenges will need high hardware costs and security.

We found a lot of examples apart from farming where modern technologies like artificial intelligence (AI), ML, the IoT, and deep learning help human beings to get their tasks done in an efficient manner. By using the IoT-enabled devices, framing may be improved using smart technologies and smart agriculture systems and demand can be successful if farmers will implement the IoT solution.

References

ADB.org. (2020) "A New Engine for Rural Economic Growth in the People's Republic of China". Available:https://www.adb.org/sites/default/files/publication/455091/internet-plus-agricultureprc.pdf. [Accessed: 15-July-2020].

agrocares. (2021) "The Most Complete, Fast, Affordable and Reliable Solution to Test Nutrients On-Site. https://www.agrocares.com/en/products/lab-in-the-box/ [Accessed: 15-April-2019 Online].

Ayaz, M., Ammad-Uddin, M., Sharif, Z., Mansour, A., & Aggoune, E.-H. (2019) "Internet-of-things (IoT)-based smart agriculture: toward making the fields talk". IEEE Access 7:129551–129583.

Chen, W. L., Lin, Y. B., Lin, Y. W., Chen, R., Liao, J. K., Ng, F. L., & Yen, T. H. (2019) "AgriTalk: IoT for precision soil farming of turmeric cultivation", IEEE Internet of Things Journal, 6(3):5209–5223.

Gaur, C. (2021), "Enabling IoT in Smart Farming Solutions and Applications" (https://www.xenon-stack.com/use-cases/iot-smart-farming) [Accessed: 28-February-2022].

Mooney, P. (2020) "Open Source Farming the next Agricultural Revolution". Available: http://mitmullingar.com/event/is-opensource-farming-the-next-agricultural revolution/[Accessed: 15-July-2020].

Nayyar, A., & Puri, V. (2016). Smart farming: IoT based smart sensors agriculture stick for live temperature and moisture monitoring using Arduino, cloud computing & solar technology, The international conference on communication and computing (ICCCS-2016).

Tu, L., Liu, S., Wang, Y., Zhang, C., & Li, P. (2020) "An optimized cluster storage method for real-time big data in internet of things", The Journal of Supercomputing 76(7):5175–5191.

Vineela, T., Naga Harini, J., Kiranmai, Ch., Harshitha, G., & Adi Lakshmi, B. (2018), "IoT based agriculture monitoring and smart irrigation system using raspberry pi", International Research Journal of Engineering and Technology (IRJET), 05 (01) (Jan-2018), p. 1417.

15

Building a Greener World: Connecting IoT with Environment towards Sustainability

Bhupal Bhattacharya and Niranjan Lal

CONTENTS

15.1 Introduction

Farming is the hand that feeds the human population, but as an industry, agricultural activity which is something often taken for granted. Pressures on the farmers to feed the booming population are increasing manifold. By 2050, it's estimated that it will be over nine and a half billion of present population. Agriculture without adoption of smart of technologies is considered to be a risky investment with tight profit margins and often unpredictable yields.

DOI: 10.1201/9781003226888-15

Climate is surely having a positive impact on global productivity. However, another major problem facing today's farmer is the shortage of seasonal labour. Many farms are losing money because they simply can't find the workers to pick their produce. Growers in particular are searching for new methods to gather their precious crops.

It is the soil from where food is raised. When land is ploughed to grow crops, only food is raised and that requires effective monitoring of resources. The natural resources are already said to have exhausted. It's not possible to carry out harvesting from only rainwater. The finding out of alternative arrangement is increasing the opportunity cost in manifold and thus requires adoption of smart technologies. Sustainable development is a development which can be sustained over a period of time, which is there for a number of years where wastages can be largely avoided in a proper judicial manner. In the Brundtland Commission Report, the concern for the common was emphasized which was published in 1987 by the World commission. The term sustainable development was used by the World commission for the first time in its report and that is for the common future.

15.2 Literature Review

AI and IoT for Sustainable Development in Emerging Countries: Challenges and Opportunities: 105 (Lecture Notes on Data Engineering and Communications Technologies), Published by Springer Nature Switzerland AG, 2020. The authors through this book summarized the collection of cutting-edge essays from practitioners and researchers engaged in a broad variety of fields where AI and IoT could create additional possibilities. AI technology and the IoT have emerged as must-have technologies in nearly every industry today. The range of AI and IoT applications is as broad as the horizon, spanning agriculture and industry. These technologies are widely employed in rich countries today, and they're still in their infancy in developing countries.

This chapter presents a great foundation and a wide range of useful applications for smart, sustainable cities and communities, as well as case studies to assist readers in comprehending IoT-driven smart city solutions in addition to the fundamentals, applications, and problems of IoT for sustainable smart cities and society. The author tried to provide readers with an overview of IoT and smart cities, as well as the communication protocols that go with them and how they can be used in a variety of smart city applications. The key concerns highlighted in this literature are in relation to IoT, including security, privacy, and authenticity.

Internet of Things for Sustainable Community Development: Wireless Communications, Sensing, and Systems 1st ed. 2020 by Abdul Salam. The importance of the IoT in building the next generation of communities is discussed in this book. The author illustrates how a research and teaching environment promotes meaningful solutions-oriented science which can assist citizens, government, industry, and perhaps other stakeholders in cooperating to make sensible, environmentally accountable, scientific-based decisions. As a result, he demonstrates how societies can deal with complex, interwoven socio-environmental issues. This book examines the fundamental interconnected difficulties that are impeding in the development of a sustainable and resilient society – each one of these issues is linked to IoT-based responses.

15.3 Sustainable Development and Green Agriculture

Sustainable agriculture is a form of agriculture that does not negatively affect future agriculture. It means sustaining your practices (Waas, T., 2011), for as long as possible (Leeuwis, C, 2000). In day-to-day life, the internet is being used to connect with other people which can be called as Internet of Humans. In a similar way when the internet is used to connect devices, vehicles, home appliances, etc., it is called IoT. The IoT area has become the main topic of discussion in the last few years, including sustainable development, green economy, and aims for sustainable development without degrading the environment. So, using a green economy means addressing the challenges of protecting the conditions of the environment. The green economy is a system that helps in economic growth while at the same time taking care of the environment. Sustainable means what is good for the economy and the future of the moment.

The advantages of a sustainable form of production are economic stability, emotional satisfaction knowing they aren't harming the environment, better physical health because of the quality of food entering their bodies and lower stress levels, preserving biological diversity, and bolstering themselves and their community against climate change (Selhub, E. M. et al., 2012).

15.4 Modern Approaches and IoT

The concept of the IoT is rapidly gaining traction in the workplace and beyond (Conway, J., 2016). Following the creation of this notion, several experts believe that its implementation has a significant impact on how people work and operate. That is due to its incalculable impact not only in the workplace but also in people's everyday lives (Ostrom, A. L. et al., 2010). The IoT is a prospective technology that uses simple machine identification tags to connect networks or items to the projected internet (Khan, R. et al., 2012). These tags contain sensors that collect data and information about the status of the agricultural object in question and others in its immediate vicinity (Khanna, A. et al., 2019).

The concept behind the IoT is to link any device to a network switch. According to several academics, there will be a total of 26 billion devices connected to the internet by the end of 2021. As a result, it coined the human-to-human, human-to-things, and human-to-things relationships (Abiodun, O. I. et al., 2021). The IoT is expected to bring a slew of benefits. Because some of its applications are already visible, it starts to rule out some of the most important applications that people consider (Eubanks, V., 2018).

The growing need predicted that there is immediate requirement of rising of 70% of agricultural activities just to keep up with demand to meet rising demand food. Producers need to turn to digital Innovations to increase their yield and farming efficiency. Technology in agriculture is thriving and attracting investment like never before. Digitization along the entire value chain is seeing tech companies forge enter to a new relationship. With the changing climate, there arises a challenge to adopt all sorts of technology addressing the needs. It's not going to be one technology that's going to help in solving all the existing problems.

The environment is deteriorating all around the planet. Food security and water availability are increasingly threatened by land degradation, deforestation, and desertification. Droughts, floods, forest fires, and other natural disasters become more frequent and have a greater impact as a result of environmental degradation (Sivakumar, M. V. K., 2007).

Industry is undergoing major developments over the last century, 100 years ago, farming looked like this today. It estimates that each year between 20 and 40% of global crop yields are destroyed by pests and disease, tiny sensors, and cameras will monitor crop growth and alert farmers on their smartphones. If there's a problem or when it's the best time to harvest, the Bonnie Rod can take a soil sample, liquidize it then analyse its pH and phosphorus levels all in real-time as a proof of concept for all this autonomous farming technology. When a troubled area is identified, machine learning can regularly improving the system's ability to differentiate between varieties of crops and the weeds that threaten the crops.

15.5 Benefits Derived from Usage of IoT in Agricultural Sectors

15.5.1 Improves Device Communication

The IoT allows devices to communicate with one another. It's a machine-to-machine exchange. Though some believe the system would be difficult to manage if it malfunctioned, the actual gadgets' connectivity suggests the opposite (Floridi, L., 2014). There's a level of absolute precision that can help machines run more efficiently (Gebreamlak, L. M., 2020).

15.5.2 Collects Useful Data

The more relevant the data, the easier it is to make the best decision possible. The amount of data collected by devices communicates with one another, assisting the consumer. By retaining openness in the operations, the machines can process the data more efficiently (Dai, H. N. et al., 2020).

15.5.3 Focused on Automation and Control

A huge degree of control and automation is possible due to physical things being connected and operated digitally with wireless support. Machines can produce faster and more timely results without the need for human participation (Vermesan, O. et al., 2013). As a result, it bridges some of the gaps between machine and human interactions.

15.5.4 Disseminating Data

The IoT makes device data more accessible. It then goes through the required stages of using a certain gadget and notifies the user in real time. It ensures consistency in the tasks at hand and preserves the service quality of each device's setup (Atzori, L. et al., 2017).

15.5.5 Monitoring

It's a good idea to keep an eye on things. Monitoring is one of the most obvious benefits of IoT. It gives the advantage of knowing what's going to happen ahead of time. This allows for easy collection of precise supply quantities, water distribution and consumption, intelligent energy management, and security distribution (McEwen, A. et al., 2013). In the event of disasters or emergencies, it also takes the required steps.

15.5.6 Time-Efficiency and Savings

Machine-to-machine contact allows for faster response times and better overall gadget performance. People can do other creative jobs since the IoT technology gives correct results promptly. Its fast-paced feature helps in saving a lot of time. Every human's daily existence can be benefitted from the IoT' potential. Everything becomes more efficient, productive, and advanced as a result of it. It is unquestionably another form of technology to which most people can look forward.

15.6 The Utilities of IoT in Sustainable Agricultural Production

Conventional farming operations were not capable to meet the increasing demands and resulted into decrease in agricultural productions. For the growth of agricultural crops and plants, IoT-driven smart devices can intelligently monitor, as well as control the climate, eliminating the need for manual intervention. Various sensors can be engaged to measure the environmental parameters according to the specific requirements. The data gathered gets automatically stored in a cloud-based platform for further processing. IoT further helps in measuring the soil temperature, volumetric water, photosynthetic, radiation soil, water, potential, and oxygen levels which are the important considerations for the proper agricultural activities. Strong, monitoring with using of IoT technology empowers farmer and producers to maximize productions, by reducing crop diseases in optimizing usage of all environmental resources. Data from the IoT sensors can be transmitted back to the central point for analysis, visualization, and trend analysis which is helpful for farming in upcoming years too. IoT is also helpful in monitoring of climatic conditions as that enable for real-time weather conditions since its collect data directly from the environment.

The application of sensor devices can equally detect real-time weather conditions, like humidity, rainfall temperature very accurately. There are several types of sensors available for the farmers, to detect all these parameters and configure therefore accordingly.

15.6.1 Water Management

The IoT makes it possible to track changes in a reservoir's water quality. The interconnection of various sensors and monitoring systems aids in the provision of water level and flood alerts (McCabe, M. F. et al., 2017), as well as the prediction of other calamities such as earthquakes and probable landslides in prone locations, allowing residents and authorities to take immediate action (Diamandis, P. H. et al., 2012).

15.6.2 Wildlife

Animal detection can also be done by using IoT. The usefulness is being felt in controlling, surveying, and preventing disease epidemics in the future. The livestock are getting fitted with specific RFID chips, and readers would be positioned in selected monitoring locations (Leskinen, S., 2014).

15.6.3 Marine Organisms

High-value species like salmon and cod are threatened by overfishing and overexploitation of aquatic variety (Ahern, M. et al., 2021). Even smart businesses that use Green Design make a significant contribution to energy reduction (Mustafa, S. et al., 2015). Solar power, for example, ensures optimum efficiency in power use and complete exploitation of renewable sources by maximising the use of daylight, rainwater capture, smart cooling and ventilation systems, and solar power.

15.6.4 Waste Management

Inefficient garbage management is one of the biggest concerns in metropolitan settings. Improper trash disposal can pose a number of health risks as well as have an impact on the environment's air and water (Rajmohan, K. V. S. et al., 2019). Machine-to-machine (M2M) or machine-to-man (M2M) systems can be set up for more intelligent trash division and disposal. Built-in sensors in trash cans or dumpsters can measure the amount of rubbish. When the garbage can is full, the signal transceiver transmits a message with the GPS location and IP address to the central command centre via internet or satellite.

Adoption of IoT in agriculture enhances the productivity by way of effectively monitoring the crops using drones, remote sensors, and computer imaging combined with continuously progressing, machine learning, and analytical tools for monitoring crops surveying and mapping the fields and providing data to farmers. Integration of IoT with agriculture seems to have contributed much in proper making management plans which saves both time and money.

The use of IoT for environmental sustainability is showing to be one of the most useful tools in our fight for environmental balance. Organizations like Smart Sight Innovations can be helpful to implement IoT processes to act more responsibly towards the environment.

15.7 The Fundamental Components of IoT

1. Sensors – It gathers information from the environment. The type of information collected might range from simple temperature monitoring to complicated video feeds. Multiple sensors can be found on a single device. GPS, camera, microphone, temperature sensors, and other sensors are examples of sensors. Some physical processes are also converted into electrical impulses by it.

2. Connectivity – The data is collected and delivered to the cloud via a medium of transport. As a result, sensors are linked to the cloud via a variety of communication methods, including Wi-Fi, satellite networks, Bluetooth, and wide area networks.

3. Data processing – Once the data has been uploaded to the cloud, the software processes it. This can range from the very basic, such as verifying temperature data on equipment, to the highly complicated, such as object identification.

4. User interface – The data is then made available to end users. This can be accomplished by sending them alarms, texts, or emails. Actuators are utilized when two devices are coupled.

It is becoming so essential to us because of one basic reason that helps us in more than one ways like security, power savings, time-savings, and convenience.

Each and everything around the whole world in environment is data and nowadays this is very needed for analysing it towards the sustainability. Moreover, the real-time data is highly desired for performing some important operations. The internet has evolved into more than just a way for people to interact with one another. It's now a platform for networked devices to connect with one another, such as refrigerators communicating with the electric utility, navigation systems communicating with traffic sensors (Gubbi, J. et al., 2013). Low-cost sensors, low-power CPUs, and broad wireless communication are among the technological developments that have enabled the IoT (Sanfeliu, A. et al., 2008). It's about creating an information-rich world more especially in supporting the agricultural activities.

It is known that the environmental changes and challenges are the whole world facing in surrounding ecosystem. Air pollutions, water pollutions, and disposal of industrial waste are the few examples of pollutions apart from these; there are many and, to tackle with it, IoT is venturing with these areas (Shim, J. P. et al., 2019).

15.8 IoT and Agriculture

Many of the cities are flooded with pollution and, therefore, to monitor the quality of air, noise level, traffic regulations, vehicle access in the city, etc. IoT monitoring systems are getting deployed. These systems and applications are capable of measuring the earthquake in the rector's scale, tsunami predictions, or wildfire warning system that speculate with IoT for the specified location (Rashid, B. et al., 2016). The countries like the United States and Italy are already earning benefits from a smart irrigation system that reduces water consumption, increases crop yields, and helps in a greenhouse.

Food or crops or pulses get spoiled or wasted during improper transportation, therefore, to save it IoT telemactics and cloud-based systems with micro-monitoring and supply chain practice if properly applied would reduce the spoilage and the cost of food.

Enterprises and government sectors are increasingly adapting IoT technologies in the real world to reconstruct the ruptured environmental balance. IoT technologies combined with blockchain with creative funding and business model can do wonders in the environmental sectors to maintain the nature-balance and save and store the natural resources (El-Bendary, N. et al., 2013). CipherHut software is already working on IoT and delivering the solution for water and air quality testing tools, animal protection, or deforestation control system, and clean indoor solution.

15.9 Major Roles IoT Is Playing in the Environment

- Critical usage is in energy efficiency
- Reducing e-waste management
- For agricultural sustainability
- Species protection
- Cleaner air
- Maximizing renewable energy

Some of the other areas where IoT is saving the environment:

- Stopping illegal deforestation
- Protecting endangered species
- Monitoring oceans to save marine life
- Combating air pollution
- Monitoring the health of the crops
- Managing waste
- Monitoring methane levels

Traditional business paradigms are being shattered by the IoT, but the technology is only the enabler. It'll be the new business models that will make a difference. The internet, for example, has expanded beyond IT departments and typical internet-enabled gadgets. Though technology is driving these new connections, business models will change across industries as they respond to the new realities of what can be supplied in anything from city-wide transit systems to smart homes (Adner, R., 2012).

The data which is present around us is in physical form, like the state of the main door, moisture level of soil in your flower pot, the current state of your air conditioner, and the electricity consumption of your refrigerator. This is the type of data which is becoming important to us nowadays and we need to access this real-time data on our mobile and to control the appliances or monitor them directly from our smartphones.

But these machines are not capable of doing these things alone, so with the help of sensors we collect this physical data from the surroundings and process this data with microcontrollers and upload this data on the internet for the accessibility. This whole process falls under the category of the IoT. With the help of this data, researcher can track the real-time state of our homes which makes our places more secure. We can control each and every thing from just a mobile phone which makes the life more comfortable. We can track the power consumption of the devices and schedule them to turn off automatically to save power. These all things along with many more help us to save time.

IoT is being used in many different areas in the present days, which include environmental monitoring infrastructure, management, industrial applications energy management, medical and Healthcare, automation, and Transport Systems etc. In growth of IoT in 2003, the ratio of connected devices to living human beings was 0.08% whereas that has increased to 1% by 2008. In fact, the number of devices connected to the internet has exceeded the number of human beings on the planet, and as of 2018, that ratio has increased manifold to 21% by 2015. In total, more than 4.1 billion devices are now connected to the internet as of the latest data available till the year 2020. Because of the new wireless technologies, the applications and usage of IoT-related advancements are also taking place. The IoT works mainly by the application of Cloud software processes, which performs an action by sending an automatic alert by adjusting the sensors or devices without the need for the user. User are also allowed to put their needed input into the system, by allowing user to do so, any adjustments or actions that the user makes are then sent in the opposite direction, through the system from the user interface to the cloud which is popularly called as the sensors.

The application of IoT in agriculture enhances the capacity of agricultural activities by improving the entire agriculture system. IoT allows effective monitoring the agricultural field in real time with the help of sensors. The IoT in agriculture has not only saved the time of the farmers but has also reduced the extravagant use of resources such as water and electricity the applications of routine farming target.

15.10 Challenges of IoT in Agriculture

Unfortunately, the connectivity still poses a problem in general in a country like India where technology has not progressed to that level as is desired for effective use of it. IoT in general as diverse system chose different protocols and data transmission methods, which requires development of 5G technology which has not yet been rolled in the third world countries. The space-based internet requires fast and reliable internet connection for every space regardless of its size and conditions which is a major task at hand.

The next challenge is to design and durability. Any IoT system used in agriculture should be able to handle not only connectivity, but also the conditions of outer space weather monitoring stations, which should have an uncomplicated yet functional design and a certain level of robustness to work in the form.

The next challenge is limited resources and time in the integration of smart technology in agricultural area within the context of a constantly changing environment. Lack of fund of the companies who design and develop IoT for agriculture is the other aspect needed to be addressed. The challenging considerations like rapid climate change, emerging weather extremes, limited land availability, and unfavourable factors like flying pollinators seem to be the other aspects of urgent attention.

Over the next two decades, the technological wave will revolutionize the efficiency of farms all over the world. It can't come soon enough by the year, 2050, the human population will be nearly 10 billion which means the production of food and crops need to have doubled.

The need of the hour is to try to create the type of opportunities for the workforce to focus on the things that require higher intelligence and things that aren't necessarily just repetitive in nature. Some sections of farmers might be concerned that technology and robots are taking jobs away. But in fact it's creating job opportunities. The visual technology really unlocks all kinds of opportunities; developments in agritech industry and farmers are already reaping the benefits in the developed nations. With mounting pressures on the food production, innovations are really needed.

According to Kerry Hinton, former director of the University of Melbourne's Centre for Energy-Efficient Telecommunications, "The Internet of Things will be the biggest, most sophisticated piece of equipment that we've deployed across the planet-ever."

15.11 Conclusion

Getting economics to align with resources is a tough thing. For achieving sustainable agriculture is to pursue a market that values sustainability. IoT if utilized in the right manner can play a key role in making this environment better as well as reversing the damages that have been already made to it. The technology is already helping to make manufacturing processes efficient thereby reducing carbon emissions, making buildings smart to deliver energy savings and making greenhouses smarter and more.

IoT is all about connectivity between devices and in turn making human really smart on the earth. It is imperative that India should shift its focus in revolutionizing the agricultural sector thoroughly to achieve this growth and for which embracement of technologies is very much essential. There is a huge opportunity for the IoT to transform the methodologies and processes followed with automation. The major benefits of using drones include crop health, imaging integrated GIS mapping which has the potential to increase yields adopting proper strategy and planning based on real-time data collection and processing.

Adoption of drone technology gives a high-tech makeover to the agriculture industry is another application of IoT in farming. IoT helps to monitor, several things including the exact location of each animal, eating habits and reproductive cycle of species, grazing and movement patterns of animals. The use of IoT devices helps further in adjusting with the conditions of devices in the environment using different sensors that measure environmental parameters. Given the expectations and requirements of future young farmers, conservation-agriculture (CA)-based ecological intensification of farming through the adoption of IoT is considered a viable alternative to green revolution (GR) agriculture. Intensification of farming with IoT-based ecological approaches is now considered to be the most appropriate option for the tropics and subtropics.

What is really going to happen is an information explosion, there will be overwhelming data and there will be no privacy as everyone going to wear digital watch, that's again going to get connected in internet of other things, tracked all the times. Understanding of the applications of IoT in its technical sense connecting with environment and societal issues can effectively implement eco-efficient farming practices.

References

Abiodun, O. I., Abiodun, E. O., Alawida, M., Alkhawaldeh, R. S., & Arshad, H. (2021). A review on the security of the Internet of Things: challenges and solutions. Wireless Personal Communications, 119, 2603–2637.

Adner, R. (2012). The wide lens: a new strategy for innovation. Penguin UK.

Ahern, M., Thilsted, S., Oenema, S., & Kühnhold, H. (2021). The role of aquatic foods in sustainable healthy diets. UN Nutrition Discussion Paper.

Atzori, L., Iera, A., & Morabito, G. (2017). Understanding the Internet of Things: definition, potentials, and societal role of a fast evolving paradigm. Ad Hoc Networks, 56, 122–140.

Conway, J. (2016). The industrial Internet of Things: an evolution to a smart manufacturing enterprise. Schneider Electric.

Dai, H. N., Wang, H., Xu, G., Wan, J., & Imran, M. (2020). Big data analytics for manufacturing internet of things: opportunities, challenges and enabling technologies. Enterprise Information Systems, 14(9–10), 1279–1303.

Diamandis, P. H., & Kotler, S. (2012). Abundance: the future is better than you think. Simon and Schuster.

El-Bendary, N., Fouad, M. M. M., Ramadan, R. A., Banerjee, S., & Hassanien, A. E. (2013). Smart environmental monitoring using wireless sensor networks. K15146_C025. indd.

Eubanks, V. (2018). Automating inequality: how high-tech tools profile, police, and punish the poor. St. Martin's Press.

Floridi, L. (2014). The fourth revolution: how the infosphere is reshaping human reality. OUP Oxford.

Gebreamlak, L. M. (2020). PKI: the key to Solving the Internet of Things security problem. Naval Postgraduate School, Monterey, CA.

Gubbi, J., Buyya, R., Marusic, S., & Palaniswami, M. (2013). Internet of Things (IoT): a vision, architectural elements, and future directions. Future Generation Computer Systems, 29(7), 1645–1660.

Khan, R., Khan, S. U., Zaheer, R., & Khan, S. (2012). Future internet: the internet of things architecture, possible applications and key challenges. In 2012 10th international conference on frontiers of information technology (pp. 257–260). IEEE.

Khanna, A., & Kaur, S. (2019). Evolution of Internet of Things (IoT) and its significant impact in the field of precision agriculture. Computers and Electronics in Agriculture, 157, 218–231.

Leeuwis, C. (2000). Reconceptualizing participation for sustainable rural development: towards a negotiation approach. Development and Change, 31(5), 931–959.

Leskinen, S. (2014). m-Equine: IS support for the horse industry.

McCabe, M. F., Rodell, M., Alsdorf, D. E., Miralles, D. G., Uijlenhoet, R., Wagner, W., … & Wood, E. F. (2017). The future of Earth observation in hydrology. Hydrology and Earth System Sciences, 21(7), 3879–3914.

McEwen, A., & Cassimally, H. (2013). Designing the internet of things. John Wiley & Sons.

Mustafa, S., & Shapawi, R. (Eds.). (2015). Aquaculture ecosystems: adaptability and sustainability. John Wiley & Sons.

Ostrom, A. L., Bitner, M. J., Brown, S. W., Burkhard, K. A., Goul, M., Smith-Daniels, V., … & Rabinovich, E. (2010). Moving forward and making a difference: research priorities for the science of service. Journal of Service Research, 13(1), 4–36.

Rajmohan, K. V. S., Ramya, C., Viswanathan, M. R., & Varjani, S. (2019). Plastic pollutants: effective waste management for pollution control and abatement. Current Opinion in Environmental Science & Health, 12, 72–84.

Rashid, B., & Rehmani, M. H. (2016). Applications of wireless sensor networks for urban areas: a survey. Journal of Network and Computer Applications, 60, 192–219.

Sanfeliu, A., Hagita, N., & Saffiotti, A. (2008). Network robot systems. Robotics and Autonomous Systems, 56(10), 793–797.

Selhub, E. M., & Logan, A. C. (2012). Your brain on nature: the science of nature's influence on your health, happiness and vitality. John Wiley & Sons.

Shim, J. P., Avital, M., Dennis, A. R., Rossi, M., Sørensen, C., & French, A. (2019). The transformative effect of the internet of things on business and society. Communications of the Association for Information Systems, 44(1), 5.

Sivakumar, M. V. K. (2007). Interactions between climate and desertification. Agricultural and forest meteorology, 142(2–4), 143–155.

Vermesan, O., & Friess, P. (Eds.). (2013). Internet of things: converging technologies for smart environments and integrated ecosystems. River Publishers.

Waas, T., Hugé, J., Verbruggen, A., & Wright, T. (2011). Sustainable development: a bird's eye view. Sustainability, 3(10), 1637–1661 (10).

16

A Novel Mechanism in Continuous Intelligence for Mining and Aggregating IoT Sensor Data

Manicka Raja M, Kiruba B, Jasmine Selvakumari Jeya I, and Manoj Kumar S

CONTENTS

16.1 Introduction

The Internet of Things (IoT) is altering the way we live, travel, communicate, work and bearing business. It is even the foundation of a new industrial transition called Industry 4.0, as well as a critical component of the digital transformation of cities, companies, and society as a whole. In IoT-based sensor network systems, information consumed and supplied continues to rise at a steady rate. This flood of data is fueling unstoppable IoT adoption, with almost 21.5 billion IoT-connected devices expected by 2025. Every day, IoT-based sensors generate a massive amount of data. Similarly, the study of this massive amount of data encircles numerous occurrences at various phases in order to total and focus the data for dynamic purposes. The IoT continuously provides, coordinates, and drives data. Data stream-oriented IoT applications are defined as applications that generate a large amount of data that must be calculated carefully and continually. When function stream handling frameworks supervise information from IoT sensors, they take measures that gradually turn raw data into useful data. The framework handles a massive amount of data streams and also handles structures that filter and regulate total information in memory. One of the key issues in IoT sensor networks is aggregating data and recognizing trends in real time. Data from the IoT sensor network is analyzed, aggregated, and transmitted to the cloud layer. Because of the diverse nature of IoT devices, most IoT devices lack computational and storage capacity for this task, making it an even more difficult problem.

DOI: 10.1201/9781003226888-16

Instead of sending data directly to the cloud server, processing of data takes place at the edge nodes, close to where the data is generated. Computing devices in this level have higher computational power and data storage capacity than IoT sensor nodes. The network's edge is an excellent location for performing an action on data before sending it to the cloud.

Because IoT sensor data is often unstructured, it is challenging to conduct research using standard analytics and business intelligence tools built to handle organized data. Typically, streaming analytics entails making analytically informed judgments in milliseconds while evaluating many thousands of events per second provided by numerous devices, which may even be augmented by many other divergent sources of knowledge. The data from these sensors usually contains substantial gaps, garbled signals, and erroneous readings that must be cleaned out before analysis can take place. Furthermore, IoT data is generally only relevant when combined with additional, third-party data inputs. The suggested technique, which includes a continuous intelligence mechanism, would analyze data received from edge nodes. This method augments human decision-making with real-time streaming data and intelligent information systems.

The chapter has been further organized as follows: Section 16.2 gives the literature review, background, related work and motivation, Section 16.3 sketches the computational model of the system, Section 16.4 presents the Gaussian mixture model (GMM) for stream data used in the work, finally Section 16.5 presents the conclusion.

16.2 Related Works

Salvatore Vitabile et al. (2020) created a system for medical data processing that uses data fusion methods. The fusion of data, processing of information, and the analytics of sensor data collected from various mobile and health devices, IoT enable sensors, and smart city components are performed at the system's edge or fog computing nodes, resulting in efficiency and low latency in the detection of precarious medical circumstances that require immediate action. Furthermore, their started system can provide a tailored health system for general comfort in which individuals can get healthcare according on their own needs. Furthermore, the authors focused on including security elements into their medical IoT sensors in order to achieve privacy and authentication.

Mamunur Rashid et al. (2015) developed a new form of behavioral pattern known as a consistently frequent sensor pattern, which specifies the outline of occurrence behaviors among sensors in sensor networks. They created a distributed data extraction technique that handles huge amounts of IoT sensor data effectively while also allowing for quicker data mining due to its parallel implementation. Their mechanism adds to the overall system's high reliability. They developed the RFSP-tree (regularly frequent sensor patterns-tree), a single-pass tree structure capable of mining frequently frequent sensor patterns in sensor datasets using a pattern growth approach. Finally, they presented RFSP-H, a MapReduced-based technique for mining RFSPs in parallel over a network of specialized nodes in order to overcome the limitations of single unit processor and primary memory-based algorithms.

Sherif Sakr et al. (2016) developed SmartHealth, an unified and complete architecture for big data analytics services in smart healthcare networks that meets the stated difficulties and limitations. Their Framework serves as a road map for research into big data analytics in smart health-care applications.

Sidahmed Benabderrahmane et al. (2017) created a recommendation system based on a hybrid model that combines modular semantic classification with time series predicting inside a big data platform. The semantic categorization of job boards and job advertising includes a textual examination of the content of the job offers using a business classification terminology given by a public French organization. The time series analysis module forecasts the best job panel for a certain offer based on the observed click values (Sidahmed Benabderrahmanea et al., 2017).

Zhang et al. (2014) proposed a privacy-preserving and priority-based data collection and forwarding method for the mobile healthcare system. Their major goal is to improve the ratio of health data delivered to the cloud. Nonetheless, they use Paillier cryptography to ensure data privacy. For tiny and resource-constrained sensors, Paillier cryptography is an asymmetric cryptosystem module based on public and private keys that are computationally demanding and an energy-efficient data aggregation approach for ensuring data confidentiality and integrity while protecting against node compromise attacks is presented. The elliptic Curve Okamoto-Uchiyama (EC-OU) and Elliptic Curve Digital Signature Algorithm (ECDSA) are used by the author to ensure data integrity during data aggregation in wireless sensor networks.

Yuwen Pu et al. (2019) presented two data aggregation techniques for IoT devices that are both safe and privacy-preserving. These two techniques can prevent users' privacy data from being disclosed, therefore protecting users' private information from being revealed. However, Scheme-I accomplishes the private-preserving aim by using homomorphic encryption and AES encryption, but Scheme-II does it by using noise technology to minimize IoT device processing and enhance efficiency. In particular, their suggested system achieves the design goals of security, efficiency, and adaptability.

Kuan Zhang et al. (2014) presented a novel cloud-based architecture for medical wireless sensor networks, as well as a control system that supports sophisticated and dynamic security rules and is built on ciphertext-policy attribute-based encryption (CP-ABE).

Daniele Ravi et al. (2017) presented a deep learning approach that syndicates inertial sensor data characteristics with balancing information from a collection of shallow structures to assist exact and real-time action categorization. Their combined technique was designed to circumvent some of the constraints of a conventional deep learning architecture when on-node processing is necessary. Before passing the input onto the deep learning framework, spectral domain pre-processing is utilized to improve the suggested technique for real-time on-node computation. The suggested deep learning approach's classification accuracy is compared to state-of-the-art approaches utilizing both research laboratory and real-life motion datasets. Their outcomes demonstrate the approach's legitimacy on various human activity datasets, outstripping other approaches, with the two methods utilized in their mutual pipeline. They similarly showed that the suggested method's calculation durations are steady with the restrictions of real-time on-node processing on cellphones and a wearable sensor platform.

Ping Jiang et al. (2017).created a wearable sensor system with an automated data forwarder. For human behavior recognition, the forwarder system employs a hidden Markov Model. As an effective technique for learning sensor patterns, locality sensitive hashing is presented. The authors have created a prototype system to track the health of scattered users. It is demonstrated that clever forwarders can offer context awareness to remote sensors. When specific behaviors occur, their suggested system sends only essential information to the big data server for analytics, avoiding overburdened transmission and data storage. The system performs admirably, providing users with piece of mind in the knowledge that their safety is being watched and analyzed.

16.3 Computing Architecture

The IoT sensor data layer is largely comprised different IoT sensors capable of measuring physical backgrounds and capturing real-time environmental variations. Humidity, temperature, accelerometer, pressure, gas, image, optical sensors, gyroscopes, radiofrequency identifier (RFID) sensors, motion sensor data, and infrared (IR) sensors are some of the most widely used IoT-assisted sensors as depicted in Figure 16.1. The microprocessor, control and interface unit, storage unit, power system, and wireless communication interface modules are the most common IoT sensors. The size, computational power, memory, networking capabilities, and storage capacity of IoT sensor devices are limited. For IoT sensor device communication, wireless communication protocols such as ZigBee, near-field communication (NFC), Wi-Fi, Bluetooth, and LTE/4G mobile technologies are widely utilized.

The monitoring nodes, also known as fog nodes, connect various IoT equipment to the server. A monitoring node acts as a server proxy and maintains the IoT system. Instead of the server, sensed data created by IoT devices is transferred to and analyzed by the monitoring node. The monitoring node handles received data and only communicates problematic conditions to the server. As a result, the server's network traffic and burden are decreased. The monitoring node controls data block by block to increase the efficiency of data search and transmission processes. A dataset contains data values, device and sensor IDs, and a timestamp to identify which IoT device created the data. Furthermore, the fog computing layer may complete direct computing processing, eliminating network transmission delays caused by sending/receiving from the faraway cloud (Gunjae Yoon et al., 2019).

16.3.1 IoT Stream Data Analytics in Cloud

Streaming analytics, also defined as event stream processing, is the study of large clusters of existing and motion data using event stream processor, which are continuous inquiries.

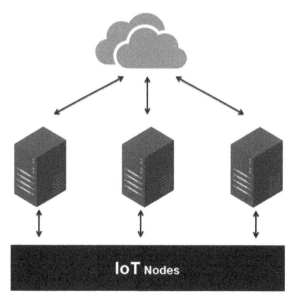

FIGURE 16.1
Generalized layered architecture of the proposed system.

FIGURE 16.2
Process flow in IoT stream analytics.

These streams are stimulated by a specific event that happens as a direct result of an action or series of activities, such as a financial transaction, equipment failure, website visit, a social post activity, or a or any other quantifiable activity (Shusen Yang. 2017). As a source of big data, IoT data may be constantly broadcast or captured. Streaming data is data that is generated or gathered at tremendously short intervals of time and must be examined fast in order to extract instant insights and/or make quick decisions. Big data refers to enormous datasets that traditional hardware and software systems are incapable of storing, managing, processing, or analyzing. Data sources include cloud applications, IoT, transactions, mobile devices, online interactions, and machine sensors (Erwin Adi et al. 2020). The complete process analysis in IoT as the streaming process is depicted in Figure 16.2.

16.4 Proposed Continuous Intelligence-Based Dynamic Gaussian Mixture Model IoT Stream Data

Streaming data is continually generated data from a number of sources. Whether the data originates from social media feedstuffs or cameras and IoT sensors, each record must be handled in such a way that its association to other data and time sequence is conserved. Real-time streaming data is generated via log files, e-commerce purchases, weather occurrences, utility service consumption, geo-location of people and objects, server activity, and other means. When there is a continual stream of data being created and collected, streaming analytics is required to make sense of the data in real time. Companies that use streaming analytics become more flexible and sensitive to the realities and settings in which they operate. It is critical to understand that streaming analytics enables companies to be proactive with real-time processing and decision-making rather than reactive to data.

16.4.1 Continuous Intelligence

Continuous intelligence is a design style that incorporates real-time analytics into company operations, analyzing present and historical data to recommend actions in response to events. It employs a number of technologies, like as stream processing, augmented analytics, and machine learning, as well as event business rule management, to provide decision automation or decision aid.

When decision-making tackles are incorporated into the business processes that generate them, continuous intelligence may help organizations streamline operations, personalize customer encounters, proactively address problems before they occur, and ultimately enhance corporate performance. This overall flow is pictured in Figure 16.3. This is known as return-on-data, and it occurs when the data that an organization invests resources in gathering and keeping is used to generate good results. To make continuous intelligence a reality, businesses must address the issues of heterogeneity, customization, and data literacy.

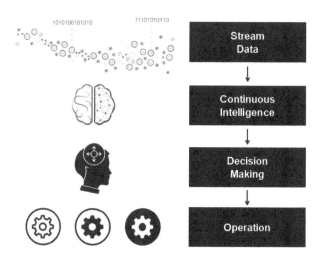

FIGURE 16.3
Role of continuous intelligence in decision-making.

IT and business teams frequently struggle to connect fundamental operational operations and gain even simple analytics insights across disparate environments. Their apps, data platforms, data management tools, and Business Intelligence tools, which have developed over decades as a result of one-off decisions, sometimes require specialist code to interoperate. New continuous intelligence solutions use open APIs to help patch things together, but they cannot entirely compensate for the proprietary restrictions of historical systems.

Enterprises can frequently standardize data intake, processing, and analysis but must still customize when it comes to operations. This is difficult since IP and operations differ greatly by industry and even business. An offshore oil drilling rig needs different IoT technologies than a car manufacturing. A commercial bank's mobile applications are not the same as those of a retailer. Many of them lack the necessary specialized programming abilities and fail to create the necessary bridges between IT and operational technicians in business units.

Data literacy is the ability to understand and use data. Many corporate and operational leaders still lack the skills required to make more data-driven choices. They require instruction in basic analytical ideas as well as how to apply those concepts to their responsibilities. They also require instruction on how to utilize continuous intelligence and Business Intelligence technologies. Businesses frequently fail to invest in the necessary educational programmes to achieve this goal.

Although continuous intelligence may assist remove some human bias from decision-making by revealing factual facts, continuous intelligence architecture can remain flexible and intuitive enough for human usage. While some firms may employ continuous intelligence to control "self-regulating" gear or software, all organizations are ultimately powered by human activities.

16.4.2 Gaussian Mixture Model

The GMM, often known as the mixture of Gaussian, is a probability distribution rather than a model. It is a model that is often used for generative unsupervised learning or clustering. It is based on the optimization method and is also known as expectation-maximization clustering or EM clustering. GMMs are intended to characterize normally distributed subpopulations within a larger population, mixture models are often employed. The advantage of mixture models is that they do not require which subgroup a data item belongs to. It enables the machine to learn the subpopulations automatically. Unsupervised learning is demonstrated here.

According to the GMM, our clustering task consists of determining the latent component c_i accountable for each v_i. For the time being, we will disregard the fact that we do not know the GMM parameters and consider how we would complete the clustering job given $(\pi, \beta_{1:k}, \Sigma_{1:k})$.

Given that a GMM with known parameters produces a joint distribution over (v_i, c_i), it makes sense to analyze the conditional distribution of each z_i given x_i:

$$\mathbf{prob}(c_i = j|v_i) = \mathbf{prob}(c_i = j)\mathbf{prob}(v_i|c_i = j)/\mathbf{prob}(v_i)$$

$$= \pi_j \varphi(v_i; \beta_j, \Sigma_j)/\sum_{l=1}^{k} \pi l \varphi(ci; \beta l, \Sigma l). \tag{16.1}$$

These conditionals reflect our updated views about z_i after we witness it: before we observe x_i, we have the prior opinion that it belongs to cluster j with probability π_j; after we observe x_i, we may update this belief based on the likelihood of x_i under each Gaussian component. A Gaussian Mixture object depicts a Gaussian mixture distribution, often known as a GMM, which defines a multivariate distribution composed of Gaussian distribution structures.

It is defined by the mean and covariance of each component. The mixture is defined by a vector of mixing proportions, where each mingling proportion reflects the fraction of the population described by a corresponding structure. Soft clustering is a clustering approach that permits certain data points to be assigned to several groups. This type of clustering with GMM is depicted in the Figure 16.4. To put soft clustering into action,

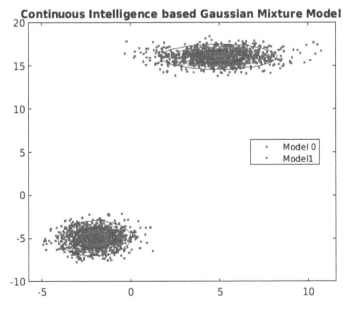

FIGURE 16.4
Clustering based of Gaussian mixture model.

do the following: (i) Assign a cluster membership score to each data point that reflects how similar it is to the archetype of each cluster. (ii) For a Gaussian mixture, the cluster archetype is the mean of the associated component, and the component can be the estimated cluster membership posterior probability. (iii) Rank the points by their cluster membership score.

A data point is a member of the cluster corresponding to the largest posterior probability in algorithms that employ posterior probabilities as scores. However, if there are additional clusters with matching posterior probability close to the maximum, the data point might be a member of those clusters as well. Before clustering, it is a good idea to set a threshold for scores that result in numerous cluster memberships.

16.5 Conclusion

The shift in the IoT sensor network paradigm toward new technologies is like cloud services, pervasive computing, edge computing, and fog computing indications to greater complexity in data processing, data synthesis, and IoT sensor data analytics. This chapter delves further into the significance of these processes. The fundamental architecture of IoT sensor data processing, fusion, and analysis has been provided to expound on the capabilities of each of these processes. Following that, the characteristics of sensor data were examined, including their large amount, real-time processing, heterogeneity, volume of data and scalability. Data analytics are present ubiquitously in the IoT, with massive amounts and types of data being created on a daily basis. As a result, acquiring real-time sensor data and executing analysis on the detected data is a difficult process. In this chapter, we have suggested the continuous intelligence mechanism for IoT sensor real-time data analysis. This method clusters various events that occur in the IoT stream using the GMM. The suggested framework was built using MATLAB® and the Azure cloud platform. The future scope of this study will involve tackling the security and privacy issues associated with IoT sensor data.

References

Erwin Adi, Adnan Anwar, Zubair Baig, and Sherali Zeadally. 2020. Machine learning and data analytics for the IoT. *Neural Computing and Applications*, Volume 32, 16205–16233.

Sidahmed Benabderrahmanea, Nedra Melloulia, Myriam Lamollea, and Patrick Paroubekb. 2017. Smart4Job: a big data framework for Intelligent job offers broadcasting using time series forecasting and semantic classification. *Big Data Research*, Volume 7, 16–30. https://databricks.com/glossary/streaming-analytics.

Ping Jiang, Jonathan Winkley, Can Zhao, Robert Munnoch, Geyong Min, and Laurence T. Yang. 2016. An intelligent information forwarder for healthcare big data systems with distributed wearable sensors. *IEEE Systems Journal*, Volume 10, Issue 3, 1147–1159.

Yuwen Pu, Jin Luo, Chunqiang Hu, Jiguo Yu, Ruifeng Zhao, Hongyu Huang, and Tao Xiang. 2019. Two Secure Privacy-Preserving Data Aggregation Schemes for IoT, Volume 2019, 11.

Md. Mamunur Rashid, Iqbal Gondal, and Joarder Kamruzzaman. 2015. Share-frequent sensor patterns mining from wireless sensor network data. *IEEE Transactions on Parallel and Distributed Systems*, Volume 26, Issue 12, 3471–3484.

Daniele Ravi, Charence Wong, Fani Deligianni, Melissa Berthelot, Javier Andreu-Perez, Benny Lo, and Guang-Zhong Yang. 2017. Deep learning for health informatics. *IEEE J Biomed Health Inform*, Volume 21, Issue 1, 4–21.

Sherif Sakrab and Amal Elgammalc. 2016. Towards a comprehensive data analytics framework for smart healthcare services. *Big Data Research*, Volume 4, 44–58.

Salvatore Vitabile, Michal Marks, Dragan Stojanovic, Sabri Pllana, Jose M. Molina, Mateusz Krzyszton, Andrzej Sikora, Andrzej Jarynowski, Farhoud Hosseinpour, Agnieszka Jakobik, Aleksandra Stojnev Ilic, Ana Respicio, Dorin Moldovan, Cristina Pop, and Ioan Salomie. 2020. High-Performance Modelling and Simulation for Big Data Applications, pp 186–220.

Shusen Yang. 2017. IoT stream processing and analytics in the fog. *IEEE Communications Magazine*, Volume 55, Issue 8, 21–27.

Gunjae Yoon, Donghwa Choi, Jeongjin Lee, and Hoon Choi. 2019. Management of IoT sensor data using a fog computing node. *Hindawi Journal of Sensors*, Volume 2019, 9.

Kuan Zhang, Xiaohui Liang, Mrinmoy Baura, Rongxing Lu, and Xuemin (Sherman) Shen. 2014. *PHDA: A Priority Based Health Data Aggregation with Privacy Preservation for Cloud Assisted WBANs*, Information Sciences, Volume 284, 130–141. Elsevier.

17

Precision Farming through IoT-Enabled Smart Irrigation System for Sustainable Development

Hitesh Kumar Sharma, Sunil Gupta, and Monit Kapoor

CONTENTS

17.1 Introduction

Agriculture is one of the most important sectors in the world. We are on third revolution in agriculture or farming. The third revolution is called 'Precision Farming'. The first revolution occurred from 1900 to 1930 [1]. In first revolution, machines were introduced for agricultural work. Second revolution was named green revolution and occurred after 1990s [2]. In second revolution, genetically modified crops were introduced to reduce water consumption, provided high quality fertilizers and pesticides to increase crop yield. In first revolution, a farmer was able to feed approximately 25 peoples, in second revolution production was increased in such a way that now a farmer was able to feed approximately 150 peoples [3, 4]. However, as population is increasing with a high speed, it is expected that by 2050 the population will be 9.5 billion [5, 6]. To meet the food requirement for this population, second revolution is not sufficient. To overcome this challenge, we have to introduce advanced technologies like IoT, artificial intelligence, computer vision, GPS-enabled drone mounted cameras and small hand held devices in agriculture.

As we know, population is increasing day by day but farming land is fix [7]. Therefore, we have to increase crop yielding in such a way that same faming land can produce the food in such a high quantity to meet the requirement of increased population. To produce high volume of food from same land need special and advanced mechanism that we are currently following to treat our farms. Individual part of the farm will be controlled and managed by different way [2, 8]. It has been noticed by the farmer that in a single farmland there are separated portions, which has different soil quality, moisture level and different soil level. If we can identify and assess these parameters for different sections of a farmland then we can treat them differently as per their requirement. The portion which has high soil level will be irrigated more which the lower section will get low water supply. This methodology is known as third revolution and it is called 'Precision Agriculture'. So precision farming is a technology-enabled farming approach where we observe, analyze and manage the need of each filed and crop individually. Sensor, robots, data analytics and satellite imagery are making precision farming a real-world project [9, 10].

In this chapter, we will describe the precision/smart agriculture/farming in detail and a complete implemented smart irrigation system for smart or précised farming. Precision farming with the help of smart irrigation system will be a useful approach for sustainable development.

17.2 Smart/Precision Farming

Smart farming is an approach where we use different set of technologies to predict the need of individual farmland and crop. Robots, data analytics, GPS images etc. can be used to get detailed information about soil fertility, soil moisture, fertilizer requirement and based upon these input a smart decision could be taken for high crop yield. It will help a farmer to produce high volume of food from same farmland.

17.2.1 Steps Involved in Smart Farming

As we have discussed in above section, smart farming is a step by step process. It has four major steps to follow (as shown in Figure 17.1). First step is data collection step, in this process the IoT-based smart sensors are used to get required information about soil type, moisture level etc. GPS-based maps provide information about the crop pattern in different section of the field [11–13]. These information about the crop and field can also be captured by moving drones with IoT and GPS-enabled sensors mounted on it.

The second step is to analyze the collected data. The data is analyzed to find crop and field condition. Several machine learning algorithms are available to find best suitable

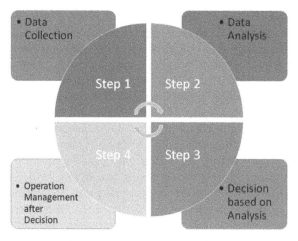

FIGURE 17.1
Four major steps involved in smart farming.

crop for given crop and filed condition. More insight can be found with the help of this step and a précised decision can be taken by the farmer. Various universities and research agencies are providing their findings with farmers to enhance their crop productivity. The third step is to take relevant decision of plating a crop as per the analytical report provided in second step. It will help the farmer to choose correct crop, correct amount of fertilizer, correct level of water level etc. If these are well known to the farmers in advance, it will help them a good production. The fourth and last step is to manage the complete process decided in third step. The number of events decided in third step needs to be managed in same way. Automated system will be used to manage same moisture level, fertilizers and pesticides usage etc.

17.2.2 Smart Farming Life Cycle

Smart farming is not a general sequential process. It is a cyclic process. The farmers need to iterate this cyclic process for high production in each production cycle (Figure 17.2). The productivity will be enhanced if the cyclic process of the smart farming is executed efficiently.

The cycle starts with collecting electronic/digital data using various types of IoT sensors for different filed and crop parameters [14]. Once the digital data is collected, then it will be stored on cloud computing storage platform for 24×7 availability [15, 16]. Once the data is stored on cloud storage servers, it will be processed by machine learning algorithms and insights will be produced after detailed data analysis. In the soil quality phase, soil parameters, crop-related parameters and weather conditions, geographic location and filed micro level map are analyzed for taking a suitable decision for planting a most suitable crop in provided filed. Once the crop is planted then automated smart irrigation system, fertilizers and pesticides controlling system will be applied on crop as per requirement. With proper management of water, fertilizers and pesticides the crop will be harvested with high production. Once the whole life cycle is completed for one crop then the same, process will iterate for next crop.

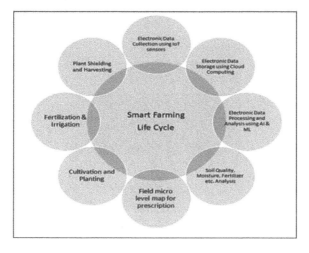

FIGURE 17.2
Smart farming life cycle.

17.3 Smart Irrigation System for Smart Farming

We need nutrients and food from the agriculture. The food we eat comes from the agricultural activities that keeps the health of these crops maintained at a good level and less affected by the insects, weather conditions and soil erosion. Most people get confused with this agriculture term, agriculture is not only regarding crops growth but it is also about the rearing of animals. Many people are in a situation who are in the field of agriculture such as farmers, transporters and agronomists. The products we obtain from agriculture are cotton, bamboo and more. They help in trading that has become source of income for many people. Good agricultural practices help in the reduction of pollution. Most of the drugs and medicines are as well produced from crops. Drip irrigation has benefitted a lot in conserving water. Dams have helped a lot in stopping wastage of water. Farmers are very much dependent mostly on the climatic conditions. The most common climatic conditions that affect these crops are either drought and flood. Sometimes damage to the crops is caused by wrong judgment of irrigation scheduling (when to water or when not to) [11]. Taking wrong decisions on irrigation scheduling results in overwatering to the crops which further leads to crop damage and sometimes it also happens that due to not having the rough idea when or when not to water the crops results in under watering. Considering these types of bad conditions, several studies have been made regarding the maintenance of the crops such that the farmers as well as the consumers (human, animals) will not suffer due to loss or inadequate crop growth. Internet of Things (IoT) [13], cloud computing and Fog computing and machine learning, artificial intelligence and apps have come into play a majorly role in preventing the crop losses with smart irrigation technologies (shown in Figure 17.3).

Taking on all these above methods, we will be discussing them one by one, looking first at IoT advantage in smart irrigation is that as we all know that IoT is the best way

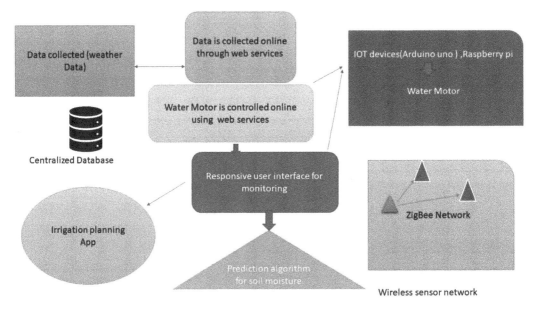

FIGURE 17.3
Smart irrigation system block diagram.

for collecting data from everywhere may it be water, land or any other sources and that also in a huge amount (Big Data). IoT has played a major role in various sectors, one of this major sector is the agricultural sector, wireless sensor networks have helped a lot in collecting the agricultural data that can be preprocessed and can be analyzed for further improvement.

Fog computing is what we call when cloud computing comes closer to the end devices which makes our lives more easier in bringing efficiency in most of the sectors or fields [10]. Fog computing along with IoT makes the agriculture sector more efficient and improved as fog computing provides storage, networking and computing services between device and cloud computing servers. It reduces the data transfer rate between device and cloud servers due to its nearby locality, saves the network bandwidth, minimizes the processing time of the cloud system. Whereas IoT collects a large amount of the agricultural data.

In addition to these technologies, we still need the machine learning and artificial algorithms that will help us to model as well as predict various trends and some of the surprising and odd patterns with the help of the data analysis process and visualization. As over the years, there has been a great advancement in the fields of machine learning and artificial intelligence through which the agricultural robots have been made for harvesting crops, monitoring crop and soil, to control the fertility of the soil.

There has been a developed app for these irrigation and agricultural purposes that helps us in various ways: provides better connections with the distributed networks of market, helps in bringing the farmers together, which helpful for chatting among the farmers even if they are located far away from each other, includes and provides agricultural videos that is best for the agricultural practices, news and government skills.

A proper Irrigation process is essential for the cultivation of the crops. Many farmers still perform the process through manual control which requires a lot of hard work and results in wastage of water and power resources. Beside these problems, farmers face unpredictable changes in weather conditions and unavailability of enough water. Therefore, we require an intelligent automated system having the capability to precisely monitor and control the water and energy consumption. Nowadays automation plays a dominant role in the human life. We implemented a smart automated irrigation system to overcome the shortcomings of traditional systems like pot irrigation or drip irrigation, which result in soil erosion and water wastage [14]. An automated irrigation method distributes water to the crops in the field by spraying all over it like a natural rainfall. Installing smart irrigation system saves time and ensures judicious usage of water. In this automated system, we have designed the system using IoT technology devices like Raspberry Pi, NodeMCU, relay module and various sensors etc. and ensured that the crops are watered appropriately when required. The water flow will be monitored and based on the data available, analysis and prediction will be done. This will help the farmers to manage water and power, indirectly reducing the cost and increasing the efficiency.

17.4 Implementation of IoT-Enabled Smart Irrigation System

In this system, we aim to effectively manage the water and power consumption of the irrigation system with the help of technological infrastructure (Figure 17.4). The presented system provides a solution, which is a smart irrigation system that takes the environmental information and determines where and when the appropriate irrigation is needed.

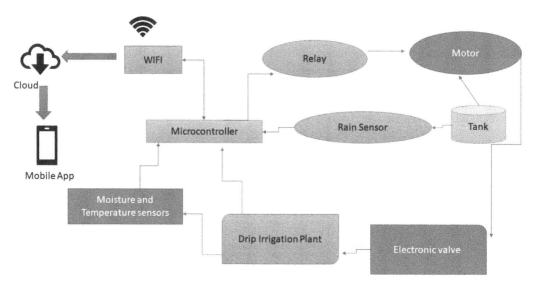

FIGURE 17.4
Smart irrigation system component diagram.

Automation makes the work of the farmer much simple and easier. The controllers in the system will monitor the soil moisture content, the temperature, the humidity etc. at the physical field site to automatically schedule the irrigation process. The system is implemented by IoT, which comprises microcontroller devices like Raspberry Pi, NodeMCU, sensors, water pumps. Hardware requirements basically included 2 GHz × 86 processor or above, 256 MB of system memory (RAM) or above, 100 MB of hard-drive space or above, monitor to display output, keyboard/mouse for data input, whereas software requirements included C-compiler (cc, gcc, egcs), Arduino IDE at the technological side and we also needed agricultural land, seeds, fertilizers, plumber, gardener, PVC pipes, electrician, electricity wirings etc. (Table 17.1).

Mentioned above is the prototype of the architecture that we have defined for our system. According to the system, we have multiple say 'n' numbers of NodeMCU units connected to the central controlling system, Raspberry Pi. Each NodeMCU is connected to moisture, humidity, and temperature sensors. In addition, our central controlling system is further connected to relays, sending an analog signal based on the readings it gets from the NodeMCU units. The relays mentioned the Figure 17.4 return operated pressure valves, which automatically get turned ON and OFF based on what signal the relay has received. Information regarding various devices used in our prototype is defined here.

Relay here is a simple and small electromechanical device consisting of a coil and few electrical components. It is an electromagnetic switch which can control a high voltage supply like AC mains by providing only a small control signal at the input. As for NodeMCU, it is an open source hardware and software development environment which is built around a low-cost SoC (System on a Chip) called ESP8266. Moreover, talking about Raspberry Pi, it is a powerful small lightweight ARM-based microcontroller with Linux operating system installed on it. It has all components for connection: input, output along with the storage capacity (circuit shown in Figure 17.5).

After the various equipment were finalized, a small prototype of the architecture was prepared about how our system is going to be and how all connections would be made.

TABLE 17.1

Smart Irrigation System Component List

S. No	Digital Component Name
1	Raspberry Pi 3 Kit
2	Display screen for pi
3	Solenoid valve
4	Rain pipes for sprinklers work
5	Node MCU ESP – 8266
6	Soil moisture sensor
7	Temperature and humidity sensor (DHT 11)
8	Relay board (12V)
9	Protoboard/Breadboard
10	Relay for water flow
11	PVC pipes
12	PVC connections
13	Electricity wires and connections
14	Water electric pump
15	Pressure pump and motor

FIGURE 17.5
Smart irrigation system circuit diagram.

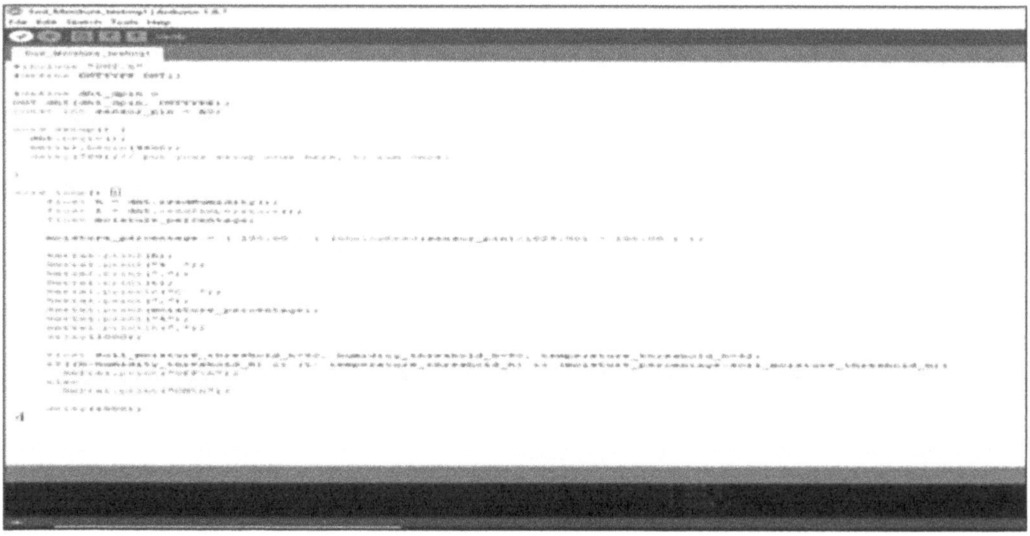

FIGURE 17.6
Coding console for Arduino IDE.

Figure 17.6 shows our programmatic logic that will help us get the values from the multiple sensors that are so deployed. This piece of code includes a pre-built header file 'DHT.h', which contains various functions to record the values from the sensor and then pass it onto another function which will save the recorded values in a. txt file.

This output displays the results of the Arduino IDE. First, thing to get displayed is the analog signal that whether sprinklers need to be ON or OFF. Second, humidity in the soil at that particular area which is measured in '%', temperature of the particular region measured in 'degree Celsius' and another is moisture content that is also recorded in '%'. Figures 17.6 and 17.7 display the programmatic logic that will help us store the recorded values from the Raspberry Pi in a. txt file.

FIGURE 17.7
COM3 serial port monitor.

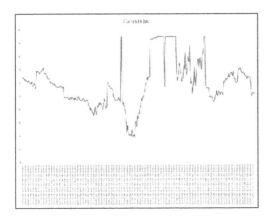
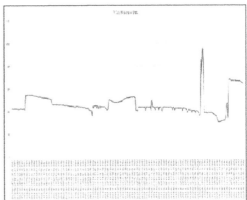
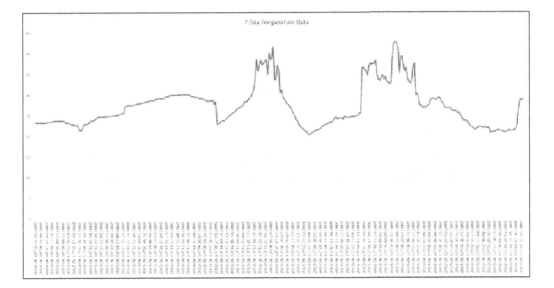

FIGURE 17.8
Graph plot for temperature, moisture and humidity data reading.

We have shown the graph plot (Figure 17.8) of temperature, moisture and humidity readings collected from IoT sensors embedded in this smart irrigation system. These plots will help to visualize the real time situation of the farming land.

17.5 Conclusion

The expected population of our world is 9.6 billion by 2030 and agriculture will serve to be the primary source of livelihood in rural areas, so the focus should be on increasing the productivity of crops without wasting another precious thing that is water. Though our country claims to have developed in terms of science and technology, erratic power supply has almost become our routine now-a-days. India has a huge untapped solar off-grid opportunity and also receives heavy rainfall. In our proposed system, we have used multiple sensor nodes (soil moisture and DHT11) and control node. The sensor nodes are deployed in the field so that they can collect respective values and the sensed data is then sent to the controller node. The controller node on receiving the data checks the sensed value with some set threshold value. The threshold value depends on the type of crop being cultivated. When the soil moisture value or temperature/humidity value is not up to the required level, the controller node sends instructions to switch ON the motor. The automated system is capable enough for automatically irrigating the field based on collected and sensed environmental data surrounding the crop. Moreover, the system can be monitored and controller remotely due to the use of Wi-Fi module present in the NodeMCU. Moreover, the power consumed by wireless network devices is also less and the system performs its function for a longer duration of time. This is a great advantage to the farmers who want to monitor the field remotely. This saves a lot of time and energy. Optimization of water usage is also achieved. In this manner, a water system framework which controls the stream according to the prerequisite alongside computerization in the water system framework is planned and comes about are accomplished agreeably. With the utilization of minimal effort sensors and the straightforward hardware makes this instrument an ease item, which can be purchased even by a poor agriculturist. This work is most appropriate for places where water is rare and must be utilized as a part of constrained amount.

In this chapter, we have tried to take a small step for precision farming and proposed a small level implementation of theoretical concept of smart/précised farming. The smart irrigation system is one component of this whole automated system on smart agriculture.

References

1. Aazam, M., Zeadally, S., Harras, K.A., Offloading in fog computing for IoT: Review, enabling technologies, and research opportunities, Future Generation Computer Systems, 87, pp. 278–289 (2018), ISSN 0167-739X, https://doi.org/10.1016/j.future.2018.04.057.
2. https://labs.sogeti.com/iot-vs-edge-vs-fog-computing.
3. https://www.embeddedcomputing.com/technology/iot/wireless-sensor-networks/how-fog-computing-can-solve-the-iot-challenges.
4. Atlam, H.F., Walters, R., Wills, G. Fog computing and the Internet of Things: A review, Big Data and Cognitive Computing 2(2) (2018). DOI: 10.3390/bdcc2020010.
5. https://www.rtinsights.com/what-is-fog-computing-open-consortium.
6. https://www.powersystemsdesign.com/articles/five-reasons-why-your-iot-application-needs-fog-computing/140/14857.
7. Alli, A.A., Alam, M.M. The fog cloud of things: A survey on concepts, architecture, standards, tools, and applications, Internet Things 9, pp. 100177 (2020).
8. Patni, J.C., Ahlawat, P., Biswas, S.S., Sensors based smart healthcare framework using internet of things (IoT), International Journal of Scientific and Technology Research 9(2), pp. 1228–1234 (2020).
9. Taneja, S., Ahmed, E., Patni, J.C., "I-Doctor: An IoT Based Self Patient's Health Monitoring System", 2019 International Conference on Innovative Sustainable Computational Technologies, CISCT 2019 (2019).
10. Khanchi, I., Agarwal, N., Seth, P., Ahlawat, P., Real time activity logger: A user activity detection system, International Journal of Engineering and Advanced Technology 9(1), pp. 1991–1994 (2019).

11. Patni, J.C., Sharma, H.K., "Air Quality Prediction using Artificial Neural Networks", 2019 International Conference on Automation, Computational and Technology Management, ICACTM 2019, 2019, pp. 568–572, 8776774.
12. Tiwari, R., Upadhyay, S., Sachan, S., Sharma, A., Automated parking system-cloud and IoT based technique, International Journal of Engineering and Advanced Technology 8(4C), pp. 116–123 (2019).
13. Shailendra, K., "NLP and Machine Learning Techniques for Detecting Insulting Comments on Social Networking Platforms", Proceedings on 2018 International Conference on Advances in Computing and Communication Engineering, ICACCE 2018, 2018, pp. 265–272, 8441728.
14. https://medium.com/yeello-digital-marketing-platform/what-is-fog-computing-why-fog-computing-trending-now-7a6bdfd73ef.
15. Tomar, R., Kumar, H., Dumka, A., Anand, A., "Traffic Management in MPLS Network Using GNS Simulator Using Class for Different Services", International Conference on Computing for Sustainable Global Development, INDIACom 2015, pp. 1066–1068.
16. Kumar, S., Dubey, S., Gupta, P., "Auto-Selection and Management of Dynamic SGA Parameters in RDBMS", International Conference on Computing for Sustainable Global Development, INDIACom 2015, pp. 1763–1768.

18

Industrial Internet of Things: Architecture and Its Applications

Pratibha Kantanavar and Sindhu Rajendran

CONTENTS

DOI: 10.1201/9781003226888-18

18.1 Introduction

The Industrial Internet of Things (IIoT) is a counterpart of the IoT which emphasizes the industrial structure by connecting many numbers of machines or devices, synchronization of connected devices using software tools, use of automated sensors, devices, and machinery at the industrial level to improve the efficiency. Connected devices are transforming industries such as mining, industrial, and logistics to energy, gas, oil, and transportation, creating a digital revolution commercially. The digitalization of industry is described in Industry 4.0 and, the technologies enabling the same are discussed in IIoT [1]. The IIoT focuses on machine-to-machine (M2M) communication, big data, and machine learning enabling organizations to access exceptional extraction of data promptly, thereby transforming the outcomes through advanced data analytics. It also comprehends a wide range of industrial applications such as collaborative robots, augmented reality (AR) devices, inventory tracking, and predictive maintenance. By the end of this year, more than 28 billion connected devices are expected to be deployed which can transmit and process data by sensing the environment or surroundings, analyzing the data, and sending it back to the environment [2]. IIoT overlays the way for a better understanding of production processes in the industry, thereby increasing efficiency and manufacturing. Industrial applications were mainly based on wireless technologies such as ad hoc solutions for connecting moving parts in the past. Recently standards are designed for the industry for to contemplate limitations of large-area coverage [3]. As we know, wireless technology such as 4G/5G connects devices over long distances with the support of licensed band and infrastructure support. In the case of IIoT, enhanced features such as energy resources, reliability, latency, security, cost, and limited hardware capabilities for connecting large numbers of devices to the internet required low throughput per node irrespective of capacity. This chapter discusses the concepts of IoT, Industry 4.0, and IIoT. The challenges associated with security issues, performance in a real-time environment, interoperability, and energy efficiency, followed by the different sectors and applications of IIoT along with the structured architecture, while conceptualizing the smart applications such as a smart farm, smart health, smart city, and smart factory emerging with the advanced industry 4.0 that enhance the quality of products as well as the quality of goods delivery in supply chain management [4].

18.1.1 Comparative Study of IoT, IIoT, and Industry 4.0

As the heading specifies, there are connections among IoT, IIoT, and Industry 4.0. IoT allows devices/things to exchange data for various aspects according to the requirement and end users. IoT is human-centered, expanding human awareness of the surrounding environment by the interconnection of consumer electronic devices by saving time and money. It can be either in the form of machine-user or server-client interactions [5]. With the advent of digital and the manufacturing of smart devices in the industry sector, IIoT is a basic pillar for data manufacturing by connecting machines, control systems, etc. by which huge measures of information gathered can take care of investigation arrangements and lead to ideal industrial operations. IoT emphasizes the design of new communication standards for connecting new devices to the internet network in a flexible way. The design of IIoT focuses on the integration and interconnection of isolated plants and machinery, thereby increasing the efficiency of production and rendering new services [6]. While comparing between IoT and IIoT in terms of connectivity and criticality, IoT is flexible as it allows ad hoc and mobile network structures, whereas IIoT employs rigid and infrastructure-based network solutions to match communication and coexistence needs and communications that are in the form of M2M to gratify requirements of time and reliability.

To summarize, IIoT is a subcategory of IoT that is explicit to mechanical applications. The assembling period of the item lifecycle is the place where the IoT and Industry 4.0 meet, starting with the IIoT. Figure 18.1 illustrates the convergences of IoT, CPS, IIoT, and Industry 4.0 [7]. As a closing comment, it must be noted that the IIoT worldview is not expected for subbing conventional computerization applications yet targets expanding the information about the actual arrangement of interest. On the contrary, as recently expressed, IIoT applications, including management, improvement, and expectation exercises, are regularly assembled into the alleged digital or cloud manufacturing (CM). The developing interest toward this point is affirmed by the wide scope of writing [7]. Many businesses are working on digital transformation; therefore, IIoT is of great interest because of its potential in taking quick and enhanced decision-making. The IIoT can help industries by giving detailed data in real time for a better understanding of the business processes and also analyzing the data coming from sensors to open up new revenue streams and make the process efficient. IIoT is of interest to transport industries, retail,

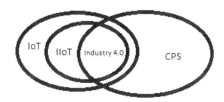

FIGURE 18.1
Venn diagram of IoT, IIoT, and Industry 4.0.

utilities, manufacturing, etc. as it gives an insight into the broader supply chain by allowing businesses to coordinate and create further efficiencies by analyzing the bottlenecks in their supply chain and includes frequent monitoring of how the production lines are considered when there is a necessity for servicing a reduction in unexpected downtime. Due to these advantages, not only businesses, but health care and government are also likely to broaden their vision in adopting IIoT.

18.2 IIoT Background

18.2.1 Benefits of IIoT

The main objective of moving toward industry IoT is in the reduction of human intervention, thereby reducing human errors and improving overall efficiency both in terms of time and money. The best advantage of the IIoT must be found in the decrease of human blunders and difficult work, the expansion in general effectiveness, and the decrease of expenses, both as far as time and money. The enhancement of IIoT shows smart quality control and maintenance [8]. To increase the automation level both in the commercial level and domestic level in IoT, it deals with large amounts of data collection, aggregation, and sending back to and from the environment. The objective of the IIoT is additionally not to supplant human work completely; it will probably improve and upgrade it by, for instance, making new income streams and plans of action with a major job for data analyses [9].

The IIoT fundamentally centers on ventures with high stakes where a human mistake could bring enormous dangers. The smart communication loop setup circle between gadgets needs ideal consideration for support issues. The protection level of the tasks is upgraded by facilitating the danger factors. To sum up, the advantages of IIoT of them are listed below: Improved and intelligent network connectivity between gadgets or machines with

- Increased proficiency;
- Cost investment funds;
- Time savings;
- Enhanced industrial safety.

18.2.2 Challenges with Industrial IoT Integration

There are some of the primary IIoT challenges that organizations need to be aware of [10].

18.2.2.1 High-Investment Cost

Indeed, one of the principle guarantees of the IoT is the potential to reduce costs through better asset management, admittance to industry knowledge, and efficiency gains. When party A is unsure of what sort of return on investment (ROI) is expected, in parallel, party B has not experienced executing the associated framework then it is very difficult for associations to legitimize the expense. As indicated by Microsoft's IoT Signals 2019 report, 29% of associations detailed that an absence of assets was one of the top purposes behind holding off on IoT reception.

18.2.2.2 Secure Data Storage and Management

IoT devices produce a huge amount of information. According to an IDC study, by 2025, the world will be a different place, there will be 160 zettabytes of information produced (10× however much the world was creating at the hour of the report), partially because of the expanded selection of modern evaluation IoT gadgets. The issue here is this enormous measure of information should be handled very quickly to identify patterns continuously. Given the degree of safety that IIoT advancements request, associations should think of an arrangement for smoothing out information checking, the executives, and capacity, considering quick reaction times to approaching dangers. This implies associations should get ready for secure, momentary capacity arrangements like edge computing, merely as a long-term solution for long-term storage (cloud/data centers). The issue is that IoT sensors may create assorted information, which is overseen through non-relational data sets. Also, for organizations to take advantage of an associated framework, enterprise resource planning (ERP) information, client records, and IoT experiences need to meet up in one, connected view [10].

18.3 Research Contributions toward IIoT

IoT stretched the arm in all manufacturing plants, which can facilitate the most efficient production flow rate. A major focus is on automation in development cycles to manage warehouses and inventories. Because of this entire enhancement, IIoT skyrocketed over the past few decades with a rise of $40 billion. The detailed investigation of core industry domain collaboration with IoT can be seen in the next section [11].

Figure 18.2 gives an insight into the approaches to IIoT in terms of Airline, Pharmaceutical, Fabrication, Insurance, Business Management, Technology and Entertainment, etc. [12]. A study of all applications considered is discussed in the next section.

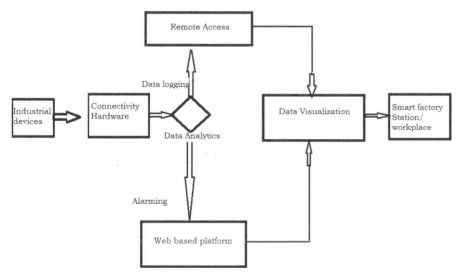

FIGURE 18.2
General approaches of IIoT.

18.3.1 Airline Industry

This sector is featured with smart monitoring of equipment and other assets. During production, IoT improves efficacy and cost-effectiveness. These things influence the customer experience and promise on-time flights [13].

18.3.1.1 Use Cases

An IoT feature emerges with baggage tracking and cabin climate control and even safety alerts are the biggest improvements. Delta airlines enhance its functioning by placing RFID cards or barcodes on the baggage help in tracking them in real-time location and the live condition of their baggage from their smartphone. Automated temperature-controlling systems using temperature sensors were fixed all over the plane, which maintains the optimal temperature in all locations and all types of weather conditions. In 2020, Virgin Atlantic's Boeing 787 used its advanced sensors such as airplane angle, velocity sensors, on-air condition monitoring, and weather monitoring sensors that were connected to an authoritative central server, which helps all parts of the airplane communicate with each other as well as monitored by concerned persons like pilots or the ground control system administrator. These features pre-handle the defective system and take care of preventive steps for the airplane. In 2021, many types of research are going on controlling the air traffic on the runway using artificial intelligence (AI) by organizing in a smart manner the plane's rescheduling of arrival and departure timings and priority setting for each function maintenance which has to be addressed first. Already EasyJet has adopted the newest IoT-enabled method as technology-enabled uniforms were given to all staff, which are equipped with built-in microphones for direct communication between technicians to passengers and within technician groups on various occasions.

18.3.2 Pharmaceutical

Temperature sensor data is integrated with remote software to monitor whether the drug has gone beyond the threshold. Other medical products industry also extends their operation with validation of quality requirements upon delivery. Temperature maintenance is a great challenge in vaccine production because of its effects on efficacy. The modern era assists the patients by sending alert messages like when it is the time to take their drug [14].

18.3.2.1 Use Cases

The pharma industries acquired a shape by IoT with the tremendous advancement in lab-on-chip, organ-in-a-chip, and cell-in-a-chip efficiently replacing human physiology. Using these features, BioLines laboratory and the University of Pennsylvania that collaboratively worked with NASA conducted some tests in space with bone-marrow-tissue chips to understand how the body fights various infections. Also, in the manufacturing units, inventory tracks humidity, gas exposure, and radiation emission parameters by enabling smart triggering an alert feature. Later it can be interfaced with AI and cloud for the future prediction on slight degradation and auto-adjustment of the environment as needed for correction. Food and Drug Administration (FDA) clearance received for the post-acute care AI-enabled monitoring system and schizophrenia and bipolar disorder treatment is delivered orally through a digitally tracked pill equipped with a sensor. Later, the pill can be investigated via smartphone.

18.3.3 Insurance

Emerging issues pertaining to health/medical-related to life insurance are providing continuous health status and are checked with the help of IoT sensors. An insurance company owner takes advantage and starts giving smart life insurance to policyholders. By making use of Fitbit wristbands, through which remotely a built-in dashboard collects the patient's health data, it reaches both policyholder and insurers [13].

18.3.3.1 Use Cases

American International Group (AGI)started with a new agenda for the insurance business, facilitating the insurance to work-related injuries. And this approach is called an investment in Human Condition Safety (HCS), where policyholder provides wearable devices and data collected that will interface with AI and cloud services, while AIG provides the insurance smartly. Aetna partnered with Apple and distributed subsidized Apple watches for their staff's everyday health monitoring. A new mobile-connected digital stethoscope and non-contact thermometer were designed in 2020, and deployed on respiratory and heart disease patients' monitoring, by Australian start-up CliniCloud.

18.3.4 Business Management

In order to start a start-up with a new product, performance analysis of that business cannot be done effectively with manual tests. It facilitates consolidated different customer's feedback on those products, by attaching the sensor to each product rack and those who purchase will automatically receive feedback messages. With that, prompt action can be taken against service problems or fault detection. These improved many industries' service levels and quality also [14].

18.3.4.1 Use Cases

Nowadays business management joints its hand with IoT and then it integrates with the cloud platform. In this regard, one recent development is the SAP HANA cloud platform automated the core business process connecting it to collaborative other sectors by delivering the value of their customers' requirements and demands. Customer relationship management (CRM) also successfully executing with IoT features in all business sectors.

18.3.5 Technology and Entertainment

An entertainment and media industry will keep an eye on successful events with a big crowd. The people's movement tracks are done by IoT sensors and collect the data on attention toward the special movement of the program. With this data analytics, the media company offers a high advertisement rate. IoT platforms monitor the turnstiles of the venues and track the attendant traffic pattern. It helps advertising companies to decide which place is suitable for casting their advertisement [13].

18.3.5.1 Use Cases

All digital media advertise companies wrap their arms around IoT; Savvy media developed retail marketing in a very smarter way to improve customer experience as well as efficient engagement of customers. Caliber media groups worked on technology consulting and end-to-end marketing services with many IoT features in the year 2021.

18.4 Integrated Sectors of Industrial IoT

To drive the industries in a better manner, simulation, analyses, and control in a single platform of automation are done to test and explore complex environments. This can also be a solution in any industrial sector to enhance its productivity and customer relationship and quality improvisation; some of the eminent techniques are discussed below.

18.4.1 Digital Twins

In the manufacturing industry, fault detection and manual product quality testing are overburdened for the workers. Digital twins replace all these manual works by its digitization. Using retrofitting of sensors, twin box collects the entire manufacturing mechanism's working conditions status. This digital data is sent to the manager for analysis. This increased the warehouse operation effectiveness and accuracy. The management system consists of a chain of processes like production, application, analytics, and network [15]. This system works better in assets and failure management.

18.4.2 Supply Chain Management

On a global scale, tracking and tracing of inventory system execute by IoT sensor system. These will monitor the supply chain by collecting estimation data out of available resources. Also provides insight into equipment working conditions, undergoing work inside that as well as its delivering status. Extended features such as the expected delivery date of the material can be predicted using IoT data analytics. Then it encourages ERP. IoT data analyzer facilitates the cross-channel visibility between managerial departments, which helps in stakeholder's examination process on different materials. It reduces the expenditure and errors in manual management and its miss data analysis [16].

18.4.3 Self-Dependent Systems

In the production environment, equipment failures and production issues are major concerns. The resolving method must design with less costly and less time-consuming. In IIoT, IoT features are merged with machine learning, enabling the machine to detect production issues and fix them automatically. When a downtime error occurs, regaining control can be done automatically. Embedded sensors will notify underlying issues to the production team. Self-dependent systems architecture with the above-discussed features can be reduced manual efforts and an effective development process. It enhances the other services and achieves faster time to market [11].

18.4.4 Workshop Mirroring

In workshops, IoT enabled manufacturing activities to execute automatically, which helps the enterprise information management systems market-readymade solutions. It addresses the production and product-related input issues concerned with connection, computing, and control [17].

18.4.5 Smart Pumping

In power plants, water management, and chemical manufacturing industries, IoT-enabled solutions are deployed with monitoring pump regulation and controlling of the pressure

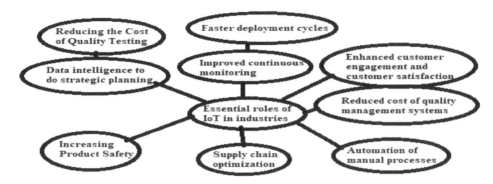

FIGURE 18.3
Essential roles of IoT in industries.

of water. It helps automatically turn off the pumps with predefined threshold values. Electricity bill reduces by taking care of unnecessary usage of pumps [17]. Analyzing and managing data from connected devices, enterprises, and third parties help identify patterns and optimize assets. Enable and manage applications to simplify the setup and operation of assets and create digital twins. Employ remote connection to industrial devices (PLC, HMI, robot) through a secure connection, control, and view of HMI panels (VNC) or PLC web servers (HTTP) on any device, live broadcasts from IP cameras [17]. Get support for industrial protocols such as OPC (Open Platform Communications), use PLC visualization, notification, and data logging. Get a well-documented API for integrating with native analytics, business intelligence tools, SAP, and other machine learning platforms. Grant the engineering-grade reliability. Achieve flexibility with code-free interfaces that allow individual users to access applications for specific tasks then Combine cloud computing, edge computing, and on-premises deployment [16]. With the above sectors' considerations, IoT plays a wide role in industries with its enhanced features as shown in Figure 18.3 [17].

18.5 Industrial IoT Architecture

The IIoT architecture tremendously altered with many signs of progress along with incremental complications. Now the time comes for focusing on challenges mentioned previously and marking meaningful strides in getting past time [18].

As shown in Figure 18.4, IoT platform architecture specific to industrial purpose is designed in such a way that it boosts effectiveness and performance to the earlier ancient industry sector.

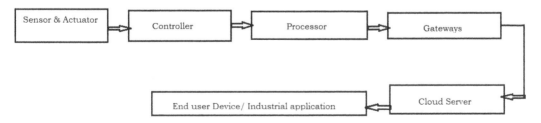

FIGURE 18.4
Architecture of IIoT.

18.5.1 Sensor and Actuators

Many analog and digital sensors along with active and passive sensors are in the mainstream of IIoT. These sensors are used for the elimination of human errors related to product defects, ease of maintenance. For the Sensor and actuator system meeting, the built-in safety and security are only challenging. In the new era with high-end verification and validation process and the use of advanced safety-compliant elements, it implies security issues in-depth with an overall result [18].

18.5.2 Controllers

An industry updated to the smart factory with many sensors and actuators, to control and monitor those controllers is required. Apart from control action, it may be helpful for the conversion of analog into digital data. The advanced control system uses Ethernet/IP, Modbus, OPC, and Profibus parallel to other end-user equipment like a computer or mobile devices using TCP/IP, HTTP/HTTPS, and JSON. Data translation and intercom processor design grab the opportunity to handle different mechanisms remotely by activating cloud-based automation infrastructure with greater convenience and marked energy saving. Activity between these two systems involves expensive middleware components like gateways, drivers, custom software, parsers, and licenses. Cost is the one of the considered backoff and other one is when data transmitted outside its immediate network increases the security issues. Edge programmable industrial controller (EPIC) reduces the security risks, the expense of installation and maintenance, and, in turn, it reduces complexity [19].

18.5.3 Processor

Processor design grabs the opportunity to handle different mechanisms remotely by activating cloud-based automation infrastructure with greater convenience and marked energy saving. A large number of sensor nodes deployed will be a restriction to the available space. It limits the microprocessor's ability to process the huge number of nodes' data and subsequential memory resources [19]. Each special functionality incorporated will be the proliferation of the processor. In the present world, processor design for the industrial purpose must compulsorily have flexibilities with all necessary hardware resources interfacing effectively. It could be a supporter for all differential IIoT systems along with a comprehensive software framework, later it can be interfacing with the cloud [20].

18.5.4 Gateways

Deployment of group of gateways along with the edge computing is to deal with distributed control systems (DCSs) or SCADA systems applications in discrete and process control industries. Generally, IoT gateway connects SCADA or DCS directly with the cloud using MODBUS, OPC, and ISA100. Wireless industrial communication protocols. ProfiBus establishes the connectivity between edges to the gateway; CoAP/MQTT will do it for the gateway-to-cloud connectivity. This chain process of connectivity boosts interoperability as well as M2M communication [18].

18.5.5 Cloud Server

Its servers the suitable and scalable network access in real-time by connecting machines to things, things to things than with the cloud. It integrates machine data from various heterogeneous computing devices. It is a huge collection of virtual resources with unlimited computational capabilities. It increases storage and the challenging task of delivering services via the internet, by managing big data/DCS sometimes accidentally attacked by SQL injection, session riding, cross-site scripting, and side channel. Here Session hijacking and virtual machine escape are vulnerable issues [20].

18.5.6 User Device

It collects real-time statistical data from within the facility or outside the facility. It furnishes the comparison between current data and memory to the manufacturing plant manager, which helps him in addressing issues related to that and can act on improvements. When sensor readings go out of the normal range will alert the system user device during continuous monitoring of sensor data. For seamless connectivity between machine and end-user devices via many devices with corporate software systems, a uniform communication format is necessary – that one aspect is IIoT communication protocols. These are the common standards for information exchange from machines to machines. The next part of our discussion is a detailed study on an overview of standard IIoT communication protocols [21].

18.6 Industrial IoT Communication Protocols

IIoT is enriched with excellent developments in improving return on investment (ROI) for each smart factory converted industry, which adopted the well-known model as three Cs–control, communication, and computation. To maintain the cooperation between the three Cs, effective communication protocols must play a vital role. If an interaction between controller system and computational devices fails, then the industry must face the challenges with system efficiency, and unnecessary usage of computational resources. The industrial environment has high-performing and high-speed control engineering, which challenges the user device's bidirectional conversation with machines. The cooperative design approach has been established in the modern IoT era with the knowledge of fundamental research and applied research approaches related to wireless communication protocols [21].

The border aspects of the wireless communication protocol stack are our discussion theme in this section. Table 18.1 explains the focused study on protocol hierarchy concerning the IIoT applications. Now, let us briefly discuss a smart look at both data and network protocols.

This helps the early-stage researcher to right choice on better performing network protocols. Taking into consideration of different wireless technical parameters such as network topology, distribution networking module, type of digital modulation, antenna coverage area, security concerns, power consumption, the new hybrid protocols are designed. Those are RFID, NFC, ZigBee, BLE, Z-wave, Sigfox, and 6LoWPAn [22]. The connection establishment from machines to machines is achieved over the network with the help of these protocols [23].

TABLE 18.1

Protocol Stack [22]

OSI Layers		Protocols		Layer Standards	
Session		MQTT, SMQTT, CoRE, DDS, AMQP, XMPP, CoAP		Security TCG, Oath 2.0,	Management
Network Encapsulation	Network Routing	6LowPAN,6TiSCH, Thread	RPL, CORPL, CARP	SMACK, SASL,	IEEE 1905, IEEE 1451
Data Link		Wi-Fi, Bluetooth low energy, Z-wave, ZigBee Smart, DECT/ULE, 3G/LTE, NFC, HomePlug GP, WirelessHART, DASH7, LoRaWAN		ISASecure, ace, DTLS, Dices	

18.6.1 Network Protocols

18.6.1.1 Radio Frequency Identification (RFID)

It works with radio waves transmission, which sends small data packets over the network within clusters. RFID tag chips are inserted in all manufacturing plants in each movable machine. RFID reader reads the data associated with the tag. The antenna emits the radio waves in both directions where the reader and tag are placed. To do cost cut down, passive antennas are generally used in many supply chain industries, but with the low power, constraint tags may not work efficiently for a longer duration. Active tags are preferred for their acceptance of cost considerations features. For lower range applications, this can be used perfectly, for example, in assessing management in many processing industries [24].

18.6.1.2 Near-Field Communication (NFC)

For very short-range communication, NFC can be used up to a maximum of 4-cm coverage area. Contactless monitoring of any harmful devices in chemical solvents, oil extraction, turbine engine, thermal power plants, and boiler sections of polymer industries can adopt this wireless protocol [21]. If all those are communicated with NFC, then power consumption is a major concern. Replacing each node with new batteries increases operational costs and may cause data damage.

18.6.1.3 ZigBee

ZigBee connected each device acts as digital radio, later all connected devices are considered in the network as routers. At the origin of the system a coordinator was placed, which scans the channel and helps in minimum interference signal transmission. Routers coordinate among the end devices rarely to save the battery power.

18.6.1.4 Bluetooth Low Energy (BLE)

Human-machine interaction allows Bluetooth Low Energy (BLE) to access the device/machine data, through which mobile phones gather the data with Bluetooth capabilities. Wherein small coverage range networking can be set up there BLE works better within 2.4GHz [21].

18.6.1.5 Z-Wave

Z wave is a quite long-range communication protocol and operates in an ISM band and servers around 4000 nodes on a single network. The basic protocol version covers a 100-m operating range per hop and it can address up to 232 devices on single mesh network. Features include long-lasting battery power to achieve lower intervention networks, massive coverage area and efficient interoperability [23].

18.6.1.6 IPv6 over Low-Power Wireless Personal Area Networks (6LoWPAN)

It lies on Ipv6, to produce transport mechanisms in complex control systems, and establishes the communications with each node in a cost-effective manner. Power is not a constraint so can be extended to any industrial application [24]. The IIoT has an extreme data exchange and a certain level of interoperability between different kinds of devices. This data can be collected locally, or it can be transferred to cloud-based applications to be summed up, stored, and analyzed [21]. Each protocol specification is listed in Table 18.2.

18.6.2 Data Protocols

18.6.2.1 Message Queue Telemetry Transport (MQTT)

Mainly it is designed for battery-powered devices with a publication/subscription model. So, it suits the best in such environments as small sensor applications, remote location applications, and all kinds of M2M connectivity applications. It blends with the new structure of tight coupling, fault-sensitive, and efficient one-to-one communication. So, it overcomes the traditional client-server model drawbacks. Using MQTT, each instance temperature or humidity sensor data can send it in batches at regular intervals of time by using truly little power. So, it always focuses on event-based communications [11].

18.6.2.2 Constrained Application Protocol (CoAP)

It operates well with multicasting also even in constrained environment parameters limited bandwidth and low power. It establishes a connection between the device-to-device and device-to-gateway. It combines with HTTP in a light version and enhances the web-based IIoT applications. In that instance sensor side CoAP works and at gateway/cloud side HTTP works. It supports content negotiation and resource discovery mechanisms [16].

TABLE 18.2

IoT Networks Protocols [25]

Protocols	IEEE Standard	Operating Frequency Band	Power Consumption	Transmission Speed	Spread Spectrum Techniques
RFID	IEEE 1451.7-2010	3–30 MHz to 13.56 MHz	˜700 nA	100 Mbps	FHSS
NFC	ISO 13157	13.56 MHz	˜50 mA	424 kbps	GSMA
ZigBee	802.15.4	868/915 MHz, 2.4 GHz	˜40mA	250 kbps	DSSS
BLE	802.15.1	2.4 GHz	˜12.5 mA	305 kbps	Adaptive FHSS
Z-wave	ITU-T	908.42 MHz	˜2.5 mA	40–100 kbps	FHSS
6LowPAN	802.15.4 and sub-1GHz ISM	2.4 GHz	˜42 mA	250 kbps	Chirp spread spectrum (CSS)

18.6.2.3 OPC Unified Architecture (OPC UA)

It allows shared access to the data as well as widening the spectrum of data sources that industrial applications can connect to the cloud, overcoming the limitations of SCADA clients which lacked this feature and archiving solutions to carry their native drivers to communicate with the devices made by various vendors. OPC UA strongly emphasizes security and information modeling [18].

18.6.2.4 Routing Protocol for Low-Power and Lossy Networks (RPL)

It works on the basic principle of distance vector protocol. To find the shortest distance among connected nodes, it follows the Destination Oriented Directed Acyclic Graph (DODAG) algorithm. It has a single route for each leaf node, through which all the traffic will be routed. At the start point, each leaf node behaves as a root and it sends an information object ready to send a message. All the leaf nodes start sending the messages simultaneously then automatically graph built, then all leaf nodes which initiate the communication will start sending destination advertisement object messages to their parental node. Then root decides where it should respond based on the destination parameter. If a new node wants to join this graph, then it has to send an Information solicitation request message. If the root is ready to accept its request, then its reply backs with an acknowledgment. Sometimes leaf nodes start tracking on their parental node. But complete knowledge of the entire graph structure is known to root. It restricts all the leaf and parental nodes to communicate through itself mandatory [24].

18.6.2.5 Channel-Aware Routing Protocol (CARP)

Especially it suits for underwater communication, in oil extraction industries CARP plays an important role. Connection establishment is based on created link quality, which is calculated on data transmission from neighboring sensor node data, and it helps in forward node selection also. In transport functionality, two major working categories are data forwarding and network initiation.

While initializing the network, a HELLO packet is broadcasted from the sink node to all other nodes in the network. Then in data forwarding, a light packet is routed from sensor node to sink node in hop-by-hop configuration. Determining individual hop is the task of the protocol. Once data is collected and finished that data forwarding then it will be discarded, cannot be reusable. If an application wants to retrieve back the previous data of any sensor node, then this protocol did not significantly. This enhancement was done in Enhance-CARP. It sends ping packets which include sensor node reply data. So drastically it reduces communication overhead [24].

18.6.2.6 The Advanced Message Queuing Protocol (AMQP)

This is one of the session layer protocols; it better suits for the finance industry. Here broker is divided into two parts: queue and exchange. The exchange broker helps in receiving publisher messages and distributing them to the queue. Queues represent subscriber data which is sensory data stored in a queue [24].

TABLE 18.3

Data Protocols [26]

Protocols	Architecture	Developers	Default Port	Header Size	Transport Protocol
MQTT	Publish/Subscriber	OASIS, Eclipse Foundations	1883/8883 (TLS/SSL)	2 bytes	TCP
CoAP	Request/Response /Publish/Subscriber	IETF, Eclipse Foundations	*5683(UDP)/5684(DLT)*	4 bytes	UDP, SCTP
OPC UA	Publish/Subscriber	Unified automation	4840	65535 bytes	TCP
RPL	Poll or Pull models	IEEE 802.15.4	RFC 6550	Undefined	UDP
CARP	Master/Slave	OpenBSD	RFC 2780	4 bytes	TCP
AMQP	Request/Response /Publish/Subscriber	OASIS, ISO/IEC	5671(TLS/SSL),5672	8 bytes	TCP, SCTP
XMPP	Client/Server	JABBER trademark	5269(server to server), 5222(client to server)	Undefined	TCP
DDS	Publish/Subscriber	Object Management Group	5100(TCP server)	124 bytes	TCP, UDP

18.6.2.7 Extensible Messaging and Presence Protocol (XMPP)

It is designed for the main serve messaging, so suits messaging service applications in supply chain management. Observed one main drawback is unguaranteed QoS service, which is not acceptable in M2M communication. XML messages use a greater number of header bits and are the same as in tag format. So, it leads to excess power consumption. With these challenges rarely it is used in IIoT [24].

18.6.2.8 DDS Data Distribution Service (DDS)

Its foundation lies on broker-less architecture, which can be achieved the best QoS and high reliability, so always implemented in M2M communication and extended with other features such as priority, durability, security, urgency, and other QoS service levels also. It includes data-centric publish and data local reconstruction sub-layers. Data-centric layer takes care of message delivery to subscribers. The publisher layer is used for sensory data distribution. In the broker, fewer architecture data reader and data writer are held responsible for data publishing in the form of topics [24]. These high-level IIoT communication protocols make it possible to do product as a service innovation and provide customer value through IoT-connected service in SCADA systems. It will also enhance predictive maintenance, service up-selling, and performance-based product and service innovation for enhanced customer value can be seen in Table 18.3.

18.7 Industrial IoT End-User Platforms

Considering the overcrowded arena as well as the escalating skills of IIoT, a few best IIoT platforms' brief introduction will be covered in this section.

Altizon Daton is provides real-time analytics, device management, and machine learning capabilities. Brain cube recommends easy export of raw data to standard applications (e.g., Excel). Deployment is complex and requires an increase in the maintenance staff. Amazon Web Services (AWS)supports gadget connectivity and control to analytics and computing along with other range of IoT services covering everything [27]. Azure IoT accumulates massive amounts of industrial machine data, processes it at the edge in real time, and transfers it to the cloud for analysis in PowerBI [27]. Flutura Cerebra provides long resource uptime and high operational efficiency. PTC ThingWorx features an attractive/adaptable interface that speeds up expansion and customization [27]. Hitachi Vantara Lumada is focused on IT systems and business applications, automated edge-to-cloud data management, archiving, advanced analytics, use-case-specific AI capabilities, and digital twin simulation. In production management systems, Oracle IoT Cloud and IBM Watson IoT highlight analytics and APIs that allow us to analyze information in real time, whether it is text or speech, social sentiment, or video. Programming AG Cumulocity includes Cloud Fieldbus, which is used to connect and control industrial resources through agreements such as Modbus and OPC UA, as well as monitor asset health and collect historical information. In detail, the description of different IoT platforms is mentioned in Table 18.4.

TABLE 18.4

Different IoT Platforms

Platforms	Applications	Associated Protocols
AltizonDatonis	Business	Serial, Modbus RTU, Modbus TCP
Braincube	Chemical, food, consumer packaged goods, paper, and oil and gas manufacturing industries	HTTPS or SFTP
Amazon Web Services	Services for industrial, consumer, and commercial solutions	MQTT over WebSocket Secure (WSS)
Azure IoT	Healthcare, retail, manufacturing, logistics and transportation	MQTT and AMQP
Flutura Cerebra	Monitoring and control of any industrial component. Particle ... machine, and big data	OPC UA
PTC ThingWorx	Automotive, insurance, and manufacturing	HTTP, REST API
Hitachi VantaraLumada	Improvement in production, quality, maintenance, supply chain, and health and safety	HTTPS, REST API
Oracle IoT Cloud	Smart manufacturing, predictive maintenance, connected logistics, workplace safety monitoring and a connected customer service	MQTT 5.0
IBM Watson IoT	Tracking and monitor of the safe and timely delivery of goods and supplies (e.g., food, medicine, and livestock) in real-time	MQTT 5.0, REST API and Node RED
ProgrammingAG Cumulocity	Remote monitoring and controlling of asset management	REST API, Edge computing

18.8 Recent Developments of IIoT

18.8.1 Limited Research on Interconnectivity and Interoperability of Industrial IoT

To address the industrial issues, we must integrate all sensors and resources associated with machines as one IoT platform. There IoT providers and interfacing platforms as well as promoting an open API are all fit for their world. They treat themselves as a single entity, so issues arise around the lack of operational things. Their interoperability with IoT-enabled devices is our discussion agenda on this topic [28]. These problems motivated me to go for Open APIs; it works well with all IoT providers. But the bottleneck is here in the market; daily IoT devices are increasing rapidly, to create a common platform for all future devices is a big challenge. Any new device that enters into the market will not be compatible with APIs [28].

18.8.2 Industrial IoT: Security Challenge

Due to the integration of IIoT technologies, industrialized companies and transportation-related industries have profited. For illustration, in water treatment companies, the maintenance can be done by installing sensors on their equipment. If any risks arise, it helps the company to predict maintenance issues by collecting and analyzing data from sensors so that operations are more efficient. As the number of devices connected and the cloud networks increase within each organization as a distributed system comes with a set of security risks for the attacks for ransomware due to which data breaches are increasing. The manufacturers need to take the stock of security challenges that differ from consumer to consumer by ensuring a network that will not compromise the consistent data breaches [29].

The IoT manufacturers must deal with the following four security challenges mentioned below: follow strict software development lifecycles, risk assessment modules, hardware integrity, and encryption

To combat the IIoT challenges, a few suggestions are listed below:

- Get the right specialists on your side. Regardless of whether you choose to work with a third-party service provider, enlist new representatives, upskill your group, or the entirety mentioned above, you'll need to guarantee that you have IT specialists to execute legitimate safety efforts, information researchers to separate the correct bits of knowledge and activities staff that realize how to function with associated frameworks.

- Set appropriate controls. Having the correct controls setup can help manufacturing groups stay away from the sorts of missteps that outcome in safety issues, property harm, and approaching security dangers.

- Integrate information properly. The integration of new IoT information within the architecture, i.e., the versatility of IIoT-generated data with current data management systems such as enterprise resource platforms, databases, and storage.

- The collection of data from legacy devices with new technologies and all these technologies work effortlessly.

There have been advancements in the manufacturing sectors of industries all over the world in recent years. However, one such prominent is the introduction of Open core

Engineering in automation by Robert Bosch, Rexroth in the year 2020.Using this Open core Engineering platform, an industrial control system like PLC can be integrated with technologies such as cloud platform, Android studio, and any open-source technology available. The graphical representation of each sensor data can be remotely accessed using any Android platform to track the unexpected downfall and also monitor the start and stop of control system over the internet, to have a fine control not over the components of the industry but even over the industry as a whole.

18.9 Conclusion

With the emergence of IoT, and the ever-growing enhancements in the industry, there was a broad utilization of IoT in businesses which has made IIoT a different examination area. Looking over IoT explicit security issues and their answers are talked about with extraordinary accentuation to IIoT. Firstly, the chapter gives an insight into the evolution of IIoT, its connection with IoT their benefits, the sectors of IIoT. Secondly, we have thrown light on the architecture of IIoT, the eminent communication protocols, and the applications of IIoT in different sectors. With the rise of IoT, there is a huge demand for new devices in the market; therefore, to interface the new gadgets with the existing open APIs or with the controller board is complex. To deal with these issues, interoperability techniques have to be incorporated. The chapter also provides the issues regarding interconnectivity and interoperability. For the interoperability issues, optimal solutions with effective cost reduction for industry are also discussed. The chapter is concluded with human-machine interface approaches. However, there are a few challenges for IIoT and a few expectations are also discussed in detail.

References

[1] Ericsson. "Cellular networks for massive IoT," January 2016, https://www.ericsson.com/assets/local/publications/white-papers/wpiot.pdf.
[2] Group, F. "Wireless HART specification," 2007, http://www.hartcomm2.org.
[3] Torry Bailey, ISA Standards Administrator report, "ISA100: Wireless systems for automation," 2009, http://www.isa.org/MSTemplate.cfm?MicrositeID=1134&CommitteeID=6891.
[4] Haque, A. K. M. B., Bhushan, B., &Dhiman, G. "Conceptualizing smart city applications: Requirements, architecture, security issues, and emerging trends," Expert Systems, vol. 39, no. 5, pp. 1–23, 2021.
[5] Palattella, M. R., Dohler, M., Grieco, A., Rizzo, G., Torsner, J., Engel, T., & Ladid, L. "Internet of things in the 5G era: Enablers, architecture, and business models," IEEE Journal on Selected Areas in Communications, vol. 34, no. 3, pp. 510–527, 2016.
[6] Bandyopadhyay, D., & Sen, J. "Internet of Things: Applications and challenges in technology and standardization," Wireless Personal Communications, vol. 58, no. 1, pp. 49–69, 2011.
[7] Wollschlaeger, M., Sauter, T., & Jasperneite, J. "The future of industrial communication: Automation networks in the era of the internet of things and industry 4.0," IEEE Industrial Electronics Magazine, vol. 11, no. 1, pp. 17–27, 2017.

[8] Akerberg, J., Gidlund, M., & Bjorkman, M. "Future research challenges in wireless sensor and actuator networks targeting industrial automation," in Proceedings of the 9th IEEE International Conference on Industrial Informatics, 2011, pp. 410–415.

[9] Gidlund, M., Lennvall, T., & Akerberg, J. "Will 5G become yet another wireless technology for industrial automation?" in IEEE International Conference on Industrial Technology (ICIT), 2017, pp. 1319–1324.

[10] Sisinni, E., et al. "Industrial Internet of Things: Challenges, opportunities, and directions," IEEE Transactions on Industrial Informatics, vol. 14, no. 11, pp. 4724–4734, Nov. 2018, https://doi.org/10.1109/tii.2018.2852491.

[11] "State of Industrial Internet of Things (IIoT) | PTC," www.ptc.com. https://www.ptc.com/en/resources/iiot/white-paper/state-of-the-iiot (accessed May 24, 2021).

[12] Palattella, M. R., Thubert, P., Vilajosana, X., Watteyne, T., Wang, Q., & Engel, T. Internet of Things. IoT Infrastructures: Second International Summit, 2016.

[13] "HPE IoT Vision," Hpe.com, 2019, https://www.hpe.com/in/en/solutions/internet-of-things.html?jumpid=ps_7cr543a6su_aid-520042866&ef_id=:G:s&s_kwcid=AL (accessed May 24, 2021).

[14] Ezechina, M. A., Okwara, K. K., & Ugboaja, C. A. U. "The Internet of Things (IoT): A scalable approach to connecting everything," The International Journal of Engineering and Science, vol. 4, no. 1, pp.09–12, 2015.

[15] Fuller, A., Fan, Z., Day, C., & Barlow, C. "Digital Twin: Enabling technologies, challenges and open research," IEEE Access, vol. 8, pp. 108952–108971, 2020, https://doi.org/10.1109/access.2020.2998358.

[16] Harrington, G. "Consumer demands: Major problems facing industry in a consumer-driven society," Meat Science, vol. 36, no. 1–2, pp. 5–18, Jan. 1994, https://doi.org/10.1016/0309-1740(94)90029-9.

[17] Kumar, A. Senthil, and Iyer, E. "An industrial IoT in engineering and manufacturing industries—benefits and challenges." International Journal of Mechanical and Production Engineering Research and Development (IJMPERD), vol. 9.2, pp. 151–160, 2019.

[18] Boyes, H., Hallaq, B., Cunningham, J., & Watson, T. "The industrial internet of things (IIoT): An analysis framework," Computers in Industry, vol. 101, pp. 1–12, Oct. 2018, https://doi.org/10.1016/j.compind.2018.04.015.

[19] Lin, J., Yu, W., Zhang, N., Yang, X., Zhang, H., & Zhao, W. "A survey on internet of things: Architecture, enabling technologies, security and privacy, and applications," IEEE Internet of Things Journal, vol. 4, no. 5, pp. 1125–1142, 2017.

[20] Rajkumar, M. Newlin, Chatrapathi, C., & Venkatesa, V. K. "Internet of Things: A vision technical issues applications and security," IPASJ International Journal of Computer Science, vol. 2.8, 20–27, 2014.

[21] Sattar, M. A., Anwaruddin, M., & Ali, M. A. "A review on Internet of Things – Protocols, issues," IJIREEICE, vol. 5, no. 2, pp. 91–97, Feb. 2017, https://doi.org/10.17148/ijireeice.2017.5217.

[22] Palattella, M. R., Accettura, N., Vilajosana, X., Watteyne, T., Grieco, L. A., Boggia, G., & Dohler, M. "Standardized protocol stack for the Internet Of (Important) Things," IEEE Communications Surveys and Tutorials, vol. 15, no. 3, pp. 1389–1406, third quarter 2013, https://doi.org/10.1109/SURV.2012.111412.00158.

[23] Salman, T., & Jain, R. "A survey of protocols and standards for Internet of Things," Advanced Computing and Communications, Advanced Computing and Communications, vol. 1, no. 1, March 2017, https://doi.org/10.34048/2017.1.f3.

[24] Woungang, I., Dhurandher, S. K., & Visconti, A. "Internet of Things design, architectures and protocols," Internet of Things, Available online July 29, 2020, 100267, https://doi.org/10.1016/j.iot.2020.100267

[25] Shyan, L.J., Wei, S.Y., & Chou, S.C. "A comparative study of wireless protocols: Bluetooth, UWB, ZigBee, and Wi-Fi", 33rd Annual Conference of the IEEE Industrial Electronics Society, pp. 46–51, 2007, https://doi.org/10.1109/IECON.2007.4460126.

[26] Hamid, H. G., & Alisa, Z. T. "Survey on IoT application layer protocols", Indonesian Journal of Electrical Engineering and Computer Science, vol. 21, no. 3, pp. 1663–1672, Mar. 2021, ISSN: 2502-4752, https://doi.org/10.11591/ijeecs.v21.i3.pp1663-1672.

[27] Sharma, A., Singh, A., Sharma, N., Kaushik, I., & Bhushan, B. Security countermeasures in web based application. 2019 2nd International Conference on Intelligent Computing, Instrumentation and Control Technologies (ICICICT), 2019, https://doi.org/10.1109/icicict46008. 2019.8993141.

[28] Industrial internet of things volume G4: security framework", Ind. Internet Consort, pp. 1–173, 2016 [online], https://www.iiconsortium.org (accessed December 28, 2020)

[29] Bhushan, B., Sahoo, C., Sinha, P. et al. Unification of Blockchain and Internet of Things (BIoT): Requirements, working model, challenges and future directions. Wireless Networks, vol. 27, pp.55–90, 2021. https://doi.org/10.1007/s11276-020-02445-6.

19

Autonomous Device Discovery for IoT: Challenges and Future Research Directions

Mehwash Weqar, Shabana Mehfuz, and Dhawal Gupta

CONTENTS

19.1 Introduction: Fundamentals of IoT

Internet of Things (IoT) is a systematic arrangement of smart objects, having embedded sensors, actuators and software technologies, which are interconnected to each other and with the internet to enable these objects to have a proper communication and exchange of data among them as well as over the internet. It is the fastest growing internetworking paradigm which facilitates human lives [1]. Figure 19.1 depicts the basic IoT architecture, where IoT devices having sensors and actuators and are interconnected via IoT gateway over internet to the computation platforms, where the data from the sensors is utilized.

IoT is now being utilized everywhere in different applications like smart healthcare systems, smart buildings, smart agriculture, smart roads, smart homes and smart cities [2]. With the increase in the development of IoT-based technologies, the number of connected devices is estimated to reach 46 billion by the end of 2021.

19.2 Device Identification and Discovery

In order to avail the maximum benefits (and complete efficiency) of smart IoT devices, it is necessary that these devices are identified and discovered in the IoT network in an efficient manner to transfer and access data. Thus, to allow these devices to be recognized,

DOI: 10.1201/9781003226888-19

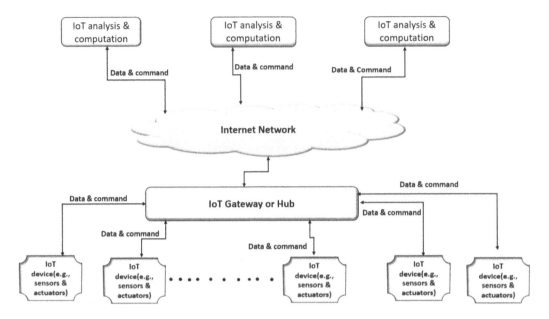

FIGURE 19.1
Basic IoT architecture.

they need to be uniquely identified by using suitable available naming schemes, which can facilitate the accessibility of these devices using their names. Many naming schemes have been proposed to support naming of IoT devices but the most commonly used are based on DNS (Domain Name System) naming schemes [3]. When the number of devices in a network increases at a rapid rate, the greatest challenge is to discover the IoT devices and connect them to the desired IoT network in a heterogeneous environment where the devices may be from different manufacturers and of different make. To make them accomplish the desired task, the identification and discovery of IoT devices can be performed in two ways: (a) Manual Device Discovery and Registration. (b) Automatic Device Discovery and registration.

19.2.1 Manual Device Discovery and Registration

The most basic and essential requirement of the IoT device is to be discovered and get registered to the IoT network to make itself accessible and achieve intercommunication with other devices and the available services. In Manual Device Discovery and Registration process, whenever an IoT device is ready to enter a network, to send data or access services, it is first registered to the network using its unique identification factors by human intervention. Figure 19.2 shows IoT Device Discovery and Registration with the help of human intervention.

During this process, many steps are performed like viewing a device then registering it using its unique id. For example, model number of the device which is given by the manufacturer can be used as its unique id. Then updating the list of the available and connected devices in the network will take place. Similar process is performed for the IoT services too. Now whenever an IoT device leaves a network then its details are also removed manually from the registered and available devices list and thereby this list is updated. This process of manual addition of an IoT device which has the steps of device identification, device registration and updating of device list consumes large amount

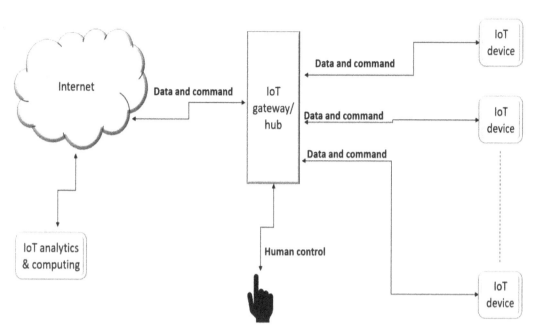

FIGURE 19.2
IoT Device Discovery and Registration by human intervention.

of time. In case of IoT networks, the number of devices entering an IoT network or connecting to an IoT application is very large, so manually performing these set of processes again and again for each and every device is very cumbersome and time consuming. This in turn increases overall request-response time of the IoT application. It also affects the efficiency of the IoT network adversely. Another challenge is the difficulties faced with respect to mobility of the device from one network to another. The process of removal from the previous IoT network and addition to the current IoT network should be easy, quick and error free. To support mobility, dynamicity and scalability in heterogeneous IoT applications, the registration of IoT devices with the DNS server should be easy and quick. These disadvantages associated with Manual Device Discovery and Registration of IoT devices lead to the requirement of Automatic Device Discovery and Registration.

19.2.2 Automatic Device Discovery and Registration

In order to overcome the challenges faced by Manual Device Discovery and Registration technique because of the ever-increasing number of IoT devices, many Automatic Device Discovery and autoconfiguration schemes have been proposed. To support mobility, dynamicity and scalability in heterogeneous, it is necessary to make the IoT devices discoverable by sharing their information on the network. For this, most of the IoT devices are registered/configured to DNS server which performs domain names to IP address translation and vice versa [4]. DNS has evolved over the period of time with new extended versions which allow auto-generation and auto registration of DNS name so that an IoT device can generate and register their appropriate DNS name and relative IP address with the DNS server, which in turn makes these IoT connected devices discoverable and accessible to users or other devices in the IoT network. To facilitate this, many autonomous Device Discovery and registration schemes have been proposed over the time.

19.3 Essential Characteristic Features of Automatic Device Discovery Techniques

The IoT devices are resource constrained in terms of computational power, battery life and storage capacity. IoT devices, most of the time, are deployed in unmanned environment where they have to sense and actuate based on the environmental conditions in an autonomous manner. These interconnected devices are mostly developed by different manufacturers with different protocols, different operating systems and variety of access technologies. In many application scenarios, IoT devices are mobile in nature, which means they frequently move from one IoT subnetwork to another IoT subnetwork rendering IoT environment dynamic and scalable. Heterogeneity, dynamicity and scalability are some challenges that need to be dealt with in order to make IoT applications more efficient and reliable in future to cope with the rapidly developing IoT systems [5]. In order to overcome heterogeneity and dynamicity challenges, IoT devices need to be autonomous in terms of either communicating with other devices or accessing services from other applications. If the IoT networks are able to automatically add and remove the devices in the networks without human intervention in a dynamic manner, it renders a flexible and scalable IoT environment.

To offer seamless applications in the quick evolving IoT paradigm, it is pertinent that the Device Discovery techniques should possess the basic characteristics which are also called IoT Device Discovery Requirements: dynamic scalability, interoperability, mobility, transparency and security. Figure 19.3 shows the basic characteristic requirement for IoT Device Discovery Technique.

These above-mentioned characteristic requirements have been analysed further which are as follows:

Dynamic scalability: IoT networks have to support billions of connected devices efficiently and flexibly in a resource constrained and unmanned environment. This means that the IoT networks should be highly scalable in order to allow the addition and removal of IoT devices in the network without human intervention in dynamic manner [5].

Interoperability: The presence of large number of connected sensors and actuators supporting different frameworks, protocols and platforms gives rise to a heterogeneous environment and to have an IoT network where the devices are capable to communicate with each other in an efficient and autonomous manner, the property of interoperability is required [6].

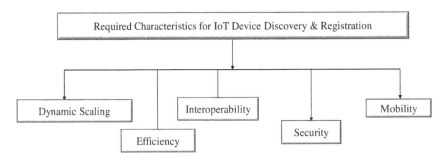

FIGURE 19.3
Basic characteristic requirement for IoT Device Discovery technique.

Mobility: In many IoT applications, like those of smart healthcare applications, vehicular networks, the sensor devices are portable and mobile. This means that in these types of cases the devices are moving from one subnetwork to another subnetwork and to support communication between these devices and services the devices need to get themselves registered and make themselves accessible in the new subnetwork that they enter in an autonomous manner, each time they change the network. Thus, mobility of devices must be facilitated in a flexible and efficient manner [5].

Efficiency: In many IoT applications, it is a pertinent requirement that the request-response time should be negligible and supports time constraints. For example, in a vehicular IoT networks where smart vehicles enter and leave the network on a regular basis, addition and removal should be done quickly supporting real-time scenarios. Another requirement to support smart transportation is for vehicles to have real-time data about the status of the traffic. Real-time data collection and control is also an essential requirement of smart grids. Therefore, efficiency becomes an essential requirement for latency-sensitive smart IoT applications.

Security: With increasing number of IoT connected devices, most of which are resource constrained and operating in an unmanned autonomous environment makes the network prone to security vulnerabilities. Hence establishing a secure connection between the devices in such a scenario becomes a mandatory requirement.

19.4 Philosophies of Recent Autonomous Device Discovery and Registration Schemes

Many Autonomous Device Discovery and Registration schemes have been proposed over the time to fulfil the requirements mentioned in Section 19.3. Some of them have been discussed in this section.

(i) To support the ever changing nature of IoT environment, DNS has also evolved over the period involving new extensions like those of mDNS (multicast DNS) and DNS-SD (DNS Service Discovery) [7]. The working of DNS-SD and mDNS in smart IoT environment was analysed in this proposal. Figure 19.4 shows the working architecture of this scheme.

The proposal has concluded that mDNS messages lead to high traffic because of multicasting a DNS request on all connected paths, so, it was not suitable for large global networks. Therefore, a lightweight implementation of mDNS and DNS-SD for resource discovery and resource directory (RD) has been recommended [8]. This scheme also enables efficient cache utilization by having minimal entries to accommodate dynamic DNS entries. Thus, dynamic scaling was the main feature which was taken into account in this proposal.

(ii) A Zero-configuration platform was introduced in [9], which used standard IPv6 protocols and RESTful web services to discover, configure and access the smart sensor devices without any human intervention. Interoperability and dynamic scaling were the features supported by this scheme. Figure 19.5 presents the basic framework of this technique.

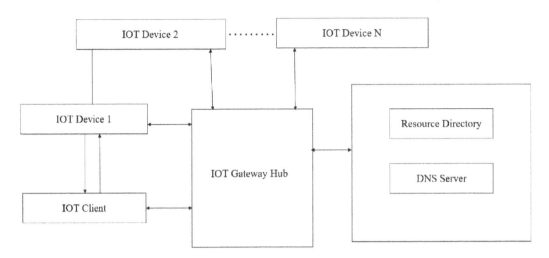

FIGURE 19.4
MDNS-based IoT Device Discovery architecture.

Implementation results lead to the conclusion that the main drawback was the presence of hop delay, thus with the increase in the number of devices (hops) request-response time increases, which lead to decrease in the overall efficiency of the IoT network and that is why this scheme is suitable for small smart networks.

(iii) To support the global naming of IoT devices in an IoT environment, a unicast DNS name autoconfiguration (DNSNA) scheme was proposed [10]. In this scheme, a DNS name of an IoT device is generated autonomously by the target IoT device i.e. the device that wants to enter the network. This auto-generation of DNS name is carried out in few steps, first DNS search list is obtained by the IPV6 host, by using either of the two protocols of IPV6 i.e. IPv6 Router Advertisement (RA) or Dynamic Host Configuration (DHCPv6).

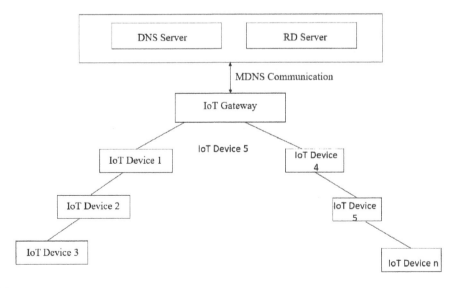

FIGURE 19.5
IoT N/W architecture supporting zero-configuration Device Discovery scheme.

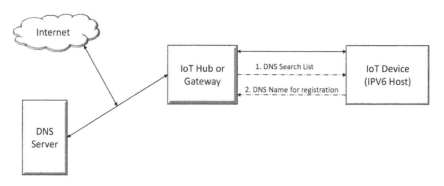

FIGURE 19.6
IoT device autonomous DNS name generation.

After this, using this DNS search list and device configuration information, a unique DNS name is autogenerated by concatenating these two entities. Figure 19.6 shows the architecture of this proposed IoT device autonomous DNS name generation technique.

When the performance of this scheme was analysed on the with respect to energy consumption, it was found that it was performing better than the previously proposed multicast DNS name generation and resolution scheme. This leads to the fact that generating less traffic at nodes leads to faster autoconfiguration of global DNS names and local names, resulting in more efficient, reliable and autonomous naming scheme for larger IoT networks. Dynamic scaling, interoperability, mobility and efficiency are the characteristic features taken into account in this discovery technique. Some drawbacks of this scheme are that it is less suitable for smaller networks like those of smart buildings but more suitable for larger networks and where mobility is required at a very fast rate like those of smart transportations. Also no security feature has been included to keep a check on some miscellaneous devices trying to gain access to the IoT network.

(iv) A new framework was proposed in [11] which performed DNSNA for IoT devices. This scheme was an enhancement over the previously proposed schemes [12]. This scheme is suitable for addressing both type of devices i.e. IPv6 IoT device and IPv4 IoT device. This was the major challenge present in techniques proposed earlier that they were compatible with IPv6 type of addressing only. For auto-identification and registration for IPv6 IoT devices, this technique uses IPv6 Neighbour Discovery (ND) protocol and for IPv4 IoT devices it uses Dynamic Host Configuration Protocol (DHCP). Using this, DNS search list is obtained containing DNS suffixes which are used by the IoT device to generate a unique DNS name. This is done by concatenating its unique device configuration with DNS suffix. Another enhancement present in this framework is that it has a security feature included in it to control any malicious device entry. This has been done by inclusion of an authentication server in the network and near field communication (NFC) card id embedded in IoT devices. Due to this, whenever an IoT device or a service wants to enter the network, it first has to send the authentication request to the authentication server, which generates an authentication key and forwards it to the requesting device. Then by using this signature key, their identification and device registration process is accomplished. Figure 19.7 shows the architecture of the proposed framework.

That is why this framework has the features of dynamic scaling, interoperability and security. The drawback of this technique is that security features work for shorter distances and cost of IoT devices increases by embedding NFC card.

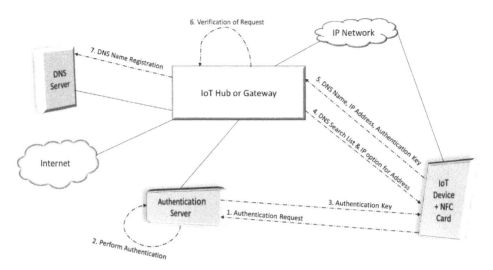

FIGURE 19.7
IoT device configuration framework of SDNSNA.

(v) Most of the IoT devices are resource constrained in terms of storage, battery power capacity, computational power and cost and usually deployed in an unmanned resource constrained environment. To address all these challenges, a consistent discovery and registration technique was proposed in [13]. This technique allows IoT devices and web services to be registered autonomously in IoT network based on Open Connectivity Foundation (OCF). A RD server is present in this framework which is used for registering and broadcasting data of IoT devices and web services. RAML (RESTful API Modeling Language) is used for registration process. IoT devices register themselves to the RD sever by sending their RAML data and the available web service providers (WSP) register themselves by sending RAML data through publishing client. Now this information present in RD server is used by the IoT client, which is an IoT user, to access the IoT device data and resources and WSP. Figure 19.8 depicts the basic architecture of this scheme containing all the basic components.

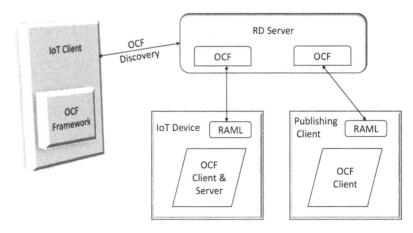

FIGURE 19.8
Consistent registration and discovery framework.

Easy registration and discovery of services from heterogeneous providers are the main advantage of this technique which results in high interoperability and fast dynamic scaling. Performance evaluation of this technique highlights some drawbacks. Firstly, the large number of interactions between different modules results in more amount of time. Secondly, the communication between the modules is supported by OCF-IoTivity framework, which is based on Constrained Application Protocol (CoAP) which is not a matured protocol and incurs delay.

(vi) The challenges faced in applying autonomous IoT device registration techniques proposed earlier were that most of these techniques took into account IPv6 addressing and were suitable for those IoT devices that are configured to IPv6 addressing techniques. However, the large number of IoT devices is based on IPv4 addressing scheme, so adapting those frameworks on a larger front is not feasible. Therefore, a novel and enhanced auto-registration and discovery scheme for IoT devices and services was proposed in [14]. In this scheme, an IoT device on first time entry into the new network performs auto-registration process, by sending a request to OCF-based IoT framework for registration process. This framework collects all the basic required essential data about the IoT device. Then with the help of this information, performs address registration of the device to the DNS sever. Now whenever an IoT user (client) wants to access the services or data from the available IoT network, the IoT user sends a resource discovery request to the available IoT nodes supported by OCF framework. It receives a response from the DNS sever containing the IP address of the desired node. After this, the user can access the desired IoT device or the service using the received IP address. Figure 19.9 shows the basic architecture of this technique.

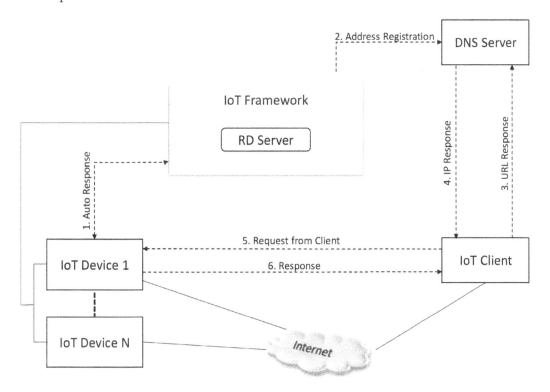

FIGURE 19.9
Auto registration and discovery based on DNS.

The main advantages present in this technique are easy adaptability and flexibility which in turn results in easy dynamic scaling of the IoT network and increased efficiency. After deploying this technique for an application in real-time scenario, it was analysed that as the number of connected devices increases in the network, the request response time increases which affects the performance of the system adversely. Another major flaw present in this technique was absence of any authentication mechanism and because of this lack of security is present. Any unauthorized malicious device can register itself and may lead to data mishandling and leakage, and denial of service (DOS) attack.

(vii) Interoperability is another basic characteristic requirement, which is about providing intercommunication between the web services and the devices supporting Hypertext Transfer Protocol (HTTP) and devices based on OCF framework supporting CoAP. These requirements led to the development of an improved scheme of IoT resource management which enables IoT device self-registration and status detection in IoT environment based on OCF [15]. In this technique, two main extensions have been incorporated, first is the addition of an IoT agent who performs self-registration for those IoT device and resources which are resource constrained and not cable to perform registration process themselves and second is the presence of an internetworking proxy which performs protocol translation and allows to maintain a communication between HTTP supported services and CoAP supported devices based on OCF. In the first step of this scheme, whenever a device joins a new network, it gets itself registered to the IoT framework, either through an available IoT agent or on its own if it is capable, by broadcasting its device details. Then using internetworking proxy present in the IoT framework, IoT resources and devices present in the OCF network can be accessed by the web client running HTTP. After the registration process of IOT devices and services, real-time management and control of these connected and registered devices is performed in a heterogeneous environment to check the condition of devices. Figure 19.10 presents the architecture of this technique.

After the deployment and analysis in real-time application, it was found out that this scheme has the advantage of IoT resource management and protocol translation which

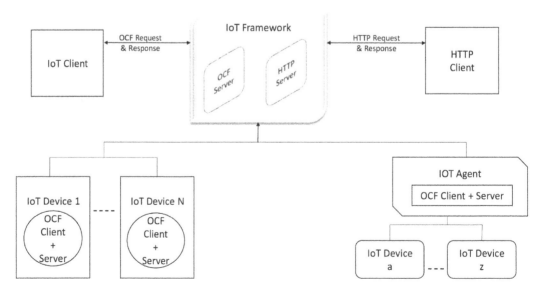

FIGURE 19.10
IoT device self-registration and resource management architecture.

makes IoT network more reliable, dynamically scalable and interoperable. But two limitations of this scheme are large packet size because of the presence of IoT agent and absence of any security feature.

(viii) The development of more and more IoT technologies and increase in the application domain of IoT devices and services has resulted in high heterogeneity in devices and services. Most of the services present in the internet are supported on HTTP web protocol, while most of the IoT devices and services in a local IoT network support protocols specific to constrained IoT environment like MQTT and CoAP. Hence in order to have a seamless communication between these two networks, supporting different protocol standards there should be a proper interconnection. Thus, there is a need to have a transparent protocol translation scheme. An upgraded technique for IoT device self-registration was proposed in [16]. This scheme has a RD based on OCF standards, which performs DNS name registration and performs protocol translation to allow transparent communication in heterogeneous environment i.e. in intra-domain and in inter-domain as well. IoT device auto registration is performed as soon as a device enters an IoT network. The registration is performed by IoT RD server using device registration framework, when it receives device configuration information. On the request of IoT client for the services from the IoT network, based on its request requirements, RD server having discovery framework performs Device Discovery and DNS name resolution. RD server acts an interface between the local IoT network and other outer networks, because of the presence of internetworking proxy module. This application module performs protocol translation. That is why any presently connected IoT device in the local IoT network based on OCF standards and supporting CoAP can be accessed by the requesting IoT user. This IoT user may be present in local IoT network based on OCF standards or may be present in internet supporting HTTP web protocol. Hence this process provides interoperability in a heterogeneous environment. Figure 19.11 shows the basic architecture of this technique.

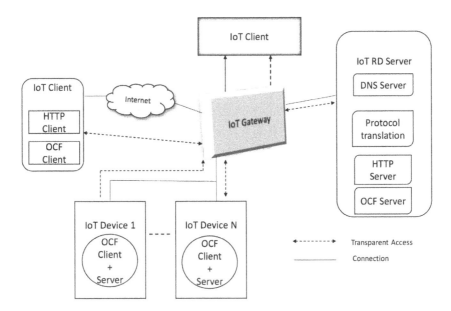

FIGURE 19.11
Name self-registration and device transparent access based on RD server.

After implementing this scheme in a real-time application, it was analysed that this scheme has the advantage of transparency in heterogeneous environment and dynamic scaling. Therefore, this technique is suitable for local networks. But by using proxy for inter-domain communication results in increase in packet size and thus request-response time increases which affects the efficiency of the network adversely.

(ix) Increasing amount of heterogeneity in IoT networks led to the requirement of transparent environment where protocol translation should be easy, quick and error free. Previously proposed device self-registration and discovery schemes consume large amount of time between request and response. Because the request from the IoT user to access a service from IoT device present in the IoT network travels through many modules before it gets responded. This challenge was dealt with in this technique, which was proposed in [17] for IoT networks based on OCF. This was an enhancement of the previous technique. In this technique, internetworking proxy is present as an outer framework, containing the application modules of the RD server, OCF server and HTTP client. This was the modification in the architecture over the previous schemes where internetworking proxy was present inside RD server. This helped in providing complete transparent environment thus enabling interoperability in a heterogeneous environment, between a resources constrained IoT network and internet. In this technique, OCF-IoTivity framework is present in the IoT devices. In this scheme, as soon as the device joins the IoT network, the application module of RD server performs autonomous registration making it discoverable by configuring its DNS name in database. After this, IoT clients request to access IoT device services and other internet services without worrying about the underlying supporting protocol and get the access to the desired service in response from internet proxy, which performs protocol translation if required, in a transparent manner. Figure 19.12 shows the basic working architecture of this technique.

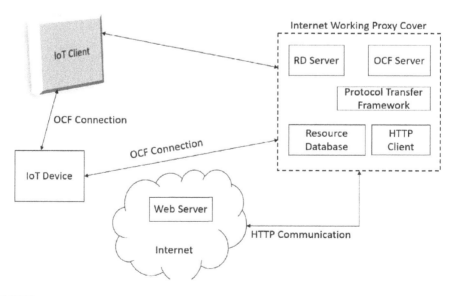

FIGURE 19.12
Internetworking proxy cover based on IoT data discovery.

Based on analysis and implementation results, it is evident that it supports interoperability and dynamic scalability. But lack of any security feature makes it vulnerable to threats, when implemented for larger networks.

(x) Many autonomous device registration and discovery techniques have been proposed over recent period of time, which can be broadly categorized into two basic categories: centralized techniques and distributed techniques. This division is based on how these frameworks perform registration [18]. In case of centralized architecture, a single server node is responsible for performing configuration, registration and discovery process. While in decentralized or distributed architecture there is no central node and each end every node is connected to every other node. In the case of performing discovery, a discovery request message is flooded from the node to its every neighbour node. This message travels until it reaches the target or time to live (TIL) has reached, whichever happens earlier [19]. After analysing both the frameworks, it was found out that centralized framework has a drawback of single point failure, which happens rarely but if it occurs, it results in total breakdown of the application system. Thus, to solve the issue, another technique was proposed in [20], which was based on distributed device registration and discovery framework. In this scheme, the complete IoT network is subdivided into smaller subnetworks, where each subnetwork contains one main node which is called discovery service node (DSN), which is responsible for maintaining the list of connected devices and the services they offer. Each DSN is connected to every other subnetwork's DSN. When a new IoT device enters or joins the network, it gets registered using its device configuration information, by the IoT gateway module, to its nearest DSN. DSN also handles the Device Discovery and service discovery request from the IoT user. Whenever a DSN receives a Device Discovery or service discovery request, it forwards this request to every neighbouring connected DSN using flood search algorithm. Figure 19.13 shows the basic working architecture of distributed Device Discovery technique based on DSN.

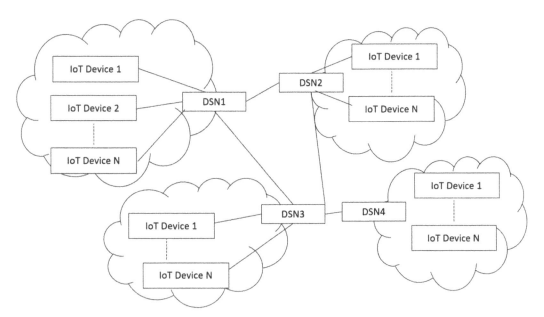

FIGURE 19.13
DSN-based IoT Device Discovery scheme.

On performing analysis on implementation results, it was observed that the main features of this technique are that it is feasible to implement, it has dynamic scaling and because of distributed registration no single point failure is possible. Some flaws are also present like packet rebroadcasting which in turn causes contention, and results in packet collisions and ultimately results in the wastage of precious limited bandwidth. Another challenge is faced when a DSN is added or removed then required updating is performed, because it contains the entire configuration information of the connected IoT nodes, which is needed to be transferred in the new connected DNS. This is indeed a cumbersome process.

19.5 Comparative Analysis of the Autonomous Device Discovery Schemes in IoT

To achieve the aforementioned features in IoT networks, many new schemes that have been proposed over the period of time for autonomous Device Discovery process have been discussed in Section 19.4. All the IoT Device Discovery and registration techniques discussed are based on the DNS. After comparing and analysing them, it was found that all the recently proposed schemes possess only few essential characteristic features. It has already been discussed earlier in the chapter that there are five important basic required characteristic features that are required to be present in the autonomous Device Discovery schemes which are interoperability, dynamic scalability, mobility, Transparency and Security. Table 19.1 shows the comparative analysis of the recently proposed relevant autonomous Device Discovery and registration techniques for IoT networks which have been presented in Section 19.4. The table is showing the advantages and features present in each technique. The table also illustrates the research gaps and flaws present in these techniques.

After analysing these schemes, it was also found out that some schemes are enhanced versions of the other. Table 19.2 shows the classification of these techniques based on their type and enhancement.

It can be concluded from Table 19.1 that most of the autonomous techniques exhibit some common features that are interoperability, mobility, dynamic scalability and efficiency but it is quite evident that no requisite security feature is present in them which leads to the presence of vulnerabilities in the IoT network. Hence any malicious IoT device may get itself registered in the IoT network and result in many internal attacks, replay attacks, DOS attack, data leakage and many more attacks. It is also evident from the performance evaluation that if a scheme includes a transparency feature, there is an extra burden included in terms of packet size which in turn affects the overall efficiency of the technique in the IoT network adversely. Hence from the comprehensive analysis and performance evaluation, it is concluded that there is a necessity to include two essential features in the autonomous Device Discovery process that is security and complete transparency in an efficient manner [21, 22]. This can be done by addition of two more application modules: (a) security frame work, for secure IoT environment (b) a smart proxy framework, for complete transparent IoT device access.

TABLE 19.1

Comparative Analysis of Autonomous Device Discovery and Registration of IoT Devices

Paper (Year)	Proposal	Parameter Taken into Account	Protocols Used	Security Feature	Research Gaps Identified	Advantages Present
1. Lightweight multicast DNS and DNS-SD (lmDNS-SD): IPv6-based resource and service discovery and service discovery for the Web of Things (2012)	1. Evaluates different ways to apply mDNS and DNS-SD for Smart Objects, 2. Recommends a lightweight implementation of mDNS and DNS-SD for resource discovery and directory.	Scalability dynamicity	IPV6, mDNS, DNS-SD, RD	Not discussed	mDNS messages lead to high traffic, not suitable for large global networks	Focus on DNS cache utilization and minimal entries to allow dynamic cache changes
2. REST Assured, We Manage your Microgrid (2014)	The zero-configuration platform, use of standard IPv6 protocols and RESTful web services for the discovery, configuration and the use of devices without any human intervention.	Interoperability, Dynamicity, Scalability	RPL, UDP and CoAP	Not mentioned	Hop delay, response time depends on hop count	Autoconfiguration. addition of new nodes is simple. Suitable for small sites.
3. DNSNA: DNS Name Autoconfiguration for Internet of Things Devices (2016)	Autoconfiguration scheme using device configuration and DNS search list	Movability, dynamicity	IPV6 RA DHCP6	Not discussed	more suitable for vehicular N/W	Good for global and local n/w. Remote controlling devices over internet is easy
4. A framework for DNS naming services for Internet-of-Things devices (2018)	DNSNA framework to support DNS naming services in different n/w	Efficiency, mobility, scalability, security	DHCP, IPV4, IPV6	Yes, if SDNSNA is used	Security feature works in shorter distances, very low data transfer rates, very expensive	name autoconfiguration of devices and services, discovery is efficient, Less no of packets travel NFC authentication access,

(Continued)

TABLE 19.1 (Continued)

Comparative Analysis of Autonomous Device Discovery and Registration of IoT Devices

Paper (Year)	Proposal	Parameter Taken into Account	Protocols Used	Security Feature	Research Gaps Identified	Advantages Present
5. Consistent Registration and Discovery Scheme for Devices and Web Service Providers Based on RAML Using Embedded RD in OCF IoT Network (2018)	An embedded resource directory (RD) server is used for consistent device and service provider's registration and publishing devices and web service provider's information in the Open Connectivity Foundation (OCF)-based IoT N/W using RAML	Interoperability and scalability	CoAP	Not mentioned	Delay of discovery by the IoT client	Easy registration and discovery of services from heterogeneous providers.
6. A Novel Approach towards Resource Auto-registration and discovery of Embedded Systems Based on DNS (2019)	IoT resource auto registration and discovery based on DNS in the OCF environment in the internet Protocol version 4 (IPV4).	Adaptability, Flexibility, mobility, scalability, Interoperability and Efficiency	IPV 4	Not discussed	With increase in no. of devices RR time increases Lack of security, unauthorized access is possible	Auto registration, reduce request-response time
7. Resource Management Based on OCF for Device Self-Registration and Status Detection in IoT Networks (2019)	AGENT device self-registration scheme. An interworking proxy is used for communications between web clients and devices	Interoperability, scalability and efficiency	HTTP, CoAP, OCF platform	Not discussed	Packet size is large. No security feature	Easy discovery and access of IoT devices, resource management Real-time status detection

(Continued)

TABLE 19.1 *(Continued)*

Comparative Analysis of Autonomous Device Discovery and Registration of IoT Devices

Paper (Year)	Proposal	Parameter Taken into Account	Protocols Used	Security Feature	Research Gaps Identified	Advantages Present
8. Improved Resource Directory Based on DNS Name Self-Registration for Device Transparent Access in Heterogeneous IoT Networks (2019)	RD (resource discovery) server is responsible for device registration, discovery, name resolution and interworking proxy of the RD server translates messages between HTTP and OCF over CoAP	Transparency, Dynamic scalability,	CoAP, OCF platform, HTTP with proxy	Not mentioned	Using proxy for outer networks increases packet size and RR time. Good for local N/W	Self-registration and transparent access to heterogeneous IoT devices.
9. Interworking Proxy Based on OCF for Connecting Web Services and IoT Networks (Feb 2020)	An interworking proxy is used to bridge a constrained network to the internet in OCF supported IoT n/w	Transparency, Interoperability, Dynamic scalability, Mobility	HTTP and CoAP	Not discussed	No security feature added/discussed.	1. Protocol translation. 2. Bridge between Client devices, IoT services and web in an heterogeneous environment.
10. Attribute-based Discovery Architecture for Devices in Internet of Things (IoT) (2019)	Gateway registers devices and services to discovery service node (DSN) using protocol or tech. Using logical attributes. Probabilistic Search Flood Algorithm is used in interconnecting DSN	Dynamicity, scalability, mobility, Distributed Device Discovery,	Not defined	Not discussed	Packet rebroadcasts, causing contention, packet collisions and ultimately wasting precious limited bandwidth	Less network traffic and query processing time, no single point failure due to distributed nature

TABLE 19.2

Grouping of Autonomous Device Discovery Techniques

Technique Number	Enhanced from Other	Type
1 and 2	2 is an enhancement over 1	Centralized
3 and 4	4 is an enhancement of 3	Centralized
5, 6, 7, 8, 9	Enhanced from 5 till 9	Centralized
10	No	Decentralized

19.6 Conclusions

The development of more and smarter IoT applications like those of smart building, smart grid, smart healthcare has led to the addition of enormous number of IoT devices, which are resource constrained in nature and deployed in an unmanned heterogeneous environment. In order to have these IoT devices function coherently and offer their services in such a difficult environment, many techniques have been proposed to enable them for autoconfiguration, self-registration and autonomous Device Discovery which possess few of the essential properties like dynamic scaling, mobility, transparency, interoperability, efficiency and security for IoT networks. But none of them has been able to attain all of them. After performing the comparative analysis in detail, it was deduced that there is a need to add an appropriate application framework which may provide thorough transparency and security features to the present autonomous IoT Device Discovery and registration techniques and to the IoT network as well.

References

1. M. Mahbub, 2020, "Progressive Researches on IoT Security: An Exhaustive Analysis from the Perspective of Protocols, Vulnerabilities, and Preemptive Architectonics," Journal of Network and Computer Applications, vol. 168, p. 102761.
2. P. Sethi and S. R. Sarangi, 2017, "Internet of Things: Architectures, Protocols, and Applications," Journal of Electrical and Computer Engineering, vol. 2017, Article ID 9324035, 25 pages.
3. S. Arshad, M. A. Azam, M. H. Rehmani and J. Loo, 2019, "Recent Advances in Information-Centric Networking-Based Internet of Things (ICN-IoT)," IEEE Internet of Things Journal, vol. 6, no. 2, pp. 2128–2158.
4. C. Hesselman et al., 2020, "The DNS in IoT: Opportunities, Risks, and Challenges," IEEE Internet Computing, vol. 24, no. 4, pp. 23–32.
5. Z. Yan, H. Li, S. Zeadally, Y. Zheng and G. Geng, 2019, "Is DNS Ready for Ubiquitous Internet of Things?", Information Science Faculty Publications, vol. 64. Published in IEEE Access, v. 7, pp. 28835–28846.
6. M. Noura, M. Atiquzzaman and M. Gaedke, 2019, "Interoperability in Internet of Things: Taxonomies and Open Challenges," Mobile Networks and Applications, vol. 24, no. 3, pp. 796–809.
7. B. Djamaa and M. Richardson, 2014, "Towards Scalable DNS-Based Service Discovery for the Internet of Things," Lecture Notes in Computer Science, vol. 8867, pp. 432–435.

8. A. J. Jara, P. Martinez-Julia and A. Skarmeta, 2012, "Light-Weight Multicast DNS and DNS-SD (lmDNS-SD): IPv6-Based Resource and Service Discovery for the Web of Things," 2012 Sixth International Conference on Innovative Mobile and Internet Services in Ubiquitous Computing, pp. 731–738.

9. A. Montanari, Y. Pignolet and E. Ferranti, 2014, "REST Assured, We Manage Your Microgrid," 2014 IEEE International Conference on Smart Grid Communications (SmartGridComm), pp. 284–289.

10. S. Lee, J. P. Jeong and J. Park, 2016, "DNSNA: DNS Name Autoconfiguration for Internet of Things Devices," 2016 18th International Conference on Advanced Communication Technology (ICACT), pp. 410–416.

11. J. Jeong, S. Lee, H. Kim and J.-S. Park, 2019, "A Framework for DNS Naming Services for Internet-of-Things Devices", Future Generation Computer Systems, vol. 92, pp. 617–627.

12. S. Lee, J. Jeong and J. Park, 2015 "DNS Name Autoconfiguration for IoT Home Devices," IEEE 29th International Conference on Advanced Information Networking and Applications Workshops, pp. 131–134, 2015.

13. W. Jin and D. Kim, 2018, "Consistent Registration and Discovery Scheme for Devices and Web Service Providers Based on RAML Using Embedded RD in OCF IoT Network," Sustainability vol. 10, no. 12, p. 4706.

14. A. Khudoyberdiev, W. Jin and D. Kim, 2019, "A Novel Approach towards Resource Auto-Registration and Discovery of Embedded Systems Based on DNS," Electronics, vol. 8, no. 4, p. 442.

15. W. Jin and D. Kim, 2019. "Resource Management Based on OCF for Device Self-Registration and Status Detection in IoT Networks," Electronics, vol. 8, no. 3, p. 311.

16. W. Jin and D. Kim, 2019 "Improved Resource Directory Based on DNS Name Self-Registration for Device Transparent Access in Heterogeneous IoT Networks," IEEE Access, vol. 7, pp. 112859–112869.

17. W. Jin and D. Kim, 2020, "Interworking Proxy Based on OCF for Connecting Web Services and IoT Networks," Journal of Communications, vol. 15, no. 2, pp. 192–197.

18. P. C. Ccori, L. C. C. De Biase, M. K. Zuffo and F. S. C. da Silva, 2016, "Device Discovery Strategies for the IoT," IEEE International Symposium on Consumer Electronics (ISCE), pp. 97–98.

19. Z. Shen, H. Jiang, Q. Dong and B. Wang, 2020, "Energy-Efficient Neighbor Discovery for the Internet of Things," IEEE Internet of Things Journal, vol. 7, no. 1, pp. 684–698.

20. S. Sharma, 2019, "Attribute based Discovery Architecture for Devices in Internet of Things (IoT)," IEEE 5th International Conference for Convergence in Technology (I2CT), pp. 1–4.

21. W. Jin and D. Kim, 2018, "Development of Virtual Resource Based IoT Proxy for Bridging Heterogeneous Web Services in IoT Networks," Sensors, vol. 18, no. 6, p. 1721.

22. A. H. Ahmed, N. M. Omar and H. M. Ibrahim, 2019, "Secured Service Discovery Technique in IoT," Journal of Communications vol. 14, no. 1, pp. 40–46.

20

IoT for ALL: Usage and Significance of IoT for Generation X, Y, and Z

Amitabh Bhargava, Deepshikha Bhargava, and Sonali Vyas

CONTENTS

20.1 Introduction

With the advent of technologies, Internet of Things (IoT) has been emerged as a technological solution capable of connecting and controlling everything. IoT is all about interconnection of physical devices, people, and networks for sharing data, providing digital

DOI: 10.1201/9781003226888-20

intelligence, connectivity, and independent communication. This low-cost solution very soon became the choice of everyone. The IoT architecture is specific to the application area and comprises a platform connected with devices, objects, and sensors over the network of network. The data from devices, objects, and sensors is integrated and further analyzed to cater to the particular need.

In daily life, we use different IoT-based applications and devices such as smart home, smart appliances, smart city, shopping, smart wearables, voice assistants, smart cars, security, smart bulbs, shopping, travel, sports, and healthcare.

Let us take a scenario of a family where members can be of any generation. Assumed members be grandparents, parents, kids, and pets. The morning starts with the alarm clock to wake up everyone. The homemaker gets busy in daily household activities and uses different smart home appliances such as a coffee maker, microwave, smart refrigerator, toaster, RO, dishwasher, and washing machine. The grandparents and kids watch smart TV in a room, while at the same time the temperature is controlled by smart AC. The other member is taking bath and using smart geezer with controlled temperature. Kids use smart watches for fitness tracking and time management. The family has a smart driverless car and use map feature to drop kids and office-going members to their destination. The house has smart bulbs and smart thermostat to save their electricity bill. The pet has smart collar to keep track of it when it goes for a walk. The grandparents have smart wearables and fitness bands to remind them medications and store their electronic health records (EHR). They can also use smart sticks to show them pathway and so on. When no one is at home, the smart security and surveillance system is activated. In daily life, each one of us uses various smart devices at home, transport, media and communication, and healthcare. This shows that every physical object can be transformed into an IoT device (Clark, 2020).

If we look back to the history of IoT, the idea was generated somewhere in the 1980s. For a decade, the ideas were around integrating artificial intelligence with sensors. For example, a bulky vending machine was connected over internet with limited communication capabilities. Further development in IoT was dependent upon cost and processing speed of processors, wireless devices, and broadband connectivity. This caused scaling up of IoT and adoption of a low-cost solution such as radio-frequency identification (RFID) tags and IPv6. The term "Internet of Things" provides digital transformation and integration of objects or devices with humans. Further developments include ubiquitous computing, machine-to-machine computing, pervasive computing, responsive and invisible computing. All these terms somehow centered around IoT. If we talk about the scale of IoT, it depends upon how many devices, objects, and people are connected. The research by International Data Corporation (IDC) shows that, by 2025, there will be more than 41 billion IoT devices that will be connected over smart home, smart city, and smart wearables. Gartner (2019) on the other hand predicts a massive rise of IoT in different sectors such as utilities, government, building automation, physical security, manufacturing, natural resources, automotive, healthcare, retail and wholesale, information, and transportation. Now, big technology giants such as Amazon, Google, and Apple leveraging this opportunity and coming up with a variety of IoT devices for smart home, virtual assistants, and personal care. However, the security of IoT devices is still a concern. The IoT device developer needs to mitigate the issues related to security and threats of IoT devices (Ranger, 2020).

20.2 Characteristics of Generation X, Y, and Z

"Traditionalists (silent generation), baby boomers, Generation X, Generation Y, Generation Z and Generation Alpha", are the commonly used terms to differentiate people falling in different age brackets and also having different characteristics than other generations.

Based on the different definitions, the generation term may be defined as the groups of people who were born, grew, and maintained their life in a certain period of time and are supposed to have common characteristics and viewpoints (Berkup, 2014). Dissimilar research/articles illustrate different age brackets for different generations.

20.2.1 Traditionalists (1900–1945)

They are also called silent generations. They are mature, experienced person, like to save and live modest life. The people falling in this generation are hard worker. In the year 2021, traditionalists are in the age bracket of 77 years to 121 years approx.

20.2.2 Baby Boomers (1946–1964)

These are the people born soon after World War II. They are workaholic and loyal to their organization. In the year 2021, they are the biggest user of traditional media like television, radio, newspaper, and magazine. In the year 2021, baby boomers are in the age bracket of 58 years to 76 years approx.

20.2.3 Generation X (1965–1979)

Generation X are the children of workaholic parents, i.e., baby boomers. The Generation X care for the personal development and open for change and have global viewpoint. They dislike a boring and stressful workplace though they suppose it as a place to develop and learn (Miller & Washington, 2011). Like baby boomers, Gen X also like to watch television, listen to radio, read newspaper, and magazine. Apart from the traditional media, they are also digital savvy and like to spend time on social media platforms like Facebook and Instagram. In the year 2021, Generation X are in the age bracket of 43 years to 57 years approx.

20.2.4 Generation Y (1980–1995/1996)

This generation is also called "millennials", a technological generation who lives with the technology. Since they live in a technological world, with high-speed internet at affordable price, the OTT have an edge over DTH while watching television. Digital news has an edge over traditional newspaper. For financial transaction, the millennials like to do digital transactions. In the year 2021, Generation Y are in the age bracket of 27 years to 42 years approx.

20.2.5 Generation Z (1996/1997–2010/2012)

They are born in techno global world and have addiction to technology and speed. The generation like to connect and socialize via internet. Smartphone is the favorite method of communication. In the year 2021, Generation Z are in the age bracket of 12 years to 26 years approx.

20.2.6 Generation Alpha (2010/2012 onward)

They are growing up with smart devices and technology in every product. In the year 2021, Generation Alpha are in the age around of 10 years.

This chapter focuses upon only Generation X, Y, and Z as they are the prime users of IoT devices (Kasasa, 2021)

20.3 IoT for All

IoT for all also referred to as IoT for everyone, which targets all stakeholders/users of IoT. The objective of IoT for all is to reach each person, society, city, government, and industry to provide technological solution and cater to their special requirements. IoT for all solutions accommodates citizen of any age, business leaders, governments, and industries in the area of education, healthcare, sustainable and energy solutions, resource management, industrial applications, to name a few.

20.4 Categories of IoT for All

The consumers of IoT devices use them for different purposes for home, entertainment, education, workplace, transport, to name a few. Let us look around different application areas of IoT (Taylor, 2021).

20.4.1 Consumer IoT (CIoT)

The IoT devices for individuals provide them convenience, security, domestic help, personal healthcare, asset tracking, wearables, and a better lifestyle at home and workplaces. It includes various IoT consumer applications such as smart butler, smart chef, robo nanny, smart Gardner, smart repairing, smart security, smart body analyzer, smart stethoscope, smart watch, smart pregnancy belt, smart vitamin analyzer, smart stress management, smart glass, pet watcher, to name a few (Team, 2021).

20.4.2 Commercial IoT/Business IoT (BIoT)

IoT solutions for commercial places such as shopping malls, supermarkets, stores, hotels, hospitals, entertainment, offices, to name few. The aim is to provide effective services, tracking, and monitoring and management of resources in smart offices/buildings.

20.4.3 Industrial IoT (IIoT)

This sector includes high-powered, fault-tolerant, and robust IoT solutions for industries, factories, or organizations, e.g. real-time monitoring, digital factory, inventory and facility management, machine-to-machine communication, sustainability, production and product flow and quality monitoring, manufacturing, energy management, staff management, plant safety and security management, supply chain management, fleet management, and predictive maintenance.

20.4.4 Infrastructure IoT (InIoT)

IoT-enabled cyber-physical systems for smart infrastructures to enhance quality of service, cost-effective, threat prevention, secure device connectivity, filtering, and processing.

20.4.5 Military Things (IoMT) or Internet of Battlefield Things (IoBT)

The military/defense applications of IoT connect naval, armed and air forces and defense equipment, devices (such as submarines, aircrafts, tanks, drones), soldiers, and military bases over a secure and robust network.

20.4.6 Education IoT (EIoT)

It includes smart school building, smart school transportation for kids, smart health for schools, smart classrooms, smart lesson plan, smart cafeteria, STEM lab, student IoT project management, student activity tracking, to name a few.

20.4.7 Government IoT (GIoT)

The IoT also facilitates government functions such as smart buildings, smart cities (planning and control), smart health, smart devices for defense and military, disaster management, smart responders for quick response management to name a few.

20.4.8 Internet of Medical Things (IoMT)

It includes IoT-enabled smart healthcare and medical solutions for doctors, patients, and hospitals such as smart wearables, smart healthcare and patient monitoring devices, electronic health and medical records (EHR and EMR), emergency care to name a few (Hernández, 2019).

20.5 Significance and Usage of IoT for All for Different Generations

The IoT for all or IoT for everything includes various applications and gadgets, which can be used by everyone. Such devices include smart homes gadgets, smart home appliances (smart coffee makers, washing machine, refrigerators, AC, TV), smart wearables, fitness bands, visual and virtual assistants, housekeeping robo-vacuum cleaners, robo-nanny for child care, IoT for elderly and disables, smart meters, bulbs; smart parking, smart cars to name a few (Cui, 2016).

For different generations such as Generation X, Y, or Z; the IoT devices fall into consumer IoT (CIoT) category. As shown in Table 20.1, let us go through different CIoT device and applications (Matthews, 2018).

20.5.1 Personal Internet of Things (PIoT)

It includes smart wearables, smart watch/fitness trackers (Fitbit), smart hearables (air pods, Google buds), smart phones, smart clothing (smart T-shirt), smart glass (Google glass) to name a few. *The most promising users of these devices are Generation Y.*

TABLE 20.1

Consumer IoT for Different Generations (Matthews, 2018)

Category IoT for All	Generation X 1965–1979 43–57 Years	Generation Y 1980–1995/1996 27–42 Years	Generation Z 1996/1997–2010/2012 11–26 Years
Personal IoT (e.g. smart wearables, watches, and fitness tracker)	Low	High	High
Smart home IoT (e.g. voice assistance, home security, robo cleaner, and smart kitchens)	Moderate	High	Very low
Vehicle IoT (e.g. personal car: security, lights, camera, locks, and GPS)	Moderate	High	High
Agriculture IoT (e.g. kitchen garden, soil management, and water management)	High	High	Very low
Health IoT (e.g. smart wellness watch, patients surveillance, care of the elderly and the disabled)	High	Moderate	Very low
Energy IoT (e.g. residential energy, home appliances, and smart meter)	High	High	Very low

20.5.2 Smart Home IoT

It includes products for making lifestyle better, e.g. Home automation products (voice assistance, smart home entertainment), smart home appliances (smart TV, smart AC, smart fridge, and washing machines, robo cleaners, etc.), smart kitchen gadgets (smart dishwasher); devices for smart home security and surveillance (Nortek security devices and accessories), and smart air products (smart sprinklers, smart air purifiers). *Generation Y mostly uses these products.*

20.5.3 Vehicle IoT

Generation Y mostly use this category. This category include smart cars equipped with security, lights, camera, locks, and GPS.

20.5.4 Health IoT

Majority of Generation X users are prime target for health IoT solutions such as smart wellness watch, patients' surveillance, care of the elderly and the disabled (Vyas & Bhargava, 2021).

20.5.5 Agriculture IoT (AIoT)

Generations X and Y consumers inclined toward home gardening and kitchen garden. They prefer IoT products for soil management, drip irrigation, etc. in their kitchen garden.

20.5.6 Energy

Generations X and Y prefer to use energy saving products such as smart light fixtures, smart bulbs to name a few.

20.6 Conclusion

IoT witnessed different emerging applications in various areas such as healthcare, social media, home, entertainment, agriculture, and energy. This chapter highlighted upon the varied needs of different generations. It is also observed that there is a generation gap in usage and significance of IoT. The Generation X inclined toward IoT products related to healthcare, energy, and agriculture. The Generation Y prefer to use IoT products for the purpose of personal care and better lifestyle. On contrary, the tech-savvy generation Z inclined toward personal and vehicle IoT products.

References

Berkup, S. B. (2014). Working with generations X and Y in generation Z period: Management of different generations in business life. Mediterranean Journal of Social Sciences, 5(19), 218–229.

Clark, J. (2020, August 28). What is the Internet of Things, and How Does It Work? IBM Business Operations Blog. https://www.ibm.com/blogs/internet-of-things/what-is-the-iot/

Cui, X. (2016). The Internet of Things. SpringerLink. https://link.springer.com/chapter/10.1057/9781137505545_7?error=cookies_not_supported&code=f7eff932-f8c3-4429-a62b-0ff9b44f6117

Hernández, M. (2019, July 31). IoT: Consumer & Commercial vs. Industrial – Main Overview. Ubidots Blog. https://ubidots.com/blog/iot-consumer-vs-commercial-vs-industrial-main-overview/

Kasasa. (2021, July 6). Boomers, Gen X, Gen Y, Gen Z, and Gen A Explained. Kasasa. https://www.kasasa.com/articles/generations/gen-x-gen-y-gen-z

Matthews, K. (2018, March 20). How Are Different Generations Using IoT? IoT For All. https://www.iotforall.com/how-different-generations-use-iot

Ranger, S. (2020, February 3). What is the IoT? Everything You Need to Know about the Internet of Things Right Now. ZDNet. https://www.zdnet.com/article/what-is-the-internet-of-things-everything-you-need-to-know-about-the-iot-right-now/

Taylor, K. (2021, April 20). What You Need to Know About Consumer IoT (CIoT). HitechNectar. https://www.hitechnectar.com/blogs/consumer-iot-ciot/#ConsumerIoTDevicesandApplications

Team, D. (2021, May 9). 6 Important IoT Consumer Applications. DataFlair. https://data-flair.training/blogs/iot-consumer-applications/

Vyas, S., & Bhargava, D. (2021). Smart Health Systems: Emerging Trends (1st ed., Vol. 1). Springer. https://doi.org/10.1007/978-981-16-4201-2

Index

Note: Locators in *italics* represent figures, and **bold** indicate tables in the text.